D1879232

A

NARRATIVE

OF THE

POLITICAL AND MILITARY TRANSACTIONS

OF

BRITISH INDIA

A

NARRATIVE

OF THE
POLITICAL AND MILITARY TRANSACTIONS
OF

BRITISH INDIA,

UNDER THE ADMINISTRATION OF THE

MARQUESS OF HASTINGS

1813 TO 1818.

BY HENRY T. PRINSEP

GYAN

Published by

GYAN

Gyan Publishing House
5, Ansari Road
Daryaganj, New Delhi-110002
Phone: 011-47034999, 9811692060
E-mail: books@gyanbooks.com

Distribution Network
gyanbooks.com
India, USA, Canada, UK, Australia

ISBN: 978-81-212-5985-9 (PB)
First Published, 1820

2nd Impression 2024

Printed at: Gyan Press, Delhi.

A NARRATIVE OF THE POLITICAL AND MILITARY TRANSACTIONS OF BRITISH INDIA

Author: HENRY T. PRINSEP

A NARRATIVE OF THE POLITICAL AND MILITARY TRANSACTIONS OF BRITISH INDIA,

UNDER THE ADMINISTRATION OF THE

MARQUESS OF HASTINGS.

1813 TO 1818.

BY HENRY T. PRINSEP,

OF THE HON. EAST INDIA COMPANY'S CIVIL SERVICE, BENGAL.

"Res poscere videtur——ut non modò casus eventusque rerum, qui plerique fortuiti sunt, sed ratio etiam causæque noscantur."—TACITUS.

LONDON:
JOHN MURRAY, ALBEMARLE-STREET.

1820.

PREFACE.

THE work, now presented to the public, pretends to no merit, beyond that of a faithful relation of the very important changes and transactions, which have occurred in India between 1814 and 1819. The labour of the narrator has been chiefly occupied in compilation and extraction from the voluminous records of the Supreme-Government, which contain the most minute details of every political or military occurrence in every quarter of India. To all these he had free access; and, thus, the only qualities requisite for the undertaking, were those of diligence in research, and discrimination in the use or rejection of the materials before him. If he shall have succeeded in selecting so much, as may render the politics of India, during the period under review, intelligible to those, who may approach the subject with motives of curiosity or utility,—if readers of this class shall retire from the perusal, tolerably satisfied with the insight it has given them into the affairs of the period, and enabled to form a fair judgment upon the propriety of the measures adopted, his grand and primary object will have been attained. At the same time, he is not ignorant, that, in skilful hands, the train of events, of which a faithful and plain relation is here submitted, might have been wrought into a form, that would have awakened a lively interest in the general, as well as the curious or interested reader. The facts recorded are both singular and important; the only circumstances, that can give a legitimate attraction to a work of the historical class. But Indian habits and occupations, as well as the example of his precursors, prevent the narrator from anticipating much success, except with those of his readers, whose attention may be excited by the recollection of Indian scenes, wherein they have themselves borne a part, or by the tie of kindred with the present actors upon that wide field for British energy.

In any other department of writing, the narrator would probably have followed the bent of his inclination, and have ventured his first literary work without the appendage of a name, which can give no title to favourable notice. But the public has a right to demand, that every thing, pretending to the character of history, should bear that certificate at least; and, in some cases, a notice of the sources of information, and of the circumstances which may have given a peculiar command of them, or a pretension to more than usual authenticity. He feels himself compelled by this consideration, in addition to his name, to state briefly, that, on the first occasion of the Governor-General's leaving the presidency in the year 1814, to make the tour of the western provinces, he had the good fortune to be selected as one of the suite of the Marquess of Hastings, then Earl of Moira, and was, during the tour, attached to the secretariat. On the occasion of his Lordship's second progress to the westward, that is to say, when he personally took the field in 1817, he had the honour of again filling the same capacity as before, and continued to form part of the suite throughout the campaign, and until his Lordship's return to the presidency.

Notwithstanding the extensive means of observation, which this employment opened to him, it never would have occurred to the narrator himself, that his time could be employed with advantage in the preparation of any thing for the press. It is not the fault of the service to which he belongs, causelessly to obtrude itself on the public in print. Its manifold duties generally give full employment to all, who might be supposed to possess the capability; and the office, to which he happened to be attached, was by no means one of the least laborious.

However, when the rise of the Mahrattas in arms, to oppose the execution of the Governor-General's plans for the suppression of the Pindarees, brought on a crisis of no common interest, it became a matter of evident importance, that the public curiosity should be satisfied in respect to the causes that had produced the juncture; and that the conduct of the Indian authorities, as well in the previous intercourse with the native powers, as in the efforts to avert the mischiefs, which then assumed a threatening aspect, should be secured from the possibility of misrepresentation, by a candid and early exposè of all their operations. In the compilation of such a memoir, if executed with but a moderate portion of skill, there seemed to be so much of public utility, as, in the narrator's circumstances, would warrant his regarding it as a point of public duty to make the attempt. Yet, though soon convinced that such a work was most desirable, it was some months before he could bring himself finally to resolve on commencing it. His employment in India, except on the two occasions abovementioned, had been confined exclusively to the internal branches of administration; and he felt the disadvantage, under which he must undertake a task that, from its nature, required a general survey of the political relations of the British dominion in the East. But, as no one of established political reputation appeared inclined to step forward on the occasion, and there was reason to fear, that, unless he took it up, an authentic account of the period might long be a desideratum, he was induced to consult on the subject with the Secretary to the Governor-General, whose idea of the importance of the matter appearing to correspond entirely with his own, he at length made the tender of his services, provided the assent of the Governor-General could be obtained, and there should be no objection to his unlimited use of the records of Government. The proposition was received by Mr. Adam with his characteristic liberality, and met with his very decided encouragement. Through him the narrator obtained the Governor-General's permission to avail himself of the records of the Secretary's office, without which, as all the most important articles of information are usually recorded while matters are still in train, it would have been impossible to execute the work, except in the most imperfect manner.

Such were the circumstances, under which the collection of materials was begun in February, 1818, when the campaign was drawing fast to a close. It has taken just a year to bring it to a conclusion. To those acquainted with the nature of the records of the Indian Government, this will not be thought an immoderate time, when it is recollected, that it was necessary carefully to peruse and note the entire proceedings of the political department for upwards of four years, before the narrative itself could be commenced. Much of the narrator's attention was besides devoted to other objects, being all the while in active employment. Thus, however desirous he may have been, that the work should appear while the curiosity of the public was yet at its height, he has found it impossible to present it at an earlier moment. As it is, in his own judgment, too much has been sacrificed to the desire of expedition.

It is necessary to premise, that the design has been, to trace the political transactions of India from the origin of the hostile spirit amongst the Mahratta powers to the final crisis of the season of 1817-18; to relate the operations of that season, and explain, as far as may be possible, the settlement resulting therefrom. Else it might create some surprise, that, while events of comparatively minor interest are dwelt upon with a minuteness, which may, perhaps, be found tedious, the particulars of the Goorkha war are passed over with a mere cursory notice. But these were in a measure foreign to the crisis in question; and, as the time had gone by, when they could be considered to have a peculiar claim to interest, it was thought best to limit the mention of that war to its influence upon the conduct of other powers, and only so far to allude to the operations of it, as might be necessary to explain that influence.

Such as it is, the work is now given to the public, with the full confidence, that it will not be regarded as a laboured exculpation of any specific scheme of policy. He can affirm, that he has not, in a single instance, designedly given a colouring to a fact, in order to make it suit the peculiar views of any class of statesmen: but he does acknowledge with some pride, that the present head of the Indian Government has claims to his personal attachment, which may have given a bias to his political views and reasonings; and further, that the habit of daily contemplating the development of his particular plans, from the moment of their conception, until they have been crowned with the predicted success, has produced a warmth of admiration, that may have warped his judgment upon the character of the system pursued. Yet has it been his exclusive aim throughout, to give a plain and candid statement of his own impressions on the events recorded: indeed, to have done otherwise would have been consistent, neither with the liberal confidence reposed in him by the Marquess of Hastings, nor with the spirit, in which he himself undertook the task.

The narrator is, at the same time, proud to own, that his situation has given him the means of verifying several points of material import, by personal inquiry at the fountain head, and that his impressions, in respect to the political measures adopted, have been submitted to the test of severe examinations, which have either confirmed their accuracy, or pointed to the means, by which they could be thoroughly sifted. Hence has resulted a further confidence, both of the authenticity of the facts detailed, and of the correctness of his own views and opinions.

The narrator does not feel himself at liberty, for the present, to obtrude his personal acknowledgments: it will suffice to declare, that he has deeply felt his obligation to the superior judgment, which has enabled him to discover errors and inaccuracies, that might have escaped his own observation; and shall consider whatever value may hereafter be thought to attach to the performance, as an authentic continuation of the political history of India through the period in question, to be more ascribable to the aid he has received in its revision, than to any pains of his own in the compilation.

Calcutta, February, 1819.

ADVERTISEMENT.

THIS work was transmitted piecemeal for publication; and its appearance has been retarded, partly by the negligence of the hands to which the manuscript was confided, and partly by some unforeseen difficulties, which it is impossible, and perhaps immaterial, to explain. For any inaccuracies of the type, or discrepancy in the spelling of Indian words and names in the map and text, the Editor's professional avocations and total ignorance of Eastern orthography must plead in excuse.—A short glossary, and a catalogue of the native princes and persons of distinction, that figure in the narrative, is added for the convenience of the untravelled European reader.

C. R. P.

Temple, April, 1820.

CONTENTS.

CHAPTER I.

INTRODUCTORY MATTERS.

STATE of India on Lord Moira's Arrival—Relations of the British with Native Powers—Alliances, subsidiary, protective—disposition towards British—of States subject to their Influence—Nizam—Pêshwa—other subsidiary Allies—of protected Allies—Independent Powers—Holkar—Sindheea—Nature of their power and administration since 1805—military force—how employed—Disposition towards British—Bhoosla—disposition—General view—Military adventurers not checked or suppressed—Pindarees in 1814—their history—settlement on Nerbudda—mode of warfare—successes—Rise of Kureem Khan—his Power in 1806—and Fall—Chetoo—Dost Mahommed—Kureem's redemption—second rise—designs, and fall—Durras in 1814—Patans—their power—locality—Relations with Mahrattas and Rajpoots—Ameer Khan—his Force in 1814 - - - - - - - Page 1

CHAPTER II.

NIPÂL—MAHRATTAS.

Nipâl War—Governor-General leaves the Presidency—Intentions respecting predatory bands—defensive plans—that adopted—reasons—intrigues afoot—Bhopâl and Sâgur alliance resolved on—condition of Bhopâl—designs of Mahrattas thereon—Chief applies for British protection—terms offered—consequent military arrangements—progress of negotiation—communication to Sindheea—how received by him—Bhoosla—and Pêshwa—influence of Nipâlese war—operations in that quarter—disasters—further preparations—successful close of the campaign—Preparations—in the Dukhun—on S. W. frontier of Hindoostan—augmentation of Bengal army—tranquillity of the season—Conduct of Bhopâl—its Vakeel dismissed—communication thereof—Reflections - - - - - - - 33

CHAPTER III.

HYDERABAD—POONA.

1815. JUNE, JULY.

Rains set in—Hyderabad—Nizam's sons seize a dependent of the Residency—guard set upon them obliged to retire—troops called into Hyderabad—their submission and confinement in Golkonda—Poona—account of Bajee Rao—of Gykwar—his relation to Pêshwa—to British—policy of Pêshwa, and claims on Nizam—on Gykwar—referred to British arbitration—award as to Ahmedabad—Trimbukjee Dainglia—Gungadhur Sastree's negotiation—Intrigues at Brodera—protest of British Resident—renunciation of the arbitration—Gungadhur practised upon, and gained over—pilgrimage to Nassick—Sastree gives offence—his destruction planned—pilgrimage to Pundurpoor—dissimulation—Sastree murdered - - - Page 59

CHAPTER IV.

POONA CONTINUED.

1815. AUGUST TO DECEMBER.

Resident—his resolves—returns to Poona—obtains proof against Trimbukjee—demands audience—presents a memorial—charging Trimbukjee—calls subsidiary force from frontier—Bajee Rao hesitates—asks proof—evades receiving it—Gykwar mission threatened—attempts to screen Trimbukjee—Hyderabad force called in—expedients offered and refused—instructions arrive—second memorial thereon—demand of Trimbukjee's surrender—Pêshwa's irresolution—seizure of Trimbukjee and surrender—reflections—effect in Guzerât - - - - 82

CHAPTER V.

NIPÂLESE—PINDAREES.

1815-16. MAY TO MAY.

Negotiations with Nipâl—terms offered—Cession of Teraee refused—Demand modified—hesitation—Treaty signed—Ratification refused—War renewed—Ochterlony takes the command—penetrates the first range of hills—Battle of Mukwanpoor—Nipâlese submit—Peace—Reflections—Pindarees—second reference to England—Army reduced—Operations of Pindarees—party surprised—successful expedition—second—British provinces ravaged with impunity—Concert of Pindarees with Mahrattas—intrigues of 1815-16—Holkar's court—Ameer-Khan - - - 103

CHAPTER VI.

BHOPÂL—NÂGPOOR.

1816. MARCH TO JULY.

Death of Vizier Mahommed—and of Ragoojee Bhoosla—consequent deliberations—Bhopâl—its alliance declined—Nâgpoor—Pursajee—his incapacity—Appa Saheb—his pretensions—character—Dhurmajee Bhoosla—his intrigues—their ill success—both parties court the British resident—who waits instructions—their tenor—alliance and terms offered—transactions at Nâgpoor—Dhurmajee confined—Appa Saheb regent—seeks British alliance—Naroba—negotiation—its progress—conclusion—and signature—reflections—Subsidiary force called in—further transactions at Nâgpoor - - - - - - Page 122

CHAPTER VII.

JYPOOR, &c.

1816. APRIL TO OCTOBER.

Jypoor alliance—orders from England—suspended—resumed—debated—resolved upon—Military preparations—Negotiation—protracted—broken off—internal condition of Jypoor—fresh overtures—and negotiation—Again broken off—Nâgpoor affairs—Sindheea's supineness—and offer to Jypoor—Pêshwa's conduct—and intrigues—Trimbukjee's escape—communications with Bajee Rao in consequence - 144

CHAPTER VIII.

PINDAREES.

1816-17. OCTOBER TO APRIL.

Nâgpoor subsidiary force moves to the Nerbudda—Pindarees alarmed—their first effort—grand expedition in three divisions—1st to Ganjam—2d to Bidur—surprised by Major M'Dowal—exploit of Sheikh Dulloo—3d to Ahmednugur—surprised by Major Lushington—Ganjam penetrated—Borthwick's pursuit—1st party intercepted—reflections—resolution to extirpate the hordes—motives—Sindheea—Holkar—Dya-Ram of Hatras—his fort invested and bombarded—his escape—fort taken 162

CHAPTER IX.

NÂGPOOR—POONA.

1817. JANUARY TO JUNE.

Nâgpoor—Ram Chundur Wâgh—Sudeek Ulee Khan—Appa Saheb goes to Chanda—intrigues—death of Pursajee—by violent means—accession of Appa Saheb—change of policy—intrigues with Pêshwa—Poona—Pêshwa's duplicity—Trimbukjee levies troops—is covertly supported—Resident's proceedings—Discussions with the Durbar —Subsidiary force called down—intercourse suspended—effect—operations against Trimbukjee—their success—Colonel Smith called in to Poona—terms of demand—refused—Poona invested—Bajee Rao submits—Governor-General's instructions—conduct of Pêshwa—New treaty signed—Its conditions—Reflections—Military movements - - - - - - - - Page 180

CHAPTER X.

GENERAL PREPARATIONS.

1817. JUNE TO NOVEMBER.

Treaty of Poona executed—cessions adjusted—vakeels dismissed—advantages to Gykwar —increase of subsidiary force—consequent cessions and exchange of territory—Governor-General's plans—Hindoostan—Dukhun—Madras army—how disposed—delays in Dukhun—Lord Hastings leaves the Presidency—Political operations—their scale enlarged on Lord Hastings' sole responsibility—he takes the field—crosses the Jumna—General Donkin moves from Agra—negotiation with Sindheea—terms proposed—demand of Hindia and Aseergurh—reasons—treaty signed and ratified—consequent general order—its execution—Treaty with Ameer Khan—and Keroulee chief—Jaloun—Sâgur—Bhopâl - - - - - - 205

CHAPTER XI.

PINDAREES—POONA—NÂGPOOR.

1817. OCTOBER TO DECEMBER.

Pindarees during rains—General Marshall from Bundelkhund—a Pindara enterprise—frustrated—operations on the Nerbudda—Sir Thomas Hislop's retrograde movement —operations in Malwa—Sir Thomas Hislop recalled thither—Poona affairs—reduction of Soondoor demanded—and effected—fresh levies of troops—Sepoys—tampered with—Kandêsh—critical situation of brigade—it moves to Kirkee—Moro Dikshut—Brigadier-General Smith on the frontier—precautions—Pêshwa's demands —Residency attacked and burnt—battle of Poona—Moro Dikshut killed—cruelties of Mahrattas—Brigadier-General Smith's move on Poona—attacks Bajee Rao's camp —city surrendered—Nâgpoor—retrospect from July—Raja irresolute—receives titles from Poona—and is publicly invested—precautions of defence—British position—attacked—pressed—and partly carried—charge of Captain Fitzgerald—restores the day—defeat of the enemy—reflections—loss on both sides—influence of these events —charge of treachery weighed - - - - - - 231

CHAPTER XII.

NÂGPOOR—HINDOOSTAN.

1817. DECEMBER.

Reinforcements to Nâgpoor—Colonel Gahan—Major Pitman—Brigadier-General Doveton—Brigadier-General Hardyman—Terms proposed to the Raja—He temporizes—and surrenders—His camp attacked—and carried—Fort of Nâgpoor occupied by Arabs—besieged and assaulted without success—Arabs capitulate—Reasons for the Raja's reinstation—terms—dissent of Governor-General—retracted—British acquisitions—Reflections—Hindoostan—Pindarees—Suspicious conduct of regular powers—effect on Lord Hastings' plans—Cholera morbus—its virulence—and symptoms—Centre division arrives at Erich—moves back to the Sindh—movements in pursuit of Pindarees—affair at Bicheetal—wife of Kureem captured—Escape through Huraotee—distress—Exploit of a Havildar—Consequent military dispositions Page 263

CHAPTER XIII.

HOLKAR—HINDOOSTAN.

1817-18. DECEMBER, JANUARY, FEBRUARY.

Brigadier-General Malcolm pursues Cheetoo—meets the army of Holkar—Falls back on Oojein—overtures from that durbar—Effect of Pêshwa's defection—army advances—Junction of the divisions of Malcolm and Hislop—negotiation tried—Regent put to death—hostilities—Battle of Mehudpoor—Junction of the Guzerat division—Terms offered—Treaty of Mundisôr—affair of Rampoora—Effect on Sindheea—Juswunt Rao Bhao—affair of Jawud—Kumulnèr and other forts taken—Final settlement in that quarter—Pindarees expelled from Mewur—surprised at Kotree—further pursuit—Submission of Namdar Khan—Wâsil Mahommed—Kureem and his son—how disposed of—Cheetoo - - - - - - - - 287

CHAPTER XIV.

POONA.

1817-18. NOVEMBER TO APRIL.

Pêshwa's flight and pursuit—is cut off from the north—returns to the south—affair at Koragâon—resolute defence of Captain Staunton—repulse of the enemy—remarks—flight of Bajee Rao continued—Brigadier-General Pritzler's pursuit—Bajee Rao turns north—met by General Smith, and pursued up the Kishna—new distribution of British force—Suttara taken—plans of Governor-General in respect to Pêshwa and Suttara Raja—reasons and reflections—instructions issued—Suttara Raja proclaimed—General Smith pursues Bajee Rao—comes up with him at Ashtee—Gokla slain—Suttara family captured—notice respecting Gokla—Pêshwa's distress—capture of his forts—desertion of his Jageerdars—joined by Gunput Rao and Ram Deen—flight to the northward - - - - - - - 310

CHAPTER XV.

HINDOOSTAN—KANDÊSH.

1818. FEBRUARY, MARCH.

Holkar—Ameer Khan—his crafty conduct—guns obtained—Troops disbanded—takes refuge in Kota—Patans taken into British service—Policy of the measure—Proceedings of Sir David Ochterlony—Troops in the field in February—exchanges with Sindheea proposed—Lord Hastings quits the field with the centre division—Sâgur—its reduction ordered—Reasons—Terms offered to Bunaeek Rao—and accepted—Dhamonee reduced—Mundela stormed—New distribution of the forces—Sir Thomas Hislop's return—Soandwara reduced—Sindwa occupied—Resistance at Talnêr—and storm—Loss of officers—Garrison put to the sword—Killadar hanged—Sir Thomas Hislop in communication with Brigadier-General Doveton - Page 333

CHAPTER XVI.

NÂGPOOR—DUKHUN.

1818. FEBRUARY TO MAY.

Nâgpoor—ministry of restored Raja—his fresh intrigues and early treachery—Resident's suspicions and measures—Governor-General's first instructions—Detection of the plots—arrest of Raja and his ministers—Bajee Rao applied to by Bhoosla for aid—consequent proceedings—marches eastward—eludes Sir Thomas Hislop's division—Army of the Dukhun broken up—progress of Bajee Rao—Brigadier-General Smith co-operates with Brigadier-General Doveton—Lieutenant-Colonel Adams—repulse of Gunput Rao—Lieutenant-Colonel Adams at Hingunghât—waits for other divisions, and advances—route of Soonee—pursuit by Brigadier-General Doveton—dispersion of Mahratta army—detention and submission of sirdars—Wusota invested and captured—new distribution of the forces—capture of other forts—affair of Solapoor—Chanda invested—its surrender - - - - - - 355

CHAPTER XVII.

NÂGPOOR—PÊSHWA, &c.

1818. MAY, JUNE, JULY.

Appa Saheb's exile—and escape—consequent measures—Bajee Rao's designs—frustrated—He sends an agent to Sir John Malcolm—is surrounded—negotiates—terms offered—intentions of Governor-General—approach of Brigadier-General Doveton—arrested—Bajee Rao submits—terms—objections—Reflections—Dispersion of Bajee Rao's army—Trimbukjee seized—Arabs refractory—General submission of the country—Review of Mr. Elphinstone's proceedings—their effect on the several classes of the population—cultivating—religious—military—commercial—Arabs of Kandêsh—their expulsion resolved—Siege of Malugâon—vigorous sally—repulsed—Assault fails—Reinforcements—bombardment—explosion of magazine—surrender of the place—mistake in the terms—Close of the campaign - - Page 383

CHAPTER XVIII.

GENERAL RESULT.

Objects of this chapter—political result—Dukhun—Suttara Raja—Bhoosla—Nizam—Hindoostan—Holkar—Nuwab of Bhopâl—Ameer Khan—Ghufoor Khan—Reflections—Rajpoot princes—Kota—peculiarity in the treaty—Joudhpoor—Oodeepoor—Captain Tod's arrangements—convention of Thakoors—and constitution fixed—Boondee—Bhikaneer—Jesulmeer—Jypoor—indecision—treaty concluded—State of Jypoor—plan for its settlement—Raja's death—New military posts in Hindoostan—Sindheea—His present condition—external relations—internal government—how remedied—Auxiliary horse—Fate of sirdars—Baptiste—Bapoo Sindheea—Effect of their ruin—Probable issue—General reflections—Financial result—character of Indian revenue—Financial condition in 1814—in subsequent years—Result up to 1818—Home supplies—Value of territorial acquisitions—Comparative view—Home territorial charges explained—General reflections - - - - 418

GLOSSARY.

Bŭneea, a merchant, or dealer.—*Sansc.*
Chelā, an elève, or ward.—*Sansc.*
Chitnavees, a private secretary.—*Pers.*
Chout, black mail; redemption from tribute; the fourth part of any thing.—*Sansc.*
Choultry, an inn, or caravansera.—*Hind.*
Coss, a measure of length; about two miles.—*Pers.*
Dāk, post for letters or travellers.—*Pers.*
Dhŭrna, sitting in, a mode of importunate demand.—*Sansc.*
Dŭrbār, the court of a prince.—*Pers.*
Dŭrrā, a horde or band of freebooters.—*Hind.*
Fŭrnăvēes, a secretary.—*Pers.*
Gooroo, a family priest.—*Sansc.*
Gŭddee, the cushion or seat of state.—*Hind.*
Hŭrkāra, a courier.—*Pers.*
Jāgeer, a fief.—*Pers.*
Jŭngŭl, forest.—*Sansc. and Pers.*
Killădār, a governor.—*Arab.*
Khutree, the military caste.—*Hind.*
Khilāt, a dress of honour.—*Pers. and Sansc.*
Kūtra, a walled town.
Lōoteea, a common plunderer.—*Sansc.*
Lūhbur, a foray or marauding party.—*Sansc.*
Moŏnshee, a linguist, or interpreter.—*Arab.*
Mŭsnŭd, the cushion or seat of state.—*Arab.*
Mōolkgērēe, conquest.—*Arab.*
Nullā, a dry torrent bed.—*Sansc.*
Petta, a town: the suburb of a fort.—*Sansc.*
Raj, a kingdom, or royal residence.—*Sansc.*
Rēsāla, a body of horse resembling a pulk of Cossacks.—*Sansc.*

Sĭrdār, a chief, or superior officer.—*Pers.*
Sĕbundee, the militia, or gens d'armerie.—*Pers.*
Sĭpāhee, or Sepoy, a foot soldier.—*Pers.*
Sōoba, a province, or government.—*Arab.*
Srad'h, a funeral ceremonial.—*Sansc.*
Sŭnnŭd, a deed of grant, or warrant.—*Sansc.*
Sŭrunjămee, military service tenure.—*Pers.*
Syce, a groom, or horse-keeper.—*Sansc.*
Vakeel, an envoy, or negotiator.—*Arab.*

TITLES.

Hindoo.

Pers.	Pêshwā, minister.
	Pêshkar, deputy.
Sansc.	Rājā, ruling prince.
Hind.	Rānā, ruling prince.
Hind.	Nānā, ruling prince.
Sansc.	Rāj-Rānā, regent, or viceroy.
Hind.	Sēna-puttee, general; title of the Raja of Berar.
Hind.	Sēna-Khas-Khel, commander of the faithful band.
Sansc.	Bhâo, prince.
	Râo, prince.
Sansc.	Rām, a title of nobility.
Sansc.	Thakoor, a feudal lord.
	Bāee, dowager princess.
	Baych, dowager princess.

Moosulman.

	Nizam, title of the Nuwab of Hyderabad originally; viceroy of the Dukhun under the Moghuls.
Arab.	Nuwab, a governor; a ruling prince.
Arab.	Vizīer, a minister of state.
Pers.	Dēwan, an administrator, or minister.
Pers.	Khān, a lord; a title of nobility.
Turk.	Bēgŭm, a dowager princess.
Arab.	Sāheb, lord; an appellation of rank.

TRIBES OF HINDOOS.

Bheels, a tribe on the borders of Rajpootana.
Jāts, a north-western tribe.
Goands, a north-western tribe, inhabiting the Mohadeo range.
Grasseas, a tribe inhabiting the Sātpoora range.
Soandees, a tribe between Oojeen and Rampoora.

Names of the principal Native Princes mentioned in the Narrative, with their respective seats of government, and the names of the British Residents.

Moosulman Princes.	Capital.	British Residents.
Nizam.	Hyderabad.	Mr. H. Russell.
Nuwab Vizier of Oude,—Ghazee Oodeen Hyder.	Lucknâo.	——
Nuwab Viziers of Bhopâl. 1. Mahommed. 2. Nuzur Mahommed.	Bhopâl.	——

Mahrattas.

Hindoo Princes.		
Raja of Suttara—Noor Nerayun.	Suttara.	Captain Grant, assistant.
Pêshwa—Bajee Râo.	Poona.	Mr. Elphinstone.
Gykwar. Anund Rao, nominal. Futteh Singh, actual.	Brodera.	——
Rajas of Nâgpoor. 1. Ragoojee Bhoosla. 2. Pursajee Bhoosla (Bala Saheb). 3. Moodajee Bhoosla (Appa Saheb.) 4. Bajee Râo Bhoosla.	Nâgpoor.	Mr. Jenkins.
Sindheea—Maha Raja Doulut Râo Sindheea.	Gwalior.	Mr. Strachey. Captain Close.
Holkar—Maha Raja Mulhar Rao Holkar.	Indore.	Major Agnew, assistant.
Nana of Sâgur. Govind Rao, legitimate. Bunaeek Rao, intrusive.	Sâgur.	——

Hindoo Princes.	Capital.	British Residents.
Rajpoots.		
Rana of Oodeepoor. ———	Oodeepoor.	Captain Tod, assistant.
Raja of Jypoor—Purtab Singh.	Jynagurh.	———
Raja of Joudhpoor—Man Singh.	Joudhpoor.	———
Raja of Kota—Kishwur Singh.	Kota.	———
Raj-Rana—Zalim Singh.		
Nipâlese.		
Goorkha Raja. ———	Katmândhoo.	Mr. E. Gardner.

DIRECTIONS FOR ARRANGING THE PLATES, &c.

	Page
Head of the Marquess of Hastings to face the title page.	
Map	1
1. Defile of Cheree—Ghâtee pass 2. Lodgment on Malaoun Hills	33
3. Ghoorkha defences 4. Position of Jyt'huk	82
5. Jypoor 6. Nâgpoor Residency	144
7. Hatras 8. Chanda	180
9. Plan of operations at Poona 10. Plan of operations at Nâgpoor	231
11. Plan of attack on Jawud 12. Plan of attack on Jubbulpoor	263
13. Plan of the battle of Mehudpoor	287
14. Kumulnèr 15. Talnèr	333
16. Plan of assault on Sholapoor 17. Plan of rout of Soonee	355

NARRATIVE.

CHAPTER I.

INTRODUCTORY MATTERS.

State of India on Lord Moira's Arrival—Relations of the British with Native Powers—Alliances, subsidiary, protective—disposition towards British—of States subject to their Influence—Nizam—Pêshwa—other subsidiary Allies—of protected Allies—Independent Powers—Holkar—Sindheea—Nature of their power and administration since 1805—military force—how employed—Disposition towards British—Bhoosla—disposition—General view—Military adventurers not checked or suppressed—Pindarees in 1814—their history—settlement on Nerbudda—mode of warfare—successes—Rise of Kureem Khan—his Power in 1806—and Fall—Cheetoo—Dost Mahommed—Kureem's redemption—second rise—designs, and fall—Durras in 1814—Patans—their power—locality—Relations with Mahrattas and Rajpoots—Ameer Khan—his Force in 1814.

THE Earl of Moira, since created Marquess of Hastings, arrived in India, and assumed the government-general, about the end of the year 1813. The relations of the British dominion with the several native powers, as adjusted during the second administration of Lord Cornwallis and that of Sir George Barlow, had continued up to this period with little variation. The attention of Lord Minto, the retiring governor-general, had been chiefly occupied, at first in preparing the states on our western frontier, to resist the passage of the French, who were then thought to meditate an expedition over-land; afterwards, in composing the discontents of the Madras army; and latterly, in wresting from the dominion of France, and the continental powers under her influence, their yet remaining insular possessions in the Indian ocean and in Polynesia. The only political operations of the eight years in question, which require notice, as anywise affecting the general system of our political relations in India, are, first, the reception of the Seikh chieftains under protection in 1809, by which measure, the British influence was extended to the Sutlej, and the rising power and ambition of Runjeet Singh materially curbed: secondly, a similar extension upon the Bundelkhund frontier, by the admission of the Rajas of Duttea and Tearee, and the Nana of Jhansee to our alliance, and by the measures adopted to curb and punish the Rewa principality, which, lying south-west of Benares, and east of Bundelkhund, had, in 1812, invited and facilitated the march of a body of marauders from the banks of the Nerbudda into the rich provinces of Mirzapoor and South Behar. In other respects, no alteration whatever had taken place in our political relations. The measures adopted for opposing the designs of Ameer Khan, which were supposed to be directed even to the subversion of the Nâgpoor government, and the establishment of a Moosulman power on its ruins, appeared, at one time, on the point of bringing about a subsidiary alliance with the Bhoosla Raja; but, for reasons, which need not be stated here, this connexion never took place; and the attempts subsequently made to accomplish it in Lord Minto's time, were frustrated by the personal jealousy and secret hostility of the Raja.

At the period of Lord Hastings's arrival, the native powers may be classed under four heads. First, those with whom the British nation had formed subsidiary alliances. Secondly, those enjoying its protection without any subsidiary contract, and consisting, for the most part, of small principalities, scarcely meriting the name of substantive powers. Thirdly, acknowledged princes, with whom the British government was at peace, and connected by the mutual obligation of treaties, but with whom it had no further intercourse or influence, except in so far as the residence of a British representative at the court was sometimes a matter of stipulation. Fourthly, independent chieftains and associations, who had never been acknowledged as substantive states, and to whom the British nation was bound by no engagements whatever. It may be useful, by way of introduction to the narrative of the late political and military operations in India, to give a brief sketch of the actual position of these respective classes, and of their disposition towards the British government at the commencement of the year 1814.

The states connected with the British power by subsidiary alliances were, the Nizam at Hyderabad, the Pêshwa at Poona, the Gykwar in Guzerat, and the Rajas of Mysore and Travancore. The Nuwab of Oude ought, perhaps, in strictness to be added to these; but the cessions, exacted of him by Lord Wellesley in 1801, had so circumscribed his territories, and contracted his means, that, although independent in the management of his remaining territories, and consequently far superior to the pageant courts of Dehlee, Moorshedabad, and Arcot, he is in too great dependence on the British government, to be regarded as one of the political states of India.

All the subsidiary alliances had been formed upon the same principles. The British nation had stipulated to furnish a specific force for the protection of the country, and for the maintenance of the sovereign's legitimate authority. This force was not to be employed in the duties of civil administration, nor in the collection of the revenues; and the British government had generally agreed not to interfere in such matters. A subsidy, equivalent to the expense of the force, was furnished by the state thus protected, either in periodical money payments, or by territorial cession, more frequently the latter; a certain native contingent was also maintained, in readiness to act with the subsidiary force, for the efficiency of which the subsidizing state was answerable. But the most material provision of these treaties was, that the states accepting them engaged to discontinue all political negotiation with the other powers of India, except in concert with the British government, and to submit all claims and disputes with others to its arbitration and final adjudication.

The engagements for the simple protection of chieftainships and principalities had the same contrôlling character, in respect to the external relations of the parties protected, with other native powers; nor did they differ materially in substance from the subsidiary treaties, except inasmuch as there was seldom any consideration exacted for the protection to be afforded, and never any obligation on the British government to maintain a specific force for the purpose. The principal members of this class were—the Rajas of Bhurtpoor and Macherree, with some other chieftains settled in the neighbourhood of Agra and Dehlee—the Bundela Chiefs, whose possessions skirted the frontier of Bundelkhund—and, latterly, the Seikhs, with several others in different parts of India. The two Rajpoot states of Jypoor and Joudhpoor had been included in this system by Lord Wellesley; but, in the settlement of 1805-6, they were left without the pale of our relations, from an apprehension that these were already too much extended. The Raja of Jypoor was considered, by his conduct in the war with Holkar, to have forfeited all claim to our farther protection; while the Raja of Joudhpoor had refused to ratify the treaty concluded with Lord Lake by his representative; so that no impediment arose out of any existing engagements with either state, to counteract the desire of the British government to withdraw from their connexion.

When mention is made of the extent of the British influence, in the estimate of the national power and resources in

India, it is in allusion to the states and principalities, whose relation with us is of one or other of the above two descriptions. These must by no means be overlooked in such an estimate; for it is one most striking feature of the connexion, indeed an express stipulation, that, in case of exigency, the whole resources of the states in alliance shall be at the command and under the direction of the British government. It must not, however, be supposed, that, of the powers thus subject to our influence, all were equally contented with their lot, or ready to afford the aid of their resources with equal zeal and alacrity. In proportion as the connexion with us had originated in motives of ambition, or interest, or necessity, or had resulted from a conviction of inability, by other means, to resist a more than transitory danger, with which their very existence was threatened from other quarters, in the same proportion were the princes, with whom these alliances subsisted, either restless and discontented at the restraints imposed on their schemes of further aggrandizement, or well satisfied with the undisturbed enjoyment of what they felt conscious they owed the possession of entirely to such alliance.

Of the subsidizing states, the Nizam was our most useful ally, and had perhaps the best reason to be satisfied with his confederates. He had formed the connexion after receiving a severe defeat from the Pêshwa, which must have produced a conviction of the inadequacy of his own means of defence, and while the power of Tippoo was a subject of constant apprehension to him. The overthrow of that prince, and the consequent augmentation of the power and influence of the British government, in some degree removed the imminency of the danger; but these events, and the transactions connected with them, naturally led to a closer intercourse between the two states, and accustomed the Nizam habitually to rely on the British government; while the annual incursions of the Pindarees served to keep alive the sense of his weakness. He had, besides, received from us in Berar, as the fruit of the alliance, an accession of territory yielding a revenue of 60 lack R^s. But gratitude is seldom a motive for the good faith of princes; our ground of confidence was the knowledge, that since forming the treaty, by which we undertook his protection, the Nizam had entirely neglected his private means, leaving his whole resources at our disposal, and allowing even his military establishment to be modelled to our will, and placed under British officers. The successor of Nizam Alee Khan was, indeed, of a weak and indolent character, and the government was in the hands of a ministry*, which, but for the constant protection of the British resident, could not have withstood the intrigues of the disaffected and designing, who abounded both in the court and in the seraglio. The secret of the Nizam's attachment and devotion to our interests is not difficult to be unravelled; the prince himself was wrapped up in pageantry and sensual pleasure; and the minister had become a creature of our own, insomuch that through him the resources and means of the state took whatever direction was pointed out by the British representative at this court. Not that the Nizam's government had thus degenerated through any design or agency of our

* The nominal minister was a relation and favourite of the Nuwab's, named Moneer-ood-d'oullah, a weak man and unacquainted with business; the real minister was a Hindoo, Raja Chundoo Lal, who, under the title of Naeeb (deputy), conducted the whole government. The introduction of this man was the result of a compromise with the Nizam; whose claim to the independent choice of his minister was admitted on the part of the British government, on condition, that the Hindoo should be made deputy, and the principal never interfere with his administration. The Nizam, for some time after this arrangement, had shown considerable ill humour, and ultimately shut himself up in his palace, and refrained altogether from meddling with public affairs. His conduct sometimes betrayed imbecility and aberration of mind, and sometimes a degree of acuteness and intelligence not incompatible with such a state of intellect.

own; on the contrary, we had more reason to deplore, than to rejoice, at this decline of its executive power, which was frequently a source of great inconvenience to us, and was continually calling in the strong arm of British authority to enforce its orders and uphold its weakness; and this in a manner, which no delicacy could disguise altogether.

The conduct of the Pêshwa had been the exact reverse of that of the Nizam: he had availed himself with the utmost art of his connexion with the British nation to recover and improve his own resources; and, instead of trusting wholly to our aid, evinced at all times the greatest jealousy of any attempt, on the part of the resident at his court, to cement a closer union, and, by detaching him from other engagements, to confirm his dependence on the support of the British government. Indeed, when the subsidiary alliance was first formed by Bajee Rao, the value of his attachment was correctly appreciated by the Marquess Wellesley. With that depth of observation, for which his lordship was so justly celebrated, he thus prophetically warned the Honourable Court of Directors of the disposition they must expect to find in their new ally. "It was evident," Lord Wellesley wrote in April, 1804, "that the Pêshwa had "only entered into the defensive alliance with the British "Government, because his highness was convinced he had no "other way of recovering any part of his just authority, or of "maintaining tranquillity in his empire. *The state of his high-"ness's affairs taking a favourable turn, his highness, supported "by the sentiments of the different branches of the Mahratta "empire, would be desirous of annulling the engagements he had "made with the British Government.*" The events of the last few years afford the best development of Bajee Rao's actual disposition towards us, after the lapse of ten years had enabled him to derive all the benefit he could reap from our alliance, towards the consolidation of his own power, and to court in security the general sentiment of the Mahratta nation, which had been thus designated as the foundation of some future rupture of this unnatural association.

At the courts of the three remaining powers, with whom subsidiary alliances had been formed, the ascendancy of the British influence was so firmly fixed, that an opposite interest could scarcely be said to exist in them. The conviction at these courts of the greatness of our power, and of the utter hopelessness of any attempt to thwart our plans, caused them to give at once into the policy of sparing no effort to secure our favour, on which rested all their hopes of prosperity. With the Gykwar, the ties were much closer drawn than with the Nizam or Pêshwa; the right of the British Government to interfere with certain qualifications in the internal administration of the country being matter of stipulation by treaty with the state *. The Mysore Raja is a prince of our own creation, and the Travancore Raja a minor: this last state, however, was never entitled to much consideration in the scale of native powers, and for some time was altogether governed by Colonel Monro the resident, on whom the office of prime minister was conferred, with the title of Dewan.

The disposition of the second class, viz. of protected states,

* The connexion with the Gykwar was anomalous. Soon after the subsidiary alliance, the utter imbecility of Anund Rao, and the confusion introduced into his affairs by Arabs and bankers, who had been security for his debts, obliged the leading men of the state to solicit the Bombay government to take that security on itself, and to give its support to Seeta-ram, son of Raojee Appajee, as Dewan with full powers, in the hope of thus restoring order and liquidating the debts. This arrangement failing from Seeta-ram's incapacity, he was deprived of power, and the administration placed in the hands of a commission, whereof the British resident was a member. Afterwards Anund Rao's brother, Futteh Singh Gykwar, was brought forward and vested with the sole direction of affairs, under the resident's advice. This arrangement continued till Futteh Singh's death in 1818, Anund Rao Gykwar living as a cypher in his own palace, where he was treated with every personal attention; but his constitutional imbecility continued.

varied of course, in a similar manner to that of those, whose connexion was of a subsidiary character. The Raja of Bhurtpoor's object, in accepting protection in 1805-6 from a power, whose whole force he conceived he had recently baffled, was to recover, without other equivalent than the nominal sacrifice of unrestrained latitude of political action, the fortress of Deeg, and the greater part of his territory, then in our hands. He has ever since viewed us with the most arrogant haughtiness, not exempt from suspicion, distrust, and fear. His whole conduct has shown him to be the most hostile in heart and disposition of all the princes of India. Feeling that his former success had made him the rallying point of disaffection from all quarters, he seemed evidently to court that dangerous pre-eminence, and to assume the attitude of one, that rather sought than avoided another occasion of trying his fortune against us: although in fact, he secretly dreaded our power in the greatest degree. His policy was displayed in openly thwarting and irritating us to the full extent of our forbearance; but conceding immediately, when he found he could safely risk no further provocation.

The other protected chiefs in that direction were generally well contented, with the single exception of the Macherree Raja, who, finding himself in the vicinity of the Jypoor state, which was distracted by internal faction and external attack, had attempted to avail himself of the opportunity of aggrandizing his own territory, at the expense of a helpless neighbour, and took occasion to seize upon some of his forts and villages. Our government, however, had interfered, and obliged the invader to make restitution; and he had been further mulcted for delaying instant obedience to the order for their evacuation.

The eastern Seikhs, whom the terror of the British name alone had saved from the arms of Runjeet Singh, and the Bundèlas, who felt indebted to it for a similar protection from Sindheea's officers, and from the marauders of the Nerbudda, were in every respect contented with the connexion, and evinced on all occasions, the most zealous attachment and obedience. But the Raja of Rewa, though he had, in the first instance, voluntarily embraced the alliance, very soon afterwards had repented of the engagement, and was evidently anxious to take the first opportunity of shaking it off. It would have been unreasonable to have expected, that the disposition of such various allies should be universally favourable, without reference to the different circumstances, attending the contraction of the alliance, or to the capricious views, which the native princes are so apt to entertain, of what is best for their present interest. In the widely extended sphere of our alliances, it was natural, that several of the confederates should be disaffected, many lukewarm, and few zealous for the maintenance of the system of general regulation we had introduced. The greatest forbearance towards all these different sentiments, and extreme moderation and consistency in our dealings, were essential to our success in the management of the stupendous machine, which we had organized: particularly with a view to the possibility of still further extension of the system at some future period.

The states and powers of the third class, that is to say, those not directly under our influence, and with whom our connexion was that of mutual amity alone, were, the Sindheea, the Bhoosla, and the Holkar families. British residents were stationed at the two former courts; but none had ever resided at the Holkar Durbar. Indeed, since the derangement of Juswunt Rao's intellect, and more especially since his death, which occurred in 1811, the power, which his personal ability had erected and maintained, was crumbling fast to pieces; while Ameer Khan, Mahommed Shah Khan, and other of his retainers, were raising themselves to consequence and independence on the ruins of the fortunes of his family. Juswunt Rao's son and successor,

Mulhar Rao, was a minor; and the intrigues of the women, superadded to the frequent mutiny of the troops for pay, and the gradual desertion of the different commanders to seek their fortune in a life of predatory adventure, were the only occurrences to be found in the reports of the news-writers at this court.

Sindheea, since the peace concluded with him in 1805, had steadily pursued the object of breaking the force and reducing the garrisons of the chiefs between the Chumbul and the Nerbudda, so as to establish and consolidate his own power in that quarter. A person little conversant in the affairs of India, and observing on the map the uniform colouring of a given space, described as forming the dominions of a Mahratta chief, would be led to suppose, that his authority was peaceably established over the whole of that space, in like manner as the British authority is established within the districts marked as its immediate possessions. This, however, is quite inconsistent with the character of Mahratta conquest. Instead of commencing with the removal of the existing government, and the general assumption of the whole authority to himself, a Mahratta chieftain begins, by appearing at the season of harvest, and demanding a consideration for his forbearance in withholding the mischief he has it in his power to inflict. The visit is annually repeated, and the demand proportionally enhanced. Whatever is thus exacted is called the *Chout*, and the process of exaction a *Moolkgeeree* (country-taking) expedition. When the same chieftain has been in the habit of continuing his annual exactions from a certain district for a number of successive years, he considers the practice of making them as a matter of right and property, and resents the interference of a stranger as an invasion of his property. In process of time, perhaps, he has a cantonment, or reduces a fort and establishes himself in the neighbourhood; his exactions swell to the full amount of the revenue; and, in the end, the authorities, that may heretofore have retained the local administration by paying these exactions, will either be superseded and reduced to mere cyphers, or be subdued and expelled by open force. The interval between the occurrence of this last act, and submission to the first exaction, will have been short or long, according as the opportunity may have been favourable for encroachment, or as the party, upon whom it has been attempted, happened to possess the sagacity to perceive, and the means to resist, the obvious tendency of such a system.

At the epoch of the settlement with Sindheea and Holkar in 1805, when the British Government engaged not to interfere with the dependencies of those chieftains lying within certain limits; that is to say, in Malwa, Mewar, and Marwar (including Kota, Joudhpoor, and Oodeepoor); the dominions of both families exhibited every variety of the intermediate state above described. The towns and villages, of which they had complete occupation, were comparatively few, and were moreover scattered about in different directions, disconnected and intermingled one with another: except in these few, the army of either chief was the whole machinery of his government, and was at all times kept in motion for the purpose of enforcing contributions from reluctant tributaries, who regularly resisted, and often successfully. Under these circumstances, the effect of the peace concluded with the British was, merely to restrict the theatre of such warfare to their own assumed dominions, and to allow the employment of the whole military power of each with greater activity against his respective dependents and nominal subjects. Thus, the confusion in that quarter of India, to which their operations were thenceforth confined, was necessarily increased, rather than diminished, by the peace; and one cannot wonder at the rapid rise of predatory hordes to power and consequence, under favour of such a state of affairs. Lord Wellesley's plan for the suppression of this system was, to extend his subsidiary alliances, which he expected would have the effect of inducing the native princes to discard their military establishments, as an useless expenditure and needless incumbrance. This plan was, however, abandoned by Sir George Barlow, so far as Sindheea and Holkar were concerned; indeed, their governments were so essentially military, that it could scarcely have succeeded with them under any circumstances, unless, in progress of time, they should assume a more regular form.

In 1805, and for some years after, Dowlut Rao Sindheea apparently took but little personal interest in the administration of his affairs. Until 1809, his government was, indeed, one of continual shifts and momentary expedients, and his durbar a mere arena for the factions of a selfish aristocracy, whereon to bring to issue their struggles for wealth and pre-eminence. The natural death of Ambajee Inglia, the too powerful Sooba of Gwalior, and the violent one of Surjee Râo, the father-in-law of Sindheea, both which occurred in 1809, enabled this prince to introduce a ministry more dependent on himself. Since that year, the control of affairs had been in the hands of a banker of the name of Gokul-paruk, recommended to office by his financial ability, and held in check by the counteracting influence and rivalry of personal favourites. By skilfully managing this balance, Dowlut Râo had asserted and exercised a more direct personal control over the affairs of his principality, during the latter period.

Up to 1810, Sindheea generally was in motion the whole of the favourable season, with the greater part of his army, employed either in punishing his own refractory officers, or in *Moolkgeeree* expeditions in Malwa, Bhopâl, or Rajpootana. Oojein was his nominal capital; but, after the forcible resumption of the Soobadaree of Gwalior from the family of his deceased vassal Ambajee, he pitched his camp a short distance to the south-west of that city and fortress; and, as his court has never been moved from the spot, except for occasional pilgrimages, a second city has arisen on the site of his encampment, rivalling the old one in population at least, if not in the appearance and structure of its edifices.

The great body of his troops have continued to be distributed over the surface of the country, enforcing tribute in the usual way, and taking every opportunity, by the capture of fortresses, and the seizure or expulsion of the petty Rajas and Chieftains in actual possession, to consolidate his power, and acquire a firmer hold of what had hitherto been more nominally than really under his dominion. The principal and most efficient of Sindheea's commanders employed on this service was Colonel Jean Baptiste Filoze, a man of ambiguous parentage on the father's side, his mother having been a common woman of a camp bazar attached to some of the French battalions. He had, however, been brought up, if not acknowledged, by the French officer whose name he bears; and the wreck of the infantry trained by the officers of that nation was placed under his command, on their desertion in the course of the war. A considerable portion of Sindheea's artillery was also attached to this force: and, in the interval between the settlement of 1805 and Lord Hastings' arrival as Governor-General, the forts and territories of Bahadur-gurh, Gurra-kota, Chanderee, Sheeopoor, with several others, had been wrested from their petty feudal lords by this commander. There were three other divisions of Sindheea's troops employed in the same manner, and commanded respectively by Bapoo Sindheea, Juswunt Râo Bhâo (successor to Juggoo Bapoo deceased), and Ambajee Punt. A fifth corps was stationed about his person at Gwalior, under command of one Jacob, a Portuguese half-cast, Arratoon an Armenian, and some other officers of distinction. The strength of each of these corps was from seven or eight to ten thousand men of all arms; but it fluctuated according to the personal views and interests of the respective commanders, who were individually answerable to their troops for pay, the greater part of Sindheea's territories being parcelled out amongst them, and assigned in lots for the subsistence of the several divisions by the discretionary levy of exactions and contributions by each within the specified limits. Under such a system, the Gwalior Durbar could not be expected to exercise a very active control over any of the Chiefs so employed; indeed, the intercourse of each with the court was an uniform series of mutual deception and jealousy.

The disposition of the prince towards the British Government must, on the whole, be considered to have been, up to 1813 *, rather favourable than otherwise. He found us punctual paymasters of the annual stipend of seven lack of rupees, agreed in November 1805 to be paid to him and his Chiefs. Nor had we, on any one occasion, interfered with the prosecution of his system of exaction upon the petty feudatories within the circle of his influence. Even when he sometimes exceeded his limits, which, by the treaty of 1805, he had engaged to consider as sacred, we had uniformly manifested the same indifference; and, though free to claim the advantage for ourselves, had never stepped forward to thwart his views of aggrandisement. Indeed he had felt, that so long as he abstained from the territories of our actual allies, he might fearlessly pursue his own schemes in any direction; and, as there was still abundant scope for his ambition, as well as of employment for his military dependents, within the limits from which we had withdrawn, he had been sensible of no restraints from our neighbourhood and superior power. This disposition resulted from

* In this year he received an emissary from the Pêshwa of the name of Ballaghee Punt.

his experience of our past conduct; but as there was no security for our continuing to act on the same system, and as events seemed fast verging to that state, which must force on us the adoption of one, that could not but interfere with his plans and interests, it was natural that he should entertain a jealousy of our views, proportionate to the sense of his own comparative inferiority.

The disposition of Holkar's court was similar; and its Sirdars seemed to consider it their policy to avoid giving offence to the British Government, even when they affected personal independence.

The resources of Ragoojee Bhoosla had been so reduced by the effects of the war of 1803, which deprived him at once of Berar and Cuttack, that he was scarcely strong enough to defend his own dominions from the aggression of the lawless predatory bands, which had collected along the Nerbudda. The military establishments of this prince, with the exception of some corps of Arabs kept near the Raja's person, were undoubtedly more defective than those of any native potentate. While fewer European improvements had been grafted on the old Mahratta system, the latter had lost all those qualities that ever had made it formidable. Indeed, so despicable was the character of his troops, that in 1809-10, Ameer Khan, a Patan officer in Holkar's service, and one of those who was aspiring at independence, planned an attack on Nâgpoor in combination with the Pindarees, and would assuredly have annihilated the power of Ragoojee, had not the British gratuitously aided him in this extremity. A simultaneous movement from Hindoostan and the Dukhun induced Ameer Khan to abandon the design. It was on this occasion, that a Madras and a Bengal force first met on the north of the Nerbudda; Colonel Sir Barry Close having advanced to Seronj, one of Ameer Khan's principal possessions, where he met Colonel Martindell from Bundelkhund.

Ragoojee's disposition towards us was far from friendly, notwithstanding the service thus rendered him: his resentment for the loss of Berar and Cuttack overpowered any feeling of gratitude for this subsequent benefit. Yet fear dictated to him the necessity of keeping on the best terms with the British Government: for the idea of his ability to call in its aid, was his main security at this time against the ambitious designs of the adventurers in his neighbourhood. Under this conviction, he was nevertheless jealous in the extreme of his political independence, and very averse to the formation of a specific defensive alliance of the same nature as those subsisting with the Nizam and Pèshwa; justly concluding it a sacrifice of his dignity and reputation among the states of India, to assume the character of dependence on a British subsidiary force.

Such being the feeling and disposition of the several great independent powers in India, there seemed little in their condition or motions calculated to excite any present alarm. As far as they were individually concerned, the object of the settlement of 1805-6 appeared to have been attained; their weakness afforded a security against any one of them meditating a separate hostile enterprise; at the same time, that the balance then established remained unaltered, and the mutual jealousies relied upon as the guarantee against a second coalition were yet unextinguished. Nevertheless, there was an unsoundness in this system of our relations, which had been predicted by many, at the moment of their establishment on this basis. Its defects had begun to be apparent some time before 1814, and it could no longer be disguised, that the settlement of 1805 was, after all, but an incomplete arrangement, which must ere long be entirely remodelled. It had become manifest that this settlement, or rather the state resulting from it, instead of having a tendency to wean the population of India from habits of military adventure, in which so large a portion of it had theretofore been bred, rather multiplied the inducements to engage in that course of life. The class addicted to such habits was evidently fast increasing. At the time of the settlement, though there were certainly some bands of marauders and brigands, associated under different leaders for purposes of general depredation, their number was not sufficient to attract notice, and it was thought that they must soon either be dissolved through want of effectual bonds of union, or be incorporated with the troops of the regular powers, or, at any rate, that these latter, as soon as they were relieved from foreign wars and expeditions, would have the means, and see the advantage, of restraining bodies of men, who professedly subsisted on the plunder of their neighbours. Instead of this result, however, either from weakness and indifference, or from some erroneous notion of the policy of favouring the lodgment, in their neighbourhood, of a military force, available as an addition to their own strength in the hour of need, without the charge of any regular pay or establishment, Sindheea and Holkar, if not active abettors of the growth of these freebooters, were, at least, very lukewarm in their efforts for their suppression. Their only solicitude was directed towards preventing aggression on themselves, and establishing a sort of nominal authority over as large a portion of the class as could be induced to acknowledge their supremacy. They even made liberal assignments of land to effect this object; and if a leader of a *durra* of Pindarees, so the associations were called, happened to make himself obnoxious, his ruin was attempted, by turning against him the arms of a rival leader; without reflecting, that such a policy must, in its consequences, rather perpetuate than suppress the evil; the ruin of one Chief serving but to consolidate the equally dangerous power of another. It is by no means improbable, that the Mahratta states viewed the increase of the Pindarees with an eye to eventual service from their arms; for they avowedly attributed the disasters of the operations of 1803 to their having imitated the European mode of warfare, and affected to believe, that, had they adhered to the Parthian method of their ancestors, the results of the contest would have been very different. The predatory hordes still pursued the old method; and the wonderful impunity and success with which they engaged in the most distant expeditions, passing the most formidable barriers of nature and of military art, and baffling every attempt to intercept their return, however well concerted, gave a colour of probability to this opinion: indeed, their calculation was erroneous,in one particular only, viz. that there were no strong holds in India which could hope to baffle our military skill, in case we should adopt the plan of pursuing the depredators to their haunts. They were ignorant of the degree in which our means were superior to those of Aurung-Zeeb; and recollecting that he, after having driven them into their fastnesses, could effect no more, readily gave into the belief, that the British power, now in its zenith, was only to be combated by the arms and arts with which Sevajee had foiled the Moghul in times of yore.

It is immaterial, however, whether accident or design had permitted the predatory hordes to gain the strength they had attained in 1814. Their actual condition at that period entitled them to be regarded as a distinct political interest of the day, requiring an equal exertion of vigilance and circumspection, as Hyder in the height of his power and inveterate animosity. The actual military force at the disposal of these associations amounted to 40,000 horse, inclusive of the Patans, who, though more orderly and better disciplined than the Pindarees of the Nerbudda, possessed the same character, and were similarly circumstanced in every respect, supporting themselves entirely by depredation wherever they could practise it. This number would be doubled, were we to add the remainder of Holkar's troops of the irregular kind, which were daily deserting the service of a falling house, in order to engage in the more profitable career of predatory enterprise, and the loose cavalry establishments of Sindheea and the Bhoosla, which were bound by no ties, but those of present entertainment, and were always in great arrear of pay. These materials formed the groundwork of an interest formidable at least to our repose, if not to our safety: and its centrical situation in India, nearly equi-distant from the dominions of the three presidencies, imposed the necessity of the most extensive annual precautions of defence, in spite of which, the territories of our allies were continually overrun. On two occasions, once when they entered Guzerat in 1808-9, and again in 1812, when the Bengal provinces of Mirzapoor and Shahabad were devastated, they penetrated into our immediate territories, which for years had been exempt from such a calamity. The spirit of enterprise evinced on these occasions had much advanced the reputation of these associations; and, although they were not now united under any single head, there had grown up among them a principle of concert in prosecution of common objects, such as a man of superior energy and abilities, had such an one chanced to arise among them, might model into the same description of force that Tymoor and Jhungeez Khan had directed to the devastation of the eastern world. The rise of Sevajee and of Hyder, both rapid and both formidable, was a proof that such things could take place in India as well as in other countries; and the whole of the unsettled spirits of central India were exactly in the condition to engender such another conqueror. They resembled the bands of Companions that swarmed all over Europe in the fourteenth century, and wanted but a leader, whose standard they could rally round with confidence. The lawless and independent character of the Pindarees, and the mode of their association, which rendered the Chiefs responsible to nobody for their acts, and made it impossible to hold any of the regular powers legitimately answerable for their dangerous existence, were the circumstances that made it necessary to watch their motions with especial caution, in order to anticipate the effects of any sudden combination. With this view, the British power had interposed at once, when Ameer Khan had attempted to collect a large body together, in prosecution of his design upon the dominions of the Bhoosla Raja; it being our uniform and avowed object to preserve things on their actual footing, and to prevent any of those fluctuations of power, which generally end in erecting a vigorous and ambitious domination on the ruins of a weak superannuated government. It was evidently not for our interest, that either the Pindarees or the Patans should build up such an edifice on the site of any of the regular states with which we were at that time connected; and it was certainly incumbent on our policy to make some effort to prevent it.

A short sketch of the origin of the predatory hordes, passing under the general denomination of Pindarees, and of the Chiefs under whom their numbers were arrayed in 1814, will lead to a more distinct view of their actual condition at that time. The name of Pindara is coeval with the earliest invasions of Hindoostan by the Mahrattas; the actual derivation of the word is unknown, notwithstanding the researches of several etymologists. The designation was applied to a sort of roving cavalry, that accompanied the Pêshwa's armies in their expeditions, rendering them much the same service as the Cossacks* perform for the armies of Russia. When the Pêshwas ceased to interfere personally in the affairs of Hindoostan, leaving that part of the Mahratta empire to the Sindheea and the Holkar Chieftains, the Pindarees were thenceforth ranged in two parties, assuming

* Pindara seems to have the same reference to Pandour that Cozák has to Cossack.

respectively the appellation of Sindheea-shahee, or of Holkar-shahee, accordingly as they attached themselves to the fortunes of either family. They still preserved, however, all the peculiarities of their own mode of association; and the several leaders went over with their bands to one Chief or the other, as best suited their private interests, or those of their followers. In 1794, the principal leaders first obtained assignments of land from Sindheea, in the valley of the Nerbudda, and amongst the hills which skirt it on the north. From that time till about 1800, there were two principal Chiefs, the brothers Heeroo and Burun, whose standards were annually raised in that valley at the season of the Dussera*, (an annual festival that takes place at the end of October or beginning of November), as a rallying point for all loose spirits and unemployed military adventurers. Here they consulted upon the best means of providing for the necessities of the year, by the exercise of rapine, accompanied by every enormity of fire and sword, upon the peaceful subjects of the regular governments. Until the close of the rains and the fall of the rivers, their horses were carefully trained, to prepare them for long marches and hard work. The rivers generally became fordable by the close of the Dussera. The horses were then shod, and a leader of tried courage and conduct having been chosen, all that were so inclined set forth on a foray or *luhbur*, as it was called in the Pindaree nomenclature. These parties latterly consisted sometimes of several thousands. All were mounted, though not equally well; out of a thousand, the proportion of good cavalry might be 400: the favourite weapon was a bamboo spear from twelve to eighteen feet long; but, as fire-arms were sometimes indispensable for the attack of villages, it was a rule that every fifteenth or twentieth man of the fighting Pindarees should be armed

* Vide Forbes's Oriental Memoirs.

with a matchlock. Of the remaining 600, 400 were usually common *looteeas*, indifferently mounted, and armed with every variety of weapon; and the rest slaves, attendants, and camp followers, mounted on tattoos or wild ponies, and keeping up with the *luhbur* in the best manner they could. It is not surprising, that a body so constituted, and moving without camp equipage of any kind, should traverse the whole of India in defiance of the most active pursuit by regular troops along the same line of march: indeed, the rapidity with which they spread their devastations to the southern extremity of the Pêshwa's and of the Nizam's territories, over an extent of not less than seven degrees of latitude from the Nerbudda, baffled every attempt to interrupt or overtake them. The cruelties they perpetrated were beyond belief. As it was impossible for them to remain more than a few hours on the same spot, the utmost despatch was necessary in rifling any towns or villages into which they could force an entrance; every one, whose appearance indicated the probability of his possessing money, was immediately put to the most horrid torture *, till he either pointed out his hoard, or died under the infliction. Nothing was safe from the pursuit of Pindarae lust or avarice; it was their common practice to burn and destroy what could not be carried away, and, in the wantonness of barbarity, to ravish and murder women and children, under the eyes of their husbands and parents.

In the infancy of the establishment of the Pindarees on the banks of the Nerbudda, their devastations were not carried to

* A favourite mode of compulsion with them was, to put hot ashes into a bag, which they tied over the mouth and nostrils of their victim, whom they then thumped on the back till he inhaled the ashes. The effect on the lungs of the sufferer was such, that few long survived the operation. Another common mode was, to throw the victim on his back, and place a plank or beam across his chest, on which two people pressed with their whole weight.

so great a distance as afterwards, when they began to feel their strength, and when the desolation of the immediate neighbourhood made it requisite to push their expeditions to a distance, in order to make them sufficiently productive. With the fruits of these expeditions, the Chiefs were from the first enabled to keep together a large military force without much territorial revenue, and to offer the occasional services of a part of their strength to Sindheea, Holkar, and other neighbouring Chieftains, at a cheaper rate than the same amount of assistance was elsewhere procurable. By means of further assignments obtained in recompense for such services, and of conquests made by the bands thus kept together upon the Grassea (aboriginal) Rajas in the mountains bordering the Nerbudda, who had never yet submitted to the Mahrattas, the Pindaree Chiefs gradually extended their influence; while, at the same time, the reputation of these successes brought additional swarms of adventurers to their standard.

About the year 1800, the two Chiefs Heeroo and Burun died either in the course of nature, or by violent means, the one at Nâgpoor, and the other at Asseergurh. Both left sons; the former, Dost Mahommed and Wâsil Mahommed; the latter, the two Rajuns; but it was not till after some time that these individuals succeeded to any part of their fathers' influence: the pre-eminence devolved, in the first instance, upon other Sirdars, according to their reputation and ability as leaders. Kureem Khan, a Holkar-shahee Pindara, was the first who rose to consequence after the death of the brothers; indeed, he was not altogether free from suspicion of having procured the death of Burun at Asseergurh. Kureem was an active, bold, and ambitious adventurer, sufficiently devoid of principle to profit by the politics of the time. He commenced his career, by joining the rising fortunes of Juswunt Rao Holkar, with a considerable party of followers, pledged to consider their own and their leader's interest as inseparable. His services proved valuable to Holkar, and were suitably rewarded. A short time after, he was bought over by Sindheea, who gave him the title of Nuwab, and several assignments of land in the valley, and above the ghâts of the Nerbudda: thenceforth he has been regarded as a Sindheea-shahee Pindara, though frequently found in arms against the adherents of his nominal superior. He enlarged his possessions by interfering in the internal affairs of Bhopâl, and in the contests of this state with the Bhoosla. After worsting the latter, he excited a civil war in Bhopâl; and giving his support to one party, was very near establishing his authority over the whole principality; but the state was saved by the personal courage and conduct of Vizier Mahommed, with the assistance of Dost Mahommed, the son of Heeroo, who began about that time to rise into notice as a rival of Kureem. During the prosecution of this ambitious course of self-aggrandisement, there was never any intermission of the systematic predatory expeditions, that still formed one of the main resources by which the chieftains maintained their military power. Sindheea himself, the Bhoosla Raja, and the Hindoo Chiefs of Bundelkhund, were the principal sufferers by their depredations at this period *.

During the troubles of the Mahratta empire consequent upon the war with the British, Kureem Khan availed himself of the opportunity to seize on some possessions of Sindheea and of the Pêshwa's jageerdars in Malwa; insomuch, that after the conclusion of hostilities in the year 1806, he was in the occupation of a territory of not less than eleven pergunnas, whereof the principal were Bairsea, Chipaneer, Ashtar, Shuja-

* The tolerance of this practice may, in part, be accounted for by the recollection, that a predatory inroad is not considered derogatory to the dignity of a Mahratta government, which avowedly regards rapine as a legitimate resource of the state.

wulpoor, Sarungpoor, Ichawur, and Sehoree, above the ghâts of the Nerbudda, together with Sutwas, and other places within the valley. His annual land revenue from this territory exceeded fifteen lack of rupees, besides compensations for immunity from plunder, which he levied on most of the neighbouring Rajas and Chiefs. He had also built himself a fort in the part of his territory acquired from Bhopâl, which was called, after him, Kureem-gurh. His power was now at the height; for though there were several Pindaree leaders who had never joined his standard, and who even affected a rivalry for the supremacy he had arrogated; still there were none whose means or influence at all approximated to those of Kureem. Though himself independent in every respect, and even an usurper upon Sindheea on more occasions than one, he still affected to be attached to that Chief's interest, and to call himself a Sindheea-shahee Pindara, for the obvious purpose of retaining some claim to protection in case of exigency. His power, however, excited that prince's jealousy; and in 1806, very soon after the settlement with the English, Sindheea, by the proffer of his aid in the reduction of a fort (that, for want of artillery, had long baffled the attacks of Kureem), inveigled the Pindara to an interview, at which he seized his person, making a simultaneous attack on his camp, which was completely plundered. Kureem's possessions were then quickly recovered; and, for five years, he was himself detained a close prisoner in the dungeons of Gwalior. His durra, in the mean time, was not broken up, though reduced to no more than two or three thousand horse, by the defection of the greater part of the sirdars of inferior note, who had been tempted, in the full tide of his success, to unite their interest with his. The fall of Kureem, however, strengthened the durras of other leaders, particularly of Chetoo or Seetoo, a Chief under whom the two Rajuns, sons of Burun, held a subordinate rank, and who had always been the avowed rival of

Kureem, though hitherto the power of the latter had greatly preponderated. The party of Dost Mahommed also acquired a great accession of strength by the ruin of Kureem, whose durra had now little else than plunder to subsist upon. The search of this, however, it prosecuted with considerable success under Kureem's deputies, and especially one Namdar Khan, who made Sindheea's territories the principal theatre of his depredations, in revenge for the treachery employed against his leader. In 1811, Kureem purchased his release from Sindheea for six lack of rupees, which were punctually paid through Zalim Singh of Kota. Returning to the scene of his former power, he immediately raised fresh levies of infantry, and invited the Pindaree Chiefs, who had before followed his fortunes, to rally again round his standard. In a very short time he recovered the greater part of the territory he had formerly possessed, and laid his plans to effect a general combination of all the Pindarees, preparatory to an expedition of more than ordinary moment. Even his rival Cheetoo was induced to unite with his durra; and the Dussera of 1811 was celebrated by an assemblage of not less than 25,000 cavalry of all descriptions, besides several battalions of infantry newly raised for the purpose. Kureem proposed to lead this force immediately against Nâgpoor, the weakness of which was notorious to all the Pindarees, whose detached parties had, a short time before, succeeded in carrying off a considerable booty from a suburb of the city itself. The Bhoosla state had fortunately won over Cheetoo by the recent grant of considerable jageers on the southern bank of the Nerbudda. He accordingly opposed the project, and retired with his durra in discontent.

This division proved the ruin of Kureem, who had a second time awakened Sindheea's jealousy to such a degree, that Juggoo Bapoo, one of Sindheea's principal officers, was sent with as large a force as could be collected, and with a reinforcement of some battalions of Holkar, to endeavour to chastise the presumption of this upstart. There is reason to believe, that this enterprise was promoted by Cheetoo, who feared the consequences of having thwarted the designs of Kureem in respect to Nâgpoor; at all events, he was the main instrument of its success, and the person who derived the greatest advantages; the major part of his late rival's possessions being allotted by Sindheea as his share of the spoil. Kureem, expecting from Cheetoo at least neutrality and indifference to his fate, advanced boldly to encounter Juggoo Bapoo. His rival, however, took an active part against him, so that he was completely defeated near Munohur-Thana, and obliged to fly with a few adherents, and seek refuge in the camp of Ameer Khan beyond the Chumbul. The strong representations of Sindheea and Holkar obliged the Patan Chief to place him in a kind of restraint, in which he remained until the end of 1816. His durra again declined to a secondary condition in comparison with that of Cheetoo, at whose cantonment of Nemawur, on the Nerbudda, not less than 15,000 horse now annually assembled at the Dussera festival, to issue forth under a leader of his nomination, in whatever direction he might prescribe.

In 1814, the following was supposed to be the relative strength of the Pindaree durras: Cheetoo 5000 good horse; total of all descriptions about 10,000, exclusive of the Holkarshahee Pindarees, mustering from 4 to 5000 more, who latterly attached themselves chiefly to his standard. The remains of Kureem's durra amounted to 2000 good horse; total of every description, at least 4000. Under Dost Mahommed 6000, with the usual proportion of the best quality; this Chief held considerable jageers above the ghâts of the Nerbudda, and usually cantoned in the Bhopâl territory. There were, moreover, at least 6 or 8000 horse, under independent leaders of inferior note, who joined one or other of the superior Chiefs, as occasion suited. The party that penetrated into the district of Mirzapoor through Rewa was of the durra of Kureem, who planned the expedition a short time before his second fall. It was led by Fazil Khan, and, turning east as soon as it reached the Mirzapoor frontier, advanced to the neighbourhood of Gya, and then disappeared up the course of the Soane, before a single soldier from any British cantonment could come up with its track. Such was the anomalous and undefinable power that had grown up into consequence out of the political settlement of 1805-6. Its leading feature was hostility to all regular governments, and of course most particularly to ourselves and our allies, insomuch as to impose the necessity of constant vigilance along the whole extent of the south-west frontier of the Bengal presidency; while, for the security of the Dukhun, the subsidiary forces of the Nizam and Pêshwa were annually obliged to move to the northern frontier of their respective territories, notwithstanding which precautions, the dominions of those states were continually penetrated and overrun.

Ameer Khan and Mahommed-Shah Khan, the two Patan Chiefs, who were rising into a similar and equally formidable pre-eminence, commanded forces of a very different description from those of the Pindaree Chiefs, though actuated by the same predatory spirit: each of them, besides horse, had large bodies of infantry and several guns. Mahommed-shah Khan's infantry were the old battalions of Tukojee Holkar, undoubtedly the best in India not under the actual command of European officers. Ameer Khan's were scarcely inferior. The cavalry were besides paid by the month, instead of living avowedly on plunder alone, like the Pindarees. Indeed, the grand difference between the two classes was, that the Patans were banded together for the purpose of preying on governments and powerful Chiefs. To this end, their force moved about with the materials of regular battles and sieges, so as to work on the fears of princes and men in power, extorting contributions and other advantages from them, by such intimidation as an efficient army only could impress. Whereas the object of the Pindarees was general rapine; they preyed upon the population at large, without arrogating an ability to cope with the established governments; their form and constitution, therefore, were framed with a view to this exclusive purpose.

Rajpootana was the principal area for the exhibition of the species of depredation practised by the Patan leaders. The nature of the principalities of that tract, each of which was a petty feodal government, at war with its neighbours and with its own vassals, seemed to mark it out as their destined prey. Nor was it a new game that they were playing in that quarter; they merely followed up what Sindheea and Holkar had long been habitually pursuing. Indeed, although the objects of the Patan Chiefs were wholly personal, and prosecuted with perfect independence of each other, still they represented the Holkar interest in the country, and had introduced their forces under sanction of that name. The very means they possessed, viz. the artillery and regular battalions, had belonged to the Holkar family, though now employed in supporting and establishing an interest virtually distinct.

Notwithstanding this virtual independence of the Patans, Sindheea did not leave them in the undisputed enjoyment of the contributions and other advantages to be extorted from Rajpootana. A division of his army, under Bapoo Sindheea, lay at Ajimeer, acting precisely on the principles of the Patans, and living on the plunder it could exact from Jypoor and Joudhpoor. Another force was stationed in the Oodeepoor territory, encroaching on the power and possessions of the Raja there, and devastating the country. The Rajpoots, however, were considerably more jealous of Sindheea's apparently consolidated power than of the Patan Chiefs, whose very loose connexion with the Holkar family gave them the character of mercenaries, who, for objects of private interest, might be hired and discharged at pleasure. Thus in 1809, when Sindheea seemed to meditate an invasion of the Joudhpoor territory with a very considerable force, the Raja called in Mahommed-Shah Khan, and took his army into pay for the purpose of repelling the attack.

This facility of tranferring their services according to their personal views, gave the Patan Chiefs the further advantage over Sindheea and his commanders, of a pretext and power to interfere in the passing intrigues amongst the Rajpoots themselves, and to become partisans of the several factions, from each of which they took care to reap some personal advantage. So long as they had the prospect of such recompense, they were not over-scrupulous of the means of earning it. Ameer Khan twice sold his services for the treacherous assassination of obnoxious persons, and accomplished his purpose on both occasions at conferences held under the most solemn guarantees. This Chief was the acknowledged head of the Patan interest. His views of ambition were, however, not confined to Rajpootana until 1814; when, finding from the activity of our preparations, whenever he seemed to be meditating an enterprise against the Bhoosla, that we were resolved to prevent his aggrandisement in that quarter, he moved from Malwa across the Chumbul towards Rajpootana; and having strengthened his interest at the durbar of Holkar (then held at Rampoora-Bhanpoora), took upon himself the supreme management of the Patan forces and interests. Mahommed-Shah Khan, Jumsheed Khan, and the other sirdars, agreed to act in subordination to him. The former of these dying about the end of 1814, the troops he had commanded became incorporated with those under the personal command of Ameer Khan. This military adventurer was thus placed at the head of a force of at least

30,000 horse and foot, furnished with an artillery well manned and served; yet he had no claim to be recognised as a substantive power, though no one of the regular governments could fairly be held responsible for his acts. The field of his operations lay in a quarter where there was every likelihood of his coming ere long into contact with the British Government, or with those under its protection.

Against this power, as well as the Pindarees, we were obliged to be continually armed, and on the alert. The want of any determinate territory or home, or of any other stake to be hazarded by the first act of hostility, left us entirely without security for their peaceable demeanour; there was nothing to restrain them but mere motives of convenience, and the sense that the calculation of the chances of success was against them. This, however, was the result of continual and most expensive preparation, the necessity of which was a part of the evil that required a remedy.

Such was the state of India at the beginning of the year 1814. In the subsequent chapters, the events which led to the final catastrophe of the year 1817-18 will be traced through the intermediate period, with as much conciseness as may be found consistent with the object of exhibiting a distinct view of the origin of those occurrences, and the share which the conduct of the British Government may have had in producing them.

DEFILE by which GENL OCHTERLONY Turned the CHEREE-GHATEE PASS.

SKETCH of GENL OCHTERLONY'S OPERATIONS to effect a LODGEMENT on the MALAOUN HILLS.

1. Lag Hill & B[illegible] Position
2. Surajgurh Fort, extreme right of Goorkha Position
3. Stockaded Posts of [illegible]
4. Ryla Peak, an unstockaded point occupied by 3 detachments on morning of 15th April 1815 [illegible] afterwards.
5. [illegible], whence Capt. Hamilton's detachment moved on Ryla.
6. Route of a Detachment of Grenadiers from Head Quarters on Ryla.
7. Route of Col. Thompson with a Battalion [illegible] on Deothul.
8. Deothul, occupied on morning of 15th and maintained against 2 desperate attacks.
9. Route of Major Lawrie with a strong detachment on Deothul
10. Support sent to Capt. Showers attack on Enemy's Cantonments
11. Goorkha Cantonment
12. Malown
13. Ruttungurh Fort whence Capt. Showers marched on morning of 15th
14. Lag Village to which Capt. Showers detachment were driven back on his being killed
15. [illegible] of [illegible]

London, Published by J. Murray 18[illegible]

CHAPTER II.

NIPÂL-TERRITORIES.

1814-15.

Nipâl War—Governor-General leaves the Presidency—Intentions respecting predatory bands—defensive plans—that adopted—reasons—intrigues afoot—Bhopâl and Sâgur alliance resolved on—condition of Bhopâl—designs of Mahrattas thereon—Chief applies for British protection—terms offered—consequent military arrangements—progress of negotiation—communication to Sindheea—how received by him—Bhoosla—and Pêshwa—influence of Nipâlese war—operations in that quarter—disasters—further preparations—successful close of the campaign—Preparations—in the Dukhun—on S. W. frontier of Hindoostan—augmentation of Bengal army—tranquillity of the season—Conduct of Bhopâl—its Vakeel dismissed—communication thereof—Reflections.

The negotiations which had been for some time pending with the Goorkha government of Nipâl *, respecting its usurpations on our northern frontier, were, in May 1814, brought to the issue of open war, by its countenance of the murder of some of our people, who had been placed in charge of the usurped and resumed villages in the Gôruckpoor district, after the British Government had recovered possession without meeting with any resistance by a military force. The extreme unhealthiness of the lowlands, stretching along the foot of the whole range in which Nipâl is situated, rendered it necessary to wait the arrival of the cold season, before commencing active operations to avenge this outrage. The Marquess of

* The reader, who wishes to know more of this new and rising frontier state, is referred to the pages of Kirkpatrick.

Hastings had previously resolved to make a tour through the western provinces of the Bengal presidency, in order to visit the different military stations, and inform himself, by personal observation, of the actual state of affairs in the interior. In prosecution of this intention, he left Calcutta in June of that year, and arrived at Cawnpoor about the end of September, proceeding up the Ganges by the usual and tedious navigation. The period of the journey was occupied in preparation for the approaching contest with the Nipâlese, and in arming the south-western frontier of the Bengal territories, and the northern frontier of our allies in the Dukhun, against the probable repetition of attempts by the Pindarees.

It had been resolved by the Supreme Government, on the eve of the Governor-General's departure from the presidency, to make a strong representation of the formidable and rapidly augmenting power of the predatory associations to the home authorities, with the view of impressing them with the like conviction of the danger to the British interests, arising from the continuance and progressive increase of bodies so capable of acquiring a mischievous pre-eminence, and of receiving their sanction for the prosecution of a systematic combination of measures, for the suppression of this growing evil. It was agreed on all hands, that the necessity of such measures would soon be forced upon us; and it was consequently essential, that those entrusted with the direction in England, should thus early be apprised of the actual posture of affairs, and of the views respecting them, entertained by those who had the means of closer observation. There seemed to be time to wait the effect of this representation; for there was no reason at the date when it was made, to expect the occurrence of any thing to demand immediate operations in the quarter where the Pindarees and Patans had fixed themselves, while the Indian government found intermediate employment in the war with the

Nipâlese. For the present, therefore, it was deemed advisable to dispose our means in a defensive attitude, sufficient to prevent or repel incursions; and neither to advance to attack the Pindarees in their haunts, nor commence that extended plan of connected movements, which, though necessary to the entire suppression of these predatory hordes, might alarm the independent states by its contrast with our recent system of general and scrupulous neutrality.

The most effectual defensive measure, and the one most desirable in every point of view, seemed to be, the establishment of a subsidiary alliance with the Bhoosla Raja, whereby the whole of our most exposed frontier, viz. the line from Bundelkhund to Cuttack, defended by the single position of Midnapore, where a regular battalion was stationed, would thenceforth be skirted by the dominions of a power in strict alliance; and a force upon the Nerbudda, communicating on one hand with the southernmost position of Bundelkhund, and on the other with the troops at the northernmost point of the Nizam's dominions, would completely guard the whole line of our possessions and those of our allies, as far as it was possible to protect them against an enemy so active and impenetrable as the Pindara. This was a project nowise novel. The British Government had, for several years, been endeavouring to prevail on Ragoojee Bhoosla to accede to such a proposition, but could never conquer his repugnance and distrust. The negotiations for the purpose, which had been open since 1812, were finally closed while the Governor-General was on his progress up the river, by a decided refusal on the part of the Raja.

The best alternative that presented itself on failure of the Nagpoor connexion was, to extend the chain of positions from Bundelkhund to the Nerbudda, by means of a connexion with the states of Sâgur and Bhopâl, and thereby draw a similar defensive line westward of the Nâgpoor territories. The necessity of adopting this alternative, should operations ever be undertaken without the co-operation of the Bhoosla, was fully acknowledged in the course of those discussions upon the practicability and mode of suppressing the predatory associations, which had preceded the representation to the home authorities; but it formed part of that extended system, which it had been resolved not to commence upon for the present, in fear of alarming the independent states. Wherefore, although Lord Hastings resolved in the end to adopt this course, he would have deferred so doing, notwithstanding the disappointment in respect to Nâgpoor, had not some indications appeared of a combination amongst the Mahratta powers, the danger of which required to be anticipated.

At the time of rejecting our alliance, it was discovered, that the Bhoosla was actually engaged in negotiating one of an offensive and defensive character with Sindheea, for the subjugation of the Bhopâl principality by their joint arms. One of the ostensible pretexts for this confederacy was, the necessity of a counter-preparation against the ambitious projects of the British Government, which were inferred, as well from the attempt to establish our influence at Nâgpoor, as from the stir of our military preparation, which denoted that active operations were meditated in some quarter or other, though the immediate direction was at that time involved in mystery. Sindheea's jealousy, ever keenly attentive to all our movements, was redoubled by this show of preparation; and it soon became evident from his conduct towards the Pindarees, that, whatever might have been his previous intention, he had now no wish to suppress them. As a further consequence of this jealousy, intrigue began to be busy at the quarters of Ameer Khan and the durbar * of Holkar, and even with Runjeet Singh, the ruler

* At the court of Holkar, affairs were at this time in the hands of Mynee Baee and Tanteea Aleek-hur, with whom Sindheea had considerable influence. The minister,

of the Punjâb Seikhs. The Pêshwa was suspected to have joined these intrigues thus early, if not to have been the first author and instigator of them; a change having been observed in his conduct some time before, which will presently be more particularly adverted to. It is difficult exactly to define the immediate objects or extent of these intrigues; whether merely defensive against any supposed designs on our part, for the further extension of our dominion, in a manner injurious to the interests of the contracting parties; or offensive also, in case of a favourable opportunity. The advance of Runjeet Singh's army to a position threatening the territory of the protected Seikhs, which took place immediately after the division at Soodeeana, under Sir David Ochterlony, was moved into the hills to attack Umeer Singh, and the concentration of the Patans under Ameer Khan, which occurred at a critical moment, and within a few marches of our Agra frontier, afford reason to suspect that the object of the confederacy was not purely de-

Tanteea, paid a visit to Gwalior early in 1815, in order to negotiate a treaty of closer union and concert between the two families, for the prosecution of common objects, under the general direction of the Pêshwa, as supreme head of the Mahratta empire. The conciliation of the Pindarees by territorial grants in the respective dominions of both the families, and the concentration of the military force of both states for the prosecution of ambitious designs against the Rajpoots, were the most striking articles of this offensive and defensive alliance, apparent on the face of the copies of this agreement, delivered in the sequel. There is reason, however, to believe that there were other secret articles, which have not even yet been divulged. Indeed it is well known, that there was one such article levelled against Ameer Khan, and more than suspected, upon many accounts, that another aimed at the diminution or subversion of the British interest. In the end, the negotiation came to nothing, from a strong surmise, that Sindheea's main object was to establish his influence at the court of Mulhar Rao, for the purpose of supplanting the family in their possessions. An opposite faction was also at work, and Tanteea Aleek-hur, with Mynee Baee, yielded very soon after to Balaram Set and Toolsee Baee, whereof the former was favourable to Ameer Khan and the Patans and jealous of Sindheea.

fensive: but this is a point it is no longer important to investigate.

No sooner was Lord Hastings apprised of these intrigues, than he saw at once that their immediate result must have been, the consolidation of the Mahratta power over the whole tract, separating the Bengal territories from those of our allies in the Dukhun, which must not only have cut off the Bhoosla for ever from any connexion with us, by rivetting his dependence on Sindheea, but have deprived us of the alternative offered in the connexion of Bhopâl, by the previous subjugation of that state. Urged by these considerations, he resolved no longer to hesitate in stepping forward to complete his defensive arrangements, by forming a connexion with Bhopâl and Sâgur, in despite of any efforts by the regular independent powers to counteract the design. It certainly was a bold stroke of policy; but it presented the double advantage of thwarting Sindheea's apparent design of establishing his influence over Nâgpoor, and of rescuing another principality, whose existence promised us many most essential benefits; moreover, it served to complete those defensive measures, which the suspected disposition of the regular powers, and their present undisguised encouragement of the predatory bands, rendered more necessary than ever for the security of our own provinces. Perhaps the very imposing boldness of the step, which exhibited a degree of vigour and resolution proportionate to the certainty of giving offence, was its best recommendation to his lordship's mind; inasmuch as it was calculated to impress on the native princes a sense of the vigilance and confidence of his administration.

A brief notice of the condition of Bhopâl will not be here out of place. The territory of this state lies in the valley of the Nerbudda, and above the hills to the north, between the 77th and 78th degrees of east longitude. The government has been vested in a Patan family since the days of Aurung-zeeb. The reigning Chief in 1814 was Vizier Mahommed, who had acquired the succession, rather by proving himself the fittest of the family to sustain its declining fortunes in arduous times, than as the lawful heir by the rules of hereditary descent. The family had preserved their political independence against the most active efforts of the Mahrattas in the fulness of their military preponderance; although their position immediately between the Bhoosla and the Sindheea made their territory the particular object of Mahratta jealousy, and presented, as long as it should remain inviolate, an effectual bar to the consolidation of the influence of that nation in this part of India. On a former occasion, when General Goddard was sent by Warren Hastings with an expedition from Hindoostan, in execution of his sagacious plan of alarming the Mahratta powers, then confederated against us, into the acceptance of his own terms of peace, by penetrating through the very heart of their possessions, the existence of this independent principality was one of the principal encouragements to make the attempt. The family are still in possession of the strongest testimonials from General Goddard of the important services rendered him by the reigning Nuwab; indeed, the ultimate success of the enterprise, and the final accomplishment of that officer's wonderful march across an enemy's country all the way to Surat, were mainly to be attributed to his having found this principality in a state of independence and hostility to the Mahrattas midway on his line of march.

The importance of saving such a friend, when a hostile combination of the Mahrattas was to be apprehended, must be obvious enough. Already, in execution of the offensive and defensive engagements between Sindheea and the Bhoosla, was the best appointed force of the former, that commanded by Colonel Baptiste, on one part of the frontier; while Sudeek Ulee Khan, with the troops of Nâgpoor, approached it on the opposite side; and another division of Sindheea's troops, that under Juswunt Rao Bhâo, was also in the neighbourhood. No time was to be lost. Sindheea had before frequently attacked this state, and even besieged its capital, but without success, owing partly to the incapacity of the commanders he employed and their general ignorance of the mode of attacking fortified places, and partly to the gallantry and skill of Vizier Mahommed's defence. The Maha-Raja, however, had never before entered Bhopâl with so efficient an army, and Baptiste's knowledge of European tactics and long and successful practice in the various sieges he had hitherto conducted, seemed to leave but little hope that the Vizier would be able to save himself and his dominions on this occasion.

His perpetual hostility to the Mahrattas had naturally made him look to us as a resource in the hour of extremity; and that hour was now fast approaching. He was accordingly induced to make a very earnest solicitation for our support; and for that purpose despatched an agent to Dehlee, who waited on Mr. Metcalfe the British resident there, and submitted, on behalf of his master, a specific proposition to be admitted within the pale of our protection. His application had reached the Governor-General a short time before he had made his determination, which was not finally resolved on until the beginning of October. When his mind was fully made up on the matter, he lost no time in instructing Mr. Metcalfe to entertain the proposition, and, in case the agent should be furnished with powers sufficiently ample and explicit, to conclude with him an engagement on the following basis—" The British Government " to afford its protection against the present designs of Sindheea " and the Bhoosla, and a perpetual guarantee for the future; " the Nuwab to be left in complete independence in the " management of his internal administration;—the British troops "to have free ingress and egress through the Bhopâl territories, "together with every facility in the provision of their supplies "and necessaries—a fortress to be delivered as a present depôt, "and, eventually, a spot to be allotted for a cantonment or per- "manent station—the Nuwab to renounce all connexion with "the Pindarees, and not to negotiate with other powers, except "in concert with the British Government, abiding by its ar- "bitration in all differences with them." However, as it was thought proper to hold out the prospect of some advantage by way of inducement to enter into an alliance of this nature, the recovery of all the territories of the state, then in the hands of the Pindarees, was to be proposed, and the Governor-General prepared himself to abandon the claim of a money consideration for the expense of defending the territory, though the demand of a proportion of the charge, if contested, was not to be hastily relinquished.

The negotiation with the legitimate Chief of Sâgur was intrusted to the political agent in Bundelkhund, Mr. Wauchope, and the basis of the connexion to be offered and concluded was precisely the same: a large proportion of the expense, it was, however, confidently expected, would be borne by the Nana. On discovery that the agent of Dehlee had not full powers from the Nuwab of Bhopâl, both negotiations were removed to Bundelkhund, which, from its vicinity to the two districts, seemed to be the most convenient spot for conducting them.

In support of the course of policy thus resolved upon, the troops in Bundelkhund were reinforced, and held in readiness; the Nizam's subsidiary force ordered to advance immediately from Jâlna to Ellichpoor, near the northern extremity of the valley of Berar; the Poona subsidiary force to hold itself in readiness to act in its support, by moving on Jafeerabad, in the neighbourhood of Jâlna; at the same time, the Bombay government was directed to draw together the whole of the Guzerat troops at some point eastward of that province. The object of these military arrangements was to overawe the Mahratta powers and predatory bands, in the event of their evincing an inclination to obstruct the execution of the treaties which might be concluded. Colonel Doveton, the commandant of the Nizam subsidiary force, began his march from Jâlna on the 3d November 1814; and it was intended that, with this army, he should penetrate into Bhopâl, to execute the protective stipulations of the treaty with the Nuwab Vizier.

The negotiations having been thus opened, Mr. Wauchope addressed a letter to the Nuwab of Bhopâl, explaining at length the terms on which the Governor-General was disposed to receive that state under protection, in compliance with the solicitations of the agent of his court, preferred at Dehlee. He hinted also at the Nuwab's bearing some part of the expense. An immediate answer was received from Vizier Mahommed, agreeing to all the stipulations proposed, with exception of the delivery of a fort for a present depôt, and of bearing a part of the expense. For the discussion of these two points, he declared his intention of deputing an envoy, as soon as the return of the person he had sent to Dehlee, which was daily expected.

Mr. Wauchope had been placed in communication with the residents at the respective courts of Sindheea and the Bhoosla, in order that he might keep them apprised from time to time of the state and progress of the negotiations: and these residents had been instructed, so soon as they should be advised of the adjustment of preliminaries, to explain fully to the respective courts the designs of the British Government, with the reasons for them, in such a manner, as they might deem least likely to create alarm. This being the first occasion of departure from the delicacy of interference we had hitherto so rigidly observed, in respect to states circumstanced like Bhopâl and Sâgur, it was deemed necessary that the British representatives at the courts of the independent princes should be prepared, both to assert the right of extending the pale of our protection to any power free to contract, and to rebut any imputation of intended injury to their interests resulting from such extension in the particular instance, by showing it to be simply a necessary precaution for the support of our own defensive system, and by no means designed or intended to thwart their respective views.

The resident at Sindheea's court (Mr. Richard Strachey), conceiving the Nuwab of Bhopâl's unqualified assent to all the fundamental articles of the Governor-General's proposition to amount to a preliminary adjustment of the terms of alliance, proceeded forthwith to make the official communication to Sindheea of the intentions of the British Government in respect to Bhopâl, on advice of the substance of the Nuwab's reply to Mr. Wauchope. Sindheea, on receiving the communication, inveighed in the strongest terms against our interference with the affairs of Bhopâl, declaring the principality to be one of his dependencies in Malwa, with which we were solemnly pledged by treaty to have no concern. The resident denied that it fell within the terms of the treaty, asserting it to be a free and independent state. Gopal Rao Bhâo, who took a prominent part in the discussion, declared the several places which had been wrested from Vizier Mahommed by Sindheea at different times, to be cessions in lieu of tribute justly due, the account of which was still unsettled, and represented our interference to prevent the enforcement of these his just dues, as tantamount to a positive declaration of war. In point of fact, according to the Mahratta notions of political justice, Sindheea had a good title to whatever he could extort from Bhopâl; and, having been in the habit of making usurpations, and levying contributions on this territory as his peculiar and exclusive prey, he conceived no one else had any right to interpose. This is the meaning he attached to the word dependency. It was notorious, however, that Vizier Mahommed had long maintained a most glorious struggle for his independence, and neither had himself, nor had any of the family before him, ever by treaty, or other act of any kind, acknowledged the supremacy of any Mahratta state. The discussions on this point grew particularly warm, Sindheea taking an active personal part in them, and using language which might have been construed into menace: and when, at the close of the interview, Mr. Strachey requested that Colonel Baptiste might be ordered to refrain from active hostility against Bhopâl, until the Governor-General's instructions upon the resident's report of the conference should arrive, the request was distinctly refused. Indeed, considering that there was yet no actual treaty concluded with Bhopâl, the demand was, perhaps, rather premature. This conference took place on the last day of November; and the tone then assumed by the durbar was nowise lowered at an interview obtained by Mr. Strachey's moonshee three days after.

Immediately on being apprised that this communication had been made to Sindheea, the residents at the other Mahratta courts resolved very properly, no longer to defer a similar explanation. The Nâgpoor Raja required time to consider of his answer; but, on being pressed by Mr. Jenkins, privately assured that gentleman, that Sudeek Ulee Khan should be forbidden to join the army of Baptiste, or to act hostilely against Bhopâl. It was farther ascertained, that this court would not oppose the advance of the subsidiary force at Ellichpoor through the portion of its territories which lay on the route from that station to Bhopâl, in case events should require its movement in that situation. A private correspondence, however, was kept up the whole time between the Bhoosla and Sindheea; and the intrigues, which had before been commenced in other quarters, were carried on with renewed activity.

The Pêshwa, on being informed of the intentions of the British Government, in respect to Bhopâl, professed to be highly satisfied, because of the security that would result to the Jageers of several of his dependants in the neighbourhood. Amongst others, the Vinshorekeer, in whose concerns he took particular interest, had large possessions about Ashta and Shujawulpoor, which the Pindarees and Sindheea's commanders were continually plundering, and of the greater part of which they had already divested him.

Notwithstanding the exterior appearance of amity assumed at Nâgpoor and Poona, which, in the case of the former, was carried so far as to produce an offer by Ragoojee of a body of his troops to be taken into British pay, and the pressure of this offer with some importunity, there was still little reason to doubt that both these courts were heartily bent upon the combination, which accounts from every quarter during the months of November, December, and January, reported to be organizing against the British power. Mahrattas, Patans, and Pindarees, seemed for the moment to have forgotten all their mutual jealousies, under the notion, that the moment was near at hand, which would give the opportunity of a successful rise against our galling superiority. The discovery that we had planned an extensive war in the hills, in which their reasonings from past history led them to anticipate our certain failure, and this anticipation was favoured by the untoward events that marked the opening of the campaign in that quarter, mainly contributed to lead all ranks to speculate on the speedy occurrence of such an opportunity. It was evident, however, that they were not yet prepared to act, nor had formed any consistent plan of future conduct.

To return to the movements of the Governor-General: at the same time that he proffered protection to Bhopâl and Sâgur, and made those arrangements in support of that measure, which have been above detailed, he put four divisions in condition to take the field against the Nipâlese; two of which, those from Meeruth and Soodheeana, had actually penetrated into the hills before the close of October. The resources for these measures had been raised by the loan of a crore of rupees (1,250,000*l.* sterling), obtained by Lord Hastings from the Nuwab Vizier, Ghazee Oodeen Hyder, who had recently succeeded his father, Sadut Ulee Khan, on the Musnud of Oude. By this supply, the treasuries of the Bengal Provinces, which his lordship had found at a very low ebb, were at once placed in a condition to support operations on a most extensive scale.

The failure before the stockaded hill and fort of Nala-panee, in which Major-General Gillespie lost his life, occurred on the last day of October. The place was breached, and a second unsuccessful attempt made to carry it by storm on the 27th November; and, though by the effect of continual bombardment, and by cutting off the supplies of water, which were derived from without, the garrison was ultimately obliged to evacuate the position, and was cut up a little in its retreat, by a party under Major Ludlow, still the sinister influence of these events, in damping the ardour of our own troops, and in giving courage to those of the enemy and hopes to the malcontents in every part of the ample surface of India, was for a long time counteracted by no one brilliant exploit of our arms. Major-General Ochterlony had yet been able to effect nothing against the strong position, in which he found Umeer Singh posted, on the heights of Ramgurh: and, although in the beginning of January, he, by a skilful manœuvre, compelled the enemy to retire to the yet stronger range of Malâoun, there was little *éclat* in such success; and, in the interim, the year 1814 had closed with failures still more unpropitious than even those of Nala-panee. On the 27th of December, Major-General Martindell, who had succeeded to Gillespie's command, made a combined movement to occupy two arms of the heights of Jytuk, whither Runjoor Singh, son of Umeer Singh, had fallen back from Nahn. The operation was well planned; but, failing on one arm in consequence of the impetuosity of the troops, the general, instead of reinforcing the other, on which he had been successful, ordered a retreat, in the face of an enemy elated with this double success. This retrograde movement was of course followed up by the enemy, and attended with the loss of many valuable lives, and was regarded by the Nipâlese as an important victory. In addition to these checks, two detachments from the main army, which had been collected in Sarun, for the purpose of penetrating into the valley of Nipâl and attacking the capital, were, on the new year's day, surprised and cut off nearly to a man: an event which induced Major-General Marly to relinquish offensive measures altogether in that direction. Major-General I. S. Wood was similarly deterred from acting on the offensive, by the result of two unsuccessful reconnoissances of the enemy's force opposed to him in the quarter north of Gôruckpoor, wherein much ammunition was expended and several lives lost, without any equivalent or the gain of a single object.

The coincidence of so many untoward events, at the precise juncture when Sindheea had assumed the decided tone which has been mentioned above, gave the Marquess of Hastings ground seriously to apprehend that the crisis was imminent: had one other important check occurred in the months of January or February, it would probably have embroiled us with the whole of the native courts. The Governor-General resolved to be prepared for the worst at all points. Instead, however, of relaxing his exertions on the northern frontier, in consequence of the suspicious aspect of things on the south and west, his judgment dictated the necessity of putting forth his whole strength in that quarter, in order, if possible, to secure some early success, signal enough to counterbalance the effect produced on public opinion, by such a multiplicity of consecutive reverses. The several divisions employed against the hill country were, therefore, reinforced to the utmost possible extent, though at the hazard of weakening the defences of the southern frontier. The Sarun division was increased to nearly 13,500 men, whereof upwards of 3000 were Europeans. The command was also entrusted to another officer; but General Marly's successor, Major-General George Wood, perplexed by the unknown dangers of the Sâl forest, which must of necessity be penetrated before reaching the hills, confined his efforts to some movements in the open Teraee, or lowland, on the hither side of the forest. The whole plan of the campaign in that quarter, as well as in Gôruckpoor, where Major-General I. S. Wood commanded, was thus immediately frustrated for the season. The dawn of success was nevertheless soon visible on the west, where Major-General Ochterlony began by reducing the forts of the Ramgurh range, which had been left garrisoned, when Umeer Singh had retired on Malâoun. This favourable outset was quickly followed up in Khumâon, by an irregular force employed in that direction, under the command of Colonel Gardiner. His attempt to penetrate to Almora, having shown this quarter to be a vulnerable point, a brigade of the regular army, under Colonel Nicolls, was pushed rapidly forwards. This officer, in the short space of less than a month, captured the city of Almora, after having defeated and slain the military governor opposed to him; and effected the conquest of the whole province. The fall of Almora, however, did not take place before the 25th of April. In the interim, the heights of Malâoun* had been carried by General Ochterlony on the 15th; and Umeer Singh, who had shut himself up in the fortress of that name, was soon afterwards reduced to such extremity, as to be obliged to surrender on terms for himself and for his son, who was

* Vide plate at the head of this chapter.

equally hard pressed at Jytuk. The whole of the hill tract, from the Gogra to the Sultej, was thus left at our disposal on the close of the campaign: a result which completely redeemed the reverses of its commencement, and raised the reputation of the British arms amongst the native powers of India, to a height proportionate to their sanguine expectations of defeat and disaster.

The reader has been conducted thus suddenly to the termination of the Nipâl operations for this season, without regard to the order of time, or occurrence of intermediate events. We left the native powers in December, 1814, under a very different impression respecting the war in the hill country, from that which was forced upon them in the following May. The military arrangements which had been made in October, for the support of the Bhopâl negotiations, were not of a magnitude to meet the extent of that combination, which seemed to be organizing against us in the course of December. Instead of being overawed by them, as had been expected, Sindheea had openly declared his resolution not to desist from hostility against that principality: and, as the Governor-General was determined to persevere in the policy he had entered upon, it became necessary to extend the scale of preparation in that quarter, as well as to the north, so as to provide against all hazards. The whole disposable force of the Madras army was accordingly ordered into the field, under the personal command of Sir Thomas Hislop; by which means a body of 13,000 men was brought together on the northern frontier of the British possessions in the Dukhun, at a point whence it could at any time move forward in support of the two subsidiary forces in advance. Reinforcements were at the same time ordered into Guzerât from the Bombay presidency; and it was his lordship's intention, in case matters should come to an actual rupture with Sindheea in confederacy with the Bhoosla and the predatory associations of central India, immediately to assume the offensive on the side of the Dukhun, while he maintained such an attitude on that of Hindoostan, as he hoped would secure him from attack. This latter object, however, was not of easy accomplishment, while the Nipâl war continued to require such extraordinary exertions. There had been at one period of the season, upwards of 45,000 * fighting men engaged either in the hills or the Teraee. The military establishments of the Bengal Presidency were, however, scarcely sufficient, even in ordinary times, to man a frontier of upwards of 1500 miles, from Soodheeana to Cuttack, in such a manner as not to expose its weakness. Indeed, the whole frontier eastward of Mirzapoor was absolutely defenceless; and the Pindaree incursion of 1812 had completely manifested our vulnerability in that quarter. In this emergency, the following were the measures adopted. It had heretofore been the practice to leave nearly all the civil duties of the western provinces to be executed by the regular army; by which means the battalions were broken into detachments, and their discipline and efficiency very much impaired. From these duties they were instantly relieved; and until provincial corps should have been formed for the purpose, the civil officers were ordered to take into their service such temporary bodies of armed men, as they might be able to procure on the spur of the occasion. An arrangement was at the same time effected, which contributed most materially to the advantageous display of the inadequate means left available for the defence of the provinces: viz. the calling out of the grenadier companies of the regiments of the line, not on actual service in the field, and forming

* According to the returns, there were at one time in the field,

Regulars - - -	33,059
Irregulars - - -	13,570
Making a total of -	46,629

them into independent battalions; while their place in the corps was directed to be filled up by supplemental companies. By this measure, an addition of seven battalions was at once made to the nominal force. Besides the above temporary expedients to meet the present exigency, considerable levies of irregular horse and foot were authorized; and Lord Hastings further determined to make a permanent addition of three regiments to the regular army, and to form six provincial corps, for the civil duties of the upper provinces. The irregular levies are of such a nature, as to be available the very moment they are raised; and as the individuals, especially of the horse, generally come from those ranks most likely to be opposed to us, their enlistment is always a measure of obvious momentary expediency. The new regiments could not be rendered fit for duty in the current season; but the motive of this augmentation was a firm conviction of the insufficiency of the military establishment, even for ordinary times; more particularly since the Goorkha power had risen to such importance, that henceforth that frontier would require as much vigilance as the southern and western. The Burmese of Ava and Arracan had also lately assumed a tone which rendered it probable that it would soon become necessary to have a permanent force in this direction likewise; and neither they nor the Nipâlese had theretofore entered into the calculations which had regulated the extent of the Bengal establishments. Inclusive of all the provincial and local corps, this augmentation would still carry the Bengal army to no higher numerical amount than about 80,000 fighting men; which would be the whole force relied on for the preservation and protection of half* a million of square miles, with a population of 40 millions, and a revenue of 12,000,000*l.* sterling.

Such were the provisions made by the Marquess of Hastings

* Including Oude and the protected states, but not the other presidencies.

to meet the crisis expected to occur in the season of 1814-15. Had it happened then, instead of three years afterwards, these preparations would have been no more than sufficient. The gloomy aspect of the campaign in the hills in January, induced his lordship to apply for two additional king's regiments from the Cape and Mauritius; and it was too late to countermand them, when the favourable turn of the tide had rendered their presence unnecessary. The more requisite precaution of recruiting the finances of the government by a second loan of a crore of rupees from the hoards of the Nuwab Vizier, contributed not a little to the facility with which these extensive arrangements were completed *.

It was, of course, some time before the above preparations could be put into a train of activity. The Madras army was not concentrated till March, when Sir Thomas Hislop assumed the command. By that time, however, it had become evident, that whatever necessity might have existed in December and January for military preparations on so large a scale, there was little chance that any part of the force assembled in every quarter would be called into active service this season. The interference we had already exerted in favour of Bhopâl, backed by such an appearance of precautionary vigilance, had proved sufficient to save the principality from attack; and the confederates not having yet gone the length of agreeing upon a specific plan of hostilities, which nothing on our part had occurred to precipitate, matters seemed, by general consent, to be subsiding into a state of repose, which, though wakeful and feverish, yet promised to last out the season. The Bhoosla Raja, on our requisition, arrested the advance of his troops; and Sindheea, notwithstanding his bullying refusal to abstain

* Upwards of half of the previous crore had been devoted by the council at Fort William to the paying off of an old loan, which imposed upon his Lordship the necessity of raising this further supply.

from hostile measures when requested by the resident, took the first opportunity of quietly withdrawing his forces. A fair occasion for so doing was offered by the violent conduct of Juswunt Rao Bhâo, whose differences with Colonel Baptiste proceeded to the length of obliging the colonel to attack and drive him off. After this, Baptiste staid some time in the neighbourhood of Bhopâl, negotiating with Vizier Mahommed; he then turned westward, ostensibly in pursuit of Juswunt Rao, leaving Bhopâl altogether unmolested.

Sindheea had before the end of December received a letter, addressed to him by the Governor-General on the subject of the discussions which had occurred at his durbar. This letter, after explaining the grounds on which Bhopâl was dealt with as a state free to negotiate and conclude alliances at will, professed a readiness to receive any statements and proofs to the contrary, that the durbar might have to exhibit; requiring, however, a suspension of all acts of hostility towards the Bhopâl territory, until the question of its political independence should have been disposed of. The court immediately caught at this proposition, having, as it should seem, already come to the resolution not to hazard an open rupture, for which it was nowise prepared: after some delay, a paper of complaints was accordingly drawn up, asserting Bhopâl to be one of the dependencies of Sindheea, but adducing no proof whatever; and further, accusing the British Government of having interfered with Sindheea's rights and possessions, by the extension of its protection to some of the Bundela Chiefs—a complaint, now preferred for the first time, though the measure had been adopted some years before. The Raja of Nâgpoor also gave in a similar paper of objections to our connexion with Bhopâl; the arguments of which were too trivial to be worth the recital.

The object of the Marquess of Hastings in inviting these durbars to the adoption of such a course of proceeding, was, to testify his adherence to that moderation and regard to the rights of others, which had been the constant aim of the British Government in its transactions with the native powers; and, by opening a door to negotiation, to prevent any sudden recourse to violent measures, likely to bring on a premature explosion. It should be recollected, that the Governor-General's principal view in proffering his protection to Bhopâl, had been to save that state from destruction, and thus prevent that union of interests between Sindheea and the Bhoosla, which must inevitably have ended in fixing the dependence of the latter on the former. The advantage of the connexion as a mere defensive arrangement against the Pindarees, however important, would scarcely have induced his Lordship to step forward at the particular juncture, had not the other two objects been so intimately blended with the prosecution of the same line of policy. The salvation of the principality, however, and the obstruction of Sindheea's apparent views on Nâgpoor, would as well be accomplished by a slow negotiation, which left things intermediately just as they were, as by the hasty employment of force, directed to the acquisition of the same objects. Should war be unavoidable in the end, still, in the then actual state of India, delay was necessary for the full development of our means, and for the removal of the unfavourable impression made by the recent occurrences of the Goorkha campaign. In every point of view, therefore, the course adopted by the Marquess of Hastings was most judicious; inasmuch as, even granting that no satisfactory result could ever be expected from negotiation, time at least would be gained; and time, in fact, was every thing. This resolution was formed early in December; and in furtherance of it, Mr. Wauchope was directed, on the arrival of the envoy from Bhopâl, to call upon him, in the first instance, to exhibit proofs of the independence of the principality.

All these matters remained in suspense the whole of the

ensuing January; during which time, the Nuwab gave out that he was under British protection, addressing letters to the commandants of the two subsidiary forces in the Dukhun, and to other British authorities, as if engagements had been actually signed and executed. At the end of January, he addressed a letter to Mr. Wauchope, informing him that his Dehlee agent had returned and acquainted him with all that had passed: that his vakeel should accordingly set off for Banda as soon as the Mohurrum * was over. No vakeel, however, was despatched before the 18th March, or appeared at Banda until the 5th April. It was positively ascertained that the Nuwab, satisfied of his security from the steps already taken by the Governor-General, imagined he might now look about for other advantages, and had employed this interval in close negotiation with Baptiste and Sudeek Ulee Khan, not only while their armies were threatening his territory, when the excuse of imminent danger might have been admissible, but even after they had retired to a distance, and there was no longer any fear of attack being meditated by the Mahrattas. Moreover, notwithstanding that it was an express stipulation of the Governor-General, to which he had distinctly declared his acquiescence, that he should not negotiate except in concert with the British Government, he gave no intimation of any intention so to act, and carefully concealed the nature of his communications; even denying the having sent an agent to the quarters of Baptiste after his retrograde movement, though the fact had been public and was universally known.

After such duplicity, it was not to be expected that negotiations, if opened at Banda, would be prosecuted with any cordiality on the part of the Nuwab. The Governor-General accordingly determined, in order both to mark his sense of the conduct pursued by the Nuwab, and to prevent his further

* A Mussulman-festival. Vide Hunter's Hindoostanee Dictionary.

trifling with the British Government, to order his vakeel to be dismissed without an audience, as soon as he should appear at Banda. These orders were executed, and the negotiation thus broken off in April. Vizier Mahommed was, at the same time, assured, that no ill-will was harboured towards him, and that it was merely because his conduct had shown that he had not a proper sense of the value of the connexion offered to him, or of the spirit in which it ought to have been received, that the British Government, for the present, withdrew from the discussion of it.

This result of the negotiation, and the insincerity of the Bhopâl prince's behaviour, which had been the occasion of its abrupt termination, were communicated in due course by the residents at the respective independent courts. It was, however, distinctly asserted on the part of the Governor-General, in reply to the objections delivered in by Sindheea and the Bhoosla, that no proof or argument whatever had been adduced, that could be construed to limit or preclude the right of the British Government to take the principality under protection on any future occasion, or to show that it had at any time been other than perfectly free and independent. No answer was made to this communication by either court; the point may therefore be considered to have been virtually conceded by the Mahratta potentates. The negotiation with the legitimate Chief of Sâgur, which was a corollary to that of Bhopâl, was abandoned at the same time; the delay and evasions of the Nana, Govind Rao, having shown, that to him also, notwithstanding his original solicitations, the connexion had become a matter of indifference.

The season was verging towards it close, ere these events were finally concluded; yet the inimical disposition which had been testified by the powers of central India had begun visibly to subside, or at least to be more guarded and disguised, through the extinction of any hope, that an opportunity of breaking out would be offered by the operations of the mountain war of Nipâl. The Governor-General felt, therefore, that it was unnecessary longer to maintain the same attitude of military preparation, which had been assumed under a different aspect of affairs. The Madras army was accordingly broken up, and the Guzerât force ordered back to its cantonments. The two subsidiary forces of the Dukhun remained for some time longer in the advanced positions they had occupied, with a view to afford as much protection to the territories of the Nizam and Pêshwa against predatory incursion, as the extended line to be defended would admit.

Thus ended the first season of active operations. The Nipâlese were soliciting peace with every appearance of sincerity; the native powers of central India had been inspired with a degree of awe that kept them quiet; and Bhopâl, though not yet linked in actual alliance with us, had been as effectually protected, as if the treaty had been signed. Moreover, the interest for its preservation, evinced on this occasion, promised to afford security for the future, by leaving the Mahratta princes under the apprehension of our again stepping forward in a similar manner to thwart a similar design. The Vizier Mahommed seems evidently to have anticipated this consequence of his application to us; indeed, his whole conduct shows that it was his intention, for his own security, to avail himself of the reputation of our power, rather than of its actual exercise; and that he never had any serious thoughts of binding himself to us in any connexion, which would interfere with his political independence. This high-minded and ambitious Chief was unwilling to forego the prospect of self-aggrandisement and extension of territory, at the expense of the regular as well as irregular powers, which hemmed him in on every side. His resort to us was a mere temporary expedient; and he wished to have no further intercourse, than was barely necessary to gain his purpose.

The policy of the Governor-General's offer of protection to Bhopâl has since been brought into question, on the ground of its tendency to give birth to those very intrigues, and that very disposition to conspire against the British domination, from which he had apprehended danger to our interests. But the previous existence of these intrigues, as evidenced by Sindheea's connexion with the Bhoosla, and by the concurring reports of the several British residents at the native courts, was the principal, and perhaps the sole reason, that induced Lord Hastings to adopt the measure; the object of which had been to anticipate, and thereby prevent, the pernicious consequences to be expected from the projects of the Mahrattas at the particular juncture. Doubtless, when the outset of the Goorkha war had been unpropitious, and when such extensive exertions were required for its prosecution, it is scarcely conceivable, that the risk of giving umbrage to the Mahratta powers and entailing fresh embarrassment would have been incurred, without a sense of most imperious exigency. But probably in the opinion of some people, the best argument in favour of the course taken is to be found in the result which actually followed, notwithstanding the unlooked-for disasters of the campaign. It will have been seen, that the establishment of Sindheea's influence over the Bhoosla, and the destruction of Bhopâl, were thereby completely prevented. Although the greater part of the force of the Bengal presidency was known to be occupied in the hill country, and daily accounts of reverses in that quarter must have been eagerly circulated, the Mahrattas were nevertheless deterred by the formidable aspect of the British preparations from resenting in any way this undisguised and direct counteraction of their views.

CHAPTER III.

HYDERABAD-POONA.

1815—JUNE—JULY.

Rains set in—Hyderabad—Nizam's sons seize a dependent of the Residency—guard set upon them obliged to retire—troops called into Hyderabad—their submission and confinement in Golkonda—Poona—account of Bajee Rao—of Gykwar—his relation to Pêshwa—to British—policy of Pêshwa, and claims on Nizam—on Gykwar—referred to British arbitration—award as to Ahmedabad—Trimbukjee Dainglia—Gungadhur Sastree's negotiation—Intrigues at Brodera—protest of British Resident—renunciation of the arbitration—Gungadhur practised upon, and gained over—pilgrimage to Nassick—Sastree gives offence—his destruction planned—pilgrimage to Pundurpoor—dissimulation—Sastree murdered.

THE preceding chapter brought down the transactions of India to the month of June, 1815. The rainy season then commences, which is usually the signal for the suspension of active warfare, and drives into cantonments the few remaining troops, that the hot months of April and May have not already compelled to seek such shelter. Yet even the rainy period of this season was not without anxieties. Whilst a large body of troops was cantoned in Behar, waiting the issue of the negotiations with Nipâl, which was to regulate its movements on the drying up of the waters, occurrences were passing in the Dukhun at the two friendly courts of the Nizam and Pêshwa, which excited the most lively interest, and developed, in a manner not to be mistaken, the real disposition of those powers.

The Nizam's sons and relations were allowed to live freely in Hyderabad; and, after the manner of Moosulman princes all over the world, collected about them all the dissolute vagabonds of the city, by whose agency they prosecuted a regular system of insult and extortion upon the rich and quietly disposed part of the community. The swarms of desperate characters and Patan bravoes, that habitually infest the streets of Hyderabad, had found in the scions of the reigning family apt leaders for all their excesses, whose influence at the palace screened them from punishment for the most flagitious crimes; insomuch that even the ministerial authority was frequently insulted, and murders openly committed with impunity. The most profligate and debauched of the princes were the two youngest sons of the Nizam, Shumsham-ood-oullah and Moobariz-ood-oullah, with their cousin and brother-in-law, Imteeaz-ood-oullah. These young men were supported in their extravagancies by Tuhneeut-oo-Nissa Begum, the mother, and Jehan Purwar Begum, the wife of the Nizam, and, shielded by this influence, carried their audacity to the utmost pitch, while the weakness and timidity of Raja Chundoo Lâl, the minister, rendered nugatory his attempts to control them. On more than one occasion, their iniquities had been the subject of a direct representation from the British Resident to his Highness the Nizam, who had ordered them to be subjected to some restraint in consequence. Their intrigues, however, baffled the minister's attempts to carry these orders into effect; and not being prepared to go the length of securing their persons, he could produce no reformation in their conduct.

In the month of August, these libertines seized an attendant of the British Resident, with a view to extort money from him. Mr. H. Russell, the Resident, immediately complained of this indignity to the Nizam; who, resolving to place the young men in actual confinement, sent a party of his reformed infantry, under the command of Captain Hare, with orders to plant sentries about the houses in which they resided. In execution of his orders, Captain Hare marched first to the residence of Moobariz-ood-oullah. On approaching it he was fired upon from the houses on either side, in which Patans armed with matchlocks had been previously posted. Some loss was sustained on the occasion; and, amongst others, an officer of the Resident's escort was killed. After carrying one or two of the houses, and putting the armed people found in them to the sword for the sake of example, Captain Hare pushed on to the palace of Moobariz-ood-oullah, where he found the gates closed, and other preparations made for resistance. He succeeded, however, in forcing open one of the gates with some six-pounders he had with him; but seeing the increased number of opponents, and that further perseverance in the attempt to execute his orders would probably cause the Patan population of the city to rise *en masse*, he retired to the house of Raja Chundoo Lâl, to wait for further instructions. Meantime the Resident had called in the whole disposable force from the adjoining cantonment of Secunderabad; but finding the brigade there too weak to act against the city, and fearing that the present disturbance might lead to a general insurrection, he kept the detachment at the Residency, and immediately despatched requisitions, as well to Colonel Doveton, to move down on Hyderabad from the northern frontier, as to the officer commanding at Bellaree, to detach a reinforcement. In the interim, he suffered matters to remain in complete suspense. This gave the princes time to reflect on the probable consequences of their inconsiderate conduct; and the violence of the Patan character soon gave way to the awful apprehension of what would be the result. Thus the ferment in the city subsided of itself, and the princes were easily induced to throw themselves on the mercy of the Nizam, in whose palace they took refuge. Mr. Russell urged the necessity of their strict confinement, and it was determined that they should be sent to the fortress of Golkonda. This sentence, however, was not carried into effect, until after repeated and very earnest solicitations of the Resident, who had to encounter the arts and intrigues of the Nizam's mother and favourite wife, as well as the indifference of the minister. When, at length, the princes were ordered off to Golkonda, the two Begums resolved to accompany them; and both actually went into voluntary confinement, hoping by this means to induce the Nizam soon to restore the offenders to favour. But his Highness coolly observed, on being informed of their departure, that they were very welcome to go, for he believed it was himself they had rather be rid of than the English; nor did he afterwards evince much anxiety to obtain the Resident's consent to the release of the culprits. The principal fomenters of the disturbance were shortly afterwards seized and executed. Mr. Russell, seeing tranquillity thus quietly restored, countermanded the march of Colonel Doveton from the frontier, but retained the reinforcements he had received from the south, thinking it necessary to maintain the force cantoned at Secunderabad in a state of greater efficiency, as a security against the evidently hostile disposition of the Patan population of the Nizam's capital. By the end of September this affair was completely settled, and order re-established on a firmer footing than before.

While Hyderabad was under the alarm of these disturbances, events and discussions of a much more serious nature were passing at Poona. It will be necessary to the due understanding of these, to enter into a somewhat detailed explanation of the character of Bajee Rao's policy, and the arts by which he had raised himself from the situation of a fugitive, to that elevation of rank and power, which finally inspired the presumptuous confidence of ability to cope with the British nation.

It will be in the recollection of the reader, that Bajee Rao was the son of *Ragoonath Rao, or Ragoobee, the uncle and

* Vide Forbes' Oriental Memoirs; also Mills' British India, and the authorities there cited.

murderer of Nerayun Rao, brother and successor to the great Madhoo Rao, who was the last of the family of the Pêshwas that wielded in his own person the undivided sovereignty of the Mahratta empire. The murderer was expelled by a combination of the Chiefs; and the infant son of the murdered Nerayun was placed on the Guddee with the name of Madhoo Rao Nerayun.

During the minority, the power of the state was in the hands of a triumvirate, Madhajee Sindheea and Tukojee Holkar exercising independent authority in Hindoostan and Kandêsh, while Nana Furnavees managed with uncommon ability the more difficult government of Poona and the southern territories. In 1795, the nominal Pêshwa, Madhoo Rao Nerayun, threw himself from a window of his palace in a sudden fit of anger, at a hasty word from Nana Furnavees, whose guardianship and strict control were becoming irksome to a prince already arrived at years of maturity. He died on the spot, leaving as next heirs the sons of Ragoonath, his father's murderer, of whom Bajee Rao, the eldest, was accordingly proclaimed: but, as he immediately commenced intrigues to rid himself of the Nana's ascendancy, a fruitless attempt was made by the latter to set up a younger brother, Chimna Appa. Bajee Rao, though young, was an adept in intrigue and dissimulation of all kinds. By calling in the aid of Sindheea, he first ruined the Furnavees; and then, by availing himself of Holkar's rivalry with that chief, set limits to the control which the latter aimed to exercise over his administration. When, after Tukojee Holkar's death in 1797, Sindheea had, by espousing the cause of one of the legitimate sons, and by circumventing and slaying the other, established his entire ascendancy over the concerns of this rival family, he made no scruple of straitening the Pêshwa's authority at Poona. To earn his favour, Bajee Rao put to death Eithojee, the brother of Juswunt Rao, both of whom were bastard sons of Tukojee Holkar. This act, which was committed in the firm belief that the Holkar interest was irretrievably ruined, occasioned the irreconcileable hatred of Juswunt Rao, and prevented a resort to the old policy of opposing the Holkar to the Sindheea, when the fortunes of the former family were restored by the abilities and activity of the surviving bastard. Thenceforward, the only counterpoise to Sindheea seemed to be the British power; and, as it was an early object of Lord Wellesley's policy, to detach the Poona state from the other Mahratta chieftains, and bring it under the influence of the British Government, it became Bajee Rao's study to affect to receive favourably the overtures made him on the subject; and, by keeping up the appearance of a secret negotiation with the British Resident, to excite Sindheea's alarms, whenever he had any point to carry. Though the intrigues and activity of Juswunt Rao, and other chiefs in Hindostan, fomented underhand by Bajee Rao himself, diverted Sindheea from the affairs of Poona and the Dukhun, about the year 1800, and left the Pêshwa more free to pursue his own projects, still he had little authority over the powerful feudatories of the empire, but such as he derived from Sindheea's countenance and superior means; so that, until the victory of Juswunt Rao Holkar over their joint forces, and his consequent flight from Poona into the Konkan, to throw himself under the protection of the English, he could be regarded as little better than a pageant in that chieftain's hands. The British army restored him to his capital and to independent authority within the Poona territory; but bound him, as a condition of the alliance, in all transactions with the Nizam and with the independent Mahratta powers, such as Holkar and Sindheea, to square his policy to our views. Amongst other matters, it was specially provided in the treaty of Bassein, that the British Government should arbitrate the claims of the Pêshwa on the Gykwar state, in case it should be found impossible to settle them by amicable adjustment. As it was out of this very adjustment that the discussions and events arose, which are about to be related, we shall be excused a short digression, for the purpose of explaining the nature and origin of the claims in question.

The rise of the Gykwar's power in Guzerât was almost contemporaneous with that of the Pêshwa's at Poona. Pillajee Gykwar, the first of the family, was Potel (managing proprietor) of a village near Poona. He entered the service of Trimbuk Rao, the Senaputtee, or general, of the Suttara dynasty, who, after the conquest of Guzerât, opposed in arms the ascendancy of the first Pêshwa. Pillajee was a principal officer of the Senaputtee, when the latter was defeated and slain in 1731. After a struggle with the Powars, and other Mahratta families, he obtained the chief management on behalf of the Senaputtee's descendants, and thus established his own power, by the same arts the Pêshwa himself had practised towards the Suttara Raja. Dying in 1747, his son Damajee succeeded to his rule, and received the additional title of Shumsheer Bahadhur, from the nominal head of the Senaputtee's family, which is the last act of authority that family appears to have exercised. The Gykwars made good their independence in the province against the Pêshwa's attempts to reduce them by force. Arms proving unavailing, negotiation was tried, in order to procure an acknowledgment of supremacy. In the course of it, Damajee engaged in a conspiracy against the Pêshwa's power, at the head of which was the Dhabareea of Tulleegâm. He marched his troops into the Dukhun in support of the conspirators; and, on their failure, was himself circumvented by a truce, pending which he was surprised and taken prisoner by Balajee Pêshwa. He was not released till he had agreed to resign the half of his possessions in Guzerât, to acknowledge his holding the other half in fief of the Pêshwa, and to unite his forces with those of

Balajee, in a joint expedition for the reduction of Ahmedabad, then in the tenure of the Moghuls. This place, if conquered, was to be similarly divided. Balajee's brother Ragoonath, father of Bajee Rao, commanded the Pêshwa's troops on this enterprise; and Damajee having executed the first part of the treaty, in spite of the opposition of the ministry, who had conducted affairs during his captivity, Ahmedabad was reduced by their joint arms in 1753. Since then, Damajee continued a faithful dependent of the Pêshwa. He was present at the battle of Puneeput, in 1761, and attended at Poona in aid of Ragoonath the regent during Madhoo Rao's minority. For his services on this latter occasion he obtained the grant of Guzerât in perpetuity, together with the title of Sena Khas khel, or commander of the special band. In the subsequent differences between the uncle and nephew, he took the part of the former; but Madhoo Rao, being successful, punished him by the imposition of an annual tribute of 5¼ lack rupees, and the furnishing of a contingent of 5000 horse. Damajee died five years after, in 1768, when the succession was disputed between Govind Rao, the second son by the first wife, and Syajee, the eldest son by the second wife; which latter was almost an idiot, set up by Futteh Singh, another son, with a view to personal aggrandizement. Pending this dispute, the Pêshwa was enabled to enhance his tribute by selling his countenance to the highest bidder; and Futteh Singh in the end carried the day, by agreeing to an annual payment of 1,779,900 rupees, and to a money compensation, in lieu of the contingent, of 675,000 rupees. With the help of the British he expelled his rival, and then paid his tribute or not according to his own ability, and to the Pêshwa's means of enforcing it. It was, however, stipulated in the treaty concluded by us with Futteh Singh, in 1782, that he should pay to the Pêshwa the same tribute, and yield him the same obedience as before the treaty. Futteh Singh died in 1789; and there have since been three successions. In 1802, Anund Rao, the reigning Gykwar, received a British subsidiary force, and made several cessions to reimburse the expense of an expedition, fitted out by the Bombay Presidency, to repel an invasion of his territory by Mulhar Rao Holkar. On the last day of 1802, the treaty of Bassein was also concluded with the Pêshwa. In 1803, territory, yielding a revenue of 780,000 rupees, was ceded by Anund Rao in lieu of the subsidy; and the force being increased in the course of the year, further cessions were added to the amount of 290,000 rupees. The British Government had since taken upon itself the guarantee of the Gykwar's debts, and the management of the greater part of his territory; and the cessions altogether amounted in 1814-15 to 13½ lacks.

While we were thus gradually and peaceably establishing a complete ascendancy in Guzerat, the Pêshwa's claims under the two engagements with Damajee and Futteh Singh were little attended to. At our suggestion, soon after the treaty of Bassein, Bajee Rao was induced to grant a farm of his share of Ahmedabad to the Gykwar for ten years. The fixed rent of this lease was regularly paid him; but no steps were taken to bring the other matters in dispute to an adjustment, Bajee Rao having never thought proper to advance his claims. The reason of this negligence may be found perhaps in the policy he was pursuing nearer home. The ten years, that followed the restoration of his authority at Poona by the British arms, were systematically devoted by Bajee Rao to the humiliation of the old Mahratta families, who, enjoying large jagheers and military tenures, on every occasion of ferment, chose their party, according as best suited their immediate interest, without conceiving themselves under the smallest obligations of fidelity and allegiance to the Pêshwa's legitimate authority. He had conceived a particular enmity against this class, from a conviction that the state, to which he had been reduced by Juswunt Rao Holkar, and the necessity he had felt of applying to the British for succour (a step most derogatory to the Mahratta name and reputation), was owing entirely to his having been deserted in the hour of need by the immediate vassals of the empire. He seems, therefore, very early to have formed the resolution of seeking every means of reducing this formidable class, and either hereafter entirely dispensing with them, entertaining what troops he might need individually, and in small bodies not exceeding one hundred under one commander, or at least of remodelling the fiefs in such a manner as should leave the vassal in the most abject dependence on his superior lord. The British subsidiary force, which was ever prompt to enforce the Pêshwa's just rights, was the engine he relied on for the re-establishment of his authority over these jageerdars; but, as this force was only available where right was on his side, he contrived to turn its name, and the apprehension created by its state of perpetual efficiency, to equal account, on many occasions, when perhaps he could not have commanded its actual service. In the course of the ten or eleven years following the treaty of Bassein, this policy had been successful in ruining by far the greater part of the old Mahratta families. The great power of the jageerdars southward of Poona, and the circumstance of their having done good service to the Duke of Wellington, in the campaign which restored Bajee Rao to his capital, rendered it necessary for him to submit to our adjustment his relative rights over these latter. He was, however, greatly discontented at the adjustment finally made by us in 1812, because it required him to renounce in perpetuity his groundless claim of sovereignty over Kolapoor and Sawuntwaree, and fixed and defined his other dues, which it is always a favourite object of Mahratta policy to keep indefinite. Of course, having accepted the arbitration of the differences, we became the guarantee of its execution on both sides. It was now found to be Bajee Rao's artifice to hold the jageerdars to the fulfilment of their part of the award with the utmost rigour, leaving, at the same time, such inducements to deviate from the letter of it, that some were occasionally found tripping, so as to forfeit our guarantee, and to give Bajee Rao a claim to our assistance towards their reduction. The case of the Rasteeas, very powerful southern jageerdars, is a notable instance. While urging to us the necessity of chastising their confirmed obstinacy and refusal to furnish their full quota of troops, Bajee Rao was privately assuring the family, that he had no design to ruin them, and thus encouraging their resistance, until their utter destruction was finally effected by our agency.

By the year 1813-14, the uniform prosecution of this crafty policy had succeeded in effecting the consolidation of the Pêshwa's authority over the whole of his Poona dominions; it had also filled his treasuries, as well by bringing into them the large revenue theretofore appropriated by individuals, as by the rigid exaction of fines and penalties. Until these domestic objects had been attained, foreign affairs did not seem to occupy much of his attention; to them he now began to devote himself. The Pêshwa's government had indefinite claims on the Nizam; amongst others, one for *chout* on the revenue of nearly his whole dominions, originating in concessions made in an hour of extremity by Nizam Ulee Khan, but neither intended nor expected to be observed, unless the same necessity should annually recur. These claims, however, the British government had engaged by the treaty of Bassein to adjust and determine; and Bajee Rao began about 1813-14 to be most importunate for some adjudication. After some time spent in pressing for a decision, the supreme-government resolved, that the senior assistant to the resident at Poona should repair to Hyderabad with the ministers of the Poona state, and a commission be there instituted, to consider and ascertain the relative rights of the parties. From this time forth nothing more was heard of the Pêshwa's claims. He ceased to urge them the instant he found in us a readiness to perform our part of the engagement for their settlement; either from distrust of our arbitration, or from an unwillingness to have his dues fixed and set at rest for ever.

The claims on the Gykwar were brought forward at the same time, and the decennial lease of the moiety of Ahmedabad being about to expire, Bajee Rao gave notice of his intention to take the management into his own hands, and on no account to renew the lease. With respect to the other matters at issue, it appeared, that four years before the conclusion of the treaties of Bassein and Brodera, the Gykwar had, through fear of Sindheea, agreed to pay up all arrears on Futteh Singh's engagement, besides fifty-six lack for his own investiture. It was on this basis that Bajee Rao expected the present adjustment of his pecuniary demands. They had been suffered to lie by so long, that, when the account came to be made up, they were found to amount to a sum considerably exceeding three crore of rupees, of which upwards of two crore were on account of arrears of the tribute and commutation money agreed to by Futteh Singh, the remainder for the moiety of acquisitions made by Damajee, subsequently to the capture of Ahmedabad, besides the item of fifty-six lack above mentioned for the investiture of Anund Rao, and upwards of thirty-nine lack in liquidation of an old account. The Gykwar had little to set off against these claims, and was evidently in no condition to make good so heavy a balance, as would ultimately have proved to have been due, if the account had been settled on this basis. At the suggestion of the British Government *, Gungadhur Sastree, the

* Gungadhur Sastree evinced extreme aversion to visiting Poona. The Pêshwa induced our government to urge it upon him, under our guarantee for

prime minister of the Gykwar state, came under our guarantee from Brodera to Poona, to endeavour to make some adjustment or compromise of these claims. He hoped also to obtain a renewal of the lease of Ahmedabad, by offering some advance of rent. This latter object was in vain attempted in every possible shape. Accordingly, in June 1814, the resident at Poona was obliged to consent to the half of Ahmedabad being delivered to the Pêshwa's officers; and orders were issued for the purpose. The soubaship was given by Bajee Rao to Trimbukjee Dainglia, who deputed an agent of his own to take charge of the Pêshwa's interests there. This Trimbukjee had risen from the meanest origin by the basest arts. He was first a menial servant, then one of the familiar companions of Bajee Rao, whose social hours were passed in witnessing exhibitions of the grossest debauchery, and had risen to favour by the conspicuous profligacy, with which he ministered and assisted at such entertainments. Though known to have been some time a personal favourite, it was not till after the above appointment, and his nomination to command the contingent, when called out in 1814-15, that he was introduced by the Pêshwa to Mr. Elphinstone, as a person high in confidence. He thenceforward regularly assisted at all conferences, assuming at them a tone of arrogance and undisguised ambition, which seemed to advance him in his master's favour, in proportion as his tone was heightened; a clear indication of the change of Bajee Rao's sentiments or designs, and of his beginning to feel the British connexion, rather in the restraints it imposed on his desire to restore the Mahratta empire to its pristine splendour, than in the security

his safety, by the holding out to us, that he was willing and able to come to an amicable arrangement, if he could have a personal communication with the Sastree. But his real object seems to have been, to remove from the court of Brodera a minister, who was sure to oppose the conspiracy then in agitation for a general league against the British power.

it gave to the possession of what remained under his immediate sway. Mr. Elphinstone early marked this change, and gave a prophetic warning to his own government, that a serious rupture must inevitably ensue, if Bajee Rao persevered in giving ear to the flagitious counsels of this abandoned favourite. The transactions of every day, after this man's influence had been established, bore evidence of the truth of this prediction; and it was further attested by the conduct of the agent whom he sent to Ahmedabad, and who there commenced a course of intrigue and aggression, from which even the subjects of the British Government in the adjacent districts did not escape unmolested.

Meanwhile Gungadhur Sastree, instead of meeting a reciprocal disposition to bring matters to a speedy adjustment, had to encounter systematic evasion and subterfuge. The Pêshwa's ministers showed no inclination to accommodate matters, and would not recede an iota from their demand. He began therefore to be sensible that his object could not be gained without larger sacrifices, either in satisfaction of the claims in dispute, or in personal gratifications to the ministers, than he felt himself authorised to consent to. This turn of the negotiation, in so far as it gave him time, which he hoped would bring the Poona court to a right understanding of his master's means, and of the futility of pretensions so much exceeding them, was not unacceptable to the Gykwar envoy. But the objects of Bajee Rao, or rather of Trimbukjee, who seems from the first to have been entrusted with the whole conduct of this negotiation, equally required time for their development.

It happened, that the Gykwar minister had a rival for his official station at Brodera, in the person of Seeta-Ram, the former dewan of our choice, who was still supported by a strong party in the palace of the Gykwar, notwithstanding that the Sastree had, on Futteh Singh's elevation, obtained the entire control of affairs, by the direct interference of the British government. Since then, Seeta-Ram had been under some degree of *surveillance*, though by no means strict. Trimbukjee, however, availing himself of the Sastree's absence from Brodera, set on foot an intrigue, the object of which was to replace his rival in the ministry, to the Sastree's exclusion, and thus to establish the Pêshwa's influence at the court of Brodera, in lieu of that of the British Government. In furtherance of this plan, an agent, named Govind Rao Burdojee, came from Seeta-Ram, in October, 1814, and was well received at Poona. A second agent, Bhugwunt Rao, came in the month of January following; and, on the Busunt Punchumee * festival, by the good offices of Trimbukjee, they both obtained a favourable reception from the Pêshwa himself, at the public audience of that day, which occurred in February, 1815. A letter was also procured in the hand-writing of Anund Rao, the nominal Gykwar, from which it would seem that he did not altogether discountenance these intrigues; and they were more openly espoused by a party amongst the women of his household. It should be observed, too, that they were most active just at the time, when the reverses at the opening of the Goorkha campaign, and the state of the negotiations respecting Bhopâl, gave the Marquess of Hastings such strong reason to apprehend the worst from the disposition of the Mahratta powers towards the British interests. On the first appearance of these intrigues in October, Mr. Elphinstone had protested against them; whereupon Bajee Rao's ministers did not affect to deny their existence, but, on the contrary, justified them on the ground that the Gykwar was a dependent of the Pêshwa, who was bound to look after his vassal's interests, that through the Sastree's mismanagement had been suffered to go to ruin. When Mr. Elphinstone argued, that his Highness's attempt to interfere was subversive of the British alliances with both states, our influence having

* A Hindoo festival. Vide Hunter's Hindoostanee Dictionary.

been instrumental in producing the existing arrangements at the court of Brodera, under authority acquired by treaties with the Gykwar, which the subsequent treaty of Bassein had formally recognised; the argument seemed to make little impression, and produced no relaxation in the activity with which the intrigues were carried on. In October, Mr. Elphinstone had confined himself to the request, that Gungadhur Sastree should be dismissed, since no good seemed likely to result from protracting an amicable negotiation with a party, whom it was endeavoured at the same time, by secret intrigue, to undermine and remove from office. However, at the Sastree's own request, he refrained from insisting on this point. Gungadhur, it seems, was himself unwilling to break off the negotiation, having still hopes of effecting an amicable compromise by delay; and he had been relieved from any fear in respect to the result of the intrigues at Brodera, by Seeta-Ram's being subjected to further restraint, at the suggestion of the English Resident at the court of the Gykwar. But in February, when it became evident to Mr. Elphinstone, that the negotiation must come to nothing if conducted in the manner it had been, and the arrival of the second agent from Seeta-Ram showed the increased and alarming vigour with which the intrigues were still pursued, he distinctly informed the Pêshwa's government, that, unless the right which had been asserted to interfere in the internal administration of the Gykwar's affairs were formally renounced, the Pêshwa must not expect the British government to arbitrate, or assist in enforcing his claims upon that state. At the same time, he demanded that the two agents of Seeta-Ram should either be delivered up, or at least discountenanced and dismissed as offenders and conspirators against the established government of the Gykwar principality; giving notice also, that unless the latter demands were complied with, he would break off the negotiation altogether, and the Sastree must return to Brodera by the end of March. As Bajee Rao was not disposed to make any renunciation of his asserted right, the negotiations, as far as the British Resident was concerned, were dropped on this ground, which was again most fully explained on the first day of the following month. Gungadhur was likewise recalled, and instructed to prepare for his departure; but he was not forbidden to enter into a private negotiation for the settlement of the matter, without the participation of the British government, if he saw a favourable opportunity, and could effect it within a reasonable time.

The bringing of matters so suddenly to this issue completely disconcerted Bajee Rao and his council; for the Pêshwa's government was in no condition to enforce any part of his claims, except by means of the British; and the main-spring of his intrigues with the faction opposed to Gungadhur was, the hope held out to them of granting in their favour better terms of settlement than Gungadhur could obtain by our arbitration. The Resident having now made the Pêshwa's abandonment of all pretension of right to interfere with the Gykwar a condition of his exerting the British influence to obtain any thing from the present ministry of Brodera, while Bajee Rao firmly persisted in the resolution not to renounce the pretension, the other party had the decided advantage; for he was at liberty either to join in insisting on the renunciation as a preliminary, and thus evade payment of any thing; or, by tendering a proposition for a separate adjustment on moderate terms, to save Bajee Rao from the supposed humiliation of publicly conceding the right to interfere. Every device was put in practice to induce Mr. Elphinstone to abandon this ground; but having once assumed it, and being sensible that, with a view to the maintenance of our existing influence and relations with the Gykwar, the right of a third power to interfere could on no account whatever be recognised, it was of course impossible to recede. The consequence was, that Bajee Rao and Trimbukjee immediately changed their behaviour towards the envoy, and now endeavoured by every art to win him over, and to induce him to remain at the durbar, notwithstanding his recal. In this object they were successful. They commenced by opening a negotiation with every appearance of cordiality, the object of which was, to compromise the whole of the Pêshwa's claims past and to come, by the cession of territory yielding a revenue of seven lack of rupees. This mode of adjustment was suggested by the Sastree himself, in order to flatter Bajee Rao's known eagerness for the extension of his personal dominions; and certainly it was the most favourable one for the Gykwar interests that could possibly be made; for, besides arrears, the annual tribute claimed, amounted, including the commutation for military service, to upwards of twenty-four lack. Having this adjustment very much at heart, the Sastree resolved to stay and pursue the negotiation, without the participation of the British resident at Poona. Had there been occasion to refer to him, Mr. Elphinstone was of course prepared to resume the ground he had before made his stand upon; but so long as the treaty could be carried on without such a reference, he saw no objection to letting it take its own course.

In this manner passed the month of March, without the dismissal of the Sastree. The negotiation continued open through the whole of April; in the course of which month, no effort was spared to win him over to the interests of the Poona court. The Pêshwa's sister-in-law was offered to his son in marriage, and the chief ministry of the Pêshwa's affairs, that is to say, the situation held by Suda-Sheeo-Bhao Mankeshur, was tendered to his acceptance. There can be no doubt that he was dazzled by these offers, and not only gave a favourable ear to them, but contracted a degree of intimacy with Trimbukjee, through whom they were made, which was very unusual amongst natives of rank, and, considering the previous animosity on both sides, rather extraordinary. In the month of May, Bajee Rao came to a determination to commence a series of pilgrimages, whereof the first was to be to Nassick near the source of the Godaveree. The negotiation for the marriage was at this time in a state of so much forwardness, as to induce the Pêshwa to take his family with him to Nassick, and to make preparations to have the ceremony performed at that place; and in this idea the journey was commenced in May. In the mean time, however, Gungadhur had referred the proposed compromise of the claim on the Gykwar to Futteh Singh, the representative of Anund Rao, on whose part he rather unexpectedly met with a decided repugnance to a territorial cession of any extent, however limited. In the hope of surmounting this difficulty, he did not candidly explain it to the Pêshwa's government, but commenced a series of evasions for the purpose of gaining time. He also put off the marriage on various pretexts, not wishing it to take place, unless the adjustment was likewise effected, which he daily found it more difficult to accomplish. This conduct had the appearance of slight; and the Sastree having refused to suffer his wife to visit the wife of Bajee Rao, on the ground of the notorious licentiousness that prevailed in the palace of the Pêshwa, all these circumstances, superadded to the disappointment of failing to gain over a man so eagerly courted, produced a second change of disposition towards him, and revived the hatred that before subsisted in an aggravated degree, and with the further stimulus of personal pique for a private injury. Trimbukjee began to feel that he had committed his master in the matter of the marriage; to break off which, after the families had been brought to Nassick for the purpose, and after all the publicity of preparation, would bring ignominy on the head of the Mahratta nation. Bajee Rao, who was naturally of a suspicious and resentful temper, seems from this time to have vowed revenge, and found in his favourite a most willing instrument. A plan was accordingly laid for the assassination of the Sastree, and prosecuted with a depth of dissimulation, which astonished even Mahratta duplicity. The terms of intimacy that subsisted between Trimbukjee Dainglia, and the object of this plot had grown so extremely familiar, while matters were running smoothly on, that the former, in an unguarded moment of friendly conversation, acknowledged, that during their previous differences, he had resolved upon the other's destruction, and had even planned his death, in case he had taken his dismissal when Mr. Elphinstone began to press it. This had been communicated by the Sastree to Mr. Elphinstone during the journey to Nassick, and doubtless was enough to have put him on his guard, by showing the character of the man he had to deal with. Yet such was the art with which both Trimbukjee and his master continued their intercourse with him to the last, that although his destruction was meditated more than a month before it was put into execution, their victim never suspected any change of sentiment towards himself. When the Nassick pilgrimage was accomplished, he assented with the utmost confidence to Trimbukjee's suggestion of proceeding to Pundurpoor on the Bheema with a smaller equipage, and sent the greater part of his escort, and half the establishment of the mission, to wait his return at Poona. Particular anxiety was shown, that Bapoo Myral, a penetrating wary Mahratta, who had been associated with the Sastree in the mission, though in a subordinate character, should not accompany the court to Pundurpoor; but this was attributed to some personal dislike, supposed to be entertained against him, rather than to fear of his prudence and foresight. It was a more important point to keep Mr. Elphinstone, who had attended the Pêshwa as far as Nassick, from proceeding further; but the resident needed no more, than to find that his attendance was not desired. While, therefore, the Pêshwa continued his route to Pundurpoor, this gentleman took the opportunity of visiting the more venerable remains of Ellora, to which the caprice of modern superstition did not attach an equal sanctity.

About the end of June or the beginning of July, Bajee Rao and Trimbukjee set off from Nassick, taking the devoted Sastree in their train. It was given out, as upon certain information received from several quarters, particularly from Nâgpoor whence an agent had arrived, that a design had been formed against the Pêshwa's life, and that Patan assassins had been engaged at Hyderabad for the purpose, who were on their way to execute their commission. Parade was made of every possible precaution against this imaginary danger. Access to Bajee Rao became more and more difficult: and he travelled, quite contrary to his usual practice, surrounded by armed attendants. When the court arrived at Pundurpoor, these precautions were further increased; and the Sastree ascertained that Seeta-Ram's agent, Burdojee, had been again admitted to favour, and had come to Pundurpoor escorted by one of Trimbukjee's people. He complained of this, but had yet no suspicion of the designs against himself. On the 14th July, the Sastree had been at an entertainment given to the Pêshwa. On his return at night, feeling indisposed, he gave orders, that any one who should come with an invitation to go to the temple, should be told that he was unwell, and unable to attend. One Luchmun Punt came with such an invitation from Trimbukjee, and returned with that answer. The message was repeated, with notice, that as the Pêshwa himself was going in the morning, the crowd had retired, and he had better come immediately with a small retinue. The Sastree, still feeling unwell, refused a second time, but sent two of his suite in his place. On their arrival, Trimbukjee, who was waiting at the temple, said to one of them (Roujee Mahratta), "I have twice sent notice to the Sastree that he had better "come to prayers now, but he refuses. I wish you would again "try to persuade him." Roujee accordingly returned, and

Gungadhur Sastree, fearing he might offend Trimbukjee by a third refusal, set off with only seven unarmed attendants. On their way inquiries were overheard in a whispering tone, "which "is the Sastree?" His attendants, in answer, pointed to the person that wore the necklace. This did not attract particular notice, having passed in the confusion of a crowd. Arrived at the temple, the Sastree performed his devotions, and continued some time in talk with Trimbukjee. On his return, he left three of his seven attendants, with an old family priest, whom he met at the temple, and walked back, escorted by a party of Trimbukjee's sepoys. He had not gone far, when three people came running up from behind, calling out to make room, and flourishing what seemed to be the twisted cloths used in clearing the way. On coming near the Sastree, one of them struck him from behind, and the blow proved to have been given with a sword. Others closed in from the front, and in an instant despatched him, wounding and putting to flight his four attendants. The *Gooroo* *, who was following from the temple with the other three, came up while the flambeaux which had been thrown away were still smoking, and found the body shockingly mangled. They had met five men with drawn swords running back to the temple, where they had left Trimbukjee just before they drew near to the spot. Indeed, there could be no doubt that Trimbukjee had contrived and superintended the assassination. His conduct, when applied to next day by the Sastree's people, who demanded an investigation for the discovery of the murderers, sufficiently evinced his guilt. He said it was impossible to discover upon whom to fix suspicion, for the Sastree had many enemies, as for instance, Seeta-Ram, who was under restraint at Brodera, and Kanojee, one of the Gykwar family confined by the English in the Carnatic, avoiding, however, the least mention of Burdojee and Bhugwunt, though

* Family priest.

the former was known to be at Pundurpoor at the time. The Sastree's people got leave next day to return to Poona, where the rest of the mission was with Bapoo Myral; and it was intimated to them, that there was no necessity for their again approaching either the Pêshwa's or Trimbukjee's quarters. In the mean time, Bajee Rao, who heard of the murder the night of its occurrence, redoubled the precautions for his personal safety. Trimbukjee too never went out without a strong guard; both evidently apprehensive of retaliation. Not only was no investigation set on foot, but the matter was prohibited to be talked of; and spies were employed to give notice of such as offended in this respect, who were apprehended under Trimbukjee's authority. Burdojee and Bhugwunt came openly to Poona, where they lived without privacy or concealment.

With these events, the month of July 1815 was brought to a close. The proceedings instituted on the part of the British Government, in consequence of this murderous outrage, will furnish the contents of a separate chapter.

CHAPTER IV.

POONA CONTINUED.

1815. AUGUST TO DECEMBER.

Resident—his resolves—returns to Poona—obtains proof against Trimbukjee—demands audience—presents a memorial—charging Trimbukjee—calls subsidiary force from frontier—Bajee Rao hesitates—asks proof—evades receiving it—Gykwar mission threatened—attempts to screen Trimbukjee—Hyderabad force called in—expedients offered and refused—instructions arrive—second memorial thereon—demand of Trimbukjee's surrender—Pêshwa's irresolution—seizure of Trimbukjee and surrender—reflections—effect in Guzerât.

Mr. Elphinstone was at Ellora, when he heard of the Sastree's violent death, and of the suspicions attaching upon Trimbukjee, though the circumstances were transmitted only by vague and indistinct report. He immediately saw the necessity of taking a decided part. The deceased was the avowed minister of an ally of the British Government, who had come to a friendly court under the security of a special guarantee, for the purpose of assisting at an adjustment, which that government had undertaken and been called upon to make. Therefore, although the British Government was no further a party to the negotiation, in which he had latterly been concerned, than is implied in his having entered upon it with the knowledge and tacit consent of the British representative, still nothing had occurred to annul the personal guarantee, on the security of which the Gykwar minister had ventured within the precincts of the Poona court. Under this impression, Mr. Elphinstone no sooner heard of the manner of his death, than he addressed a letter to the Pêshwa, expressive of his concern at the event,

Second Stockade.

SECTION

of the Second Stockade.

Third Stockade.

SKETCHES of the GOORKHA DEFENCES in the CHEKRERA-GHATEE PASS.

London, Published by J. Murray, [illegible]

A. [illegible] Range.
B. [illegible] Mortar Battery of British Force.
C. [illegible] Hill.
D. Mortar Battery British Force.
E. Goorkha Cantonment.
F. Jythuk.
G. Advanced Battery British Force.
H. First Battery British Force.
British Encampment.

STOCKADED POSITION of the GOORKHAS at JYTHUK.

and demanding a rigorous investigation, with a view to the speedy detection and punishment of the murderers; he at the same time forwarded the intelligence to the Governor-General, soliciting special instructions for his guidance in every possible event; and expressing his intention, in the interim, to hasten back to Poona, and, if his examination of the Sastree's people should fix the guilt on Trimbukjee, and it should be found inexpedient to wait the arrival of instructions, immediately to accuse that favourite, and demand of the Pêshwa his arrest and trial, in vindication of the insult offered to the British name and authority. He did not think it necessary or advisable to travel out of his way, in order to fix upon Bajee Rao himself a charge of participation; conceiving it more prudent, and, at the same time, quite as effectual for the sake of example, that the prince's minister and favourite, the adviser and instrument of the act, should be visited with the entire responsibility. Having formed this resolution, and called back the subsidiary force from Jâlna, where it was then cantoned, to Seroor, in order to be prepared for the worst, the Resident directed his assistant, who had remained behind at Poona, to offer his unqualified protection to the remainder of the Gykwar mission, and even, if it should be necessary, to announce a rupture of the subsisting alliance with the Pêshwa, as the consequence of any further attempt at violation. He then set off direct for Poona, where he arrived on the 6th of August. On the route, he met groups of pilgrims returning from Pundurpoor, all of whom agreed in giving the same account of the transaction, and in ascribing the perpetration of it to Trimbukjee. The Sastree was a Brahmin * of the highest caste, and of great reputation for sanctity of character; the manner of his death, therefore, in a holy city, in the midst of a pilgrimage, at

* For some account of the sacrilegious horror, with which the Hindoos regard the murder of a Brahmin, the European reader is referred to the narrative of Nerayun Rao's murder by his uncle Ragoonath, contained in Forbes' Oriental Memoirs.

which myriads were collected, and in the very precincts of the temple of their resort, had inflamed the superstitious minds of all who witnessed it with more than ordinary horror and detestation of the crime. Returning to their homes in every direction, they communicated their feeling wherever they went, till it became the general sentiment of the Mahratta nation and Hindoo sect, to a degree quite unusual in a country, where the means of diffusing information are so limited. Arrived at Poona, Mr. Elphinstone made a very particular examination of the Sastree's people, and of every one likely to afford evidence or information. The result was, the clear establishment of the facts and circumstances above related; and the evidence was so minute and consistent in all its parts, as not to leave a shadow of doubt in respect to Trimbukjee's direct participation and actual superintendance of the assassination.

Mean time, Trimbukjee and his master had augured from the resident's demand of investigation, as well as from the protection afforded to the remainder of the Gykwar mission, and the whole conduct of Mr. Elphinstone, that it was his resolution to take a decided course in the matter of the Sastree's murder. Both were consequently in the utmost alarm and suspense respecting his intentions, and began immediately to raise troops, and take every possible precaution for their personal safety. Trimbukjee hurried home to Poona, where he arrived on the 7th August at night. One of his personal adherents, who had charge of the city in his absence, had waited on Mr. Elphinstone in the course of the day, apparently to sound his intentions; but on being directly questioned as to what investigation had taken place, and how it was that Bhugwunt Rao and Burdojee were living at large, he was confused, and could give no answer. The Pêshwa himself entered Poona on the 9th by stealth, under cover of the night, in a close palanquin, without previous notice, without the troops being drawn out, or any one's going forth to meet him. This was the more extraordinary, because it was the day of the Dukshina * festival, when money is bountifully distributed among the Brahmins, thousands of whom were collected for the purpose; and the Pêshwas had never yet been known to fail of presiding at the largess.

The whole city was in alarm at these unusual demonstrations. The rest of the Gykwar mission under Bapoo Myral were shunned by every one, and apparently regarded as victims already devoted to destruction. In vain were the utmost efforts made to quiet their fears. In this state of things, Mr. Elphinstone saw the necessity of taking his measures without waiting the Governor-General's orders, which, at the earliest, could scarcely arrive in a month from that date; an interval that would have allowed Trimbukjee to complete his preparations, and to remove, intimidate, or cut off the witnesses, and must infallibly have driven the Pêshwa to make common cause with his minister; since, while the suspense continued, they both had common fears. On the 11th August, therefore, the resident demanded an audience, which was refused on the ground of indisposition. The demand was repeated next day, and evaded on the pretext, that an infant daughter had died, which rendered his highness impure for three days. Unable longer to brook these subterfuges, especially as his object was to remove the cause of them, by relieving Bajee Rao from his state of suspense and personal alarm, he resolved to send a written note, which he had drawn out to be presented at the audience, in case one could have been procured. The paper was sent to Suda Sheeoo Bhâo, the usual channel of communication before Trimbukjee's late appointment; but he declined to present it, as did every other minister that was applied to. At last Mr. Elphinstone resolved to send his Moonshee with it openly, but

* For an account of this festival, see Scott-Waring.

all means of getting it delivered were still unsuccessful. Two people came, however, on the Pêshwa's part, apparently to sound the resident as to its contents. He accordingly opened himself so far as to let it be seen, that the paper only affected Trimbukjee, and that Bajee Rao was not personally involved in the charge, and would be so only in the event of his continuing to countenance and support that favourite. After this explanation, the written paper * obtained a reception on the 15th August. It began with expressing a conviction, that the Pêshwa must have been desirous of revenging the foul murder of a foreign minister and a Brahmin like himself, had his ministers suffered the truth to reach his ears; but as it was evident they had not done so, and, under the circumstances, could not be expected so to do, it had become necessary that it should reach his highness through an unbiassed channel, on which account the British resident addressed him upon the matter. The memorial proceeded to charge Trimbukjee with direct participation in the murder of Gungadhur Sastree, showing how the universal voice of the nation marked him out as the guilty person, while the circumstances of the transaction, his uniform conduct before and after it, his suppression of all investigation, even after it had been demanded by the British resident, and his actual encouragement of those, who would otherwise have been objects of suspicion, brought the charge home to him in

* Those who would ascertain the real merits of Indian diplomacy, and would possess themselves of the secret necessary to those employed in such negotiations, for baffling the arts, deceptions, and subterfuges of the treacherous Mahratta and wily Brahmin, should obtain the perusal of Mr. Elphinstone's unassuming account of his part in these negotiations, in the record of his original correspondence with the Indian government. It is to be hoped these valuable papers will not be for ever withheld from public curiosity. The whole of the account here given of the Poona affairs is but a meagre abstract of that correspondence. Mr. Elphinstone's letter of the 16th of August, on that part of the transactions now detailing, is perhaps as interesting a document as ever found its way into a record-office.

the clearest and most undeniable manner. After recapitulating the proofs, it thus continued:—" On all these grounds, I declare " my conviction of Trimbukjee Dainglia's guilt, and I call upon " your highness to apprehend him, as well as Govind Rao Bur- " dojee and Bhugwunt Rao Gykwar, and to deposit them in " such custody as may be considered safe and trustworthy. Even " if your highness is not fully convinced of the guilt of these " persons, it must be admitted, that there is sufficient ground " for confining them; and I only ask of you to do so, until his " excellency the Governor-General and your highness shall have " an opportunity of consulting on the subject. I have only to " add my desire, that this apprehension may be immediate. A " foreign ambassador has been murdered in the midst of your " highness' court. A Brahmin has been massacred, almost in " the temple, during one of the greatest solemnities of your " religion; and I must not conceal from your highness, that the " impunity of the perpetrators of this enormity has led to im- " putations not to be thought of against your highness' govern- " ment. Nobody is more convinced of the falsehood of such " insinuations than I am; but I think it my duty to state them, " that your highness may see the necessity of refuting calumnies " so injurious to your reputation. I beg you also to observe, " that while Trimbukjee remains at large, his situation enables " him to commit further acts of rashness, which he may under- " take on purpose to embroil your highness with the British " Government. He is at the head of the administration at " Poona, and has troops at his command. He is likewise in " charge of your highness' districts, which are contiguous to the " possessions of the British Government, the Nizam and the " Gykwar; and, even though he should raise no public dis- " turbances there, I cannot but consider with uneasiness and " apprehension, in what manner your highness' affairs will be " conducted. For these reasons, it is absolutely necessary, that "immediate steps should be taken; as your highness will be "held responsible by the Governor-General for any acts of "violence, which Trimbukjee may commit after this intimation. "I therefore again call on your highness to adopt the course "which I have pointed out to you, as the only one which can "restore confidence to the public ministers deputed to your "court. They cannot otherwise enjoy the security necessary "to transact business with your highness; nor can they with "safety even reside in the city: and every body will be obliged "to take such steps as he may deem necessary for his own pro-"tection. One consequence of this will be, an interruption "of your communication with the British Government, until "the measure I have recommended shall be adopted. I beg "that your highness's reply may be communicated through "some person unconnected with Trimbukjee Dainglia." The memorial concluded with assuring his highness, that the British Government had no design whatever of interfering with the freedom of his choice of a successor to Trimbukjee, or with the independence of his internal administration; which the Pêshwa might perhaps have suspected was the ulterior object of this attack on his minister.

Nothing could have been better adapted to work on Bajee Rao's hopes and fears, and induce him to screen himself by sacrificing his favourite, than this memorial. The subsidiary force marched into its cantonment at Seroor on the 17th of August. Mr. Elphinstone had taken the precaution of strengthening the brigade of this force, which was regularly cantoned at Poona, by having another battalion marched in, as if to relieve one of those composing the brigade. But as soon as the memorial was received, he suffered the relieved battalion to join the main body at Seroor, thinking such a display of confidence would have a good effect this time.

The Pêshwa was evidently embarrassed and irresolute. He

sent a messenger to say that he was considering the memorial, and to propose a distant day for an interview. The resident declared himself particularly desirous of an audience, but intimated that he could not go to the palace, if he was to meet Trimbukjee there and at large. A day or two afterwards, a message came from the Pêshwa, through Suda Sheeoo Bhâo, declaring that Bajee Rao believed Trimbukjee innocent, but that if Mr. Elphinstone would undertake to prove the three distinct invitations, he would have him arrested. That gentleman at once closed with the proposal; but, though he did not cease to press the execution of the Pêshwa's part of this offer, it was perpetually evaded. The excuse set up by Trimbukjee for not ordering an immediate investigation on the night of the murder, was, that he was so busy sweeping the temple, that he did not hear of it in time. He thus admitted his having been at the spot, whence the assassins issued, and to which they were seen to return after the act was perpetrated.

During this discussion, the situation of Bapoo Myral and the rest of the Gykwar mission became very critical. Mr. Elphinstone had, some days before, advised their coming and encamping close by the residency; but Burdojee and Trimbukjee had been tampering with the escort, and had gained over the greater part, so that a strict watch was set on all their motions. On pretence of sending off the Sastree's children and family, the whole were marched a little way out of the city without disturbance; but when it was proposed to move next morning to the residency, the escort broke out into open mutiny, and, under the pretext of demanding an advance of pay, surrounded Bapoo Myral and his people in such a manner, that escape was impossible. The difficulty of their position was manifest; but to have attempted a rescue by the British troops at Poona, would infallibly have produced the massacre of the whole; —the excuse of some disturbance being all that was needed to

N

bring matters to this extremity. He contented himself, therefore, with sending his guarantee of what money Bapoo Myral might promise; and, with this security, the latter was enabled to win over half the mutineers, and to get quit of the other half without bloodshed. The arrangement, however, cost a lack and a quarter, which was advanced by the resident in bills on the Gykwar treasury.

On the 20th August, hearing that the levy of troops was going on with increased activity, Mr. Elphinstone remonstrated, declaring, that if this measure were not discontinued, he should be obliged to call in the subsidiary force to Poona, and take such measures for his own security, and for the interests of his government, as must lead to a rupture. In reply, a bullying message was received, stating, that however desirous the Pêshwa was to preserve the alliance, the person accused in this case was one of the greatest consequence, having 10,000 horse and 5000 foot at his devotion, besides fifty or sixty forts, and a territory yielding seventy-five lack of rupees; that therefore it was necessary to proceed with caution, as there were many difficulties in the way of the course recommended by the resident. Direct attempts were at the same time made to intimidate and buy off the witnesses, whose evidence was known to constitute the proof possessed by Mr. Elphinstone. A further message was sent, declaring it not to be conformable even to English law to imprison before conviction; and that as yet no proof had been offered, that the assassins were in Trimbukjee's service, or otherwise connected with him. These, and other arguments verbally adduced, were answered at length in a written communication, the matter of which it would be superfluous to detail.

In the mean time, the indications of an intention on the part of Bajee Rao, either to make common cause with the favourite, or to abet his flight into the country, where, under the pretext of rebellion, he might place the resources of the Poona state in direct hostility to the British Government, were growing daily more strong and conclusive. Mr. Elphinstone in consequence applied to have the Hyderabad force marched from the valley of Berar to Jâlna, where it might be in readiness to act according to occasion. This application was nearly simultaneous with Mr. Russell's recall of that force to Hyderabad, for the settlement of the disturbance then excited by the princes. Hoping, however, that nothing serious would arise at that court, the resident at Poona repeated his request for a light force at least, to take up the pursuit, in case Trimbukjee should fly before Colonel L. Smith, the commandant of the Poona subsidiary force. The Hyderabad commotion having subsided altogether in the interim, the whole of Colonel Doveton's army moved upon Jâlna at this requisition.

During the remainder of August, attempts were made by the Pêshwa to induce the resident to forego his demand of Trimbukjee's arrest, by the offer of several expedients, none of which went further, than that the accused should absent himself from court and from Poona, pending the judicial investigation of his guilt or innocence, and lose his office. Of course none of these offers could be listened to; but he waited with some anxiety the receipt of the first orders on the subject from the Governor-General, before taking any further step. Those orders arrived on the 1st of September. They had been made out immediately on receipt of the first intelligence of the murder, which had been despatched from Ellora about the end of July, and had reached the Marquess of Hastings at Futtehgurh, in the middle of August. His Lordship's instructions, assuming that there would be found sufficient evidence to fix the crime on Trimbukjee, had provided specifically for every possible case of his surrender, or support by his master. In the event of his being delivered up for trial and punishment at the resident's requisition, the British representative was authorised to gratify the Pêshwa, if necessary, with an assurance that the life of the offender was not sought by the British Government, and that perpetual confinement would be the utmost severity exercised. But, in the event of that prince's refusing to bring his favourite to trial, or of his affecting to consent to an investigation, and taking underhand means to render it nugatory, or of his refusing to deliver him up to punishment after the establishment of his guilt, Bajee Rao was to be held distinctly and personally responsible for the act: so, likewise, if he should abet Trimbukjee's escape from Poona, in order to raise the country, unless the flight should be attended with such circumstances as should acquit his Highness of any knowledge or participation. In the event of this responsibility being incurred, all communication was to be stopped, and preparations made to secure his person, or at least to prevent his leaving the capital; but extreme measures were not to be resorted to, unless it should be hazardous to delay, or absolutely necessary to anticipate his Highness's designs. A letter was addressed to the Pêshwa himself by the Governor-General, in further support of the Resident's proceedings, which it was left to his discretion to present or not as he might deem expedient.

Thus assured of the Governor-General's unqualified support in the course he had adopted upon his own judgment, Mr. Elphinstone prepared a second memorial, which he delivered on the 4th of September, together with the Marquess of Hastings' letter. This memorial began by setting forth the tenor of the instructions just received, and declaring Bajee Rao to have already incurred the responsibility adverted to in the Governor-General's letter, by systematic neglect of all investigation, and by evasion of the demand for the arrest of Trimbukjee preparatory to his trial and punishment: it proceeded to require the immediate delivery of Trimbukjee to the British Government, alleging his instructions to warrant the demand of capital punishment; but, out of regard for his Highness, and because he (the resident) thought the expression of his Highness's anxiety might yet prevail with the Governor-General to spare his life, he should be contented with his delivery, until the receipt of further orders. The memorial went on to declare the alternative of a refusal of this demand to be, a suspension of all communication, and the calling in of the troops to Poona, where Mr. Elphinstone stated his intention still to remain, until he should be made acquainted with the ulterior wishes of the Governor-General, unless an attempt on the part of his Highness to leave Poona, or the continued levy of troops by his Highness, should render active hostility necessary in the interim.

Up to this time, Mr. Elphinstone had contented himself with demanding that the Pêshwa should himself hold Trimbukjee in restraint, until his trial should take place, as had been offered by Bajee Rao himself. The advance of this demand to that of the unqualified surrender of the accused to the British Government had become absolutely necessary: for, with the disposition evinced by the Poona prince, it was evident that any investigation, which might now be set on foot by his authority, would be the merest mockery in the world. It was most fortunate, that the Governor-General's instructions, warranting such an advance of demand, arrived at the particular juncture; for Bajee Rao was still evidently hesitating between the surrender of his favourite and the rupture of the alliance; and the obloquy attending the former alternative seemed to have by far the most weight with him. At one time he had resolved to make common cause with Trimbukjee, and relays of horses had been placed for their joint flight from the capital; from which course he was dissuaded only by Gokla, a southern jageerdar, and one of the best military officers in his service. The second memorial of the 4th of September, with the Governor-General's letter, found the Pêshwa in this state of suspense; and it was further communicated, on the part of the Resident, that unless Trimbukjee should be seized in the course of the following day, the alternative threatened would be resorted to. His eyes seem to have been opened by this communication to the real danger of his situation. Nearly the whole of the night of the 4th of September was spent in consultation with the Bhâo, Gokla, and another person high in confidence, viz. Balooba, dewan of the Vinshor jageerdar. On the following morning the Bhâo was sent with a message, that his Highness would confine Trimbukjee, on the condition that neither his life nor his surrender should be demanded. Mr. Elphinstone returned for answer, that he could hear nothing until the offender was seized. However, he thought it right to explain to the Bhâo, that he conceived the surrender of Trimbukjee to the British Government, and of Burdojee and Bhugwunt to that of the Gykwar, would satisfy all parties, and set the whole affair at rest; that no advantage would be taken of any disclosures by Trimbukjee after his confinement, and that the investigation should be urged no further. These assurances seemed to be necessary to quiet Bajee Rao's personal apprehensions. The result of the conference was reported by the Bhâo, the same morning, and the whole of this day also was spent in consultation. In the night, it was resolved to send Trimbukjee to a hill fort, and the selection being left to him, he was sent off to Wusuntgurh, under an escort of 200 Arabs and a body of horse. The Bhâo next morning waited upon the Resident, to acquaint him with what had been done, and to request that the Gykwar negotiation might be re-opened, and every thing go on as before. Mr. Elphinstone declared, that now Trimbukjee was in confinement, the Pêshwa must be answerable that he did not escape or create disturbances; but that, before the matter could be considered as settled, he must be actually given up to the British Government, according to the demand made and the present instructions of his own court, for that he daily expected further orders, in answer to subsequent communications, those now acted upon having been issued before the late evasive conduct of his Highness was known; and he could not answer for what the next might contain: that, when received, he should be obliged to obey them to the letter, however injurious to his Highness's interests, unless the present demand should have been complied with in the interim; in which case, he should of course suspend their execution, till the Governor-General was informed of the compliance with his first demand. The confinement of Trimbukjee was believed throughout Poona to be a mere device to gain time; and the mode of it, together with the continuance in office of all his adherents, confirmed this impression.

The Bhâo returned on the 7th of September, with an endeavour, by working on Mr. Elphinstone's feelings, to induce him to forego the demand for the delivery of Trimbukjee's person. He claimed himself the merit of having induced the Pêshwa to confine that favourite, stating that he had succeeded only by engaging personally that this would satisfy the British Resident. If, therefore, the further demand were still persisted in, he was himself in a dilemma, from which poison alone could extricate him. It was hardly credible, that, knowing his sentiments and resolutions so fully as the Bhâo must have done, he would so have pledged himself; but it was resolved, at all events, not to recede. The attempt was repeated next day with the same ill success: yet the Bhâo survived his difficulties. Secret intrigues were also set on foot through every medium likely to have influence at the British Residency; but threats, entreaties, and persuasions were alike ineffectual. Levies of horse and foot were still making every where; and positive information was received, that it was the Pêshwa's intention to fly to the fort of Wye, and there raise the standard of the Mahratta empire. Mr.

Elphinstone accordingly resolved no longer to delay calling in the main body of the subsidiary force from Seroor, and gave the Pêshwa notice of his having done so. This produced a message of remonstrance through the Bhâo, which was answered in such terms, as seemed most likely to fix the Pêshwa's wavering resolutions for the sacrifice of Trimbukjee. His surrender, it was announced, would be all the satisfaction expected; for that, except perhaps some atonement to the Gykwar for the murder of his minister, nothing further would be demanded by the British Government; that one word from his Highness now could accomplish this: but, if he hesitated much longer, or attempted to leave Poona, an amicable settlement would be no longer possible. While this message was on its way, the Pêshwa had sent for Major Ford, an officer of the Company's service, who had raised and disciplined a brigade of infantry for his Highness, as part of his contingent. On his arrival, he was left with Chimnajee, Bajee Rao's brother, and Moro Dikshet, a minister who latterly had been growing into favour. These two consulted him on the best means of re-establishing the former terms of intercourse; and on his recommending the delivery of Trimbukjee, as the only measure he could suggest, went with his advice into the next room, whence they brought his Highness' consent. The mode of his delivery was accordingly arranged. A party of Major Ford's brigade was to bring him from Wusuntgurh, and the Pêshwa (as the Resident was told next day) had no objection to a party of the British troops accompanying, but this was declined. At the close of the conference with the Major, Bajee Rao appeared in person, and confirmed what the other two had agreed to, requiring Major Ford's engagement, that the act of surrender should replace every thing on the former footing; and that any fresh orders from the Governor-General should be suspended, even should they arrive before he could acquaint Mr. Elphinstone. Gopâl

Punt, the manager of the brigade business at court, accompanied Major Ford to the Residency, and carried back thence the assurance, that, on the delivery of Trimbukjee, every thing should revert to its former state; and that, except perhaps some satisfaction to the Gykwar, which must still be left to the Governor-General's discretion, no further demand or proceeding should be instituted in consequence of the Sastree's murder.

On the 11th of September, 850 men of the brigade marched from Poona, under the command of Captain Hick; and on the 19th they received charge of Trimbukjee; along with whom Bhugwunt Rao and Govind Rao were delivered up at Poona, on the 25th; and next day the three prisoners were sent down to Tanna fort in Salsette, under charge of a light battalion and a regiment of cavalry, from the subsidiary force. The main body of that force, under Colonel L. Smith, returned on the 29th to Seroor.

Thus was accomplished, by negotiation, without a rupture of the alliance, and entirely through the spirit, firmness, and diplomatic ability of the British Representative, the important object of vindicating the honour and reputation of his nation, which had received the grossest insult, in the murder of an ambassador, negotiating under its guarantee of protection. The Pêshwa had submitted to the humiliation of sacrificing his minister and favourite, in atonement for an act, which had evidently been committed with his concurrence and participation. He had in vain tried every artifice and subterfuge to avert or delay the moment of submission; and when every attempt of this description had been baffled by the firmness and vigilance opposed to him, there can be no doubt that his inclination was, rather to risk a rupture of the alliance, than to submit. But his own good sense, and the representation of the Sirdars in whom he placed his principal trust, satisfied him of the present insufficiency of his means to cope single-handed with the British power. It was evident, however, that henceforward we had nothing to expect but rancorous and malignant hate; and that the same fear, which had produced the important result on this occasion, would require to be constantly kept alive, in order to curb the natural bent of his mind. Mr. Elphinstone's conduct throughout the whole of this negotiation met with the Marquess of Hastings' particular approbation; and his Lordship felt, that the successful termination of the affair was mainly attributable to the prompt and decisive tone assumed and maintained from the outset to the close of the discussion.

On the whole perhaps it was fortunate, that the short sighted violence of Trimbukjee brought matters thus prematurely to a crisis between his master and the British Government. The uniform conduct of that favourite's administration, proceeding from ignorance, either real or affected, of the actual relations of the Pêshwa at this period, had already given rise to so many infractions of the subsisting engagements, and of the treaty of Bassein in particular, that it would have been impossible to have suffered them to pass much longer without notice *. His

* In proof of this it may be sufficient to mention, that, on the 27th of the preceding May, soon after the court arrived at Nassick, the Resident had found it necessary to present a remonstrance against Trimbukjee's measures. The most important infraction of the treaty of Bassein was, a treaty made with a Gôandwana Raja, the preamble of which declared it to be offensive against both the Nizam and Bhoosla; this had been negotiated by Trimbukjee himself, after marching a hostile force into the Nizam's dominions and occupying several of his villages. The affair took place about the preceding February, when Trimbukjee had been sent with some troops in pursuit of the Pindara, Sheikh Duloo. The whole proceeding, however, was not only without the participation of the British Government, as required by the treaty of Bassein, but the troops had driven away an agent sent by the Resident to Nâgpoor, to endeavour to settle a boundary dispute, that had occurred in the neighbourhood between the officers of the Nizam and Bhoosla; and Trimbukjee had put himself in possession of the disputed lands. Many similar infractions of the subsisting engagements, which had been produced by the conduct of his agent at Ahmedabad, were also brought forward in this remonstrance. Mr. E. then

measures must soon have come to the pass of compelling the British Government to demand the displacement of the minister, as a pledge, that the frequent acts of offence, which had occurred under his administration, were without his Highness' countenance. In such an event, Trimbukjee would have been backed by popular feeling, and have been regarded as the victim of our displeasure, for honestly preferring his master's interests to ours; and, at the other native courts, the Pêshwa would have made a strong case of the indignity put upon him, and represented it as a warning of the consequence of too close a connexion with a power so constituted as the British. In the issue, to which matters were brought by the Sastree's murder, we stood forth in the character of avengers of the death of a Brahmin ambassador, and had the full advantage of the popular voice on our side, even among the Pêshwa's own subjects. This favourable impression lasted beyond the immediate occasion; insomuch that two years afterwards, when a rupture occurred with nearly all

attributed these acts rather to the ignorance and Mahratta habits of the favourite, than to any deliberate design of breaking with the British Government. But it cannot be denied, that the tone assumed at some of the discussions of that time was such as to indicate the most ambitious views. In one conference, the rights of the Pêshwa coming under discussion, Trimbukjee went so far as to assert his master's right to the *Chout* of Bengal, under the cession of Aleeverdee Khan, and to that of Mysore, agreed to by Hyder Alee: such was the temper of the man, who had been specially appointed a short time before to conduct the business on behalf of the Pêshwa with the British Representative at his court. The high favour he still enjoyed made it difficult not to identify the Pêshwa with his minister. Had the Mahratta powers risen against the English in the year 1814-15, there can be little doubt, that Bajee Rao would have seized the first occasion to shake off his subsidiary connexion with us and take his station amongst them: but he was not yet prepared to take the lead himself, and offer an example for their imitation in the manner he did in 1817-18. Naturally suspicious and timorous, he would probably have preferred to take no active part, until he had seen what success attended others. The bolder plan he ultimately adopted, he was goaded to by the continual loss and disappointment he incurred, in the prosecution of that course of insidious attack, which he commenced from this time forward.

the Mahratta states, the cause of the British nation derived a vast accession of strength in public opinion, from recollection of the foul murder of this Brahmin, in which the quarrel had originated; and the indifference manifested upon the subsequent downfall of the Pêshwa's dynasty was owing, in a great measure, to its being regarded as a judgment on the reigning head of the family for his participation in this crime, polluted as he was already by the yet unexpiated murder of Nerayun Rao by his father Ragoonath.

The Sastree's death, as might have been expected, excited a considerable sensation throughout Guzerât. Futteh Singh and the party of the deceased, though they lamented the loss as irreparable, hoped from it, at any rate, the entire exoneration from all demands of the Poona government. On the other hand, the party in communication with Trimbukjee hoped, by his means and through the Pêshwa's influence and power, to bring about a revolution in the affairs of the court of Brodera. Seeta-Ram and his adherents were raising troops, and making preparations to act according to the turn events might take at Poona; a body of men under a marauding chief in Seeta-Ram's interest approached from Dhur so near as Dawud; and the two managers in Ahmedabad were acting in concert, and both levying horse and foot. Under these circumstances, the Bombay government had thought it advisable to detain the Guzerât force, which, on its presence becoming unnecessary in central India, had before been destined to the adjustment of affairs in Kutch, whence some of the border tribes had been latterly in the habit of making predatory incursions into Guzerât. Every thing remained in a state of the most anxious suspense, until the amicable settlement of the discussions at Poona was known. It produced a simultaneous effect at Brodera and Ahmedabad. In the interim, Gungadhur Sastree's son was appointed to all his father's offices, rather in demonstration of the sense entertained of the services of the deceased, than out of regard to any superior qualifications the son was thought to possess. After the delivery of Trimbukjee and the two agents of Seeta-Ram to the British authority, the two latter were transferred to the Gykwar, and confined in hill-forts within the dominions of that state. The Bombay government, however, resolved to prevent the occurrence of similar intrigues, by taking Seeta-Ram into their own custody; an arrangement to which the court of Brodera was not induced to accede without extreme difficulty.

The question of the degree of compensation to be afforded the Gykwar, for the murder of his minister and the representative of his court, was, in the following January, thus decided by the Governor-General, to whose arbitration it had been referred. Assuming the surrender of Trimbukjee, the actual perpetrator, to be an entire exculpation of the Pêshwa's government from any share or participation in the act, his Highness was declared to be exonerated from further responsibility, and, therefore, from the obligation to offer any specific atonement to the offended state. The resident was, however, instructed to endeavour by persuasion to lead his Highness to make some handsome provision for the family of the Sastree, as a spontaneous act of generosity: for the supreme government did not conceive itself to possess a right to make a special demand on this head. As a natural consequence of this view of the question, the negotiation for the settlement of the Pêshwa's claims on the Gykwar was directed to be re-opened at the point where it had been broken off, in the same manner as if the murder had never taken place. The Pêshwa occasionally revived it, but with little sincerity or interest; his mind being apparently engrossed with the prosecution of an object nearer his heart, which, from this time, he will be found to have pursued with more consistency and determination; viz. * to bring about a general and secret combination of the Mahratta princes, directed against the British ascendancy. In the course of the negotiations respecting the surrender of Trimbukjee, Mr. Elphinstone was more than once assured that such a thing had been in agitation in the preceding season; but the Poona Government assumed to itself credit for having abstained from giving direct encouragement to the project. Bajee Rao certainly was not then prepared to put every thing to hazard on such a risk; but from this time he seems to have resolved to do so, and himself to head the confederacy, as soon as it should be organized.

While these events were passing at Poona, and, indeed, during the remainder of the year 1815, nothing of moment occurred at any of the courts of southern and central India. It was ascertained, however, that confidential agents, men of family and name amongst the Mahrattas, were still intriguing at each Mahratta durbar, with such secrecy, that the object of the intrigues could only be gathered from suspicion and rumour. Bajee Rao occupied himself in incessant endeavours to obtain, through Mr. Elphinstone, the release of his captive favourite; but all his efforts directed to this end were of course unavailing. In January 1816, the Governor-General addressed a letter to his Highness, in such terms, as it was thought would be most effectual to extinguish all hope, that the British Government would ever consent either to release or give up the custody of this eminent offender.

* This design originated at an earlier period. By confession of Trimbukjee, the conspiracy was in progress before the arrival of the Sastree at Poona.

CHAPTER V.

NIPÂLESE—PINDAREES.

1815-16, MAY TO MAY.

Negotiations with Nipâl—terms offered—Cession of Teraee refused—Demand modified—hesitation—Treaty signed—Ratification refused—War renewed—Ochterlony takes the command—penetrates the first range of hills—Battle of Mukwanpoor—Nipâlese submit—Peace—Reflections—Pindarees—second reference to England—Army reduced—Operations of Pindarees—party surprised—successful expedition—second—British provinces ravaged with impunity—Concert of Pindarees with Mahrattas—intrigues of 1815-16—Holkar's court—Ameer-Khan.

After the settlement of the affairs of Hyderabad and Poona, the negotiations with Nipâl were the object which most engrossed the attention of the Supreme Government. Those negotiations had been opened at the close of the first campaign in the preceding May; Gujraj Misur, the Gooroo (family priest) of the Raja, having come down to the army in Sarun, with powers under the red seal for the purpose. The loss of the whole of the hills west of the Gogra, it seems, had opened the eyes of the Goorkha Chiefs to the real danger of a war with the British, and had proved, that the confidence of security in the ruggedness of their mountains was a vain illusion. The leading party amongst them was, consequently, desirous of peace, and anxious to know the terms on which it would be granted.

The Marquess of Hastings' conditions were hard enough; the perpetual cession of all the hill country taken in the campaign, and as well of such parts of the low land as were in dispute before the war, as of the whole line of Teraee to the very foot of the hills. A fort and territory, which had been seized from the Sikkim Raja before the war, was also demanded; for, having in the course of it formed an alliance with that Raja, and taken him under protection, we had become pledged to restore the integrity of his dominions. Besides these terms, a resident was to be received at Katmândhoo, which, to their prejudices, appeared the first stage towards absolute subjection. Immediately on learning these conditions, the Gooroo broke off the negotiation, declaring he could not treat on the basis of any further cession of the low land, except perhaps the disputed tracts. In its desire for accommodation, and from a hope of being less hardly pressed by other negotiators, the Goorkha government had made a second overture through the late Chief of Almora, Bumsah, who was in communication with the Honourable E. Gardner, the British commissioner for the management of the conquered province. This also was broken off on the same ground. In August the negotiation was re-opened by the Gooroo; and it having been ascertained, that the main objection to giving up the Teraee was, that most of the principal officers of the court of Katmândhoo enjoyed considerable jageers in that territory, the Marquess of Hastings was induced to offer the grant of similar possessions, or of an equivalent in money pensions to the amount of two or three lack of rupees, to be left at the distribution of the Goorkha court. In September, the Gooroo again broke off the negotiation on the same ground, declaring, that the Goorkha Chiefs would never accede to a cession of the Teraee or low land, which was alleged to be the main source of their subsistence, the hills themselves being comparatively unproductive.

It seemed evident from what had passed, that the demand of the Teraee was a bar to the re-establishment of peace, which no advantage we had to offer in any other shape, could compensate to the Goorkha government. Its repugnance to this cession was solely owing to the estimate of its pecuniary value at present entertained by the court of Katmândhoo, and was not in the least ascribable to any feeling of pride, or objection to the humiliation of the cession. The British Government, on the contrary, insisted on the demand, rather from a sense of honour, and a desire to visit with marked severity the act of gross violence and insult, which had arisen out of former disputes about the Teraee, and had been the immediate cause of the war, than from any expectation of profit from the lands. The experience of a season's occupation of a considerable portion of them proved them to be of extremely difficult management and inconsiderable advantage in revenue; while the climate was so noxious, as to render the continuance of troops, and even of civil officers upon them, utterly impracticable for one-half the year. Under these circumstances, the supreme government, balancing the advantage of a restoration of peace against the gratification of forcing on the Goorkhas the sacrifice of an object extremely valuable to them, and only so to us in an inconsiderable degree, came to the resolution of relaxing the rigour of the original demand. A draft of a treaty was accordingly prepared and transmitted to Lieutenant-Colonel Bradshaw, appointed to negotiate on the Sarun frontier, to be delivered openly to the Gooroo, in case of his expected re-appearance with a fresh overture; accompanied by a declaration, that it contained the only terms on which the British Government were willing to make peace with the Nipâl state. In this draft, the Teraee from the Kalee, a branch of the Gogra, to the Gunduk, was all that was insisted on, and of the rest so much only as was in our actual possession. Pensions to the extent of two lack were still offered to the Sirdars of the court; and a stipulation to that effect was contained in one of the articles of the draft. When this draft was submitted to the Gooroo, and to Chundur Seekur Opadhea, another Brahmin associated with him to treat on the part of

Nipâl, they declared without hesitation, that they did not feel themselves competent to accede to such terms, without first submitting them to their court. They promised, however, that a definitive answer should be returned in fifteen days. The period expired, yet no instructions had been received. It was ascertained also, that the deliberations on the acceptance or rejection of these terms had occasioned some ferment at Katmândhoo. The stipulation for the allotment of pensions was particularly obnoxious and unpopular with one party, which represented it as placing the Raja's subjects and ministers in direct dependence on a foreign power. At the head of this party stood Umeer Singh and his sons, who had lately returned to Katmândhoo, after the total loss of their provinces west of the Ganges. They had opposed the commencement of the war, as promising little success; but now it had been begun, were for continuing it to the last extremity. The Goorkha negotiators being unable to redeem their pledge by producing the definitive answer of the Raja within the time specified, offered a submissive apology, but begged the negotiation might not be finally broken off, until they should have proceeded to Katmândhoo and ascertained the cause. The Gooroo offered at the same time to sign the treaty provisionally, if the portion of the Teraee occupied by the British between the Koosa and Gunduk were substituted for the pensions proposed. This was refused, and the negotiation broken off; but the Goorkha negotiators declared, that they would return in twelve days with the treaty signed. This occurred on the 29th October.

The Supreme-Government, on hearing of the continued reluctance on the part of the Nipâlese, called on the several authorities in charge of the contiguous districts, for their opinion of the value of the several portions of the Teraee occupied by its officers since the commencement of the war, and the means of obtaining a good frontier line, by the retention of part only of what had been acquired; thus preparing itself to make some further gratuitous concessions, either in lieu of the pensions, or in addition to them, in order better to gratify the Goorkha chiefs, and to leave them in a disposition to execute and maintain the treaty when made. In the mean time, however, Gooroo Gujraj Misur returned from Katmândhoo, and signed the treaty according to the draft before submitted to his court. This was done at Segoulee on the 28th November; and, by the terms of it, the ratification of the Raja was to be delivered in fifteen days. On being apprized of this event, the Supreme-Government determined notwithstanding, to make those further concessions which had before been in agitation; and it was considered fortunate, that the execution of the treaty without them would most decisively mark the concessions to be a gratuitous act of bounty towards a fallen and suppliant foe: while their conciliatory effect on the Goorkha Sirdars would be much enhanced by their not feeling themselves indebted for them to their own successful obstinacy, either in war or in negotiation.

The fifteen days, however, expired, without any appearance of the ratified treaty: and it was ascertained, in the course of December, not only that the Gooroo would fail to produce it, but that the war faction had prevailed, and, in consequence, that preparations were making for the recommencement of active hostility, and positions in the forest of the Teraee already taken up. The fact, indeed, was, that having in the past season baffled entirely the feeble attempts made by the British commanders on the Sarun and Gôrukpoor frontiers to penetrate into the mountains east of the Gogra, which now formed their whole remaining dominions, the Nipâlese were not without a presumptuous confidence of their means of successful resistance for a much longer period; and, though desirous of peace, the terms offered were such, that they hoped more advantage from the continuance of war. But not being altogether without apprehension, it thenceforward became their game, to endeavour to amuse the British Government with hollow discussions and negotiations, in order, if possible, to get over the season without the renewal of active operations.

During the whole of the rains, the large body of troops cantoned in Behar had been kept in readiness; and towards the close of them, Major-General Ochterlony had been called down from the westward to take the command, preparatory to an advance direct upon Katmândhoo, so soon as the passage of the forest should be practicable. Unfortunately, upon the signature of the treaty, the activity of preparation was a little relaxed; and the commissariat department, in particular, had been authorised, for the purpose of an early reduction of expense, to cut down the establishments provided for the convoy service, and to sell the greater part of the grain which had been stored in depôts: insomuch, that when war became inevitable, there was reason to fear the efficiency of the force would be cramped by these efforts at economy. However, by dint of extraordinary exertion in every department, civil as well as military, the army was enabled to take the field in the Teraee by the end of January, without being delayed on this account. Perhaps no occasion ever produced a more satisfactory display of the real extent of the resources and energies of the local Indian administrations, when called forth by a popular commander in a popular cause. General Ochterlony hastened to the frontier, to assume the entire direction of political and military affairs in that quarter, under special orders for the purpose from the Supreme-Government. Before his arrival, the Gooroo, unable to produce the ratified treaty, had made a second visit to Katmândhoo; but, instead of returning with it, brought some new propositions, which of course were inadmissible after what had passed. The General accordingly dismissed the negotiators immediately on his arrival in the Teraee, making them the bearers of a letter from the Governor-General to the Raja, expressive of his Lordship's sense of the insincere conduct of the Nipâl government, and declaring the renewal of war in all its activity. General Ochterlony immediately pushed a portion of his force across the forest, which it passed without opposition, encamping at the foot of the Chereea-ghâtee * pass, which leads from Bicheeakoh through the first range of hills, directly into the valley of Mukwanpoor. This pass, which was strong by nature, in common with all the passes of this mountainous tract, had been stockaded and well manned. The General, however, who followed close upon the advance, proceeded to make his dispositions for turning it; and, in a few days, led a light division in person across the range, by a very difficult pathway unknown even to the enemy. Nothing could exceed the patience, with which the toil and privations of this march were endured by the troops, many of whom were for two days almost wholly without provisions: the rapidity of the movement, added to the ruggedness of the ground, rendering it impossible to bring up the supplies. This judicious manœuvre produced the immediate evacuation of the pass, which was forthwith occupied by the main body of the army, which had continued encamped in front of it. After spending a few days in clearing and improving it, and in establishing a depôt and line of communication through it with the plains, the General marched direct upon Mukwanpoor, where the enemy's whole army was strongly stockaded. A simultaneous movement was arranged of two other columns of infantry; one to the west under Colonel Nicol of H. M. 66th, which, meeting with little opposition or difficulty, except from the ruggedness of the route, succeeded in joining the Major-General in the valley on the 29th February; and another under Colonel Kelly of H. M. 24th, which moved upon Hurreehurpoor, a strong hill fort, commanding a pass into the Mukwanee valley

* Vide plate at the head of this chapter.

eastward of Bicheeakoh. On approaching this fort, Colonel Kelly observed an eminence that seemed to be within commanding distance of a stockade near the fort, from which a party of the enemy, that at first had occupied it, had been observed to retire. A detachment of light companies was immediately sent to seize the point; but they were no sooner in position, than the whole force of the Goorkhas advanced from the fort and other stockades to recover the ground they had abandoned. A severe struggle ensued, attended with some loss on the part of the British, and a very heavy one on that of the enemy: the position, however, was maintained until the arrival of reinforcements, when the Nipâlese were driven back at all points. This affair took place on the first day of March, and the fort was evacuated very soon after.

Meanwhile, General Ochterlony had penetrated to the neighbourhood of Mukwanpoor, where his force had, on the 28th February, a rencontre with the enemy, precisely similar to that above described, but considerably more serious, from the greater numbers engaged on both sides. The companies which had been detached in the first instance to occupy a position * at Mukwanpoor, from which the Goorkhas had similarly retired, were very nearly overpowered, when the first reinforcement arrived; and, as the Goorkhas repeated their attacks each time in greater strength, it became necessary to reinforce the position in the same proportion, till, in the end, several battalions were employed, and the enemy were finally driven back only by the charge of one of them along the ridge. The whole of the Nipâl army at Mukwanpoor, in number upwards of 3000 of their disciplined Sepoys, exclusive of their irregulars, was engaged in the course of this day; and by their own subsequent acknowledgment, their loss exceeded 800: that of the British amounted

* This point was a village, called Seekhee Khutree, at the end of the ridge on which Mukwanpoor was situated, and along which the road ran. The Goorkha army was stockaded between it and the fort.

to 45 killed, amongst which was Lieutenant Tirrell, the officer who commanded the party sent to occupy the village in the first instance. There were also 175 wounded, including another British officer.

This trial of strength and exemplary failure reconciled the Nipâlese to make a tender of unqualified submission. On the 3d March Khajee Buktawur Singh, one of their principal officers, wrote to the General, to say he had the ratified treaty in his possession, and would send it by Chundur Seekur. The General returned for answer, that the Goorkha government must not expect the same terms now, as before the recommencement of hostilities, but that he had no objection to receiving Chundur Seekur, if they thought fit to send him with full powers. In the interim, he pushed on his approaches to within 500 yards of the fort of Mukwanpoor, and threw up a battery in readiness to open upon it. Chundur Seekur soon appeared with the ratified treaty, and pressed it earnestly on the General's acceptance. The latter had previously resolved not to insist on harder terms, in case he found the enemy sufficiently humbled by their late reverses, to make it safe to rely on their sincerity. Accordingly, on Chundur Seekur's arrival, having ascertained that the spirit of hostility was completely annihilated, and that unqualified submission was the course for which all parties were now prepared, the General accepted the treaty, explaining to Chundur Seekur, that whatever disposition the Supreme-Government might have had, before the late operations, to extend its bounty to the Nipâlese beyond the letter of the engagement, the same must not be now expected. As the intention to exhibit a further generosity had been expressed to the Goorkha envoys after the Gooroo's signing the treaty of Segoulee, Chundur was called upon to give a specific note in writing, declaratory of his now having no such hopes, together with an assurance, that a similar declaration should be made in a letter under the red seal, to the Governor-General. This was agreed to with the utmost readiness; and the General having accepted the treaty, the contest with the Nipâlese was thus brought to a final close in the beginning of March. Sir David Ochterlony waited to receive the orders for delivery of what remained to be ceded under the treaty, particularly the fort and district of Nagree and Nagurkoh to the Raja of Sikkim, and the disputed lands in Gôrukpoor, which had not yet been occupied by us. He then returned with his army into Behar.

Preparations had been made to extend the military preparations above described, by a combined attack from the west, where Colonel Nicolls was to have penetrated into the hills by a pass from the Gôrukpoor district into the province of Sâleeana; while a force should move into Dotee from Almora, under Colonel Adams. This was, however, rendered unnecessary by the decisive activity of Sir David Ochterlony, which thus closed the campaign and the war, in the short space of little more than a month.

The articles of the treaty were punctually executed by the Goorkhas according to agreement. The Supreme-Government thought, notwithstanding what had passed, that it would be a politic act of conciliation, to cede such of the Teraee as had been before contemplated, in lieu of the pensions stipulated in the treaty; accordingly the Governor-General, after every article had been executed, gave notice to the Raja of his intention to send the Honourable E. Gardner as resident, and to empower him to conclude an arrangement on this basis. It was subsequently carried into effect. That part of the Teraee, which skirted the dominions of the Nuwab Vizier, was, however, specially reserved; and this, together with a pergunna of Rohilkhund, valuable to the Vizier from its situation in the Teraee eastward of the Gogra, but yielding under our management an inadequate revenue, was ceded to his excellency in extinction of one of the loans of a crore of rupees that had been obtained of him during the war.

The Goorkhas had shown themselves, in the course of the past two years, to be as formidable a power as any that existed in India. But the conditions of the peace now concluded were calculated to undermine their power, not only by their present direct effect in weakening their resources and curtailing their dominions, but, more particularly, by taking away, for the future, the means of gratifying their ambitious views, and pursuing those plans of conquest and extension, which the superiority of the Goorkhas in courage and military science over their neighbours, had hitherto enabled this nation to follow with no inconsiderable success. By our possession of the hill tract westward of the Gogra, and by the protection afforded to the Sikkim Raja to the east, the Goorkha territory has been reduced to the form of a parallelogram, three sides of which are in immediate contact with the British power, while the fourth is bounded by the stupendous mountain barrier of the Humachul range, on the other side of which is the frontier of the Chinese empire. Since the Goorkha government can never be prepared to venture in a second contest with either of these powers, so long at least as they maintain their present strength, its natural policy hereafter will be, to forego altogether those military habits, which no longer hold out the same prospect of advantage.

The Marquess of Hastings had returned to the Presidency towards the close of the rainy season of 1815, more fully convinced than ever of the necessity of early undertaking the suppression of the predatory hordes, for which as yet no authority had arrived from England. Anticipating that the Nipâl war would have closed with the first campaign, his Lordship had prepared himself to devote, if not immediately, at least in the subsequent year, the unreduced strength of the armies of the Bengal Presidency to the accomplishment of the important object of securing the peace of central India by the destruction of these lawless marauders. The assent of the home authorities to this undertaking could not appear doubtful to any one in Bengal; and, anticipating its arrival, he was desirous of acting while the late additions increased so much his military means, and before the extraordinary resources obtained from the Nuwab Vizier should have been frittered away in expensive annual preparations of defence. But, as the expected sanction of the authorities in England to the adoption of this course of policy had not arrived, his Lordship did not feel himself at liberty to undertake the proposed measures. After some discussion, however, it was resolved to submit a second and more earnest reference of the question for the consideration of the authorities, to whom the Supreme Government was responsible, and, in the interim, it was deemed necessary, as soon as the Goorkha war should be terminated, to make every possible reduction of the military establishments, which was done by breaking up the grenadier battalions and other temporary arrangements of the preceding year.

Meantime, the dussera of 1815 had been celebrated at Cheetoo's cantonment of Nemawur by a greater concourse of Pindarees, than had ever before been assembled at one point. Preparation was evidently making for an expedition of more than ordinary interest, in which every durra was to have its share. On the 14th October, a body of nearly 8000 of all descriptions was ascertained to have crossed the Nerbudda, and to have taken a southward direction. It soon broke into two parties, one of which was heard of as it passed the valley of the Taptee, and was beaten up in its bivouac on the 24th October by a party of the Nizam's reformed infantry under Major Fraser, in number about 300, accompanied by about 100 horse. The completeness of the surprise allowed the infantry time to fire several volleys, by which the Pindarees suffered some loss before they could gallop off and disperse: but the horse would neither attack nor pursue, nor even (which is yet more extraordinary) join in collecting the booty. Indeed, no efforts could get them from between the advance and rear guard of the infantry, so that the loss suffered by the freebooters was comparatively trifling. This, and other examples of the degree of reliance to be placed on the Nizam's cavalry, induced the Supreme-Government shortly afterwards to authorise the resident at Hyderabad to exert his influence in procuring a similar reform, to that already introduced by British officers into the infantry establishments, to be extended to the cavalry also, which were, of the two, deficient in perhaps the greater degree. A plan for the reform of the Nizam's horse was drawn up by Captain Sydenham, an officer employed in a diplomatic situation at Aurungabad: and, since its introduction, these troops have been distinguished by more courage and activity, and are now in nothing inferior to the irregular horse of other establishments. The routed party of Pindarees were not deterred by the surprise they had suffered from continuing their depredations in a southerly direction till they reached the banks of the Kishna. The other party, which had proceeded south-eastward, had been heard of at Ramtikee and Choupara in the Nâgpoor dominions. It thence had traversed the Nizam's territories from north to south, till it also appeared on the northern bank of the Kishna, where no such danger was apprehended. The territories of the Madras presidency lay on the southern bank, and were only preserved from devastation by the fortuitous circumstance of the river continuing not fordable for horses so unusually late as the 20th of November. Finding the Kishna impassable, the freebooters took a turn eastward, plundering the country for several miles along its populous and fertile banks, and committing every kind of enormity. On approaching the frontier of Masulipatam, they shaped their course northward, and returned along the line of the Godaveree and Wurda, passing to the east of all Colonel Doveton's positions, and making good their route to Nemawur, with an immense booty collected in the Nizam's dominions, and with utter impunity. The plunder obtained in this Luhbur was greater than that of any previous expedition; insomuch, that merchants were sent for from Oojein to purchase many of the valuables obtained, those of Nemawur not being sufficiently wealthy.

Elated at this success, a second expedition was planned and proclaimed very soon after the return of the first. Pindarees again flocked in from every durra, to join in it; and, by the 5th of February, ten thousand under different leaders had again crossed from Nemawur, and were on their way S. S. E. in the route, by which the former party had returned. The first that was heard of this body, after its crossing the Nerbudda, was its appearance on the western frontier of the district of Masulipatam, under the Madras Presidency, on the 10th of March. From this point it shaped its course southward, and next day made a march of 38 miles, in the course of which it plundered 92 villages, committing in each the most horrid cruelties upon the unarmed and inoffensive inhabitants. The following day (12th), after a march of 38 miles, and the destruction of 54 villages, the horde arrived at the civil station of Guntoor, where they plundered a considerable part of the town, and the houses of all the civil officers. The government treasure and the persons of the British Residents were protected at the Collector's office, by the exertions of a few troops and invalids kept at the station for civil duties. It being, however, no part of the design of the Pindarees to risk the loss of time or of lives, they immediately moved off with what they could get; and before night there was not a single strange horseman in the neighbourhood. The whole had hurried off westward, making a march of 52 miles the next day. This body of marauders continued on the whole 12 days within the Company's frontier; and, after leaving Guntoor, swept through part of the Kuddapa district, and recrossed the Kishna on the 22d of March. A squadron of the Madras 4th native cavalry, detached against them from Hyderabad, arrived on the opposite bank just after they had made good the passage. It happened that a considerable force was at the time in the field a little further to the west, for the settlement of a disputed succession to the Kurnool Jagheer; but, though it sent out detachments in every direction, and others were despatched from Hyderabad in their rear, the plunderers escaped from all with impunity. After recrossing the Kishna, the Luhbur seems by agreement to have separated into several bodies, in order the better to baffle pursuit and scour the country. The greater part moved westward, along the north bank of the Kishna, passing south of Hyderabad, until they approached the Pêshwa's dominions: when, turning short to the north, the whole retraced their steps to the Nerbudda in several divisions and by various routes. The advanced guard of one body, led by Bhee Koo Seyud, was heard of by Colonel Doveton, and overtaken, as it was passing the Adjunta range at Dewal Ghât, by a party of Mysore horse, detached for the purpose. The Colonel himself had moved at the same time under the guidance of a prisoner to intercept the main body; it escaped, however, by a singular chance, and contrary to all expectation. The other parties, which had taken a more easterly course, met with no obstruction on their return; and it was ascertained that nearly the whole of those who had passed the Nerbudda, in February, to engage in this expedition, had recrossed before the 17th of May, bringing a second immense harvest of booty within the year, and without having suffered any loss worthy of mention. Some idea may be formed of the extent of ravage and cruelty, which marked the track of these banditti, from what was found to be the damage sustained by the Company's district, during the 12 days that they remained within its frontier. It was ascertained by a committee sent to the spot for the express purpose of the investigation, that 182 individuals had been put to a cruel death, 505 were found severely wounded, and no less than 3603 had been subjected to different kinds of torture. The private loss of individuals was estimated by the committee at two lacks and a half of perjodas, about 100,000*l.* sterling.

It would seem that the Pindaree leaders had this season come to a resolution to respect the territories of the Mahratta chiefs, and to direct their ravages chiefly, if not exclusively, against those of the Nizam and of the British Government. This had been publicly given out in the hordes: and some of the few stragglers that were left behind and taken, stated the same thing on their examinations. Such a resolution may have been the result of the secret negotiations carried on by the Mahratta agents, particularly Balajee Koonjur, a person of high repute, and formerly a minister of the Pêshwa. This man having left Poona some years before in apparent disgrace, had latterly visited all the Mahratta courts, where he was received with marked attention, and evidently had some important business in hand. He was known to have had communication with the Pindarees, on his way to Nâgpoor from Sindheea's camp, in the early part of 1815, and from that city he went to Cheetoo's cantonment at Nemawur, as if purposely to make them a party to the intrigue he was conducting. It was an insidious kind of hostility, thus, under the mask of friendship and professions of attachment, to instigate the attacks of these irresponsible unacknowledged bands; but it is not on that account the less likely to have been suggested, by the hatred and fears of the Mahratta chiefs, or recommended by their notions of morality. Perhaps the Mahrattas had discovered the full extent, to which we were disposed to carry our consideration of their fellow feeling towards the freebooters, and our intention to act upon the principle of refraining to suppress this common pest of all regular governments, through fear of giving them umbrage, and thence derived an assurance of safety and impunity in this course for some time to come. If any proof were wanting, that these enterprises of the Pindarees were undertaken in concert with the Mahratta powers, it might be found in the circumstance of the latter having afterwards chosen the particular moment of our prosecuting measures for the suppression of the predatory associations, to rise themselves against the British supremacy. Without some assurance of such support, whenever our strength should be put forth against them, the Pindaree leaders would scarcely have commenced, at this particular juncture, a plan of systematic depredation, pointedly aimed at the only power they had reason to fear. And, if the plan of directing the Pindarees against us originated in the councils of the Mahratta durbars, it must be traced to intrigues anterior to those which accompanied and followed the discussions at the Poona court; although these may doubtless have helped to exasperate the national feeling against us.

A brief notice of the intrigues that passed in the season of 1815-16, will here perhaps be acceptable. While the Pêshwa was hesitating, whether to abandon his favourite, or the British alliance, he was naturally desirous of ascertaining how far he might reckon on the other Mahratta courts. He accordingly had taken measures to sound the Bhoosla and Sindheea; but the answer of neither arrived, until Bajee Rao had been forced to make his election for the surrender of his minister. It was ascertained, however, that both had given him to understand, that, if he were willing fairly to commit himself and take the lead, he might depend on their co-operation, though, until he did so, they were not disposed to trust him, or to come forward, at the hazard of taking the whole consequences on themselves. Baptiste's force was specially applied for by Trimbukjee, through Sindheea's agent at Poona, the channel used by the Pêshwa to sound the disposition of that durbar. The answer was written in the form of a banker's letter to his correspondent. After assurances that Willoba Naeek (the Pêshwa) might have drawn at pleasure, the letter proceeded: "This banking-house is the "Naeek's own; while your house is in want of cash" (meaning troops), "you must submit to the importunity of creditors" (the British). "The Naeek ought, therefore, to go about for some "time on pretence of pilgrimages; but let him write a bill in his "*own hand*, and, after that, wherever money is required, thither "it shall be sent without delay." The letter was dated 11th of September, at the time the discussions were at their height; and it is not difficult to discover both the advice, the assurance, and the distrust conveyed under this puerile disguise. The interest excited by these discussions, and by the state of the wars and negotiations with Nipâl, were the matters which engrossed the chief attention of all the Mahratta powers during the season of 1815-16. Holkar's troops were collected and held in some state of preparation during the month of September; but the pecuniary embarrassments of that court were growing every day greater; insomuch, that, in December, the two regent widows, Meena Baee and Toolsee Baee, were obliged to fly with their ward, Mulhar Rao Holkar, to take refuge with Zalim Singh, the manager of Kota, until the mutinous disposition of the troops, who had for some time been sitting *dhurna** on the court for pay, could either be quelled, or their demands satisfied. They effected their escape on horseback after the young Holkar had been carried in procession with the Tazeea (the bier of Hoosein), during the Muhurrum†, and thus got off unsuspected to Zalim Singh's fort of Gungerial. Before April 1816, the two widows, connecting themselves with different parties, came to a final rupture; and Meena Baee, suspecting that Toolsee Baee's party had a design to seize her person, fled back for protection

* Vide Hunter's Hindoostanee Dictionary.

† A Moosulman festival—Vide Ditto.

to a body of the discontented troops. These, however, at the suggestion, it was supposed, of Toolsee Baee and Balaram Set her adviser, placed her under restraint, demanding their arrears from some private treasure she was suspected to be possessed of.

Ameer Khan did not seem disposed to take any further advantage of this confusion, than by the more complete establishment of his own independence. But his influence was exerted in favour of Balaram Set, and contributed materially to aid him in supplanting Tanteeaa Aleekur, who was very justly disliked and suspected by the Patans. In the earlier part of the season of 1815-16, Ameer Khan had been employed in settling the amount of the contribution he was to receive from Joudhpoor. The Raja, Man Singh, first employed his minister, Singhee Indraj, to negotiate this point, and then, from jealousy of his power and influence, intrigued with Ameer Khan to have him murdered. This was effected at a conference within the citadel, where two Patans were admitted to adjust with the minister the amount to be paid. The assassins were protected from the populace by the Raja, and sent back in safety to Ameer Khan, who, by agreement, held one of the gates of the city during the conference. This was the second assassination committed by the Patans at the suggestion of Raja Man Singh. Towards the end of the season, having adjusted matters with Joudhpoor, Ameer Khan made preparations for a serious attack on Jypoor, as will hereafter be more particularly mentioned.

CHAPTER VI.

BHOPÂL—NÂGPOOR.

1816. MARCH TO JULY.

Death of Vizier Mahommed—and of Ragoojee Bhoosla—consequent deliberations—Bhopâl—its alliance declined—Nagpoor—Pursajee—his incapacity—Appa Saheb—his pretensions—character—Dhurmajee Bhoosla—his intrigues—their ill success—both parties court the British resident—who waits instructions—their tenor—alliance and terms offered—transactions at Nagpoor—Dhurmajee confined—Appa Saheb regent—seeks British alliance—Naroba—negotiation—its progress—conclusion—and signature—reflections—Subsidiary force called in—further transactions at Nâgpoor.

WHILE the Pindarees were engaged in the second enterprise described in the preceding chapter, two events occurred, most propitious to the British interests in the quarter whence those marauders had issued, had but the Indian government been prepared to take advantage of them: the death of Vizier Mahommed, Nuwab of Bhopâl, on the 17th March 1816, and that of Ragoojee Bhoosla on the 22d of the same month. The former was succeeded by his son, Nuzur Mahommed, a very young man—too young, it was to be feared, for the perilous circumstances of the principality, superadded to the troubles of a new succession. There was every reason, therefore, to apprehend, that either the Mahrattas or the Pindaree chieftains in the neighbourhood would attempt to avail themselves of the occasion, to interfere in the concerns of Bhopâl; in either of which cases, a second and more sincere application for our permanent protection of its legitimate prince was to be expected as a natural consequence. Ragoojee's successor was his only son, Pursajee Bhoosla, known before his accession by the name of Bala Saheb. The intrigues and passing occurrences of that court likewise promised equally to give the long-sought opportunity of establishing a subsidiary connexion with the Nâgpoor state. The question, whether or no the supreme-government should now direct its efforts to the accomplishment of these two objects, was thus forced upon the consideration of the Governor-General in council in the month of April 1816.

There was but one opinion in respect to the policy of forming the connexion with Nâgpoor, which was accordingly resolved upon the moment the question was brought forward. That with Bhopâl had hitherto been regarded rather as an alternative to be adopted in consequence of the impossibility of forming one with Nâgpoor, or as a necessary precaution against the designs of a hostile Mahratta confederation: now, however, it presented itself in a new light; and the point to be determined was, whether, having the means of establishing the British influence at Nâgpoor, the advantage of extending it in the direction of the Nerbudda, whenever the occasion offered, by the annexation of Bhopâl, the territories of which lay so opportunely contiguous, and presented such advantages both of offence and defence against the Pindarees, did not call for its adoption yet more strongly than before. It was now recommended, not only as a measure ancillary to the Nâgpoor alliance, but also as a means of gaining a vantage ground for striking a blow at the predatory associations, which the supreme-government was still left free to inflict, should any opportunity offer of catching their bands beyond their proper boundaries. The objections urged against forming such a connexion had their foundation apparently in the apprehension of the risk of giving umbrage to the Mahratta powers, which the steps taken in 1814-15 had proved to be an object of exaggerated alarm. Moreover, if the Nâgpoor Raja were gained over to our side, that risk could scarcely be said to exist, or, at the most, was a matter of comparative indifference to the British, after the successful close of the Nipâlese war. At the same time, having once established an alliance with Nâgpoor, and obtained from it a position for a considerable force on the Nerbudda, the defence of Bhopâl might be provided for by an additional brigade, in communication with that position; and this could be so chosen, as to form a connecting link with the force in Bundelkhund. The advantage of securing the resources of this state in our own interest, and depriving the Pindarees of the means they derived from it, especially when this could be accomplished with such apparent facility, were strongly felt by the Governor-General, who perceived the incalculable benefit of this arrangement, both to the present interests of his government, and to the ulterior prosecution of a systematic plan, for the entire suppression of those dangerous and rapidly increasing hordes of adventurers and banditti.

The Marquess of Hastings could not, however, consider these advantages, certain and considerable as they were, sufficient, in the actual state of things, to warrant a departure from the policy that seemed most acceptable to the authorities in England. Towards the close of the month of April, therefore, a short time after the Nâgpoor connexion had been resolved upon, his Lordship came to the resolution not to seek the Bhopâl alliance, even should the negotiations, which were then opened at Nâgpoor, be brought to a favourable issue. The political agent in Bundelkhund, as well as the resident at the durbar of Sindheea, both of whom had solicited instructions for their guidance, in the expectation of new overtures from Bhopâl, or of further attempts against that principality on the part of the Mahrattas, were accordingly desired to refrain from giving to such overtures any encouragement, and to maintain, on behalf of the British Government, the strictest neutrality and indifference in regard to what might be passing at Bhopâl. They were, however, warned, that there was no occasion to make public profession of this determination; as any such declaration would infallibly have the effect of needlessly inviting the cupidity and ambition of the turbulent neighbours of the principality, who probably might else be restrained by the fear of a second protective interference. These instructions were strictly followed: and when, in the course of 1816, indirect overtures were made by the young Nuwab, they were answered by commonplace expressions of courtesy and goodwill, without meeting any further encouragement whatever*.

Affairs were in the meantime hastening to a crisis at the court of Nâgpoor. Ragoojee's successor was nowise capable of conducting the government that had devolved upon him. He had been all his life reputed to be of a disposition flighty and impatient of control; but a recent sickness had deprived him of sight, and he had lost the use of one of his arms by a stroke of the palsy, that had left him, moreover, completely bedridden. His mind had also been affected by these bodily afflictions, and was frequently observed to wander, insomuch as scarcely to be sensible of what was passing. Several instances of this were current in the way of public conversation: for instance, during the ceremony of burning his father's body, he made very indecorous complaints of its length, and accused the

* In the beginning of 1817, an agent of the Nuwab, named Inayut Museeb, went over to Nâgpoor, and there delivered a specific proposition, in writing, to Mr. Jenkins, the resident, soliciting, on the part of Nuzur Mahommed, that the state might be admitted to the British protection, on the terms offered to Vizier Mahommed. This was followed up by a letter to the same effect, from the Nuwab himself to Mr. Wauchope, the political agent in Bundelkhund. On reference to the supreme-government, it was still determined, after some deliberation, to adhere to the above resolution: but the Marquess of Hastings took the occasion to put his opinions on the question upon record, and to bring the subject to the special notice of the authorities in England.

Brahmins of having some sinister design in thus detaining him. He publicly charged Appa Saheb of attempting his life, when some consecrated water happened accidentally to be sprinkled over him; and on one occasion, in full durbar, expressed impatience as to what had become of his *mustaches*, forgetting that they had been shaved off, as a necessary circumstance of mourning for his father's death. There was, indeed, but one opinion respecting his utter incompetency to exercise the functions of his station; and all seemed to agree upon the necessity of an immediate resort to a provisional form of administration.

The next heir to the Raja was Moodajee Bhoosla, commonly called Appa Saheb, son of Vincojee Bhoosla (Nana Saheb), the only brother of Ragoojee. The claims of an infant son of a daughter of Ragoojee were not held to come into competition with those of Appa Saheb, the nearest in the male line, except, indeed, in the case of his adoption by Pursajee; marriage being considered, by some classes of Hindoos, to transfer the bride to her husband's family, and to cut off herself and her descendants for ever from any claim on that of her own parents. Appa Saheb was of an age and character to possess public consideration, and was naturally the person entitled to assume the regency; but he had been on ill terms with his uncle, Ragoojee, for some time before his death, in consequence of the Raja's having attempted the resumption of a large territory which the nephew had inherited from his father. It had been preserved to him, at last, by the aid of a remonstrance of the British Resident at Nagpoor; and this circumstance not only produced an irreconcilable difference between the two princes, but induced Ragoojee to have recourse to a series of measures, calculated to annoy and distress his nephew in every possible way. On his death-bed, however, Ragoojee, aware of his son's incapacity, sent for Appa Saheb, and placing his son's hand within that of his offended cousin, said, he made him the depositary of the family honour; endeavouring, by this tardy confidence, to secure his good offices towards Pursajee. But the ministers and favourites, who had been the instruments, if not the originators, of Ragoojee's persecution of his nephew, were not so easily reconciled to the idea of his assuming the supreme direction of affairs. A strong party accordingly formed itself, to oppose the claim of the heir-presumptive to the regency. It was headed by Dhurmajee Bhoosla, a *chela* or *elève* of the deceased Raja, who had risen to such favour with him, as to be entrusted with the charge of a great part of his public and private treasures, amounting, as was supposed, to about a crore of rupees. This man was an unprincipled libertine, and had been the instigator and chief actor in those measures of extortion which had marked the close of Ragoojee's life, and latterly rendered it dangerous for any man of wealth to reside or come within his dominions. Besides the large influence resulting from the control of the treasury, Dhurmajee had several partizans in the *mahul*, or women's apartment, and enjoyed a considerable share of popularity among the Arab mercenaries, who guarded the palace and person of the new Raja. The principal officers of the late prince's ministry joined this party, and formed a scheme for vesting the regency in Buka Baee*, the favourite wife of the deceased, and further, for inducing his successor to adopt the infant grandson of Ragoojee, to the perpetual exclusion of Appa Saheb from all share in the administration, and ultimately from the succession itself. The intrigue first showed itself, in an attempt to have some other than Appa Saheb nominated to officiate at the *sradh* of the deceased Raja, a ceremony always required to be performed by the nearest male heir, who being incompetent in the present case, the nephew, as next in the male line, had some sort of right to preside on his behalf.

* Not Pursajee's mother, who was not then living.

Hearing of this intrigue, Appa Saheb openly expressed the highest indignation, professing his determination to resort to force, sooner than submit to be so superseded. His party at the same time talked loudly of the necessity of rescuing the government and public treasures from the hands of the worthless and designing individuals, who, under the colour of the name, were usurping the authority of the young Raja. The popular voice was so strongly in his favour on this point, that Dhurmajee's party, not being yet prepared for extremities, disclaimed having ever meditated the supersession of the presumptive heir, or appointment of another person to officiate for Pursajee at the approaching *srahd*. A readiness was at the same time expressed to admit Appa Saheb to a share in the government on certain conditions; and efforts were made to bring about a reconciliation, but thwarted underhand by Dhurmajee. The *srahd* was quietly performed on the 1st of April, the nephew of the deceased officiating as principal actor in the ceremonies.

While matters remained in this unsettled state, both parties expressed the strongest desire for the return of Sreedhur Pundit, who was still the nominal prime minister at Nâgpoor, but having found his influence with Ragoojee on the wane, had retired some months before the death of that prince, on pretence of a pilgrimage to Benares, where he still remained. This man was regarded as the head of the English party at Nâgpoor; and the object of these professions of intention to abide by what he might determine was, to prevent a more active interference on our part in their favour. Of this, both seemed apprehensive, though nothing was farther from the Resident's thoughts. Dhurmajee had however an ulterior object in view: for so long as this suspense should continue, the power, as well as the treasures, of the government, would remain at his disposal, in the same manner as they had been at the time of Ragoojee's decease. Thus every one seemed earnest in his protestations to Mr.

Jenkins, the British resident at Nâgpoor, of desire to maintain the best understanding with the English. Appa Saheb, in particular, made direct overtures through Juswunt Rao Ram Chundur, who was the negotiator of the treaty of Deogam, and had since been the appointed channel of communication between the resident and this court. He proposed to accept the terms before offered to Ragoojee, and to receive a subsidiary force, on condition of support against the designs of the opposite faction.

Mr. Jenkins refused to interfere in this scene of intrigue until he should receive special orders from the Governor-General, but lost no time in laying before the Supreme Government the real position of affairs at Nâgpoor, asking instructions, as to how far, in the actual state of the Raja's intellects, he might consider himself warranted in receiving the overtures, and listening to the propositions of the presumptive heir, previously to his acquiring any direct ostensible share in the government. This was a question that depended on the degree of Pursajee's incapacity. If it were such as to prevent his being considered a free agent in the choice of the responsible functionaries of his government, then, of course, any faction that should attempt to exclude the next heir, being of fit age, from a share in the administration, could only be regarded as usurpers, assuming the Raja's name as a mere cloke to their illegal proceedings. In submitting this question, Mr. Jenkins had evidently so decided an opinion of the malady of the reigning Raja, as to think it would be usurpation in Dhurmajee's party, if, representing themselves as the ministers of Pursajee's choice, they refused to allow Appa Saheb the exercise of a fair portion of control over their acts of administration. Wherefore, on the same principle as the latter would have been warranted in the employment of force to obtain his right, would he likewise be free to solicit foreign aid for the purpose, and the British at liberty to connect themselves with his party, if solicited so to do, and to support his claims against the opposition of Dhurmajee, or of the other ministers of the late Raja.

By the way, it is observable, that the turn taken by these intrigues and divisions at Nâgpoor had a direct and obvious tendency to introduce a foreign influence, at the invitation of either party, or of both. If, therefore, we refrained from stepping forward, it was to be feared, that either Sindheea or the Pêshwa, or some of the Pindaree leaders, would succeed in establishing themselves to our perpetual exclusion: at the same time, since the contention lay entirely between the factions of Appa Saheb and of Dhurmajee, the legitimate Raja having no greater interest on the one side than on the other, we seemed to have no other object of solicitude, than to connect ourselves with the rightful cause, which appeared undoubtedly to be that of the cousin and presumptive heir.

In the month of April, as before mentioned, the Supreme Government came to the resolution of seizing the first opportunity to form a subsidiary alliance with Nâgpoor. On hearing of the state of parties at that court, as described in the despatches of the resident, the government further resolved, that in case Pursajee's malady should prove to be such, as to render him utterly incapable of conducting public business, or of exercising the judgment requisite in the selection of fit persons for administrative affairs, the next male heir, if of mature age and possessed of the requisite qualifications, should be considered to possess an inherent right to represent the sovereign authority of the state, and that the British Government would consequently hold itself free to negotiate with him directly, without any inquiry whether he derived his authority from the nominal and hereditary prince, or otherwise. Wherefore, if Pursajee should appear to be incapacitated by the malady under which he laboured, in the degree stated, a point which must unavoidably be left to the discretion of the resident and the general feeling of those attached to the court, and if Appa Saheb should be the next male heir in legitimate succession to Pursajee, Mr. Jenkins was instructed to negotiate with him as the rightful head of the state, and if practicable, to conclude a treaty on the basis of affording the aid of the British Government in support of his just pretensions, upon the conditions of a subsidiary alliance. The utmost caution was, however, directed to be observed, in ascertaining the precise degree of Pursajee's incapacity; and some further inquiry was ordered into the other point, how far the heritable claims of the nephew were recognised by the Mahratta law of succession, as preferable to those of the grandson by the daughter of Ragoojee. The first instructions on this subject were forwarded on the 15th April. The division of the Hyderabad subsidiary force, then at Ellickpoor in the valley of the Poorna under Colonel Doveton, was placed at Mr. Jenkins's disposal, in case he should find it necessary to call for the whole, or any part of it, in support of the cause of Appa Saheb, under the conditional authority conveyed in his instructions, or for the execution of the treaty of alliance and subsidy, in case the negotiations should be brought to this issue.

The terms of alliance to be proposed to the Nâgpoor prince varied in nothing from those which it had been attempted to establish in the lifetime of the late Raja. The Bhoosla state was to be incorporated in the league for the defence of the Dukhun, already subsisting between the British Government, the Nizam, and the Pêshwa; and was to be ready with its whole resources, when required for the purpose of promoting or securing that object. A contingent was at all events to be maintained in permanent efficiency, and ever ready to act with the British subsidiary force, and to consist of not less than four battalions of infantry, a regiment of cavalry, and a due proportion of artillery; which contingent was to be posted somewhere in the neighbourhood of the Nerbudda, and of which the Bhoosla was to bear a proportion of the expense. His court was also to refrain from negotiation, except in concert with the British Government, and to abide its arbitration of all differences with other powers. In short, the conditions were the same as have been explained in the first chapter, to constitute the relations of such other states as had accepted subsidiary alliances; the main object being to bring the Bhoosla into this class. In subsequent instructions regarding the conduct of this negotiation, the Supreme Government declared its wish, in the present instance, that whatever subsidy should be agreed on, should be stipulated in the shape of periodical money payments; with a proviso, however, for the eventual substitution of a territorial cession in case of irregularity of payments, or of the occurrence of such a change of circumstances as should render an arrangement of this nature more desirable than at present. The reason for this unusual preference of money payments was, that this subsidiary force must necessarily be thrown so much in advance upon the frontier, and be so continually in the field in chase of the Pindarees, as to raise a probability of embarrassments arising, from its having also to protect a territory of considerable extent, specifically assigned for its own support. Had a cession been demanded in the first instance, it could only have been granted somewhere in the neighbourhood of the position to be occupied by the subsidiary force, for there were no other lands belonging to the state conveniently situated for the purpose.

Before Mr. Jenkins received any of these instructions, almost indeed before he was informed of his own government being prepared to contract the alliance, the contest had been brought to a crisis at Nâgpoor, which produced renewed overtures of such a nature, as he did not hesitate to entertain on his own responsibility, from their consonance to the spirit of the orders, under which he had acted upon former occasions. It has been mentioned before, that a reconciliation, which was attempted between the two rival factions, miscarried in consequence of Dhurmajee's secret counteraction. He not only induced Buka Baee, the regent proposed by his party, to reject with scorn the paper of reconciliation, when submitted to her for signature; but, after first agreeing to sign himself, next day retracted his assent, unless upon the condition, that Appa Saheb would give him the security of the Punnee Patans. This is a class of Mousulman assassins, whose existence would not be tolerated under any other civil institutions, than those engendered by the misrule of the Nizam and the Mahratta princes. The singularity and binding force of their contracts consist in this, that, if once their pledge is given for any one's personal security, they are notorious for never failing to redeem it, by the secret murder of the aggressor upon the person guaranteed.

The distrust of Appa Saheb, intimated in the assumption of such a pretext for rejecting the reconciliation, joined to the known profligacy of Dhurmajee's character, made every one suspicious of his real designs. It was also discovered, that Dhurmajee had sent invitations to men of this description to come over from Hyderabad and Ellickpoor, a thing which gave great disgust to the leading people of all parties at the Nágpoor court. His behaviour was moreover offensively overbearing to every body; insomuch, that all but men of desperate fortunes were alienated and disgusted. Appa Saheb was encouraged by this posture of affairs to take measures for seizing him in the palace where he resided; and having secured the concurrence of the principal people about the person of the Raja, as well as of Pursajee himself, who seems to have been brought to declare himself in favour of his cousin, and consent to his acting in this, as in all other matters, as he might think best, a body of Appa

Saheb's personal retainers was marched into the fort of Nâgpoor, and Dhurmajee secured without resistance or difficulty, together with his public and private treasures. This measure was effected on the evening of the 11th of April, 1816; having been precipitated by a sense of the necessity of crushing this intriguer, before his command of treasure and connexion with the Punnee Patans should have made him formidable. Pursajee showed more energy on this occasion than could have been expected from his usual habits: for, when Appa Saheb's party was approaching the palace, there were not wanting some who represented their coming as hostile and dangerous to himself, and endeavoured to procure an order from the Raja for their being resisted, which the Arab mercenaries were well enough inclined to obey. Pursajee, however, had no personal alarm, and forbad any resistance; declaring that Appa Saheb had full power in all things.

Three days after Dhurmajee's apprehension, the ceremony of seating the Raja on the Guddee, which is the formal act of installation, was publicly performed, and Appa Saheb was on the same day solemnly declared to be vested, by the Raja himself, with the sole and entire conduct of the public affairs, under the title of Naeeb-o-Mokhtar—Deputy with full powers. The English gentlemen at Nâgpoor were present at the ceremony, and Mr. Jenkins was the first to offer his own congratulations and those of the government he represented, upon the auspicious commencement of the new reign.

Though Appa Saheb had thus quietly obtained the apparent object of his wishes, in being publicly acknowledged regent with full powers, he was still by no means so certain of retaining the quiet enjoyment of the dignity, as to cease to regard a subsidiary connexion with the British, as a most desirable measure of security, in the unsettled state in which he found all around him. The chief offices of the government were still held by the ministers of Ragoojee, the greater part of whom had joined in the conspiracy for his exclusion. There was danger in attempting their immediate displacement, lest they should declare Pursajee's competency to resume the reins himself, and, by alarming him with fears for his life, obtain from him a formal revocation of the late nomination to the regency. The ministers, indeed, though professing their ready acquiescence in the late arrangement, assumed a tone of independence by no means compatible with the Asiatic notion of the deference due from a minister to his master. Thus Naroba, the Chitnavees, or secretary of state, took an early opportunity to wait upon the new regent, in order to inform him, that if he wished to be served zealously by himself, it would be necessary that the course of foreign policy, pursued by Ragoojee in the latter part of his life, should be maintained, particularly alluding to the communications that had for some time been passing between Ragoojee, on the one hand, and the Pêshwa, Sindheea, and Holkar, on the other, the object of which was to promote a spirit of concert and union amongst all the Mahrattas, directed against the British ascendancy. Naroba adverted also to another intrigue, which, it seems, had been in train some time before the death of Ragoojee, and had in view the endeavour, through the medium of English gentlemen returning to their native country, to open a direct communication with the King of England, in order to procure the restoration of the provinces of Cuttack and Berar, for a present consideration of 30 lacks of rupees. Such an intrigue, it is firmly believed, never had being, except in the machinations of a wily Mahratta of the name of Pursaram Rao, who, understanding a little of the English language, had address enough to persuade the deceased Raja, that nothing was easier than to open such a channel, and had procured considerable sums of money, under pretence of forwarding the project. In this intrigue Naroba wished the government of Nâgpoor to persevere, being himself the dupe of Pursaram's imposture.

The regent was induced, by distrust of Naroba, immediately to communicate what had passed to Mr. Jenkins, hoping thereby to secure his active support, in measures directed to the removal of this man, whose office he intended for his private dewan Nagoo Punt. Naroba, however, had induced Sudeek Ulee Khan to accompany him, when he made this communication of his views and principles; and, as this man was one of the principal commanders of the Bhoosla military, upon whose affection he knew he could place no reliance, Appa Saheb felt himself under the necessity of temporizing with the Chitnavees, not feeling sufficient confidence in his own means to take the decided part his inclinations prompted. The desire of removing this, and others of his uncle's ministers, for the purpose of introducing men of his own choice, joined to the necessity he felt of disbanding, or at least re-organizing the military establishments, which caused him so much alarm, were the motives that urged him to the determination of connecting himself in a subsidiary alliance with the British Government, on the terms which had been offered to the late Raja. He was apprehensive, however, that, in the event of his forming such a connexion, an effort would be made to impose upon him a ministry made up of the party of Sreedhur Pundit, which it was supposed that Mr. Jenkins favoured. Accordingly, although the regent had resolved upon the alliance, he would not employ Juswunt Rao Ramchundur in the negotiation of it, knowing his anxiety for Sreedhur's recall and restoration to favour and authority. This point Juswunt Rao had frequently pressed, both upon Appa Saheb and upon the resident. Indeed, he was rather disappointed at the lukewarmness evinced by the latter's refusing to make an earnest representation of the necessity of the immediate recall of his patron to settle the affairs of the court.

The persons employed by Appa Saheb were his private dewan, Nagoo Punt, and Nerayun Pundit, a minister of the late Raja, who had early espoused his party. The negotiation was commenced by a visit of Nerayun to the Resident on the night of the 22d April, the very same day on which Appa Saheb had consulted Mr. Jenkins about the removal of Naroba from office. Great mystery was observed upon the occasion; and, in the course of the interview, Nerayun presented a paper, written in the regent's own hand, signifying "that Nagoo Punt and Nerayun Pundit enjoyed his entire confidence, and were commissioned to open his (Appa Saheb's) inmost wishes to Mr. Jenkins, if he were disposed to meet them with equal cordiality." Having shown this paper, Nerayun invited the Resident to declare the views of his own government. Mr. Jenkins explained, that he was in daily expectation of receiving detailed instructions from the Governor-General; but that the views of his government were sufficiently apparent, from what had passed in the previous negotiation with Ragoojee, and as he had no reason to believe that they had undergone any alteration, he should be prepared to meet the negotiators on the part of Appa Saheb, without waiting the arrival of fresh orders. It was accordingly agreed, that both Nagoo Punt and Nerayun Pundit should have a conference with Mr. Jenkins, at the residency, on the night of 24th April.

Now that the heir-presumptive's pretensions were backed by Pursajee's late nomination to the regency, and he had thus become the recognised head of the Bhoosla state, our representative had no doubts as to the propriety of receiving his overtures; and in the absence of any ground for supposing that the views of his government in respect to Nâgpoor had changed, since the miscarriage of the negotiations in 1814, he resolved to renew them on the same basis without further delay. He was naturally desirous of availing himself of this favourable disposition while it lasted; a course particularly necessary, considering the wavering characters of the native princes, and the total absence of any thing like systematic policy in most of their acts and resolutions.

The conference took place, according to appointment, on the night of the 24th. Nagoo Punt explained candidly his master's motives for desiring the alliance; but after much unreserved discussion on both sides, it was agreed to proceed no further, until Mr. Jenkins should have received his instructions. On the same evening, Appa Saheb himself sent for the Resident's moonshee, and after mentioning his desire to contract the alliance on the terms proposed to Ragoojee, declared, that besides the four battalions and a regiment of cavalry before proposed to be stationed on the Nerbudda, he must have another battalion at Nâgpoor for his personal security.

Mr. Jenkins received his first instructions on the 25th of April; and a further conference was held on the 27th, when a Persian draft of the treaty proposed to Ragoojee being produced, the conditions were fairly discussed article by article. The basis of the negotiation was at once agreed to; and the only points remaining to be settled after the first conference were—the strength of the subsidiary force—the amount of the subsidy—and the nature and strength of the contingent to be furnished by the Bhoosla state. A further question was agitated by the Mahratta negotiators, viz. the mode in which the regent was to be assured of the personal support of the British Government against the designs of the domestic factions of Nâgpoor. As both parties were equally sincere in their desire for the alliance, it was not long before all these points were satisfactorily adjusted. The strength of the subsidiary force was fixed at six battalions and a regiment of cavalry, the increase being made on the application of Appa Saheb, who was informed that less than two battalions could not safely be cantoned at Nâgpoor without support, in case he required a British force at that point. An article was further inserted in the treaty, by which it was stipulated, that two of the battalions of infantry should be stationed near the court of the Raja, one of which might be elsewhere employed on emergency, but not less than one complete battalion should always remain for his Highness' personal security. The subsidy demanded was, an equivalent to the field charges of the force to be furnished, which was estimated at eight lack of rupees; and this amount had been agreed to, and a territorial cession fixed upon as the mode of payment, when Mr. Jenkins ascertained from his instructions, that, in the present instance, money payments at Nâgpoor were to be preferred. In order to procure this substitution, an abatement of half a lack of rupees was made in the amount; and it was stipulated, that the expediency of commuting this for a territorial cession at a subsequent period should be considered and determined by mutual consent, but that the British Government should be entitled to demand such cession, in the event of any irregularity in the payments. With respect to the contingent, 5000 horse and 3000 foot was at first mentioned; but in consideration of the poverty of the state, which was strongly represented by the Mahratta negotiators, it was finally fixed at 3000 horse and 2000 foot, in the regulation of the discipline and internal management of which the British Resident at the court was to have the right of offering advice.

Some difficulty occurred in settling the mode, in which the regent was to be assured of the support of the British Government to his personal interests. Some such assurance seemed to be a *sine quâ non* with the Mahratta negotiators. It was at last agreed, that the treaty should purport to be concluded "with

"Moodajee Bhoosla (Appa Saheb) exercising with full powers "all the functions of the government on behalf of the Maha-raja "Pursajee Bhoosla," thus involving a complete recognition of the authority of Moodajee; in addition to which, Mr. Jenkins engaged that the Governor-General's answer to the formal letter, to be written on its ratification, should contain a distinct assurance of support to Appa Saheb's administration of affairs, so long as Pursajee might remain in his present state of mental incapacity. The Mahratta negotiators were very urgent to have a stipulation introduced, that cows and bullocks should not be killed within the Nâgpoor territory. But this was refused as unusual; and they were obliged to rest satisfied with a verbal assurance, that the custom which prevailed at Poona should also be observed here, and no bullocks or cows be killed on any account within the city itself; but the troops, when in the field, or at a distance, were not to be restricted in this particular. All matters having been thus satisfactorily adjusted, the treaty was finally executed on the 27th May. Appa Saheb's signature was affixed with great secrecy in the night at the house of Nagoo Punt, one of the negotiators; and it was agreed not to make it public, until the approach of the subsidiary force, which Mr. Jenkins promised immediately to call in from Ellickpoor, should remove every apprehension for the consequences of the expected displeasure of the adverse factions.

It may be proper to mention, that early in the negotiation, and with a view to expedite its conclusion, the resident had promised, on the part of the British Government, a pension of 25,000 rupees a year to Nagoo Punt, the chief negotiator, and of 15,000 to his colleague, both to commence from the signature of the treaty, and subject to the approbation of their master. Written engagements to this effect were accordingly delivered to both in the regent's presence, immediately on receipt of the signed treaty. These were to be commuted for sunnuds under the Governor-General's seal, which it was engaged to procure. Appa Saheb seemed well pleased with the arrangement: indeed, a similar one had followed the treaty of Deogam, when Sreedhur Pundit and Juswunt Rao Ramchundur obtained similar pensions of thirty and fifteen thousand rupees. The treaty was ratified by the Governor-General in council on the 15th June, and the assurance of personal support to Appa Saheb's administration, during the continued incapacity of Pursajee, was conveyed in the letter of congratulation addressed to that prince on the 13th July following.

Thus was accomplished the most important extension of the system of our relations with the native powers of India, that had taken place since the general settlement of them ten years before. On our part, it was hoped, that the alliance would have the effect of detaching the Bhoosla for ever from the other members of the Mahratta confederation, at the same time that it gave us a most important vantage ground, whence to launch our operations against the Pindarees and those who might venture to support them. Judging from subsequent events, it would seem to have been regarded by the other contracting party as a mere stepping-stone to absolute authority in internal affairs, a necessary expedient at the moment for breaking a formidable aristocratic faction, backed by a still more formidable soldiery; but one that might be rejected with scorn, so soon as the object should have been securely gained. The parties obtained, each of them, much of the advantage calculated upon, though the result entirely answered the views of neither.

Immediately after the execution of the treaty, an express was sent off to summon the subsidiary force to Nâgpoor. The resident had previously acquainted Colonel Doveton with the progress of the negotiations, and prepared him to receive a summons of this nature. That officer had accordingly held in readiness a force of the exact strength agreed upon in the treaty, giving the command to Colonel Walker of the 3d Madras cavalry. This force left the neighbourhood of Ellickpoor on the first of June; and crossing the Wurda at Amner on the sixth, arrived at the distance of one march from Nâgpoor on the eighth of June. Here the main body halted; and two battalions, brigaded under the command of Lieutenant-Colonel Scott, marched in to the Bhoosla capital on the tenth, Colonel Walker accompanying them. The treaty, which had not till then been so much as suspected, was published in the city on the preceding day. On the 18th June, a cantonment was fixed upon for the Nâgpoor brigade about three miles to the west of the city. It was the resident's intention, that the remainder of the subsidiary force should move immediately to Pandoorna, there to canton during the rains, before it took up its final position on the banks of the Nerbudda near Hoshungabad. The continuance of the intrigues at Nâgpoor, however, induced our new ally to request that the departure of the main body might be postponed. Not only Naroba and his faction, but the Baees of the Muhal, and, amongst the rest, Kashee Baee Pursajee's wife, complained loudly of the conclusion of the treaty by Appa Saheb, without previously consulting them, declaring it to have been a condition of their acquiescence in his nomination to the regency, that they should be consulted in all matters of importance. The treaty itself was not the ground of their complaint; on the contrary, they avowed their readiness to give more advantageous terms, and made distinct overtures for the purpose to Mr. Jenkins. But the regent's breach of personal faith awakened all this virulence; and so rancorous was the enmity, that at last, fearing assassination, and having been dissuaded from accepting a personal guard of our troops, Appa Saheb on the 27th June went to live at a garden-house adjoining the newly-chosen cantonment of the brigade, as the only place where he could feel himself in security. The issue of these dissensions will be detailed in a subsequent chapter.

CHAPTER VII.

JYPOOR, &c.

1816, APRIL TO OCTOBER.

Jypoor alliance—orders from England—suspended—resumed—debated—resolved upon—Military preparations—Negotiation—protracted—broken off—internal condition of Jypoor—fresh overtures—and negotiation—Again broken off—Nâgpoor affairs—Sindheea's supineness—and offer to Jypoor—Pêshwa's conduct—and intrigues—Trimbukjee's escape—communications with Bajee Rao in consequence.

THE Nâgpoor alliance was not the only object, which engaged the attention of the Supreme Government during the hot season and the rains of 1816. The Goorkha war had no sooner been brought to an end, than it was resolved to endeavour to bring the state of Jypoor within the sphere of British protection; and the negotiations and military arrangements, commenced for this purpose, were simultaneous with the occurrences at Nâgpoor, detailed in the preceding chapter.

The circumstances, under which the first connexion of the British Government with Jypoor was formed in 1803, and broken off in 1806, will be familiar to those at all conversant with the political history of India. They are recorded in the work of Sir John Malcolm, * which appeared in 1811. One good effect of that publication was, that it produced a revolution in the sentiments of those intrusted with the home administration of the affairs of our Indian empire, in conformity with the spirit of whose policy, the previous treaty with Jypoor had been

* Political History of India.

JYPOOR FROM THE SOUTH-WEST.

SEETABULDEE HILLS & RESIDENCY OF NAGPOOR FROM THE WEST.

dissolved, and the principality abandoned to the oppression and exaction of the Mahrattas and Patans. Regretting the policy adopted towards this state in 1806, the secret committee issued orders from England on the 23rd December 1813, for taking it again under protection. These arrived on the 10th June 1814, at the time when the Supreme-Government had found itself forced into war with the Nipâlese, and had prepared to refer the expediency of offensive measures against the predatory associations to the previous consideration of the authorities in England. When the execution of these orders came to be discussed, it was agreed, that the renewed connexion with Jypoor might well form part of the comprehensive plan proposed for the reduction of the freebooters; that singly it was an object of little importance, while it might involve us with the Mahrattas, and prematurely bring on the necessity of the immediate prosecution of the very course it had been resolved to defer. These arguments prevailed; and the home authorities afterwards admitted the propriety of this postponement of the execution of their orders at the particular juncture.

On the Governor-General's return from the western provinces, in September 1815, conceiving the Goorkha war to be near its conclusion, his Lordship came prepared with a proposition then to carry the measure into effect. However, the suspense in regard to Nipâl, and the ultimate renewal of war in that direction, prevented the matter from being immediately taken up. After the final termination of hostilities towards the end of March, the proposition was renewed; indeed, the question was forced upon the Indian government, by the increasing distresses of Jypoor, and by the earnest applications of its Raja, to be received under the wing of protection.

In the course of that month it had been ascertained, that Ameer Khan was collecting the whole of the Patan forces for the attack of Raja Purtab Singh in his capital of Jynagurh *,

* Vide plate at the head of this chapter.

ostensibly to force upon him a change of ministers, but evidently with the design of reducing the state, if possible, to complete subjection. There was no reason, therefore, to doubt the Raja's sincerity in the pressing overtures he made to Mr. Metcalfe through his agents at Dehlee, accompanied by an offer to submit to any sacrifices that might be demanded. These were soon followed up by similar solicitations and offers made directly to the Supreme-Government by the Raja's resident vakeel at the presidency.

Under these circumstances, it became necessary forthwith to decide upon the course of policy to be adopted in regard to Jypoor; and the question was fully considered and discussed. It was again urged, that the proposed alliance ought to form a part of the general plan of operations against the predatory bands, and therefore should be suspended till the sanction of the home authorities should allow that plan to be commenced upon—that the premature adoption of this insulated measure, by immediately involving us with Ameer Khan and the Patans, and possibly also with Sindheea, who made equal advantage of exactions from Jypoor, which a connexion with the British must put an immediate stop to, would necessarily bring on that extended scale of operations, and produce that change in the political relations of our eastern dominions, which had been regarded with so much alarm—that the committee's approbation of the postponement by the Supreme Government of execution of their previous orders was to be regarded as a virtual recal of them, or at least, as an acquiescence in the opinion, that the measure should only be prosecuted as part of a general system, without being desirable on its individual account. Giving to these arguments all the weight which they derived from the respectable quarter whence they proceeded, the Marquess of Hastings, nevertheless, considered the government to be free to take Jypoor under its protection, in obedience to the orders of 1813, whenever the measure might be deemed expedient;—and that this freedom of action was not in the least affected by the approval of postponement at a juncture, when circumstances were obviously unfavourable. His Lordship thought also, that the measure was highly desirable in itself, abstracted from any general plan of operations, inasmuch as it would cripple the resources of one of the predatory powers, and save a fine and eventually useful territory from ruin and devastation. At the same time he conceived, from former experience of Sindheea's disposition, that it was not likely to involve us in extensive operations, as it was easy to overawe both that chieftain and the Patans, by demonstrations similar to those which had proved effectual pending the former negotiations with Bhopâl. He also considered the actual difficulties of Jypoor to have arrived at a crisis, that rendered the delay of a further reference quite inadmissible.

In conformity with his Lordship's opinion, it was resolved to entertain the Raja's overtures; and orders were issued to Mr. Metcalfe to that effect on the 20th of April 1816. The terms were to correspond exactly with those offered to Bhopâl in 1814-15: but Jypoor having greater resources, though for the present in a most exhausted condition, was to be called upon to defray eventually the greater part of the charge to be incurred in its protection. To carry into effect the alliance, in case of its being formed, troops were to assemble in the neighbourhood of Muttra and Rewaree, sufficient for the formation of two armies of 9000 men each. It was intended, that Sir David Ochterlony should take the command of one of them; and that both should be ready to advance on the first requisition of the resident at Dehlee, in order to drive the Patans beyond the Jypoor frontier. With a view at the same time to hold Sindheea and the Mahrattas in check, the troops at Cawnpoor and in Bundelkhund were directed to be on the alert; and the four subsidiary forces were ordered respectively to positions, whence they might overawe the whole of Sindheea's and Holkar's dominions, while they covered, as far as was practicable, the territories of our own allies. The Guzerât force was to move to Brodera; the Poona subsidiary force to Jâlna; the Nizam's to Ellickpoor; and the Bhoosla Raja's, immediately on its then expected establishment, to the banks of the Nerbudda. There would thus be a display of nearly 40,000 infantry and 12,000 cavalry, besides artillery, in readiness to put down any disposition that might be shown, to obstruct the execution of the plan determined on by government.

It may be right to mention, that the Jypoor territory lay entirely to the north and west of the Chumbul; and the principality, so far from being included amongst those Rajpoot states, with which we had bound ourselves by treaty with Holkar and Sindheea not to interfere, at the time of forming those treaties was actually under British protection, the resolution to dissolve the alliance having been subsequently formed: wherefore, there was evidently no argument arising out of our relations with the Mahrattas, on which our right to renew the alliance could be disputed.

Before the military arrangements above specified were brought to any forwardness, the negotiation had already been some time in progress. To return to it, Mr. Metcalf, on receipt of his instructions, took an early opportunity of communicating to the Jypoor vakeel, that he was ready to receive the overtures of the principality, in case an agent duly empowered to conclude engagements on its part should present himself. Notwithstanding the earnestness with which entreaties were made to be taken under protection, while it was understood to be a matter of principle with us not to extend our political relations beyond their existing limits, it became evident, after this communication, that there existed no corresponding desire to bring matters speedily to a point. Ameer Khan only threatened Jypoor, when Mr. Metcalfe made this offer to negotiate. He had actually invested the capital, before the negotiators arrived at Dehlee furnished with full powers. As long as the Patans continued to press the siege, the negotiation proceeded with apparent alacrity. Every thing indeed was soon agreed to, except the amount of subsidy to be paid by the Raja: this point also was at length settled. Mr. Metcalfe had begun with a demand of twenty-five lack rupees, the amount of the total charge of the troops to be furnished for the protection of the state. He was afterwards induced to lower his demand to fifteen lack rupees for the permanent subsidy, with the accommodation of considerable remissions during the first five years, in consideration of the impoverished condition of the territory. Pending the siege of Jynagurh, the negotiation was kept in that state, that an hour's time would have sufficed for its completion. It seems, however, that a separate negotiation was kept up all the while with Ameer Khan; and the threat of bringing down upon him a British force, which a mere signature could instantly effect, was held out as an inducement to his raising the siege. He withdrew early in the month of July, after having failed in several attempts to carry some strong positions necessary to cover his approaches to the city; but not without exacting a stipulation to receive a sum of money as the ransom of the Raja's territory from plunder, and as the consideration for reducing Madhoorajpoor, a town in the jageer of one of the Raja's family, then in rebellion against him. The two first items were observed on neither side; but Ameer Khan, with part of his troops, moved down to reduce Madhoorajpoor, in execution of the last article; doubtless with the object of appropriating it to himself. Other bodies of the Patans immediately spread themselves over the surface of the country, plundering, as before, in every direction.

About the time that these terms were made with Ameer Khan, every thing had been settled at Dehlee; but the Jypoor agents were forthwith instructed to bring forward a new demand, viz. that our troops should reduce Tonk and Rampoora, and re-annex them to Jypoor, in addition to the other stipulations. These places had been taken by us from Holkar, and restored at the peace of 1805. They were now held on his behalf by Ameer Khan, whom we had agreed to expel from the Raja's own possessions; and, as these towns had at some distant period been subject to Jypoor, this was the ground of their reduction being now demanded. The negotiation was of course broken off upon the advance of this new demand. Indeed, the Supreme Government had previously directed it to be brought to some decided issue, on first observing the insidious way, in which it was conducted by the other side. The indifference manifested by the durbar of Jypoor on this occasion to the advantages attending a closer union with the British, is perhaps in part attributable to the general reluctance felt by the petty independent princes to make any indissoluble alliances, on terms apparently calculated to interfere with the unrestrained latitude of political action they had hitherto enjoyed. All our alliances with states of this description have necessarily a character of dependence on their part, and on that account are not very palatable. Yet a more obvious mode of accounting for the disinclination experienced on this occasion may be found in the actual circumstances of the internal government of Jypoor. The whole territory was parcelled out into hereditary tenures of the nature of the fiefs or baronies of the feudal system: over these the Raja, a weak man, had much about the same degree of influence and authority, as was possessed by the weakest of the kings of England, when the same system prevailed in that country. The continual war of factions was prosecuted with the utmost virulence. Since the preceding November, the

Jypoor ministry had been twice changed. Manjee Doss's party, which was the most aristocratical and most hostile to the Patans, had ultimately gained the ascendancy; and the strong national spirit it succeeded in exciting amongst the Rajpoots, was one of the principal instruments, by which the enterprise of Ameer Khan was successfully resisted. No member of this aristocracy, however, would willingly exchange a state of things, which leaves so wide an opening to his hopes and ambition, for the perpetual repose and tranquillity that must result from the introduction of our influence. This disposition might be expected to have prevailed, even if we had offered a settlement on the basis of leaving matters as we found them; but there was reason for the aristocracy to suspect, that our guarantee of maintaining the Raja's authority comprehended the enforcement of his just dues from themselves; and their suspicions naturally made them oppose the completion of the alliance. Besides, their success in baffling the Patans with their native means alone, had added much to the pride of their independence, and increased their aversion to allow the interference of a foreign power in their concerns.

It was in the beginning of August that Mr. Metcalfe broke off the negotiation, dismissing the agent, Sunkur Doss, who had been sent on behalf of Purtab Singh. The Supreme-Government had hopes, that some little longer experience of the excesses of the Patans would produce a better feeling in the leading men of this principality; and not wishing to punish the duplicity of their past conduct, by making it a ground of perpetual exclusion from the benefits of future alliance, empowered the resident to receive any new overtures that might bear the aspect of more sincerity. It was resolved, at the same time, thenceforward to make no military preparations, until a treaty should be actually signed and executed, in order to prevent the recurrence of a fruitless expense. Before the close of September, the knowledge of the final rupture of the negotiation produced a stir amongst the factions of Jynagurh; and a considerable party expressed great dissatisfaction against Manjee Doss, to whom the failure was attributed. To quiet the murmurs of this party, for the event showed it was with no real design of completing the alliance, agents were again sent off to Dehlee, the minister's brother being associated with Sunkur Doss in the mission. On the 17th of November they arrived at Dehlee, and soon after waited on the British Resident. At the first audience they declared, that, knowing the wishes of the British Government, from what had passed at the former negotiation, they had come to conform to them, and to sign the treaty before proposed; but that they wished first to submit a few requests to the Governor-General, leaving it to his generosity to accord them or not. The reduction and delivery of Tonk and Rampoora was their first request; this Mr. Metcalfe refused to forward or listen to; the second was for jageers or pensions to the negotiators, similar to what had been granted at Nâgpoor; and the third for a promise, that they should always have a good-tempered gentleman as Resident. The request for pensions, as a matter of stipulation, was absurd, considering that the negotiation was not on the footing of reciprocal advantage, and that there was no object to be acquired by the British worth a pecuniary sacrifice; the occasion of our treating at all being the compliance with their solicitation for salvation by our means from impending ruin. Mr. Metcalfe having combated these points rather with ridicule than argument, proceeded to state an omission in the draft of treaty before discussed, viz. the stipulation for our arbitration of all foreign disputes and claims, either for or against the principality. The greatest objections were raised to the insertion of any such article; the chief of which appeared to arise from an apprehension, that it might extend to the adjudication of the title to the Raj of Jypoor, to which there was more than one claimant.

against Purtab Singh, particularly a pretender still living, who had been supported at one time by Sindheea. The scruples of the negotiators in respect to this article could not be got over, even although this construction was disavowed. The conference accordingly broke up, with a distinct explanation to Sunkur Doss and his colleague, that the insertion of this new article was insisted upon under special orders from the Supreme Government; consequently, that the point could on no account be conceded. Two days were allowed them to consider of it: the third was fixed for a second conference, at which they would be expected to sign the treaty, with this article introduced, either in the form proposed, or so modified as might be agreed upon in the interim; or, if matters could not be adjusted by that time, the negotiation would be dropped altogether. This restriction in point of time was necessary, to prevent the government of Jypoor from again making its advantages of the show of negotiation, without any intention to bring it to a point. Continued opposition being manifested to the stipulation for our arbitrament, it occurred to the Resident, that the secret reason might be, the fear lest the liquidation of certain bonds, given at different times to Patan Sirdars, would be comprehended under its terms. To exclude this interpretation, he agreed so to word the article, as to confine it to claims of tribute or other demands on the part of Sindeea and Holkar as independent powers. In this form the negotiators waived their objections to the stipulation. But when the time came for the treaty to be signed, a new and extraordinary objection was started to the usual engagement to procure the ratification of Raja Purtab Singh within fifteen days. The negotiators seemed to wish our representative to be satisfied with their signature, and to act upon their treaty, without requiring its ratification by their master. They were told, however, in answer, that, if they objected to this article, they must take their immediate departure; and as they made no other reply than to solicit a delay of twenty days for the discussion of the point, not for procuring the required confirmation, the treaty was a second time abruptly terminated, with no more successful issue than the former.

It was now most evident, that the object of the Jypoor administration was, to keep open a negotiation, not to conclude a treaty. Manjee Doss, a short time after the return of the agents, declared publicly to the British news-writer at Jynagurh, that he had never authorised the negotiators at Dehlee to agree to any stipulation for a money payment. It is difficult to conceive what could have been the object of this extraordinary communication; but it was supposed to arise from a wish to ingratiate himself with the party adverse to the British alliance. He lost nothing in their eyes by this public profession of duplicity; and on its being made matter of remonstrance by the resident at Dehlee, replied only by evasion and further falsehood; declaring, that the amount of subsidy was what he had not agreed to; although, when the agents presented themselves the second time, it was distinctly explained beforehand, that, unless they were empowered to sign the treaty before proposed, of which the specific money stipulation formed an item, they could not be listened to; and the negotiators, after this intimation, declared, at their first audience, that they had come empowered to sign.

Immediately on the rupture of the first negotiation in August, the military preparations which had been made for its eventual support were suspended; and the troops destined for this being now available for other service, a force was directed to be formed under Lieutenant-Colonel Adams, of the 10th B. N. I., and to hold itself in readiness to proceed to the Nerbudda at the close of the rains, in order to relieve the Madras troops there stationed under Colonel Walker, of which for the present the Nâgpoor subsidiary force was composed.

In the mean time, Appa Saheb, who in June had taken refuge at a garden-house adjoining to the new cantonment, as mentioned in the preceding chapter, became relieved from his alarms. Having seized and confined Naroba, the secretary, and established another of the widows of Ragojee in the control of the interior of the palace, and care of the Raja's person, in the room of Buka Baee, he returned to the city, and his authority was in appearance firmly established by the end of August. Goojaba Dada, who had likewise been an opponent of the regent, but was in the main a moderate man, and besides a relation, was merely debarred from indiscriminate access to the Raja's person; and Svdeek Ulee Khan, seeing the turn affairs had taken, paid assiduous court to the Naeeb, and in a very short time acquired an influence seemingly little inferior to that of Nagoo Punt and Neragun themselves. The two last mentioned favourites, indeed, complained to Mr. Jenkins, that the interested counsels of this officer had induced Appa Saheb to renounce his original design of reducing and reforming his military establishments, by which means Sudeek Allee Khan had preserved to himself the chief military authority, with all its corrupt emoluments. In October, however, the old advisers of Appa Saheb so far prevailed, as to induce him to apply for a battalion, to be raised and disciplined by British officers, on the model of the reformed infantry in the Nizam's service. The Governor-General acquiesced at once in the proposal, and nominated officers for the purpose. The object of this application was, to provide a further counterpoise to the Arabs, whose fidelity to himself he still mistrusted, on account of their known personal attachment to the son of Ragoojee, their late master. Yet this step seemed to indicate a degree of confidence and cordiality towards his new allies, little consistent with the treachery of his subsequent conduct. To say the truth, there is ground to conclude, from this and other symptoms, that Appa

Saheb, while Pursajee remained alive, was not engaged in the conspiracy, which had been for some time in progress for a general rising of the whole Mahratta nation.

In the beginning of October, Colonel Walker moved to take up the position assigned to him, on the banks of the Nerbudda. His operations in that quarter, and the effect of the appearance of a British force so near the immediate haunts of the Pindarees, together with their plans and expeditions for the season of 1816-17, will more properly form the subject of a separate chapter. But it may first be necessary to notice briefly what was passing during the rains at the other Mahratta courts.

Sindheea made no effort to avail himself of the distractions at the Bhoosla court, consequent upon the death of Ragoojee: indeed, the expedition with which the treaty of subsidiary alliance was negotiated by Mr. Jenkins, and the secrecy observed in the conduct of that affair, had left no time for the operation of foreign intrigue, much less for the machinations of a durbar, so slow in its deliberations as that of Gwalior. In the same manner this chieftain refrained entirely from further interference in the affairs of Bhopâl; so that the young Nuwab, having retained his father's counsellors in their offices, continued to make head against the Pindarees, and to command their respect: keeping up at the same time an active correspondence with the political agent in Bundelkhund, explaining every thing that passed between him and the freebooters, and professing his desire to become, or at least to be considered, a dependent of the British dominion. Neither did Sindheea make any effort whatever, in the course of 1816, to curb or reduce the Pindarees, notwithstanding that the subject was specially brought to his notice by the British Resident, on more occasions than one. His constant reply was, that repeated orders had been issued, prohibiting their violation of the British territories; and that time and negotiation were necessary to bring the refractory chiefs to implicit obedience. It was explained in private to the Resident upon one occasion, that Sindheea's plan was to inveigle the chiefs to an interview, and, by seizing their persons, to deprive the durras of their leaders, and cause their dissolution. It was evident, however, from the general tenor of his conduct, that he began to be alarmed, lest he should be visited with the whole responsibility for an evil, which his weakness had suffered to grow up within his dominions. He was moreover beginning to have a more accurate notion of his relative strength than he had entertained before the discussions in 1814, when he thought, by the loftiness of his tone, to restrain the British Government from interfering with Bhopâl. In short, anxiety and alarm were fast succeeding to the jealous rivalry and contentious spirit, which the violent among his courtiers still vainly flattered him was the policy, warranted and demanded, by his relative position amongst the powers of India. To this cause, and to habitual tardiness of judgment, is to be attributed the supineness with which Sindheea witnessed the extension of our influence over the dominions of the Bhoosla, and which, though it in the end produced the determination to temporize with both parties, and, if possible, to keep well with both, till he could see the probable issue of affairs, yet prevented any exertion to court our favour by a vigorous and early effort against the Pindarees, the common enemy. Another reason for his want of energy at this juncture may be found in the circumstance, that his best troops, under Baptiste, were fully employed in the siege of Ragoogurh, a fort belonging to a Rajpoot, named Raja Jysingh. That active chief, while his own strong hold was closely invested, succeeded in a sudden surprise of Baptiste's fort of Sheeopoor, where the son and part of the treasure of the Colonel had been deposited for safety. This passed in the beginning of June; and, though the fort of Ragoogurh fell in the following August, Jysingh, as a partisan, gave full occupation to the whole of Baptiste's division, and had good success in several light skirmishes and attacks on detachments and convoys during the whole of the rains, and even up to the close of the cold season. At length, having lost his late conquest of Sheeopoor also by the treachery of his garrison, he went off with his followers to form a new band of Pindarees, and was not unsuccessful in his depredations on the territories of Sindheea, more particularly on Baptiste's assigned lands.

Yet notwithstanding the indifference manifested by Sindheea to the passing occurrences at Nâgpoor and on the Nerbudda, the opening of the British negotiation with Jypoor seemed to waken him to the policy of a counter-exertion, for the purpose of securing some personal advantage. He accordingly opened a similar negotiation, tendering the assistance of his military means towards restraining the Patans; and, in furtherance of this object, sent a reinforcement to Bapoo Sindheea at Ajimeer, to add to the efficiency of his establishment in that quarter. The Jypoor durbar amused Sindheea for some time with the hope of accepting his protection, pretty nearly in the same manner as they amused the British Government; but the Mahratta meeting this conduct with reciprocal duplicity opened a further negotiation with Ameer Khan, and in proportion as coolness was evinced on the part of the Raja, pretended a cordiality with the Patan, in the hope of alarming the Jypoor ministry by the apprehension, that his weight would be thrown into the opposite scale. But Jypoor had no real design of connecting itself with any one; and while it relied on the known disposition of the British to afford it protection, as a sufficient resource against any extremity the united efforts of the Patans and Sindheea could reduce it to, reckoned also upon the deterring influence of this knowledge, as its best protection against any actual design on their part to drive it to this last resort. Sindheea's plans came, therefore, to the same issue with the British negotiations; that is to say, produced no result whatsoever.

At the court of Poona nothing particular occurred; but the conduct of the Pêshwa's government was an alternation of concessions, subservience, and conciliation, and of a spirit of recrimination and litigious opposition. The prince himself assumed either character, with a versatility, that seemed to baffle every attempt to penetrate his real disposition and intentions. In this spirit, at one time he ordered extensive levies of horse and foot, and at another reduced his establishments to the lowest possible ebb: at one time he complained of the delays thrown in the way of the adjustment of his claims on the Nizam and Gykwar; at other times himself created new and very childish ones. All the while, every nerve was strained to procure the release of Trimbukjee, and every advantage, personal as well as national, was offered to Mr. Elphinstone through various channels, to engage him to forward this grand object of his desire. Active intrigues were at the same time carrying on in Hindoostan and Guzerât, and special agents deputed to all the Mahratta courts, to persuade them to join the proposed coalition, promising advantages to those who were not prepared for open hostility, if they would but aid, by keeping up the appearance of concert, whence he anticipated a reduction of our tone, and a greater degree of deference to the general wish of the Mahratta nation. The British residents exerted themselves with activity to penetrate into all these intrigues, and generally with complete success. Those of the Pêshwa at the court of Holkar, were made the subject of a special remonstrance, and produced abundance of protestations, but no change of conduct. Even Futteh Sing Gykwar was a party to these designs, and gave way for some time to the dangerous counsels of low companions and men adverse to the British connexion; but this disposition was overcome in him without any resort to strong measures, by the operation of his own good sense and experience of the solid advantages of the alliance, and by the judicious advice and moderation of the resident at his court.

On the 12th of September, to the surprise of all, Trimbukjee Dainglia succeeded in escaping from his confinement in Tannah, notwithstanding that the precaution had been taken of garrisoning the fort entirely with Europeans, of whom a guard was continually mounted to observe his personal movements. The escape was effected at eight o'clock at night, through a hole in the wall of the privy, which being detached from the place of actual confinement, communicated on the other side with a stable belonging to one of the officers of the garrison. By accustoming the sentries to attend him to this place at the same hour of the night, their suspicions were lulled to sleep, and he was suffered to enter alone, while the sentry with the light remained without, in a situation, whence he could not see what passed within. The preparations for this escape were made by a man who had, with this design, taken service as *syee*, or horsekeeper, to the officer living in the adjoining premises, and who disappeared along with the prisoner. His communications with Trimbukjee are supposed to have passed while he was leading the horse under his care near the prison-door and the terrace, on which Trimbukjee was allowed to walk: for at these times this *syee* was generally observed to be singing Mahratta songs, which the European sentries did not understand nor suspect. It was some minutes before the escape was discovered, and the night being dark and rainy, Trimbukjee had slipped off his clothes and crossed the rampart by a rope previously attached to one of the guns, before the alarm was given, and thus gained the other side of the narrow and shallow channel separating Salsette from the Mahratta territories, before measures could be taken to intercept the passage.

The resident at Poona was informed of this event by express. He immediately communicated the news to the Pêshwa, declaring that the Governor-General would expect the utmost efforts to be made by his Highness for the re-apprehension of this delinquent, as a necessary proof of attachment to the British Government; while to afford him protection either overtly or underhand, would infallibly produce the mischiefs that had been avoided by his surrender. Bajee Rao wished to avail himself of the escape, to alter the terms on which his favourite had before been given up, and to make his own exertions for the re-apprehension conditional, on receiving a promise, that the prisoner should hereafter remain in his own custody. This attempt was of course resisted: but the fugitive for some time eluded all efforts to discover the place of his retreat; and there could be no doubt that Bajee Rao abetted his concealment, notwithstanding his open professions to the contrary.

Thus have the political events of India been traced to the close of the rainy season of 1816, about the middle of the month of October of that year.

CHAPTER VIII.

PINDAREES.

1816-17, OCTOBER TO APRIL.

Nâgpoor subsidiary force moves to the Nerbudda—Pindarees alarmed—their first effort—grand expedition in three divisions—1st to Ganjam—2d to Bidur—surprised by Major M'Dowal—exploit of Sheikh Dulloo—3d to Ahmednugur—surprised by Major Lushington—Ganjam penetrated—Borthwick's pursuit—1st party intercepted—reflections—resolution to extirpate the hordes—motives—Sindheea—Holkar—Dya-Ram of Hatras—his fort invested and bombarded—his escape—fort taken.

Early in October 1816, Lieutenant-Colonel Walker had moved, as abovementioned, with the main body of the Nâgpoor subsidiary force, to take up the position assigned to him on the southern bank of the Nerbudda. By the 25th of the month, his defensive line was completed. It extended from Soonee, which lies 27 miles S. S. W. of Hoshungabad, to Sirinugur, 120 miles east of the same place. With all the advantages of favourable ground, the force, consisting of but five battalions of infantry, and one regiment of cavalry, was evidently unequal to the defence of so extended a line; more especially as the Raja's contingent was in no present condition to afford effectual assistance. One of Colonel Walker's posts was no less than 90 miles distant from its nearest *appui*. But the first appearance of a British army in the valley of the Nerbudda spread consternation amongst the Pindarees; and Cheetoo's durra, which occupied the cantonment of Nemawur, on the northern bank, a little lower down the river, prepared to retire with their families in the direction of the Ghâts into Malwa. In the apprehension of an immediate attack, the preparations which had been making for an expedition to the south, when the river should be fordable, were suspended: and some time was lost by the chiefs of durras, in forwarding intreaties to Sindheea for an asylum for their families in some of his numerous strong holds, while they prepared for a desultory contest with the army, whose approach they daily expected. Sindheea openly rejected all such applications, notwithstanding that they were accompanied with an intimation, that unless he helped them in this emergency, his territories should no longer enjoy immunity from ravage. Some of his military commanders, however, and a party in his ministry, privately gave them hopes of ultimately obtaining their object, in case matters came to extremity; assuring them that all public acts and professions were merely intended to save appearances with the English.

Emboldened in some measure by these assurances, and by observing that the British troops did not cross the Nerbudda, the several durras came to the resolution of pushing small parties between Colonel Walker's posts, and round his flanks, and thus pursuing the same system of predatory incursions into the British territories, that had in the past year been so productive and successful. On the 4th of November, a party crossed near Hindia, half of which proceeded on the Boorhanpoor road, and the other half towards Tamboornee. Colonel Walker immediately moved with a light force upon Hurda, to intercept their route; and, after a vain pursuit for some distance along the Boorhanpoor road, succeeded by a sudden march eastward, in falling in with the latter party, while bivouacked in the jungle on the night of the 5th. This body suffered an inconsiderable loss, and fled precipitately back across the river. Similar attempts to pass were not renewed till the 13th, when the plan which had been agreed upon by the chiefs, in the interim, was carried into execution. Cheetoo's durra still continued in force to the west. At the same time, large bodies moved to the east, and upwards of 5000 passed the river in sight of the infantry post, on the extreme right of Colonel Walker's line, with a rapidity of movement, which baffled the efforts of the infantry to impede or harass their march, and the regiment of cavalry was on the opposite flank. In this manner the passage was effected, in sufficient numbers to form two *luhburs*, (expeditions), one of which continued its progress due east, and, penetrating by the route of Mundela, Chuteesgurh, and the forests and mountains forming the northern and eastern frontier of the Nâgpoor dominions, burst suddenly into the Company's district of Ganjam, with the evident and avowed intention of turning thence to Cuttack and Juggernauth. By good fortune, the turbulent character of the Rajas and landholders of Ganjam had caused the district to be well furnished with troops, and the *luhbur* was driven back before it could penetrate to any distance, as will presently be mentioned more particularly. The other body of these Pindarees took a southward direction, and passed within 20 miles of Nâgpoor with impunity, notwithstanding that an effort was made to intercept them, by a light detachment from the infantry brigade remaining at that city. They then crossed the Wurda into the Nizam's territory, before Colonel Doveton could bring up troops for the defence of that line, from the position he occupied to shut the Ghâts in the valley of the Poorna, in which quarter he was looking out for these marauders. This body, which at the lowest estimate amounted to 6000, was on the Godaveree, at Neermul, on the 15th of December, and at Bidur on the 21st; up to which point it had marched leisurely without interruption, or fatiguing its horses, plundering a broad line of country on either side of its track. The *luhbur* continued some time in the neighbourhood of Bidur, while the chiefs remained indecisive, as to the prosecution of the ulterior design of penetrating into the Company's ceded districts on the other side of the Kishna and Toomboodra. Their indecision proved the ruin of the enterprise, as it afforded time for a light force, detached from Hyderabad for this purpose, under Major M'Dowal, to give the main body a complete surprise, about 30 miles to the west of Bidur. This occurred before daylight in the morning of the 15th of January; and such was the security into which the Pindarees had been lulled by their hitherto uninterrupted progress, that the infantry were close in upon the tents of the chiefs before they were discovered, and hardly a man of the party was mounted, by the time the first volley was discharged. The greater part of the horses and booty of the main division of this *luhbur* was abandoned on the rapid advance of the infantry. One leader, however, indignant at the want of energy betrayed by those vested with the chief command of the expedition, had carried away a body of from 3 to 500, a few days before this discomfiture; and, passing rapidly across the Pêshwa's territory, descended into the Konkan by the Amba Ghât in the western range, and thence shaped his course due north, plundering the western shores of India, from the 17th to the 21st degree of north latitude, and returning by the valley of the Taptee, and the route of Boorhanpoor. The conductor of this bold enterprise was a man named Sheikh Dulloo, and the singular hardihood of the exploit, joined to the uncommon skill and rapidity with which it was conducted, saved it from the fate which overtook every other expedition of the kind this season. The only loss Sheikh Dulloo sustained from British troops was, when, on his return to the Nerbudda, in the following March, he found the ford, by which he hoped to re-cross to Cheetoo's durra, guarded by a havildar's party of our sepoys. Several of his men were shot in attempting to dash across; but Sheikh Dulloo himself, with his main body, and best mounted followers, retiring from the ghât, boldly swam the river lower down, though not without a further loss of men and horses, several of whom were drowned in the attempt. The ill mounted and less daring of the band dispersed and fled into the jungle on the southern bank of the river, where the greater part were cut off by the wild inhabitants of the neighbourhood: so that, of 260 Pindarees of the first and second classes, of which the band had consisted when it separated from the *luhbur* at Bidur, only 110 joined the durra; but these carried a rich booty in their saddles; and the brilliancy of the achievement added even more to their reputation than its success had done to their wealth.

Besides the above two bodies of Pindarees, which had turned the right flank of Colonel Walker's line, another detachment from Cheetoo's durra had succeeded in making good its route by the Boorhanpoor road, as above mentioned. It was subsequently reinforced, and succeeded in passing the valley of the Taptee and ghâts of Berar, notwithstanding the dispositions made for their defence. This body passed between Aurungabad and Jâlna on the 28th of November, and moved direct upon Ahmednugur. The Poona subsidiary force was not wholly in position for the defence of the Pêshwa's frontiers against such incursions, a considerable part of the light troops having been called down to the south, where their presence was required to awe Appa Dussaee into submission. This man was a powerful southern jageerdar, who had subjected himself, by continued contumacy, to the penalty of a forfeiture of one-third of his jageer; and the forfeiture was enforced by calling down a British detachment at the close of the rainy season, which did not completely effect the object until the middle of December 1816. On the 25th of this month, while on his route to the northward with the 4th Madras native cavalry, which had formed part of the force employed to the south, Major Lushington obtained intelligence that this body of Pindarees was on the S. E. of Poona. He was at the time at Pupulwaree, twenty-five miles distant; but as the Pindarees were ignorant of his being in the neighbourhood, and were plundering at their leisure in fancied security, there was every hope of falling in with them: at all events, he resolved to make the effort. After an unremitting march of upwards of fifty miles, from one o'clock in the morning of the 26th, the Major succeeded in coming up with the *luhbur*, at the time the Pindarees were cooking and eating after a long march. The surprise was complete; and, as the ground was favourable for the pursuit of cavalry, a very large proportion was cut up. The loss of the freebooters was estimated to be very great, as between 7 and 800 were left on the field. The only casualty on the part of the British was the death of Captain Darke, who received a spear through the body. A man of his troop had turned from the charge of a Pindara, armed in this manner; and, indignant at the sight, this spirited officer himself rushed forward, and fell a victim to the superiority of the weapon in skilful hands. The Pindara was immediately cut to pieces by Captain Darke's men. This *luhbur*, and that surprised a few days afterwards by Major M'Dowall, both suffered so severely, that they broke up, and fled back to the Nerbudda in the utmost confusion. However, before they could arrive on its banks, the passes and ghâts were so well guarded, that the greater part of the fugitives perished, and but few reached the durras they had left in November. A remnant of the party surprised by M'Dowall, was conducted across the river with great skill by its leader, who succeeded in making his way by the Charwa road, before the party sent to interrupt him by Colonel Walker arrived to occupy it.

The Ganjam expedition is the only one that remains to be accounted for. This body was composed almost entirely of men from Wâsil Mahommed's durra. It crossed the British frontier in the middle of December, marching upon Kimmedy, to which place Lieutenant Tweedle, who was on the frontier with a company of Madras native infantry, retired as the *luhbur* advanced. Emboldened by this, the Pindarees attacked the town, and succeeded in burning and plundering part of it on the night of the 19th of December, though Major Oliver was there with three companies of infantry. Having ascertained that their camp was but two miles distant, this officer determined to surprise it before morning, and met with complete success, occasioning considerable loss to the *luhbur*, notwithstanding the smallness of his force and his utter want of cavalry. In the course of the following morning the whole band moved off, taking the direct road to Ganjam, before which they appeared on the 25th. They plundered part of the town in haste, and retired through Goomsir. Lieutenant Borthwick instantly commenced a most active pursuit. On the 27th he fell in with about 1000, of whom he destroyed twenty men and fifty horses; but, not satisfied with this success, he resolved to beat up the Pindara camp, which, in their confidence, from knowing the British troops to be infantry only, he rightly judged would not be far off. Leaving a jemadar's party to pursue the direct road, he himself, with fifty men of his company, took a circuitous route, so as to fall upon the enemy from the opposite quarter. His success was very brilliant; and soon after the Pindarees disappeared from the province, abandoning the hope of being able to penetrate into Cuttack, and disheartened by the losses already sustained.

In the mean time, the advance division of the Bengal troops, destined to relieve Colonel Walker, had moved down to the Nerbudda; and Major M'Morine, who commanded, leaving a detachment at Jubulpoor on his arrival at that point on the 1st of January, so disposed the rest of his force, under Colonel

Walker's orders, as to extend the defensive line thence to Sirinugur, and allow of the Madras troops before stationed at the latter point being called in to strengthen and complete the chain of posts from Sirinugur to Hoshungabad and Soonee. Wâsil Mahommed, seeing these further preparations, became apprehensive for the safety of the *luhbur* he had sent out, and despatched *hircaras* in every direction to warn them against returning by the same route, with positive injunctions to keep well to the north. This, however, availed them little; for Lieutenant-Colonel Adams, who was in the course of January moving down in the same direction with the main body of the Bengal troops, sent forward parties to occupy the ghâts and passes from Chandya northwards to Bundelkhund, so as effectually to intercept the return of any body of marauders from the east towards the Sâgur district, near which Wâsil Mahommed had fixed his head-quarters. These arrangements completely answered the purpose. On the 24th of January, Captain Caulfield, who was furthest in advance, heard of the approach of the *luhbur* from Ganjam, and fell upon them in the night with a squadron of the 5th Bengal cavalry, while attempting to return by the Chandya road. He captured 400 horses; and the number of the slain was estimated at the same amount. Ramzan Khan, the leader of the party, was ascertained to be amongst these: the chief next in rank had previously fallen in one of Lieutenant Borthwick's attacks. The fugitives, after this discomfiture, made an effort to escape by a pass further to the north, where, on the 26th, they fell in with Major Clarke and the main body of the 5th Bengal cavalry, who cut up about 150 more. This expedition, therefore, which was the only one that penetrated the British frontier, suffered yet more severely than either of the other two. A small part of the advance, that had passed between Chandya and Jubulpoor, before Colonel Adams's detachments had taken up their positions, were all of those engaged in it who escaped unmolested in their return homewards *.

No further attempt was made this season to pass into the Dukhun, or to get beyond the defensive posts, connecting the frontier of our possessions in Bundelkhund with those of the Bhoosla Raja. From January forward the Pindarees carried on their trade of plunder for mere subsistence, and exclusively above the ghâts in Malwa; while such was the alacrity of the troops occupying the defensive line, that, towards the end of the season, a band from Wâsil's durra having ventured too far to the eastward, to ravage the country between Bundelkhund and Sâgur, was surprised and driven back with loss by the rapid advance of a squadron of the 4th Bengal native cavalry, under Captain Ridge, from their post at Lohargâon. A party that came to the bank of the Nerbudda to reconnoitre, and ascertain the practicability of a passage, was in like manner stopped by the guard on the southern bank, while Major Clarke (the Bengal troops having by that time completely relieved those of Madras) crossed the river with cavalry at a different ford, and cut them up as they retired across the valley in their way to the hills that form the barrier of Malwa.

Such were the proceedings of the Pindaree hordes during the season of 1816-17, and such the military operations against them. Their plan of depredation this year embraced a more ample expanse of territory, than had ever before been attempted, extending from shore to shore of the peninsula of India, and including all the intermediate provinces that had been spared the ravage of the preceding year. The report of Lieutenant-General Sir Thomas Hislop to the Marquess of Hastings represented their different columns as amounting by his estimate

* This party was hotly but unsuccessfully pursued by infantry from Jubulpoor, under Major Popham.

to 23,000 horse. This inroad had been foreseen to the full extent, and the precautionary measures of the British were consequently on a proportionate scale of magnitude. After the Bengal troops had crossed the Nerbudda to relieve Colonel Walker, there were no less than 32,000 regulars of the King's or Company's forces between that river and the Kishna, besides the reformed infantry and cavalry of the Nizam and the Pêshwa's brigade, which, though paid by our allies, were in effect devoted to the same service with their officers. In addition to the above force in advance, the utmost efforts had been made to arm the northern frontier of our immediate possessions in the Dukhun, to guard against a similar attempt to that of the preceding year; so that altogether the military effort on the side of Madras was nearly as great, as it would have been in the event of operations of the most decisive kind. Notwithstanding all this, it was rather to good fortune on our part, and to a relaxation of vigilance and activity on that of the enemy, than to our own exertions, that we must attribute the overtaking of the two larger bodies, and their severe chastisement by Majors Lushington and M'Dowall. So, likewise, the opportune march of Colonel Adams to the south most materially contributed to afford the means of completely intercepting the third expedition, which had penetrated into Ganjam. Thus it was accident, not the merits of our defensive policy, that had yielded us so much more brilliant successes this year than the last, and no argument could be drawn from them in favour of the security of any combination of defensive arrangements. To build a system for the future upon the experience of this season, that should provide only for similar results, would involve an annual preparation on the same enormous scale of expense; and even by the most favourable calculation, would not secure our provinces from invasion, and our subjects from the horrors of Pindara devastation, although we might, in some cases, happen to inflict signal vengeance on the marauders, on their way homeward incumbered with spoil.

The insufficiency of stationary posts of defence was abundantly shown by the early success of the Pindarees in penetrating Colonel Walker's line; and it stands to reason, that if a light assailant of this description be allowed time to ascertain precisely at what points the covering force may be expected to be found, he will always be able so to choose his line of route, and to regulate the length of his marches, as to baffle the utmost vigilance of such stationary defenders, when they are under an interdict not to advance and meet the danger, or crush it in the embryo. The conviction of this disadvantage produced an alteration of policy before the close of the season: for Colonel Adams obtained permission to cross the Nerbudda, and the officers in post to the south of Bundelkhund to advance westward even into Sâgur, in case an enemy should approach: whereas antecedently, the southern bank of the Nerbudda, or more generally the frontier of our own territories and that of our protected allies, had been fixed as the limit of their operations. The two successful affairs of April were attributable to this judicious alteration.

The policy and views entertained respectively by the British Government and by the native potentates of India regarding the Pindarees in the course of this season will now be shortly explained. The Governor-General in council had, as before mentioned, come to the resolution of waiting the arrival of the sanction of the home authorities to commence offensive measures for their suppression. In the interval Lord Hastings trusted, that the advantage of defence acquired by the Nâgpoor alliance might, in some degree deter, or at least enable us to repel aggression, either on ourselves or our allies. Early in the season, however, he became sensible of the futility of such expectations; and even before the storm had burst upon Ganjam, the council came to the unanimous resolution to defer no longer the extirpation of these banditti. On the 21st of December 1816, this determination was formed, and Lord Hastings gave immediate notice of his intention to proceed in person to the scene of action, and to spare no efforts to accomplish the object in spite of any obstacles that might be raised by open or secret foes. With respect to the time, it was resolved not to commence until the following season, unless the formation of the Jypoor alliance should require operations against Ameer Khan, in which case his Lordship proposed to enter upon immediate action. This not having taken place, his departure for the upper provinces was fixed for the following rains, that is to say, the month of June or July. It was still considered doubtful, whether Sindheea would be induced to co-operate with us in this important object, or yield to the importunity of alternate entreaty and menace, addressed to him from the several durras. The certain opposition of Ameer Khan, or at least of his Patan mercenaries, and the probable secret counteraction of the Pêshwa, were confidently anticipated: but with the resources of the Nizam and of the Bhoosla, who was supposed to be equally staunch, added to our own strength in that quarter of India, there appeared little hazard of failure. But his Lordship resolved to place himself above that little, by calling into play the whole disposable means of the three presidencies, according to a comprehensive plan, which will hereafter be particularly developed. The resolution to undertake active measures was formed not only without any assurance of support from the home authorities, but at a time when the Supreme Government had reason to believe that a contrary disposition prevailed at the India House.

It must be observed, that there had not yet been time to learn their sentiments on receiving information of the storm having burst upon their own district of Guntoor. This intelligence arrived in the course of the month of September 1816.

and seems to have wrought an immediate change in their aversion to offensive operations. When the Supreme Government resolved to wait no longer for the expected sanction from home, no answer to its second reference had yet been received.

The repeated violations of our own territory, and the experience of the utter futility of defensive arrangements, irresistibly impelled the Governor-General to this course; and his Lordship felt confident, a confidence justified by the result, if the result of a measure can ever be admitted to afford a fair test of its merit, that a knowledge of these circumstances would awaken the authorities in England to a sense of the magnitude of the evil, and the imperative duty and necessity of eradicating it. The reasons for postponing the commencement of operations till the close of the rains, unless prematurely brought on by the issue of the Jypoor negotiation, will be obvious, when the time requisite fully to prepare so extensive a plan of military and political movements, and the vast advantage of commencing with the whole of the fair season to look forward to, are taken into consideration. The current of events appeared also to be daily tending to produce a state of public feeling and opinion more and more favourable to our views. The successes against the Pindarees, the increasing alarm and anxiety of Sindheea, the prospect of further improving our connexion with Nâgpoor, and of comprehending Jypoor within the circle of our influence, as well as the time thus given for the newly-formed pacific relations with Nipâl to take effect, all contributed to recommend that government should reserve the execution of its resolve, until the following season. There was every prospect, that the work would then be accomplished in one campaign; and the event has shown that the expectation was just. Wherefore, although the effort for this purpose must necessarily be on the largest and most expensive scale, still the ultimate saving of charge and increase of reputation, from avoiding a warfare protracted indefinitely from year to year, were objects worth any sacrifice, and only to be ensured by having an entire season to act in, after a due allowance of time for previous preparation.

It will not be necessary to detain the reader, by stating at length the views of the several native princes, in respect to the Pindarees. Their aggressions on ourselves and our allies were more than once brought to the notice of Sindheea, by order of the Supreme Government; and in proportion as we became earnest in representing the evil, this chief redoubled his protestation of hostility to the hordes, while his generals and ministers continued to give them even open encouragement. A commander was at last appointed to conduct an expedition, that was to extirpate the whole race of Pindarees: but, when the army was to be collected, delays and difficulties began to be started in such number, that, in the end, Balajee Inglia, the officer nominated, never stirred from Gwalior. Some anxiety was shown, when the apprehension of our immediately advancing to the north of the Nerbudda was most lively; and care was taken to have troops in readiness to act according to the course of events. Beyond that point, the activity of this durbar did not reach. But we so far availed ourselves of Sindheea's professions and general policy, as to assume, that we were at perfect liberty to pursue the freebooters beyond his frontier, though it was not thought expedient to define the matter, by desiring any formal recognition of the right.

Holkar's durbar, during the season 1816-17, was agitated by a violent struggle between the party of Ameer Khan, whose agent Ghufoor Khan was at the head of the Patan interest, and had the regular battalions at his beck, and that of the native Mahrattas, who had followed the fortunes of the family, and into whose hands Toolsee Baee the regent had latterly thrown herself and her ward, the young Mulhar Rao. The former minister, Balaram Set, having been thought to favour the Patan faction, was arrested and put to death in prison; and the differences between the two parties went so far, as to produce what was called a battle, though it amounted to no more than a distant cannonade. The season passed without reconciliation or the complete reduction of either party: and Sindheea, who had at one time shown a disposition to interfere, in order to effect an accommodation, refrained in the end, and withdrew the force he had kept in the neighbourhood for the purpose. One consequence of these disturbances was, the release of Kureem Khan, the most noted of the Pindaree leaders, who had hitherto been kept under the appearance of some restraint.

The occurrences at the courts of Poona and Nâgpoor, during the season 1816-17, will be given in the following chapter. The operations against the fort of Hatras in the Dooab, as they had considerable effect in calming the public mind of the native population of our own western provinces, and preparing them for the events that were to follow, will here find its proper place of notice. Soon after the Supreme Government had determined on the suppression of the predatory bands, indeed before the close of the month of December, the continued contumacy of Dya Ram and Bhugwunt Singh, two zemindars of the Dooab, was brought particularly under the notice of Lord Hastings and the council, together with some further recent acts of unprovoked aggression upon peaceable residents within the Agra district. The rank of both these chieftains was that of mere talookdars, or renters of portions of land, but they held very strong forts; and the government, on its acquisition of the province from Sindheea, the possessions of both lying in the Aleegurh district, behaved towards them with its usual consideration, and, so long as their quota of revenue was regularly paid, a strict conformity with the equalizing laws of our system was not enforced upon them. Presuming upon this moderation, and upon the strength of their fortresses of Hatras and Moorsan, they both levied arbitrary duties, harboured thieves and robbers, and, disregarding the authority of the courts of judicature, which they were bound to respect, sported with the persons and properties of the peaceable and well-disposed in their neighbourhood. At last, the Supreme-Government felt itself called upon to resent this conduct; and it was particularly politic not to pass it over at this time, as a rising of the Patan population of Rohilkhund a few months before, to oppose an usual ordinance for the regulation of the police of cities and towns, showed the minds of the people in this part of our dominions to be very unsettled. That insurrection had, indeed, subsided on the failure of the armed mob to overpower a small party of but three* companies of Sepoys, which had been marched into the city of Barellee, where the green flag of Mahommed had been hoisted by the malcontents. Still, in the probability of extensive war with the Mahrattas and Patans, necessarily involving the risk of a successful inroad from beyond our frontier, the mischief would be incalculable, if the slightest idea of the internal instability of our power were suffered to go abroad. It was therefore important to strike a blow, that should impress all ranks with a proper estimate of our vigour and military means.

Hatras † was reckoned one of the strongest forts in India. Dya-Ram was a Jât, and derived no small accession of confidence and estimation, from being a relation of the Bhurtpoor Raja, with whom he claimed equality of rank. The fort was kept in the completest state of repair, and every improvement that was

* The exemplary conduct of this detachment and of Captain Boscawen its commander would deserve a much more particular notice, if the plan of this narrative would allow of such a digression. The Rohillas penetrated the square, into which the detachment was compelled to form itself, before the fourth side could be completed by the falling in of the picquets and light infantry They were literally blown out again by the bold manœuvre of turning one of the guns at the angles inwards, loaded with grape.

† Vide plate at the head of the next chapter.

introduced into our neighbouring fortress of Aleegurh, such as preparing a covered way, raising a glacis, and levelling the height of the ramparts, was carefully copied by this suspicious chief. At the close of 1816, it was resolved to reduce both Dya-Ram and Bhugwunt Singh to the level of subjects, and to employ an overwhelming force for the purpose, as well to bear down all opposition, as to give *eclât* to the measure. The divisions from Cawnpoor, from Meeruth, and from Muttra, were accordingly ordered to concentrate upon Hatras, and place themselves under the immediate command of Major-General Marshall, the commanding officer in the field. On the 11th of February, the place was invested on all sides. Dya-Ram was then summoned to surrender a gate of his fort and allow of its being dismantled. After some evasion on his part, and a negotiation, which lasted till the 16th, he finally refused; when the siege immediately commenced. The Kutra, or fortified town, was breached and evacuated on the 23rd. Approaches were then made to the fort, and batteries erected under a smart, though ineffectual fire from the ramparts. By the first of March, the works of the besiegers were completed, and on the following morning forty-two mortars and three breaching batteries of heavy guns began to play on the fort. Such powerful means had never yet been employed against any fortified place in India. The effect was beyond measure destructive and astonishing to the garrison. The batteries continued to play till the evening, when, at five o'clock *, a magazine disproportionally large blew up within the place, destroying half the garrison and nearly all the buildings. The effect is described to have been awful. Dya-Ram with a few horse made his escape in the dark the same night; and, though challenged and pursued by a picquet of the 8th dragoons, got off with little damage. The rest of the garrison, in attempting

* The other magazine, one of yet larger dimensions, was likewise found penetrated by a shell; but the fuse had dropt out.

to follow, were driven in and obliged to surrender at discretion. Bhugwunt Singh agreed to dismantle his fort on the first summons; and thus was this important object gained, without any sacrifice of lives; the casualties * of the assailants in the siege being too inignificant to mention; while the impression of the utter futility of resistance spread far and wide through Hindoostan, and even through the remote Dukhun, where it materially influenced the subsequent conduct of the Mahratta chiefs and kuladars.

* Killed—one European, five natives.

CHAPTER IX.

NÂGPOOR—POONA.

1817. JANUARY TO JUNE.

Nâgpoor—Ram Chundur Wâgh—Sudeek Ulee Khan—Appa Saheb goes to Chanda—intrigues—death of Pursajee—by violent means—accession of Appa Saheb—change of policy—intrigues with Pêshwa—Poona—Pêshwa's duplicity—Trimbukjee levies troops—is covertly supported—Residents proceedings—Discussions with the Durbar—Subsidiary force called down—intercourse suspended—effect—operations against Trimbukjee—their success—Colonel Smith called in to Poona—terms of demand—refused—Poona invested—Bajee Rao submits—Governor-General's instructions—conduct of Pêshwa—New treaty signed—Its conditions—Reflections—Military movements.

EVENTS, that led to very important results, were passing at Nâgpoor and Poona, while the British were engaged with the Pindarees in the manner above described. At the former court, a party had been rapidly rising into favour, which threatened completely to undermine the influence possessed by those of the ministry, who had been instrumental in bringing about the subsidiary alliance with the English. At the head of this party was Ramchundur Wâgh, the commander of Appa Saheb's private troops, before his elevation to the regency; a man who had the character of a daring, deep-designing Mahratta. The Naeeb was himself of a restless disposition, and a great lover of intrigue; and it was not long before he showed a decided preference to the counsels most suited to this turn of mind. Instead of giving his attention to the reform of his internal administration, the object which the moderate men endeavoured to press upon him, he greedily listened to schemes for the concentration of all power

HATRAS FORT, FROM THE TRENCHES.

CHANDA.

in his own hands or those of his immediate dependants. Nagoo Punt was of that class; but Nerayun Pundit was one of the old advisers of Ragoojee; and having been the immediate instrument, whereby the British alliance had been effected, he was early thought to be too much attached to that nation, and to have its objects more at heart than those of the Bhoosla principality. So long, however, as Pursajee lived, and as there was a party in the state possessed of influence not derived from himself, Appa Saheb felt his dependance on his English allies, and did not venture to break finally with Nerayun, who was supposed to enjoy their fullest confidence. A plan was therefore laid to relieve the Naeeb from every source of apprehension on this head: and, in the course of January 1817, the following expedients were practised to carry it into effect.

It will be recollected, that Sudeek Ulee Khan had been received into apparent favour by Appa Saheb, instead of being degraded along with Naroba, the late secretary. He had contrived to make his peace through Ramchundur Wâgh, but was too independent in power and influence for the reconciliation to be complete. The large assignments of territory he enjoyed were also an object of envy, as well to the prince, as to the favourites by whom he was surrounded. Nagoo Punt and Nerayun were in the mean time, at the Resident's desire, continually urging a reform of the contingent furnished to the British under the treaty. The duty of providing and maintaining the stipulated force out of his assignments had been thrown upon Sudeek Ulee Khan; and its notorious incompleteness and inefficiency had afforded ground of continual remonstrance. After having for some time seemingly favoured the system as well as the individual, Appa Saheb resolved to avail himself of these complaints for the ruin of Sudeek Ulee; whilst, by making it appear that the measure was forced upon him by the British, and by leaving the execution to them, he hoped himself to escape the odium that would infallibly attend it.

On some slight pretence, towards the end of January 1817, the Naeeb left Nâgpoor, and went to the strong fort of Chanda *, situated about seventy miles south of the capital. Immediately after his departure, Nagoo Punt waited on Mr. Jenkins, with pressing instances, that he would take the opportunity of seizing the person of Sudeek Ulee, by means of the British troops at Nâgpoor. He declared, that Appa Saheb's principal reason for leaving the city was, to allow of this arrest; and showed a written authority, in the hand-writing of the regent, in proof that his sanction had been obtained. The paper, it is true, contained only an assurance, that Nagoo Punt had his entire confidence, and that a communication from him might be considered as authentic; but it is very unusual for Mahratta princes to give more specific credentials to those, whom they entrust with communications of the highest importance. The first overture on this subject was made on the 22d of January. On the Resident's hesitating to afford his direct interference, the request was repeated at subsequent interviews, when both Nagoo and Nerayun were earnest in soliciting him to act. Some further credentials were shown in testimony of Appa Saheb's desire in the matter; and as Sudeek, hearing that intrigues for his ruin were afoot, had begun to fortify his house, and make other defensive preparations, this circumstance was urged, together with sundry proofs that had been obtained of his being in correspondence with the Pindarees, to enforce the immediate necessity of strong measures. After some reflection, Mr. Jenkins finally resolved not to stir in a case of so much importance, without a written or verbal application from the prince himself, which should prevent the possibility of his afterwards disavowing

* Vide plate at the head of this chapter.

the act or pretending to be dissatisfied at it. But he strongly advised the ministers to execute the arrest with their own people, assuring them of his support in case it should be necessary, and only requiring that they, as the ostensible ministers, should take the responsibility of the deed in the first instance on themselves. For this Nagoo Punt was not prepared; for he knew, that though Appa Saheb would have been glad enough to have seen the ruin of Sudeek, he was far from wishing that it should appear to be his own act. Finding himself, therefore, unable to move the resident from this judicious resolution, he immediately rejoined his master at Chanda, leaving Sudeek Ulee Khan, for the present, without further molestation. The ruin of this officer was, however, only part of the plot, with the mature concoction of which the retirement of Appa Saheb to Chanda was connected. On the morning of the 1st of February, Pursajee Bhoosla, the reigning Raja, was found dead in his bed, without any alteration for the worse having been observed in his general health, or in the particular complaints under which he had for some time laboured. At the moment, no suspicion attached to any one; and though it was whispered about, that the Raja had met his death by violent means, Mr. Jenkins, who made private inquiries to ascertain the fact, could trace the reports to no certain source. He accordingly concluded them to be no more than the common rumours, which in India always attend the sudden death of a man in power; and, as the previous ailings of Pursojee made it less extraordinary that he should come to such an end, he treated the reports so lightly, as not even to mention them in his despatches to the Supreme Government, announcing the event. Afterwards, however, when upon Appa Saheb's deposition, free access was obtained to the servants and women of the interior of the palace, it was positively ascertained, that Pursajee was strangled about two o'clock in the morning; and there was reason to believe, that an unsuccessful attempt had previously been made, to administer poison in an offering of prepared betel leaf*, presented to him early in the same night by one of the Baees of the palace. Ramchundur Wâgh himself appears to have come to the palace about midnight, and to have given directions for the perpetration of the deed. Its actual execution was entrusted to a man named Mun Bhut, who afterwards rose to great power, and was a prime mover of the treacherous attack made on the residency in the November following.

Pursajee was 39 years of age. His body was burnt on the 10th of February; and his wife, Kashee Baee, ascended the funeral pile, and sacrificed herself upon it. Appa Saheb was immediately proclaimed successor to the Raja, by the name of Moodajee Bhoosla. The day of good omen for the new Raja's formal installation was not declared until the 21st of April following; but this did not prevent his at once assuming the titles and dignities of the head of the Bhoosla state.

Upon Appa Saheb's accession and return from Chanda, Sudeek Ulee Khan was received with marked attention; and, as Nerayun, one of the ministers, who had pressed the British Resident to complete his downfal, was treated with a coolness equally pointed, it was for some time matter of doubt, whether the plot for the ruin of the former had really originated with his Highness. It was soon afterwards pretty evident, that his secret disposition was as little favourable to the one as to the other: but some motives still existed, for practising deception towards the Moosulman soldier; while his elevation to the undivided honours of the Raja, under the sanction and formal recognition of the British Government previously obtained, rendered it no longer necessary for the prince to keep on terms with the minister, whom he suspected of favouring the British interest. About the end of February, Nerayun Pundit was especially removed from the conduct of the department of com-

* Pursajee rejected it, finding it bitter.

munication with the British Resident; and at first Purseram Rao, the very person whose intrigues in the lifetime of Ragoojee, Appa Saheb had himself betrayed to the Resident, before his own elevation to the Regency, was appointed in his stead. Mr. Jenkins remonstrated against the causeless removal of Nerayun, observing, that the disgrace of this minister had the appearance of being occasioned by his having exerted himself to induce his Highness to execute faithfully the treaty of alliance, especially that part of it which provided for the maintenance of the contingent in a state of efficiency; that the default in this respect, and the removal of the minister who had attempted to prevent it, were calculated to give the British Government a very unfavourable impression of his disposition towards the alliance; which was yet further increased by the selection of such a man as Purseram, to conduct the public communications with the English Resident. Appa Saheb was bent on the removal of Nerayun, and therefore would only listen to the remonstrance so far, as to nominate Ramchundur Wâgh to the office, instead of Purseram, who was obnoxious on such plausible grounds.

Reference being made to the Supreme-Government, it was determined not to authorize any more pressing instances for the restoration of Nerayun, through fear of increasing the new Raja's incipient dislike of the alliance. His sacrifice was, therefore, submitted to, notwithstanding that it was considered most evident, that his disgrace was owing to his exertions to procure the punctual execution of the treaty. Immediately on the fall of Nerayun, Nagoo Punt combined with Ramchundur Wâgh; and, in a very short time, every official station was filled by the new Raja's personal dependents. A persecution was also commenced against Goojaba Dada, who, fearing for his life, took refuge first with Nagoo Punt, and afterwards at the British Residency, whence he was ultimately conducted in safety to

Allahabad. In the mean time, negotiations were openly kept on foot with the resident vakeels of the Pêshwa, of Sindheea, and of Holkar: and, although circumstances arose at Poona, which placed Bajee Rao for a short time on a footing of direct hostility with the British, his representative at Nâgpoor received daily letters and had daily audiences with the new Raja, making communications, the substance of which was withheld from the British resident, in direct violation of the treaty concluded only twelve months before. Indeed, from the time that Appa Saheb felt himself secure in the full possession of the honours and authority of the Raja, he ceased to regard the British alliance as a necessary prop to his rule, and began to be sensible of the humiliation of appearing to the Mahratta nation, as the first of the Bhoosla dynasty who had made a voluntary sacrifice of political independence. It is true, there had not yet been time for the alliance to operate as a restraint on his personal direction of internal or external affairs; but it was not difficult for the designing men about him to convince him, that it must ultimately have that effect. He, therefore, eagerly listened to the invitations of the agents of the other Mahratta powers, to unite with them for the purpose of shaking off the connexion: nor was his personal vanity insensible to the flattery with which his alliance was courted, or to the distinction of being thought of so much consequence to the success of the coalition. Henceforward he lent himself wholly to the designs of Bajee Rao; and, in April and May, when matters were on the eve of a rupture with the latter, it was ascertained, that assurances of mutual support had passed between the two courts. But it is now time to state specifically the nature of the occurrences at Poona, to which allusion has more than once been made.

Trimbukjee Dainglia's escape, in September, has been already noticed. The place of his retreat could not be traced; but, during the early part of the ensuing cold season, he remained in perfect quiet; and though, as might have been expected, his master made no exertions to seize him, still it could not be discovered, that he either harboured or gave him ostensible support. There was consequently no interruption of the good understanding maintained by his Highness with the British Government. On the contrary, studious efforts were made by him to win Mr. Elphinstone's confidence; and, in this view, he solicited to be made a party to the plans which were, in the course of the season, supposed to be meditated by us against the Pindarees, and made a parade of issuing orders to his agent at Sindheea's camp, to refrain from intrigues, and only to meddle in the politics of that durbar, as far as they might have relation to his claims in Hindoostan; and even in them to do nothing without communication with the British Resident. He also professed a disposition to be satisfied with a very moderate composition for all his demands on the Gykwar, taking six lack of rupees a year, and giving up every thing else, but the right of investiture. The display of such an accommodating spirit, at a time when it was scarcely expected, was not at first attributed to a design in Bajee Rao to deceive the British Government. It was thought rather to have its origin in the desire to keep well with us at all events, however hostile his secret inclinations might be. The Marquess of Hastings resolved to encourage this disposition; and accordingly a copy of a remonstrance, made in January to Sindheea, on the subject of the late incursion of the Pindarees into Ganjam, was forwarded to Poona, together with some explanation of the grounds on which the British Government proposed to take early measures for the suppression of these hordes. This communication his Highness received in the course of February, with every demonstration of satisfaction at the confidence thus reposed in him.

In the mean time, the plot he had contrived was drawing to maturity. In the course of the months of January and February, Mr. Elphinstone heard of the collection of troops in the Mohadeo hills, to the south of the Neera, and about 50 miles south-east of Poona. He early represented the circumstance to the Pêshwa, who, with every appearance of alacrity, sent out a party of Gokla's troops to quell the supposed insurrection; protesting all along that he had himself heard nothing of the matter, and did not believe the existence of any thing of the kind. The detachment went to the spot, and reported that no insurgents were to be found or heard of; though it lay for some time encamped in the neighbourhood of the Mohadeo temple, holding daily communication with the armed bodies that had been there assembled. Early in March it was distinctly ascertained, that Trimbukjee was himself in that part of the country, and had for some time been making extensive levies. The 18th of March was talked of as the day appointed for his open appearance in arms; and the direct participation of Bajee Rao was evident, as well from general report, and from the conduct of the detachment sent to suppress the insurrection, as from positive information received of actual interviews between his Highness and that delinquent at Phoolshuhur, a village about 15 miles from Poona, which he gave many frivolous reasons for making the place of a lengthened stay. Large remittances of money, to the parts in insurrection, were also traced through several hands, in a manner that left no room to doubt their having been made from Bajee Rao to Trimbukjee and his adherents. The Pêshwa and his ministers persisted in stoutly denying the existence of any insurrection, or levy of troops, in the neighbourhood of Mohadeo. At the same time, all his Highness's forts were ordered to be put in a state of complete repair, and extensive levies of horse and foot were going on even at Poona and the vicinity; besides which, agents were sent with money into Malwa and other quarters, to invite men to the Dukhun, in order to enter his service.

Up to the 24th of February, Mr. Elphinstone had considered the insurrection as levelled equally against the Pêshwa's government and the interests of the British nation, and his communications with the Durbar were made in that belief. On that day, however, the reply of the Pêshwa's officer sent to quell it was put into his hands, which, combined with the other circumstances alluded to, satisfied him of the necessity of taking up the matter in its proper light, that is to say, as an underhand attempt of the prince himself to shake the British power. The early part of March was spent in remonstrances on one side, and on the other, in denials of the existence of any insurrection or assemblage of troops, and in protestations of readiness to do any thing that might be suggested, and to send troops to any place that might be named to put it down. Mr. Elphinstone declared he wanted no troops, that he should employ the British troops in dispersing the insurgents, and that the presence of those of his Highness would only lead to confusion: he demanded other proofs that the insurrection was not encouraged underhand; such as the placing Trimbukjee's known adherents and the members of his family under restraint, instead of which they were continued in office and in favour. He demanded also, that the enlistment of troops by his Highness should be discontinued, and the late extraordinary levies disbanded; that the repairs of fortresses, and the measures that were taking for storing them with grain and ammunition, should cease; adding, that while such things were going on, there could be no reliance on his Highness's sincerity, as such preparations could be meant against no other than the British. On one occasion early in March, Bajee Rao remonstrated against the style of the resident's communications, declaring them to be of a threatening nature, and calculated to produce a rupture. Generally, however, he met them by an outward show of acquiescence. Thus, on the 11th of March, part of Trimbukjee's family was placed under nominal restraint, and other ostensible measures taken of the same cast; while the most liberal promises were continually made, to discontinue every thing which gave offence. But the preparations continued with the same activity and more secrecy, as well at Poona and its neighbourhood, as in Kandêsh and other parts; and Trimbukjee's insurrection in the south was growing every day into more importance. About the middle of March, Mr. Elphinstone resolved to call down the subsidiary force, and to employ it forthwith in the suppression of the insurrection, and eventually against Poona, in case Bajee Rao's conduct should render it necessary. On the 21st of March, he solicited special instructions for the case of a continuation of these hostile preparations, and of the covert support of Trimbukjee's rebellion; stating it to be his intention to break off all communication with his Highness in the interim, and to announce the present relations of amity to be at an end, leaving it to his Lordship in council to restore them, with such demand of security for the future, as he might deem it proper to require. In communicating this to the Pêshwa, he stated his intention to assure him there was no design of committing acts of direct hostility, unless his Highness's preparations should render such proceeding necessary, or unless his Highness should attempt to leave Poona; in either of which cases, hostilities against himself would be commenced, without waiting the Governor-General's orders.

On the 1st of April these intentions were carried into effect: the continued preparations of Bajee Rao, which went the length of even collecting gun bullocks for the artillery in his arsenal at Poona, and of sending all the treasures, jewels, and wardrobe of his palace there to his strongest fort of Rygurh, having rendered it necessary no longer to defer bringing matters to this issue. Accordingly, on that day the resident sent in a note, wherein, after reproaching his Highness with the wantonness of the aggression on the British Government, which he had been abetting underhand, and after recapitulating the abundant proofs of his so doing, and of his preparing for hostility throughout his whole dominions, he notified the intention of immediately employing the subsidiary force for the suppression of the insurrection, and eventually for the support of the British interests against his Highness himself; declaring, that the good understanding between the two governments was now at an end, but that his Highness had one chance left of restoring it, that of disarming and waiting the Governor-General's determination, which if he showed a disposition to try, no act of hostility would take place against himself, though any attempt to leave Poona would be held a decided indication of war. The Poona brigade was ordered to hold itself in readiness, and Colonel Leighton, its commanding officer, was desired to take such precautions as he might deem necessary for the security of the residency and cantonment. Affairs were left in this posture at Poona, while the main body of the subsidiary force, which had previously been put in motion from the frontier, was formed into several divisions, whereof, one lightly equipped, and under Colonel Smith's personal command, hastened down to the southward to operate against the insurgents. Major M'Dowall, with the detachment that had beat up the Pindarees on the 15th of January, being still in the neighbourhood of Bidur, was at the same time called into Tooljapoor to co-operate; and another force, under Lieutenant-Colonel Thompson, was also summoned northward from the ceded districts of the Madras presidency. Mr. Elphinstone, in placing matters on this footing with the Pêshwa, acted in conformity with the instructions he had received from Lord Hastings during the first discussion respecting Trimbukjee, which had provided for the case of his leaving Poona, and raising disturbances in the country under the covert support of his master, and had prescribed the particular course now adopted in that event. The circumstances were completely analogous; the only difference being, that the delinquent had escaped into the interior, after having been surrendered to us, instead of before.

Bajee Rao was greatly alarmed when he saw matters brought to this issue. He sent his ministers to assure the resident of his disposition to do any thing that might be required, in order to restore things to their former state. It was distinctly explained, that this was now become impossible, as it depended entirely upon the nature of the instructions that might be received, in which most probably securities for the future would be made a condition precedent to the renewal of the former terms of friendship between the governments; that his Highness had to choose between two lines of conduct; if he resolved to accede unconditionally to what the Governor-General might determine, he would disband his new levies, and place his forts in their former condition, bringing back his treasure, and showing other signs of confidence: if he only waited the arrival of instructions to make up his mind, whether he would declare war or not, and wished to be understood so to do, he would leave things exactly in their present posture, but must take the consequences of the further loss of confidence resulting from the preference of the latter course. In the progress of the month, it was communicated to him through Major Ford, who still continued to be consulted and treated with confidence, that if his Highness seized and delivered up Trimbukjee before the arrival of the Governor-General's expected instructions, as he had done before, his conduct might again warrant the resident in suspending their immediate execution, and restore at once to the former relations of amity. The month was consumed in insincere negotiation on the part of the Mahratta court, evincing alternate resolutions to submit and to resist. More than once preparations were made for his departure from Poona; but the natural indecision and timidity of this prince's character kept him fixed to the spot to the last moment, in anxiety to know the extent of the demands that would be made upon him. Yet, instead of disarming in the interim, he increased the activity of his preparations.

During this suspense, the troops had begun to act against the insurgents. On the 7th of April, a body of 100 newly raised troops were traced to the village of Jumta, and there disarmed by Colonel Smith, and their chief confined. This was all that was done to the south of Poona; for the Pêshwa's influence had so completely set the country against us, that although that officer, with the light divisions, scoured all the neighbourhood in which the insurgents had been collected, no information or assistance could be got at any of the villages, nor could any other party of their force be discovered. They had, indeed, decamped from that part of the country immediately on the approach of the troops, with the design of removing the seat of war into Kandêsh. A body of 4000, chiefly horse, after having got clear off from Colonel Smith, was heard of in its way to the north by Major Smith, who commanded one of the detachments posted to cover Poona on the east. It was instantly pursued, and after a chase of 150 miles in four days, the Major succeeded in overtaking the party, about a march westward of Toka on the Godaveree. This body had fallen in with and cruelly murdered Lieutenant Warre, an officer of the artillery, travelling with a small escort. When attacked, they made little resistance, but dispersed with the loss of no more than fifty or sixty, for want of cavalry to pursue.

A more brilliant affair occurred in Kandêsh, where Godajee

Dainglia, a relative of Trimbukjee, was busily collecting partisans. Upon calling down Colonel Smith to the south, measures had been taken to put the Nizam's troops and the Hyderabad subsidiary force in motion, to counteract the designs of the insurgents to the north. Captain Sydenham, the political agent at Aurungabad, being apprised of Godajee's operations, despatched Captains Davies and Pedlar with a *resala*, in number about 600, of the reformed horse, and a small party of the reformed infantry of the Nizam, to the frontier of that prince's dominions in that direction, giving them instructions, if they should hear of the collection of troops, and could find an opportunity of striking a blow, to attack and disperse them without ceremony. Such an opportunity occurred on the 20th of April, when, after a rapid advance of fifty miles into Kandêsh, Captain Davies succeeded in falling in with a body of 2000, whereof near 300 were Arab infantry, the whole under Godajee himself. They took up a good position, and showed face; whereupon Captain Davies resolved not to wait for the infantry, but at once to charge sword in hand with the horse he had in advance. The charge was completely successful, insomuch that the loss of the enemy was not less than 400 left on the field. It should be noticed, that these were the same troops that two years before had refused to advance against a body of routed Pindarees. But they were now acting under the influence of the confidence inspired by an able commander, and impelled by the sense of duty created by the novel assurance of regular pay. Of Captain Davies's men, seventy-four were killed and wounded. Both the officers were amongst the number of the latter, a circumstance not to be wondered at; for the nature of the service required the example of a personal exertion on their part, which neither was of a disposition to spare. The new distinctions of modern warfare, which assign the use of the arm to the private soldier, and that of the head only to the superior, had not yet found their way amongst the class of men led by Captain Davies on this occasion. Several of the enemy fell by his own hand before he received his wound, which fortunately was not severe. Captain Pedlar's was more so, but still not dangerous. Nothing could be more creditable to the national character, than the exhibition, afforded by this conflict, of the superiority of troops similarly modelled, armed, and disciplined, and differing in no respect whatever from the enemy, except in the circumstance of their being led by the cool judgment and enterprising courage of British officers.

Mean while, affairs were coming to a crisis at Poona. On the 20th of April, Mr. Elphinstone found it necessary to increase the British force there, by calling in Colonel Smith with his light division. He gave notice to Bajee Rao that he had so done, stating the reasons, but assuring him that it would produce no alteration of his resolution to commit no act of direct hostility, unless his Highness compelled him to it, and to wait the receipt of his expected instructions. Discussions with the ministers and emissaries of his Highness continued as before, without producing any satisfactory result. On the 25th of April a private letter reached the residency from Mr. Secretary Adam, which opened in some degree the views of government, by showing the unconditional surrender of Trimbukjee, in case nothing should have been done by the Pêshwa in the interval, to be an indispensable preliminary to any new accommodation with him. The full instructions, which were despatched only the day after, the 7th of April, were detained for a fortnight, by an insurrection which broke out in Cuttack, and at this unlucky moment interrupted the Dâk* communication between Calcutta and Poona. Colonel Smith had arrived at Poona on the 26th, and taken up ground at the village of Kirkee. On the 3rd of May, the resident heard of the insurrection in Cuttack, and of the Dâk

* Dâk—post, conducted by native carriers on foot.

communication being cut off; he accordingly resolved to wait till the 6th for the chance of receiving the desired instructions, and, if not then arrived, to act on the imperfect intimation he already received of the Governor-General's wishes. On that day, no further despatch having arrived, Mr. Elphinstone solicited a private audience of his Highness the Pêshwa, in order to apprise him, that the only terms on which the British Government could consent to any accommodation with his Highness, after what had passed, were, his engaging to surrender Trimbukjee within a definite period, and his giving substantial security not to fail in this particular. Bajee Rao, who seemed prepared for the communication, distinctly refused the preliminary proposed, with the appearance of very unusual coolness of determination. He did not rest his case on his want of ability to apprehend the fugitive, for he would not even bind himself to make exertions for the purpose. On the next day, a written note was sent in to the same general purport as the verbal communication, but specifically requiring a covenant to surrender Trimbukjee within one month, and to deliver the three hill forts of Singurh, Poorundur, and Rygurh, as pledges for its performance. Twenty-four hours were allowed for his Highness to come to a final determination on this proposition; if not in the affirmative, immediate hostility was denounced. The note was received with apparent indifference, nor were its contents noticed until the morning of the 8th, when the time had nearly expired, and the troops were marching from the cantonment of the Poona brigade and from the village of Kirkee, to take up positions, according to a plan previously settled, so as completely to invest the city. The fears of this irresolute prince then predominated. None of his advisers, excepting Gokla and the commandant of his artillery, recommended a resort to arms. About ten o'clock in the morning, he sent vakeels, promising to agree to the terms, and to surrender the forts without delay. They were accordingly taken possession of in the course of that and of the following day. Rygurh was a place of peculiar strength, as indeed were both Poorundur and Singurh: but no difficulty was made in the delivery of them under the stipulation. On these preliminary terms, the Pêshwa was admitted to throw himself upon the ultimate determination of the Governor-General in council, as to the conditions on which a final accommodation should be made with him; but he was given to understand, that he must not expect the treaty of Bassein to be implicitly renewed.

On the 10th of May, arrived the instructions of Lord Hastings in council. They prescribed exactly the course already adopted, so far as it had gone; but provided distinctly for the three cases: first, of the actual surrender of Trimbukjee or sincere efforts of his master to seize him, before the arrival of the instructions; secondly, of the positive inaction of the prince; and thirdly, of his refusal or evasion, after receipt of the instructions, of compliance with the enhanced demand to be made upon him in the second case. In the first case, the relations of the treaty of Bassein were to be restored, and every thing placed on the footing of the previous settlement, made on the surrender of Trimbukjee in 1815. In the second case, the demand of the surrender of that delinquent within a time specified, and of hostages for performance was to be a positive preliminary to any accommodation; with the further understanding, that no renewal of friendship could take place, without the delivery of greater securities for the future, than the treaty of Bassein afforded. In the last case, that of decided war, the person of the prince was to be seized, and a temporary arrangement made for the government of the country. The further securities, to be insisted on in the second case, were, cessions of territory, including the fort of Ahmednugurh, to the extent of twenty-nine lack rupees, applicable to the raising and pay of a force of 5000 horse and 3000 foot on our own establishment, to replace the contingent of his Highness's troops, stipulated in the treaty of Bassein, but never furnished in full upon any one occasion: also, the surrender to the British of all claims on Guzerât, Bundelkhund, and in Hindoostan; and, generally, a renunciation of the supremacy of the Mahratta empire. The renewal of the farm of Ahmedabad to the Gykwar, and the restoration of affairs in that quarter to the footing established by Colonel Walker, were to form part of the new arrangement; and the opportunity was to be taken of settling some points of minor importance, which had for some time been the subject of mutual irritation. The Resident prepared himself to execute these instructions, as soon as the month assigned for the apprehension of Trimbukjee should expire. But he informed Bajee Rao of their arrival, and of the intimation therein, that his Highness had so far lost the Governor-General's confidence, as to have incurred the demand of greater securities for the future, without acquainting him with the probable extent of this ulterior demand. In the early part of the month, no sincere efforts were made to seize Trimbukjee, notwithstanding the security given; indeed, on the night of the 13th of May every thing was ready for the prince's flight from Poona, and he was on the point of departure; even so late as the 17th, he issued pay to his troops and kept up the appearance of a resolution to break finally with the British. On the 20th, however, he made up his mind to the opposite course. The adherents and family of Trimbukjee were put in durance, and proclamations issued in every direction, offering two lack rupees and a rent free village of 1000 rupees a year guaranteed by the British Government to any one, who should bring in the person of the fugitive. Copies of the proclamation were given to the Resident, that he might aid in their circulation. This conduct satisfied every body of the Pêshwa's present sincerity: indeed it placed Trimbukjee's apprehension, in a manner, beyond the influence of his master's caprice. Mr. Elphinstone accordingly resolved to consider these exertions as a sufficient atonement, and to accept his submission at the end of the month, if his conduct were not changed in the interval, whether the culprit should be seized or not, for delivery according to the letter of the covenant. On the 28th of May, Major Ford was authorised to acquaint the Pêshwa of the general nature of the demands that were to be made upon him, under the Governor-General's late instructions; and on the 1st of June following, the Resident went in person, and explained, article by article, a draft he had prepared of the new treaty. This varied from the instructions in some few points of minor importance; and in one material item, the amount of the cessions, fixing them at thirty-four instead of twenty-nine lack rupees, in order to cover extraordinary expenses of staff equipment, &c. of the forces to be raised and substituted for the Pêshwa's contingent, provision for which had been overlooked in the former estimate.

The Pêshwa and his minister endeavoured, with much dexterity, to reduce the sum of these demands, taking the ground of intreaty, and reliance on the compassion and generosity of the British Government. It was urged by the ministers, that their master's offences, whatever they might have been, did not deserve so heavy a punishment, or one so grating to his Highness's feelings; that we seemed to expect a strictness of fidelity beyond all reason, and more than a native potentate had it in his power to observe; and that, if we enforced so rigorous a fine, the world would cry out against us, and accuse his Highness of folly, in having originally formed the connexion with us. As proof of the wide scope of Bajee Rao's machinations against our interests was pouring in from every quarter, Mr. Elphinstone was inflexible in insisting on every article of his draft. On the 7th of June, the month allowed for the apprehension of Trimbukjee having expired, he demanded that the treaty should immediately be signed, the only proof of submission that could now be given; no reduction having been made in the levies of troops, and Trimbukjee not having been delivered up as agreed upon. Six days more were consumed in further discussion of the several items, and particularly in disputes respecting the districts to be ceded and the rates at which each should be taken. At length, on the 13th of June, the treaty was signed according to the original draft. The following is the substance. Article 1st renounces Trimbukjee Dainglia, engages to punish his adherents, and to surrender his family to the British Government, as hostages for his never being again countenanced. Article 2d re-establishes the treaty of Bassein, except as now modified. Article 3rd explains more specifically the former engagement not to take Europeans or Americans into the service of the Pêshwa. Article 4th engages, in further execution of the previous stipulation, respecting his Highness' conduct to other native powers, not to receive or send vakeels, or communicate in any manner, except through the British Resident: further, renounces the character of supreme head of the Mahratta empire. Article 5th commutes his Highness' past claims on the Gykwar for an annual payment of four lack rupees, in case Anund Rao should consent; if he should not, arbitration to be made under the treaty of Bassein: renounces all prospective claims unconditionally. Article 6th exchanges the proviso for the Pêshwa's contingent of 5000 horse and 3000 infantry, for an engagement to furnish to the British Government the means of maintaining an equal force. Articles 7th, 8th, 9th, and 10th, provide for the transfer and *arrondissement* of territories to be ceded for this purpose, with their forts, according to a schedule, and for the date and operation of the cessions from the 5th of June, the commencement of the Hindoo year. Article 11th authorises the discretionary increase of the subsidiary force and its employment in reducing the ceded districts.

Article 12th cedes Ahmednugurh with a glacis of 2000 yards, and engages to furnish pasture lands for the subsidiary force. Articles 13th and 14th cede to us rights over Bundelkhund and Hindoostan, or in Malwa. Article 15th renews the farm of Ahmedabad to the Gykwar, for an annual payment of four and a half lack rupees; exclusive, however, of the Katteewâr tribute. Article 16th ratifies the settlement of Pundurpoor, made the 6th of July 1812, for the adjustment of the Pêshwa's relative rights over the Jageerdars, and restores the Rasteea's forfeited Jageer. Article 17th stipulates the restitution of Melghât, an usurpation of Trimbukjee from the Nizam, in violation of the treaty of Bassein. Article 18th provides for the exchange of the ratifications in the usual manner.

The schedule alluded to in Article 7 specifies the following territories: 1st, the Konkan, or country between the sea and the western ghâts, to the north of the high road from Poona to Bombay, rated by Mr. Elphinstone at eleven lack rupees, but alleged by the Pêshwa's minister to yield considerably more; 2d, the whole of the Pêshwa's possessions in Guzerât, estimated at ten lack rupees, exclusive however of Ahmedabad Oolpar and the Gykwar's commutation-payment for past claims; 3d, the Katteewâr tribute, taken at four lack rupees; 4th, the forts of Darwar and Koosigul, with sufficient territory in the neighbourhood and south of the Wurda to make the entire annual revenue ceded equal to thirty-four lack rupees. The cessions were to be immediate, except the lands in the Carnatic, the extent of which would depend upon what might be found to be the value of the Konkan; but the two forts named were to be surrendered forthwith.

This treaty was ratified by the Governor-General on the 5th of July, 1817. It contains provisions for the settlement of all those points, that for a long time before had been the subject of acrimonious discussion at the Poona durbar, as well as for securing the British Government, as far as seemed possible, against a continuance of his Highness' treachery and secret hostility. The engagement being avowedly compulsory, and involving an aggrandizement of our own territories at the expense of our late ally, the first that had been made upon any Mahratta state since the settlement of 1805-6, was undoubtedly calculated to increase the apprehension and alarm, with which our power and policy were regarded. But the measure was exacted and warranted by Bajee Rao's indisputable perfidy; and the detection of it at the moment, when we were on the point of entering on a connected plan of operations, directed to the extirpation of the predatory hordes, would have justified a still further reduction of the means of this prince than was actually effected, nay, perhaps, have warranted his entire suspension from the exercise of any kind of authority and influence pending those operations. Subsequent events showed the danger of restoring him to any share of power, until the projected measures had been completed. It was hardly to be expected, that his pride could ever forgive the humiliation he had been subjected to, or that the sense of comparative weakness, which had been the motive of present submission, could for a moment influence his speculation on those ulterior chances, held out by the enterprise in which we were about to engage. This speculation, not his present condition, was the obvious source of all his subsequent treachery, and of all his past intrigues. Yet perhaps the risk was unavoidable; for an attempt to remove the head of the Mahratta nation entirely from power and consideration would, at this juncture, have been productive of much confusion, and must have contributed to exasperate the hostile disposition of that nation to an earlier and probably a more general ferment, at a moment too when we were less prepared. On the whole, there was equal moderation and justice in exacting, by way of safeguard against an ally of detected perfidy, whose services to a certain extent we were entitled to expect, that in lieu of the contingent he was himself bound to furnish to the cause, he should provide the means of maintaining an equal body at our own immediate disposition. As for the appeals made to our liberality and compassion after the final resolution to submit was taken, these were very justly allowed to have no weight in mitigating the terms imposed: such motives can have no legitimate influence, until confidence be completely re-established; and no part of the Pêshwa's conduct, from the time of our first connexion with him, had left an impression of his character, that entitled him to be restored to it in the former degree. The cessions now demanded, though extensive, were by no means a dead loss to his Exchequer; for he would henceforward be saved the expense of supporting, from his own resources, the force they would enable us to keep up. It should be recollected, that Bajee Rao had for ten years enjoyed the benefit of the British subsidiary force, without any corresponding pecuniary sacrifice on his part: for the cession of his Bundelkhund revenues, by way of subsidy, was a surrender of what he never had really possessed, what required an expensive military force to occupy, and what any other power would have been free to undertake the conquest of. For these reasons, it is fair to presume, that Bajee Rao will not be thought to have been too hardly dealt with on the present occasion.

The subsidiary force returned to Seroor immediately after the execution of the treaty, in order to prepare itself to take a part in the general operations of the ensuing season. One battalion, however, was detached to take possession of the cessions in the Konkan. The force that had moved into Kandêsh, under Colonel Doveton, succeeded in keeping under that part of the country, and ultimately in expelling from it Trimbukjee and his adherents. What most contributed to this was the gallant storm of a strong hold occupied by them, of the name of Dorana. Colonel Scott, of the 22d Madras native infantry, appeared before it with a detachment on the 10th of July, and resolved immediately to attempt an escalade. Making ladders of his tent-poles, he forthwith attacked the Petta, and carried it in several places. The garrison retired into the fort; which, alarmed at observing the further preparations for storming that point also, they likewise surrendered. After this, Trimbukjee's adherents ceased to make head, and he himself retired to Choolee Muheshwur on the Nerbudda, where he spent the rainy months with a few followers. Colonel Doveton moved back to his cantonment of Jâlna on the 17th of July.

CHAPTER X.

GENERAL PREPARATIONS.

1817, JUNE TO NOVEMBER.

Treaty of Poona executed—cessions adjusted—vakeels dismissed—advantages to Gykwar—increase of subsidiary force—consequent cessions and exchange of territory—Governor-General's plans—Hindoostan—Dukhun—Madras army—how disposed—delays in Dukhun—Lord Hastings leaves the Presidency—Political operations—their scale enlarged on Lord Hastings' sole responsibility—he takes the field—crosses the Jumna—General Donkin moves from Agra—negotiation with Sindheea—terms proposed—demand of Hindia and Aseergurh—reasons—treaty signed and ratified—consequent general order—its execution—Treaty with Ameer Khan—and Keroulee chief—Jaloun—Sâgur—Bhopâl.

The rainy season of 1817 was spent in preparations for a great military effort against the Pindarees, and whatever powers of central India might support them; and in arrangements for giving immediate effect to the several stipulations of the treaty of Poona, particularly those relating to the territorial cessions of the Pêshwa.

Less difficulty or evasion was experienced, in obtaining the punctual execution of the treaty, than might have been expected from the known personal character of that prince: but our continued possession of his three forts of Singurh, Rygurh, and Poorundur, to which, from their strength and vicinity to Poona, he was known to attach a high value, was a powerful motive for alacrity; since, without the unequivocal display of good faith on his part, he could scarcely have hoped for their restoration. The formal orders for the delivery of the forts and territories of Guzerat and the northern Konkan, together with those for Koosigul and Darwar, were obtained by the 18th of June; and as, with exception of the killadar of Darwar, none of the subordinate officers made any demur to implicit obedience, the whole of these districts were in our hands before the end of July, and the sole point remaining to be settled was, the value at which the Konkan should be taken, whence the extent of the further cessions to the south was to be regulated. It had been agreed to rate the Konkan at what the Pêshwa's accounts of the average for the past twenty years might show to have been the actual receipts from it, clear of all deductions, and with an allowance for the expense of collection. On reference to these, instead of their exhibiting a product of more than eleven lack rupees, the rate Mr. Elphinstone had been willing to allow, the net value was not found to exceed seven lack; so that, to make up the 34 lack rupees, a territory producing 13 would, under the treaty, have been demandable in the Carnatic, instead of nine as at first assumed. In consideration of his former offer to accept nine, the Resident, though he saw no reason why he should not draw the actual advantage, in the same manner as he must have abided the loss, still thought it right to act with some indulgence, and not to press with too much severity. Accordingly, he limited his present demand to 11 lack, notwithstanding which, many obstacles and delays were thrown in the way of the assignment of specific territory. The Resident, seeing this, made a written demand of Ranee Bednore, Soondoor, and some other districts, estimated to yield that amount: but, while this matter was under discussion, receiving intimation of an arrangement on foot with Futteh Singh Gykwar, to obtain Ahmedabad for the Company, he so far modified the demand as to take the 4½ lack rupees of rent, payable for the Pêshwa's moiety of that place by the Gykwar, instead of an equal cession towards the Carnatic, leaving 6½ lack only to be made good from that quarter. On this basis, an agreement was finally concluded in August; Darwar and Koosigul being taken at 84,000 rupees, and the Pêshwa's territories, south and eastward of the Wurda, to make up the remaining 566,000 rupees.

The other articles of the treaty had previously been executed. The resident vakeels of foreign states received their formal dismissal, at the time the first orders for surrender were delivered. Bajee Rao himself, after admitting Mr. Elphinstone to an audience, at which he seemed very sullen and dejected, quitted Poona on the 18th of June, on the pretence of his annual pilgrimage to Pundurpoor, leaving all minor arrangements to be settled by his ministers. The vakeels, though dismissed, were many of them natives of the Pêshwa's territories, and had, therefore, claims to be allowed a continued residence there, notwithstanding their dismissal from public employ. Hence, it was impossible to prevent the continuation of their intrigues; and, even if they had themselves been removed, other unacknowledged instruments and emissaries were at hand in abundance. Nevertheless, there was this advantage in the strictness of the 4th article of the treaty, that besides abolishing the formal character of the communications that passed between the Pêshwa and other powers, it imposed the necessity of concealing the instruments and existence, as well as the nature of the intrigues afloat; for it would thenceforward be a sufficient ground of complaint, that such things were passing, without waiting for proof of a hostile purpose, before they could be noticed. Thus, intrigue became much more hazardous to Bajee Rao; though he was not of a disposition to be deterred by such hazards. This, however, was not the only object contemplated at the time of imposing this humiliation. It was conceived to be the most public and effectual mode of proclaiming to the other princes of India, the new condition, in which the former head of the Mahratta empire was to be considered as having placed himself. The case was not one in which feelings of tenderness towards the pride of Bajee Rao were entitled to much weight: but, since it was of importance to eradicate in him the disposition to regard himself as the rallying point of the Mahratta nation, and, if possible, to remove this dangerous notion from others, the public dismissal of vakeels was thought to be a most effectual means of promoting the end, and in this view it was desirable to require it on this occasion.

The treaty of Poona, independently of its advantageous compromise of all past claims by the Pêshwa on the Gykwar family, for an annual payment of four lack rupees, gave the latter a most profitable lease of Ahmedabad, and remitted in perpetuity all tribute or compensation for military service, extinguishing thereby all pretensions of feudal superiority. These benefits, which together were reckoned considerably to exceed 20 lack rupees a year in value, were about to be accorded to the Gykwar, for no other merit or claim on his part, except the murder of his minister and representative, for which deed this might be considered as a just atonement exacted from a prince, who had by his conduct identified himself with the actual perpetrator of the crime. The Bombay Government, thinking the moment of our having made such considerable acquisitions for this ally favourable for urging separate objects of mutual advantage to the two states, determined, at the time of imparting the above benefits, to attempt to procure Futteh Singh's consent to provide funds for an increase of the subsidiary force, and thus to bear a more just proportion of the general charge incurred in the defence of Guzerât, than had hitherto been contributed by the Gykwar. The proposed addition to the subsidiary force was 1000 infantry and two regiments of cavalry for the Guzerât force. The troops subsidised at present consisted only of 3000 infantry, with no regular cavalry of any kind. With a frontier so exposed, as that of Gykwar, on the east, the north, and the west, such a force was obviously a very insufficient protection. Indeed, its acknowledged inadequacy obliged us always to keep a body of our own troops in the neighbourhood; many of whom, particularly a regiment of dragoons, (the King's 17th), were constantly acting with the subsidiary force, without any demand upon the Gykwar for the expense of a reinforcement so necessary to its efficiency, though he derived the whole advantage. Under these circumstances, and in consideration of the very flourishing condition into which the affairs of the principality had been brought since the establishment of our influence, as well as of the many advantages at different times secured by us for the family, the Bombay Government thought itself warranted in asking an increase of subsidy on this occasion, sufficient to make the force kept up strong enough to act independently in support of our interests in that quarter. It was resolved, at the same time, to urge a further reduction and reform of the irregular and efficient, though very chargable military establishment maintained by the Gykwar himself. The Supreme-Government signified its entire approval of the proposition, if Futteh Singh's assent should be obtained.

The provision for this additional subsidy, most desired by the Bombay Government, was the moiety of the Katteewâr tribute, realized by its own agency for the Gykwar. The other half of this tribute had been enjoyed by the Pêshwa, and was included in the cessions of the treaty of Poona; consequently, it was an object to exclude all foreign influence but our own from that part of the country. To this, however, Futteh Singh showed a decided repugnance; but the advantages of the farm, just obtained of Ahmedabad, were tendered in lieu of it, and ultimately accepted, with some further rents of inferior importance, to complete the sum required for the increase of subsidy. A further arrangement was afterwards made for the exchange of the interest in Ahmedabad, held by the Gykwar, independently of the farm, for three pergunnahs of our own, situated inconveniently near to Brodera. These were Dubhoee, Bhadhurpoor, and Saolee, yielding altogether near three lack, an amount which was expected to exceed the value of the interest accepted in exchange. Other advantages also had accrued to us from the treaty of Poona, affording the means of advantageous exchanges; and the opportunity was taken of improving our frontier, and consolidating our scattered possessions in Guzerât, so as to avoid the frequent collision of a divided authority, which existed under the former relations with the court of Brodera. The negotiation was conducted on the principle of equal exchange: but such are the habitual delays of a Mahratta durbar, and such the pertinacity with which it seeks to drive the hardest bargain possible, that the treaty was not concluded until the 6th of November, 1817, and much further matter yet remained to be adjusted; insomuch, that the agreement was not forwarded for the final ratification of the Governor-General, until the November following. The mutual transfers then amounted to 578,848 rupees: amongst them, in addition to what have above been mentioned, the British Government ceded its moiety of the town of Pittawud for the Gykwar's moiety of Oomrut, by which, and other similar exchanges, the possessions of both were consolidated and improved. The hitherto indefinite frontier of our immediate territories in Guzerât was fixed by these arrangements. The pergunnahs of Gogo, Bhaonugur, and Sehoree, are the most southernly; thence a line through Ranpoor to Patree on the lesser Rin, and eastward from Patree through Vurungam, Ahmedabad, and Kuppurwunj, to Bala-Sinore and Beerpoor on the Myhee, forms our western and northern boundary; the Myhee is our boundary to the east.

The only other changes consequent upon the treaty of

Poona, which are of sufficient importance to require notice, were those which arose out of the cession of the Pêshwa's rights in Hindoostan and Bundelkhund. But, as the settlement of these fell in with the preparations and general plan of the ensuing campaign, it is better to leave each separate case to find its place amongst the transactions, that brought us into contact with the party whom it concerned. The cession of these rights by the Pêshwa, just at this time, gave us a great advantage in the subsequent operations: had they remained vested in Bajee Rao, as they would have done in the event of no rupture having occurred with him, and the expectation of thus acquiring the disposal of them could not have been anticipated, the peaceable settlement of central India would have been embarrassed and impeded by long and intricate disputes, and clogged at every step by endless intrigue and irritating discussion. The disposal of these benefits was desirable, rather as a means of effecting other objects by their exchange, than with a view to appropriate the whole to ourselves, as was abundantly verified by the actual result. Proceed we now to explain the general plan of operations, devised for the execution of the Supreme-Government's determination to suppress and extinguish for ever the existing mischief of predatory associations.

The plan of Lord Hastings embraced the whole circle of the reserved possessions of Sindheea and Holkar, including likewise a great part of Rajpootana. Within these limits, it was his intention, if possible, wholly to confine the campaign, by surrounding them with a cordon of efficient corps, which should converge simultaneously towards a common centre; making provision, however, for the possible event of the enemy's passing this barrier, and by no means neglecting the defence of our own territories. On the side of Hindoostan, it was his Lordship's intention to have four divisions in the field, each of sufficient strength to act independently under any circumstances; besides two corps of observation, to guard the most exposed part of our frontier, in case the enemy should find the opportunity of undertaking an offensive enterprise. The points at which the several corps were ordered to collect were, Kalinjur in Bundelkhund, some point on the Jumna midway between Calpee and Etâwa, Agra, and Rewaree. The two corps of observation were to be stationed, one about Rewa, to the south of Mirzapoor and Benares, and the other further eastward, in the southern extremity of Behar *. On the side of the Dukhun, his Lordship expected to have in the field at least four substantive corps and a reserve, each of strength enough to act independently. In Guzerât a corps was also to be formed, to penetrate in a north-easterly direction, and complete the cordon of the intended area of operations.

It was his Lordship's design to assume the personal direction of the different movements, and to fix his head-quarters with the centre division of the Bengal army, appointed to rendezvous between Calpee and Etâwa; and it was deemed necessary, with a view to ensure a due consistency of action on the side of the Dukhun, to request the Commander-in-Chief of the Madras Presidency to take the personal command of the troops between the Nerbudda and Kishna; and to regulate the disposition of the forces to be there collected, so as to fall in with his Lordship's projects on the side of Hindostan. Sir Thomas Hislop accordingly took the field, under the Governor-General's orders, on the 21st of June; and was vested with full political powers, in addition to his military command. Colonel Sir John Malcolm, an officer of the Madras Establishment, of high name and merit, had returned to India in the beginning of 1817; and,

* Beyond Behar to the east, the Bengal southern and western frontier was considered to be sufficiently guarded by the troops already in position at Midnapoor and Cuttack; but, on the defection of the Nâgpoor Raja, a reinforcement was sent from the Presidency, in which a squadron of dragoons was included.

happening to come to Bengal to wait upon the Governor-General, just at the time when the plan of operations for the ensuing season was under deliberation, he was thought a fit person to be employed as the political agent on the part of the Governor-General, to aid Sir Thomas Hislop in that capacity; but with a commission to act separately, with the concurrence of Sir Thomas Hislop, whenever circumstances might require it. This officer was in consequence made acquainted with the whole of the plans in contemplation, and returned to the head-quarters of the Madras army early in July, carrying with him the commissions of Brigadier-General for himself and Colonels Doveton, Smith, Floyer, and Pritzler. Sir John Malcolm immediately set out on a tour to the several native courts, in order to concert measures with the respective British residents; while Sir Thomas Hislop was engaged in making the military dispositions for the approaching campaign.

Lord Hastings was extremely desirous of having two corps at least upon the Nerbudda by the close of the rains, if possible; wishing rather to fall upon the Pindarees, while their power of rapid movement would be cramped by the swollen state of the rivers. Colonel Adams, with the Nâgpoor subsidiary force, was already at Hoshungabad: the other force was to be assembled at Hindia, lower down the river. A movement from both these points, in combination with the left division of the Bengal force from Bundelkhund, in the direction of Sâgur, would effectually drive the Pindarees from their usual haunts above the ghâts into Malwa.

The troops under Sir Thomas Hislop's command, exclusive of the reserve, which was ordered to collect in advance of Adoni, and placed under Brigadier-General Pritzler's direction, amounted to four battalions of European and thirty-one and a half of native infantry, eight regiments of native cavalry, a squadron of dragoons, two of horse artillery, and seven and a half companies of foot artillery. Besides the above, there were six battalions of the Nizam's reformed infantry, and 4000 horse, under European officers: also 4000 Siladar horse, raised for the campaign by the Raja of Mysore, under the stipulations of the treaty contracted with him; and the troops of Salabut Khan, a powerful jageerdar of the Nizam, settled under our guarantee at Ellichpoor in Berar. The following was the disposition made of these extensive means: Colonel Adams was already at Hoshungabad with the Nâgpoor subsidiary force, which was constituted the fifth division of the army of the Dukhun. To Hindia Sir Thomas Hislop intended to proceed in person, with a division, to be called the first, composed of a squadron of dragoons and two regiments of native cavalry, one European and six native battalions of infantry, with field artillery, but no battering train. A brigade of the Nizam's infantry, the Mysore horse, and Salabut Khan's troops, were, with a few regulars, to be formed into a separate division, the third, to proceed in advance, under the command of Sir John Malcolm. Colonel Doveton's force was constituted the second division, and appointed to manœuvre in Berar, in support of Sir Thomas Hislop, and for the security of the Nizam's territories. Colonel Smith's force was destined to form the fourth division, and to operate in Kandêsh to the south of the Sâtpoora range of hills, which divides the valleys of the Taptee and Nerbudda, keeping in communication with Colonel Doveton on one side, and with the Guzerât force on the other. Sufficient provision was thought to be made for the doubtful disposition of Bajee Rao and the Poona Mahrattas, as well as for the Nizam's weakness and the turbulence of the Patans of Hyderabad, by leaving three native battalions, reinforced by half the Bombay European regiment, at the former place, and a force similar in every respect at the latter; both under the support of the reserve assembling in advance of Adoni, and capable of being further supported by the divisions of Brigadier-Generals Smith and Doveton, who were purposely held back from the most advanced line of operation, that they might be available in either direction. At Nâgpoor the force was smaller; consisting of only two weak Madras battalions, and three troops of Bengal cavalry. There was certainly no hostile appearance in the conduct of our allies, at the time the above military dispositions were made. Yet Mr. Elphinstone leaned to the opinion, that the irritated feelings of Bajee Rao, while the humiliations put upon him by the treaty of Poona were fresh in his memory, rendered it unsafe to carry the subsidiary force to a distance from the capital. But he yielded to the more confident judgment of Sir John Malcolm, who, on his arrival at Poona on the 5th of August, finding the Pêshwa still absent, went out by dâk, a distance of ninety miles, to meet him; and, after having been received with great attention at two audiences, returned with the avowed conviction, that his Highness could not be meditating any fresh hostility. He urged also the advance of Colonel Smith to the north at an early period, as of material importance to the success of the general plan.

The arrival of the Madras forward divisions at the points assigned to them was retarded by a continuance of heavy rain beyond the usual season, as well as by an attack of illness, of which Sir Thomas Hislop recovered with difficulty, and some other untoward circumstances: so that the first division, instead of arriving at Hindia by the beginning of October, as was intended, did not reach that point until the 10th of November. The operations on the side of Hindoostan were in some degree retarded in consequence. It is necessary to mention them more in detail.

The Marquess of Hastings embarked a second time on the voyage up the Ganges on the 8th of July, 1817. He arrived at Cawnpoor in September, having stopped nowhere on the route, except for a very few days at the city of Patna, whither a complimentary deputation had come down from Katmândhoo, to which it was thought politic to show every possible attention. In consequence of the delay on the side of the Dukhun, the Bengal troops were not put in motion till the middle of October; the 10th of that month being fixed upon for the rendezvous of the Bundelkhund army, and the 20th for that of the centre and Agra columns. The Rewaree force was intended to act as a reserve, and was therefore not required to be so early in motion.

In the interval, the political operations had commenced. The Supreme-Government felt itself authorized, by the instructions already received from England, to undertake active measures for the suppression of the predatory hordes, so far as the dislodgment of the Pindarees from their haunts in Malwa and Sâgur, and to make such arrangements with the chiefs in the neighbourhood, or those to whom we might restore the lands recovered from the Pindarees, as should secure us against their re-establishment in that part of the country. The Marquess of Hastings had himself always been of opinion, that, without a complete reform of the condition of central India, that is to say, without so altering the relations of the several princes and associations one to another, as to remove all inducement to predatory and ambitious adventure, on the extensive scale on which it was now prosecuted, no partial measures, however brilliant or successful on our part, and distressing to the adventurers for the time, could prevent the speedy recurrence of the evil, and probably in a more formidable shape. His Lordship saw plainly, that with mere temporary expedients, the work would be left to be done over again, and that there could be no security for the future in any plan that did not settle, or provide the means of settling, every one's pretensions to dominion, so as to leave a broad line of demarcation between the Chief of a regular government and the leader of lawless banditti. The whole of central India was at present the arena of a general scramble for dominion. It was requisite at length to fix who should be acknowledged as the lawful possessors now and from this time forth. His mind was fully convinced, that without doing this, and without binding the recognised possessors in such a league, as should on one hand check their disposition to encroach on each other, by the prospect of certain loss of the stake each possessed, and, on the other, should unite them all by a sense of common interest against a common depredator, little would have been done towards the eradication of the prevailing habits of predatory adventure, which were the grand object of anxiety and alarm. He did not despair of being able to form such a combination, by offering the general guarantee and protection of the British Government; though it was evident, that nothing short of that inflexible rigour of control and irresistible power of enforcing obedience to its award, which the British Government alone could exercise, could possibly impose a due degree of restraint on the passions and ambition of a host of greedy pretenders, aspiring by right of birth, or of the sword, to the territorial sovereignties of this wide expanse.

His Lordship hoped, that the principal Chiefs, Sindheea and Holkar, would voluntarily second the design upon a proper invitation, for both had reason by this time to know, that the fortunes of their families were on the wane; and though the invitation promised to gratify no ambitious views of aggrandizement, at any rate it would rivet their dominion over their remaining territories, and ensure to their families the entire inheritance, instead of a dilapidated succession, fast decreasing, day after day, by waste and usurpation, similar to what had been witnessed for the last ten years. The great officers of both families, who had already tasted of these usurpations, and probably expected further to gorge their appetite, were the persons from whom the most serious opposition to the plan was to be feared; but even they might be won over by the proffered guarantee of their past gains against the caprice of a master and the fickleness of fortune; and then, in fact, the needy and desperate alone would heartily oppose the execution of the design. To Ameer Khan it was resolved to offer such a guarantee immediately: his actual independence of Holkar might fairly be assumed, from his whole conduct since Juswunt Rao's death. Sindheea's sirdars, on the contrary, could not be separately treated with, unless the temper of that prince should be declaredly inimical.

Such was the outline of the policy which Lord Hastings determined to observe towards the Mahratta powers of central India. In furtherance of it, he did not hesitate boldly to assume the principle, that in the operations against the Pindarees, no one could be suffered to be neutral, but all should be required to join in the league for their suppression, under conditions, securing their active co-operation, as well in the present measures of cure, as in the ulterior preventive efforts against the future rise of these or similar associations into dangerous importance. The independent principalities, like Bhopâl and some of the Rajpoot states, were likewise to be included in the league, on the condition of a moderate tribute, sufficient to defray the expense of our general protection of all; but in all cases where Sindheea or Holkar could establish the right to a separate tribute, that also was to be confirmed to them under British guarantee. The orders for the simultaneous execution of this extensive plan of concert throughout every part of India, were issued towards the end of September. It had been originally intended to wait till the armies were in the field; but the discussions respecting the march of part of Sir Thomas Hislop's army by the route of Sindheea's territory of Boorhanpoor, rendered it necessary that the communication of our designs should not be longer delayed: suspense in respect to them being always more prejudicial than a direct knowledge of the worst that is to happen.

The negotiations with Holkar, Ameer Khan, Jypoor, Joudhpoor, Oodeepoor, and the other Rajpoot states *, were entrusted to Mr. Metcalfe, the resident at Dehlee. Captain Close, the resident at the durbar of Sindheea, was appointed to conduct the negotiations at Gwalior. The revision of our relations with the Bundēla Chiefs, who owed tribute or allegiance to the Pêshwa, viz. those of J'hansee, Sumtar, Jaloun, Dutteea, and Tearee, and the settlement with Benaeek Rao, who, on behalf of a Mahratta woman, administered the affairs of Sâgur † proper, were confided to the political agent in Bundelkhund, Mr. Wauchope. The resident at Nâgpoor was directed to tender to the acceptance of Nuzur Mahommed of Bhopâl the terms which had been proposed to his father in 1814-15, and to require him, in case of his acceding to them, to forward without delay a written paper containing the several stipulations, preparatory to the advance of Colonel Adams through his territories. Nuzurgurh was named as the fort to be required of him for a depôt. The arrangements of detail were left to Sir Thomas Hislop and Sir John Malcolm, whose arrival on the Nerbudda was then shortly expected.

In communicating the course he was about to adopt to the council at Fort William, the Marquess of Hastings briefly de-

* Kota, Boondee, Banswara, Bikaneer, and Jesselmeer. There was also a late dependent of the Pêshwa's, the Keroulee Chief, with whom engagements were to be made at this residency.

† The Jalounman, Nana Govind Rao, was the hereditary Chief of Sâgur; but as it was a principle with us not to disturb occupancy, unless the occupant should range himself on the side of the enemy, Benaeek Rao was to be permitted to engage for what he held of Sâgur, notwithstanding the abstract right of Govind Rao.

clared his reasons for deviating from the more limited views that seemed to be entertained in England, and at the same time expressed a confident hope, that the enlarged plan he had laid down for the secure and permanent attainment of his object would meet with the assent of the most considerable princes of central India. "It was his boast," he said, "to have "an earnest desire to accomplish every thing by pacific means, "and to be able to declare with sincerity, that the exclusive "object of his present preparations was to get rid of the greatest "pest that society ever experienced." He did not hesitate to take upon himself the undivided responsibility of acting without the full sanction of the home authorities; for he felt confident the result would justify his determination in the eyes of those authorities, and of the British nation at large.

On the morning of the 16th of October, the Governor-General took the field in person, and on the 20th reached the rendezvous of the centre division of the grand army, which was appointed to assemble at Secundera on the Jumna. The next day the force was reviewed. It consisted of two battalions of European and seven battalions of native infantry, five squadrons of European dragoons, and eight of native cavalry, besides two troops of a newly-raised corps mounted on dromedaries. There were also three troops of horse artillery, together with a light and heavy train, and every equipment for a siege, in case it should be found necessary to undertake any enterprise of that nature. The number of fighting men of the regular army attached to this division exceeded 12,500. On the 26th of October, this force crossed the Jumna on a bridge of boats constructed for the purpose, and thence proceeded in its march direct upon Gwalior, by the route of Jaloun and Seonda. The right division under Major-General Donkin, in strength about 4000 infantry and 3000 cavalry, including an irregular corps, moved simultaneously in the same direction from Agra. The time of movement was so calculated, that the centre division should arrive at Seonda on the Sindh on the same day that General Donkin reached the Chumbul at Dholpoor Baree; after which both forces would advance on Gwalior, or prosecute other operations, according as circumstances might require. Their approach accelerated and fixed Sindheea's determination to agree to the terms, upon which his co-operation in the campaign had been demanded. Yet he did not sign the treaty till the 5th of November, when the two armies were respectively within but one march of the point assigned to them on his frontier. It will be necessary to give at some length the particulars of the negotiation.

In the month of September, the resident first mentioned in durbar the march of our troops from the Dukhun to the Nerbudda by the route of Boorhanpoor, and applied, as a matter of mere form, for orders to his Highness' officers on the route to allow a free passage, and to afford every aid and facility due to us as friends and allies. At this period, the military at Gwalior were more tumultuous than ordinary, having actually beset the quarters of the Chief with the clamorous demand of immediate payment of arrears, and held him in personal restraint. The talk of Bajee Rao's positive determination to break with the English was general through the camp; and the wish for Sindheea to join him in hostility was evidently the prevailing sentiment, insomuch that it was greatly feared he would be driven to this course. It seemed very doubtful, however, what line of conduct it was the real intention of Sindheea to adopt. The reply of the durbar to the application for passes contained an assurance, that his Highness had not given up the intention of himself taking measures against the Pindarees; and a hope was expressed, that, on hearing this, the march of the troops might be stopped, till it was seen what could be done. This being declared impossible, after what had occurred in the last two years, the passports were prepared and despatched on the 1st of October.

The knowledge of our preparations on both sides of India augmented the ferment and confusion amongst the troops of Sindheea, and completely distracted the mind of the chief. In the hope of allaying this in some degree, it was resolved, as above noticed, not to defer the communication of our views and designs to the durbar, until the military preparations should be more advanced. Accordingly, between the 10th and 15th of October, the Governor-General's views were completely unfolded to his Highness, by the presentation of a note prepared and sent for the express purpose from head-quarters. This exposè, after remonstrating with Sindheea for having harboured the freebooters, that during two successive years had ravaged our territories, and for having fed us with empty promises of punishing the perpetrators of these enormities, while both before and since he was in constant correspondence with them, and was even supposed to share the booty, went on to combat the plea he had advanced, of inability to control their acts. Admitting it as a personal exoneration of his Highness, it was nevertheless declared to constitute a virtual dissolution of the treaties, concluded with him under a different impression respecting the efficiency of his government; more especially to annul those stipulations, which left his Highness free and independent in his dealings with all feudatories and dependents in Malwa, Mewur and Marwar, and prohibited our interference in their affairs. Of course, the moment he ceased to have the power of restraining the hostility of such dependents, when directed against ourselves, the restriction upon our taking measures for the purpose could no longer be suffered to have a binding effect. The note professed, that the British Government sought no objects of private advantage, but merely the suppression of the Pindarees, and the final and total extinction of such associations; and asserted, that to this object its plans would be exclusively directed: and his Highness' hearty co-operation was demanded, in the mode which the Resident would explain. It was further notified, that any harbouring of the Pindarees, or reception of them into his ranks, or any encouragement of others in such conduct, would be regarded as an act of unequivocal hostility. A hint was thrown out, that, if his Highness could not control the acts of any of his more immediate subjects or officers than the Pindarees, the British Government was willing to engage to lend its aid for the purpose of enforcing obedience. But, if they should assist or give asylum to the freebooters, it would be indispensable that they should be dealt with as enemies to both governments.

Captain Close was instructed, in case Sindheea agreed to the propositions of the above note, to submit to him the following terms of concert. His troops to be at our disposal entirely, and either to be stationary, or to be employed, at our option, with a British superintending officer attached to each division. Funds to be provided for the punctual payment of the force to be employed, and which was fixed at 5000 horse, by assignment for three years of the stipends receivable from us under the treaty of November 1805, and of the tributes demandable from Joudhpoor, Boondee, and Kota. Doulut Rao himself was not to move from Gwalior, or such other station as might be indicated; but this and some other points of less moment were not to be made the matter of direct stipulation, lest they should have too humiliating an appearance. It was thought indispensable to require some security for the good faith with which Sindheea might enter into the above stipulations. The demand of the two forts of Hindia and Aseergurh, to be retained during the war, was accordingly resolved upon. The only material difficulty, experienced in the negotiation, was, in procuring the cession of Aseergurh. Objections were, indeed, started to the assignment of the stipends and tributes, on the ground, that the former had been already assigned to individuals, and that of the latter there were arrears due, for which it was desired to obtain our guarantee. These points were, however, given up comparatively without difficulty: but with respect to the stipulation for the surrender of Aseergurh, which was considered one of the strongest forts in India, and the key of the Dukhun, the greatest repugnance was evinced. The discussions were brought, in the end, to the single point, who should bear the expense of its reduction, in case of the Killadar's resistance, and to whom the fort should belong, if captured under such circumstances. At first, the ground of pride had been taken, and the humiliation of the cession was objected; but this was got over by the Resident's agreeing to allow his Highness's flag to fly, and a nominal garrison and Killadar to remain in ostensible possession, if our troops were admitted in such numbers, as to amount to a substantial occupation. At length it was settled, that, even should the Killadar resist, the property of the fort should not be lost to Sindheea, unless his collusion should be clearly detected. But a firmer stand was made upon the other point, viz. who should bear the expense of reducing it in that case; for Captain Close, having reason to suspect that orders had early been issued to the Killadar to resist at all hazards, was urgent to throw the burthen of the consequences of such treachery upon the guilty party. The expense of taking Aseer, if resistance should be offered, was finally made chargeable upon the stipends and tributes to be ceded; which was, in fact, nearly equivalent to a concession of the point on our part; this fund having already been placed beyond Sindheea's control by the other stipulations. For, although we had engaged, at the end of the three years, to render an account of the appropriation of this money, and repay any balance that might remain, beyond the actual expense of the 5000 horse, still we were to have the ordering of the expenditure; and, as it would be our interest to see that the whole fund was employed in this way, for the horse would be efficient, in proportion as their pay was liberal, it was evident Sindheea could not expect that any part would be left unappropriated. Thus, it mattered little to him what further charges were thrown upon it.

With respect to Hindia, a place of little strength, though of some consequence from its commanding some of the best fords and passages of the Nerbudda, no difficulty whatever was made; and it was surrendered by the Killadar on the first summons. The subsequent occurrences in the Dukhun prevented the Governor-General from allotting a force to the immediate reduction of Aseer; indeed, the course of events showed, that its possession was not of the importance that had been supposed on the one hand, nor requisite on the other to keep in check the court of Gwalior. It was well, however, to have the right of demanding it, should circumstances have rendered it expedient in any possible turn the war might have taken. The public declaration of Sindheea's assent to our occupation of it was moreover advantageous, inasmuch as it marked his entire acquiescence in our plans, and abandonment of the cause of those, who were prepared to offer opposition. It was demanded, partly as a safeguard against treachery and vacillation; and doubtless some security was necessary; for we were already possessed of proof of Sindheea's intrigues with Bajee Rao and the Pindarees; besides which, a secret correspondence between him and the court of Katmândhoo had very recently been detected*. But a much more substantial security

* Accident led to this discovery. A full-size impression of Sindheea's seal happened to drop from the turban of one of his emissaries, while in the act of crossing the Ganges at Bithoor. Suspicion was of course excited, and he was stopped along with his companion. On searching them, letters, written with the design of stirring up the Goorkhas to make common cause with the rest of the

for Sindheea's conduct than the surrender of any number of forts could give, was to be found in the proximity and disposition of our armies. Had he delayed the signature of the treaty another day, orders had been issued to the Resident to advance his demand, by requiring the perpetual cession of the Ragpoot tributes, together with the district of Ajimeer, in addition to the other stipulations. He affixed his signature on the very day these orders arrived, and thereby avoided these fresh demands.

On the 6th of November, the day after the treaty was executed, it was ratified by the Governor-General, and the circumstance was communicated to the army under Lord Hastings' command, in the following short but expressive general order.

" The Governor-General has great pleasure in announcing " to the army, that the Maha Raja, Doulut Rao Sindheea, has " signed a treaty, by which his Highness engages to afford every " facilitation to the British troops, in their pursuit of the " Pindarees through his dominions, and to co-operate actively " towards the extinction of those brutal freebooters. In conse- " quence, the troops and country of his Highness are to be " regarded as those of an ally.

" The generous confidence and animated zeal of the army " may experience a shade of disappointment, in the diminished " prospect of serious exertion; but the Governor-General is " convinced, that the reflection of every officer and soldier in

independent powers of India, were found neatly pasted between the leaves of a Sanscrit book of the Vedas, which one of them, travelling in the character of a student, was carrying with him. Several sealed and some open letters from the chief himself were found upon them. The former were sent by his Lordship to be presented to his Highness in full durbar, unopened and without comment, in order that he might not suppose us to be ignorant of the intrigues and machinations afoot, and might be cautious not to provoke our vengeance by any overt act of hostility.

"this army will satisfy him, that the carrying every desired "point by equity and moderation is the proudest triumph for "the British character."

Officers were immediately appointed to proceed to Sindheea's several corps. Major Bunce of the king's 24th dragoons was sent to Bahadhur-gurh, Baptiste's head-quarters; but Baptiste had gone off to Gwalior before his arrival, and the second in command said he could not receive the Major without express orders from his superior. Major Ludlow was ordered to Ajimeer, where Bapoo Sindheea was stationed; and Captain Caulfield to Juswunt Rao Bhâo's camp at Jawud; but neither the state of that part of the country, nor that of the troops of this chief, were such as to allow of his joining for some time; as will hereafter be more particularly mentioned.

Although Sindheea was thus compelled to sign the treaty, it was not to be expected, that he would heartily join in the cause; and he endeavoured for some time to evade its stipulations, by every means in his power. For the first six weeks or two months afterwards, no effort whatever was made by him to furnish the 5000 auxiliary horse stipulated for; nor was any disposition shown to give us effectual co-operation. He was evidently on the watch for some insight into the probable result of what was passing with the other Mahratta powers, all of whom brought matters to the extremity of open war, in the course of November and December. Bajee Rao took the lead, by attacking the Residency and British troops at Poona, on the very day of the signature of the treaty at Gwalior. As long as the other Mahratta chiefs continued in this disposition, it was of course necessary to maintain towards Sindheea the same attitude which had compelled him to accept our terms; for, until some decided blow should be struck, no efficient restraint but the certainty of immediate attack could be placed on his natural desire to set aside the engagements he had entered into.

This had been fully contemplated; and his acceptance of our conditions was valued more for the effect it was expected to have, in paralyzing his underhand or open efforts against us, by exhibiting him to the world as one who had deserted the cause of our enemies, than from any hope of benefit from his co-operation. As soon as our success in other quarters should have confirmed Doulut Rao in his resolution to abide by his engagements, the treaty was so drawn, as to give us every advantage we could have desired at his hands, as will be abundantly evident in the sequel.

Ameer Khan followed the example of Sindheea; and an agent, whom he had sent to Dehlee to negotiate, signed the treaty, proposed to him by the Resident there, on the 9th of November. The terms were, a guarantee on our part to himself and family of all territories Ameer Khan might be in the actual tenure of, under grants from Holkar: the Patan army immediately to be disbanded, and the artillery to be given up for an equitable compensation: other articles secured the aid of Ameer Khan for the suppression of the Pindarees. In the negotiations respecting this treaty, it was agreed, that the compensation for the artillery, which was fixed at five lack rupees, should be paid down in advance, to enable Ameer Khan to disband his army, which he could not effect without an advance of money. The son and heir of this chief was to come to Dehlee, and reside there as a hostage for his father's fidelity; and, on his arrival, two lack rupees were to be paid, the remaining three lack to be afterwards remitted, as soon as the Resident was satisfied that Ameer Khan was diligently employed in the work of disbanding his troops. It was also settled, that territories belonging to any of the Rajpoot states, and forcibly occupied by him, should be given up on our requisition.

This treaty was ratified by the Governor-General, on the 15th of November. A month had been fixed as the period for the counter ratification to be procured from Ameer Khan; but, before the expiration of that period, the rise of the Pêshwa and Bhoosla in arms to oppose our measures had occurred, and there was time within the month for him to learn the event of their first efforts against us. This chief had, therefore, all the advantage of waiting to see the probable issue of affairs in other quarters, and he availed himself of this advantage to the utmost: insomuch, that it was for some time doubtful whether or not he would abide by the act of his envoy. His own interest and inclination undoubtedly prompted him to secure to himself independent dominion, as soon as possible; but this was offered him at the price of the sacrifice of his army; and his control over that army was not such as to enable him to disregard its feeling, which, until the ill success of Bajee Rao and Appa Saheb became known, was too decidedly hostile to the British propositions, for him to venture to declare himself in opposition to it. In the end, finding himself placed between General Donkin's force, and that assembled at Rewaree, under the command of Major-General Sir David Ochterlony, he felt both the necessity of coming to a decision, and the advantage of choosing his side, while the proximity of our divisions gave him the means of setting the feelings of his own retainers at defiance. He accordingly ratified the treaty in the course of December, and thenceforth entered heartily into the cause, adopting readily all our plans, and abiding by our suggestions.

The Keroulee chief, formerly a dependent of the Pêshwa, signed a treaty, by which he placed himself under our protection, and lent us the use of his means, on the same day with Ameer Khan. The tribute he owed the Pêshwa being only 25,000 rupees per annum, was remitted in this case, in consequence of our past experience of his favourable sentiments.

On the 8th of October, Govind Rao, the Nana of Jaloun, had signed a treaty, whereby the Pêshwa's right of tribute and of military service, now transferred to us, was commuted for the cession of Mahoba, a pergunnah of 43 villages that jutted into our Bundelkhund frontier, and four other villages on the banks of the Jumna. Benaeek Rao of Sâgur rejected the offer made to negotiate with him, in order to fix the relative situation he was to hold towards the British Government, now that it had acquired the Pêshwa's feudal superiority over that principality. The Nuwab of Bhopâl, on the contrary, accepted at once, and with eagerness, the terms offered to him, and proved himself to the extent of his ability a stanch and zealous ally; by which conduct he ultimately reaped abundant advantages, while Benaeek Rao brought on his own ruin.

The circumstances that attended the opening of the campaign against the Pindarees, and the crisis brought on by the sudden rise of Bajee Rao and Appa Saheb in open hostility, have been specially reserved for a separate chapter.

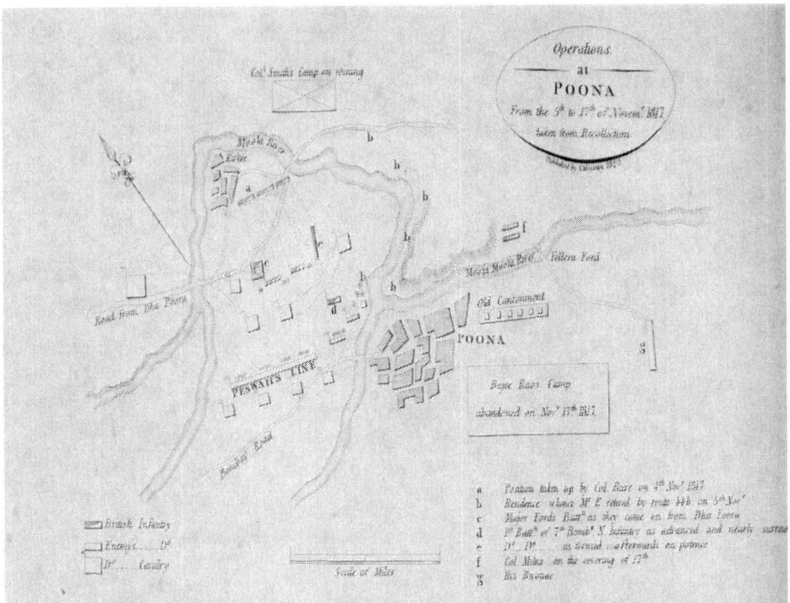
Operations
at
POONA
From the 5th to 17th of Novemr. 1817
taken from Recollection
Col. Smiths Camp on arriving
Road from Dhu Poora
Old Cantonment
POONA
PESWAH'S LINE
Bapu Raos Camp
abandoned on Novr. 17th 1817
British Infantry
Scale of Miles

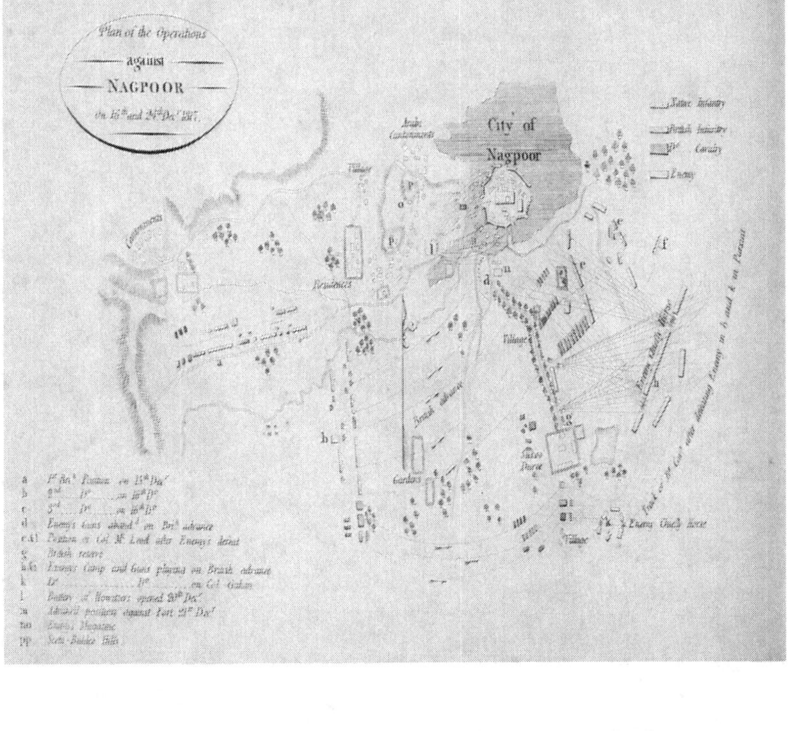
Plan of the Operations
against
NAGPOOR
on 16th and 24th Decr. 1817.
City of
Nagpoor
Native Infantry
British Infantry
Cavalry
Enemy
Residence
Village
Gardens
British Reserve
Enemys Camp and Guns playing on British advance

CHAPTER XI.

PINDAREES—POONA—NÀGPOOR.

1817. OCTOBER TO DECEMBER.

Pindarees during rains—General Marshall from Bundelkhund—a Pindara enterprise—frustrated—operations on the Nerbudda—Sir Thomas Hislop's retrograde movement—operations in Malwa—Sir Thomas Hislop recalled thither—Poona affairs—reduction of Soondoor demanded—and effected—fresh levies of troops—Sepoys—tampered with—Kandêsh—critical situation of brigade—it moves to Kirkee—Moro Dikshut—Brigadier-General Smith on the frontier—precautions—Pêshwa's demands—Residency attacked and burnt—battle of Poona—Moro Dikshut killed—cruelties of Mahrattas—Brigadier-General Smith's move on Poona—attacks Bajee Rao's camp—city surrendered—Nàgpoor—retrospect from July—Raja irresolute—receives titles from Poona—and is publicly invested—precautions of defence—British position—attacked—pressed—and partly carried—charge of Captain Fitzgerald—restores the day—defeat of the enemy—reflections—loss on both sides—influence of these events—charge of treachery weighed.

The Pindarees cantoned for the rains of 1817 in three bodies, under Cheetoo, Kureem Khan, and Wâsil Mahommed. The durra of the former occupied the position furthest to the west, and shifted its ground several times in the season, from about Ashta and Ichawur westward to the Kalee-Sindh. Kureem, who had resumed the command of his durra from Namdar Khan his lieutenant, lay about Bairsea, due north of Bhopâl. Wâsil Mahommed, brother and successor to Dost Mahommed, deceased, was at Garspoor, westward of Sâgur. It was generally known throughout the durras, that the English meditated offensive operations against them in the approaching season. Kureem was therefore particularly active in recruiting his durra, and raising fresh infantry, with a view to enable him to meet the emergency. He was desirous also of concerting a general plan of defence with the leaders of the other durras; and a meeting was accordingly appointed on the 15th of September for that purpose. The ill-will that subsisted between Cheetoo and this Chief was, however, too rancorous to allow of any cordiality between them. At the same time, though the Chiefs received general assurances of support in the hour of need from all quarters, there was no one of the native princes yet willing openly to take their part, or to incur the responsibility of admitting their families into any forts capable of affording them protection. Thus the rainy season passed without their having been able to disencumber themselves of their families and baggage, or to fix upon any consistent plan of action for the campaign. Sheikh Dulloo, the most adventurous of all the Chiefs, declared his intention of joining Trimbukjee at Choolee-Muheshwur, and seeking his fortune in another expedition to the Dukhun. The rest were distracted, and inclined to wait the issue of the expected rise amongst the Mahrattas in support of their cause. The spirits of Kureem's durra were damped by a destructive fire that accidentally broke out in their cantonment on the 17th of September, and consumed the greater part of their valuables. In the present temper of their minds, this was regarded as an omen of ill-fortune.

Mean time, the left division of the grand army from Hindoostan, consisting of two strong brigades of infantry and a regiment and irregular corps of cavalry, assembled on the 10th of October at Kalinjur, under the command of Major-General Marshall. It immediately advanced on Punna in Bundelkhund, and thence continued its march to Hutta on the way to Sâgur, where it arrived on the 28th of October. While this army was on the advance to the south, a bold enterprise was attempted from the durra of Wâsil Mahommed at Garspoor, whence an active *luhbur* was sent out in a north-easterly direction to plunder our own provinces of Bundelkhund. It penetrated by the Heerapoor ghât to the westward of General Marshall's route, and ravaged the territories of some Bundela chiefs as far north as Mow, near Raneepoor. From this town the party was beaten off; but as they were thought to have thence taken a direction eastward, some alarm was felt at Banda, the civil station of Bundelkhund, which was at this time totally without protection, all the troops of the province having marched to the south with General Marshall. The Marquess of Hastings hearing of this bold enterprise on the 1st of November, when he was at Jaloun with his division, detached two squadrons of the seventh native cavalry with the dromedary corps and two light companies to proceed with all expedition under the command of Major Cumming of the seventh native cavalry, so as to cover Banda, in case of that station being threatened. The marauders got intelligence of this detachment, and retired again to the south-west without doing farther mischief in Bundelkhund. Major Cumming was, however, reinforced, and ordered to remain with his detachment about Kyta, in order to cover our frontier on that side, and more effectually to keep open the communication between General Marshall and the centre division under his Lordship's personal command.

During this diversion, the left division continued its advance from Hutta to Rylee, where it arrived on the 10th of November, and thence opened a communication with Colonel Adams at Hoshungabad. Wâsil Mahommed retired from Garspoor westward to Gunj Basouda, as this division advanced. On the same day that General Marshall arrived at Rylee, Lieutenant-General Sir Thomas Hislop reached Hurda, and took the command of the first division of the army of the Dukhun. Brigadier-General

Sir John Malcolm had arrived in the valley of the Nerbudda some time before. Every thing was therefore now in readiness for the combined movement, that had been concerted to drive the Pindarees out of Malwa. In expectation of it, the Guzerât force had by this time advanced to Dohud or Dwahud, to intercept their escape westward; and Lord Hastings having concluded the treaty with Sindheea, moved his own division to a position that should prevent their penetrating to the north or east; while he ordered General Donkin to advance from Dholpoor in a south-westerly direction, so as to guard the left bank of the Chumbul, and cut off any retreat on that side. It had been planned, that one of Sir Thomas Hislop's divisions should penetrate into Malwa by marching straight upon Ashta, while another moved by Oonchôd, further to the west; that Colonel Adams should at the same time move upon Ressein, while General Marshall marched from Rylee westward on Sâgur and Ratgurh.

The execution of this plan was, however, interrupted by intelligence which had reached Sir Thomas Hislop of the Pêshwa's having risen in arms. After some deliberation as to the course to be adopted in this perplexity, the Lieutenant-General resolved to send forward Sir John Malcolm with the third division, reinforced by a brigade of regular troops, while he himself returned by the Boorhanpoor route towards the Dukhun, to support the divisions of Brigadier-Generals Doveton, Smith, and Pritzler, the two latter of which had previously been directed on Poona. In furtherance of this determination, Sir Thomas Hislop thought it advisable to employ himself in the first instance in summoning Aseergurh, the orders for the surrender of which had recently been forwarded to him, and in laying siege to it in case of resistance. This opinion was founded on the assumption of our interests in the Dukhun being more seriously endangered than the event showed them to have been. It is likewise true, that recent communications from Mr. Jenkins had described the Raja of Nâgpoor as likely to follow the example of Bajee Rao; which had obliged him to detain a brigade of Colonel Adam's force, and to order a battalion and additional troops of cavalry to hold themselves in readiness to march on Nâgpoor, as a reinforcement to the troops there: nor was it long before he was obliged to avail himself of their active services. However, even in the worst event, the force of Brigadier-General Doveton was applicable in this direction, without the necessity of holding back a second division for the purpose.

It was under these, circumstances that Sir Thomas Hislop, conceiving the safety of our interests in the Dukhun to be a consideration paramount to all others, resolved to divert the strength of his division from the suppression of the Pindarees, which he regarded as a minor object, and to devote his chief exertions to the support of those interests. Accordingly, the first division of the army of the Dukhun began to retrace its steps towards Boorhanpoor on the 19th of November: Sir John Malcolm having previously been despatched with the third and Colonel Adams with the fifth division, to prosecute alone the operations against the Pindarees. The former crossed the Nerbudda on the 16th of November, the latter on the 14th. A movement had been combined with General Marshall, so as to bring the three armies respectively to Ashta, Ressein, and Ratgurh, all on the same day, which was fixed for the 22d of November. They all reached their stations without fail. Three other points, Tullain, Bairsea, and Gunj-Basouda, were then designated and occupied respectively by the three divisions on the 26th of November. The freebooters were by these operations driven entirely out of their usual haunts; and, as the divisions advanced, their agents were expelled from the several towns and villages, which were taken possession of or restored, according as there appeared to be claimants with a valid title or not. All that belonged to Sindheea or Bhopâl were immediately delivered over to the agents of these chiefs in attendance with the divisions. The Pindarees had hitherto retired in masses, with all their property and families, carefully keeping beyond the reach of a surprise. The durras had not yet joined, but they had converged in their retreat. After this, however, Kureem and Wâsil Mahommed effected a junction about Seronj, and retired together on the high road leading by Nya-Seraee to Gwalior. Cheetoo moved westward, towards Holkar's army, which had by this time taken the field.

During these movements, the Marquess of Hastings on the 14th of November received advice of the state of affairs at Poona, and the certainty of a rupture with the Pêshwa. Apprehending the possibility of Sir Thomas Hislop's suspending his advance into Malwa in consequence of the intelligence, his Lordship immediately issued the most distinct and positive instructions for his adherence to the original plan of the campaign, thinking Brigadier-Generals Smith and Pritzler strong enough to operate against Bajee Rao, while Brigadier-General Doveton's position in Berar would overawe or enable him to act against the Nâgpoor Raja, in case of his defection also. He declared it to be, at all events, of vital importance to the success of the general plan, that the first division should advance to the support of Sir John Malcolm, who might else be opposed by an accumulation of force, with which he would scarcely be competent to cope. These instructions were enforced in several subsequent communications, particularly one of the 21st of November from Erich. They reached the head-quarters of the Madras army, when they had already retrograded as far as Charwa. On receiving them, the Lieutenant-General immediately retraced his steps; and on the 26th of November again began his march to the north, with intent to move by Oonchôd direct upon Oojein, to which point he ordered Sir John Malcolm to look for his support.

But ere we pursue further the narrative of occurrences in Hindoostan, it will be necessary to give some account of the important events that had taken place in the interval at Poona and Nâgpoor.

After the execution of the treaty of Poona, Bajee Rao had retired, and still continued, on different pretences, to absent himself from his capital, whither he did not return till the end of September. His ministers had, in the interim, been very urgent for the performance of an old promise we had given, to reduce for him the rebellious feudatory of Soondoor. It was a case of disputed succession, in which Bajee Rao had declared for Juswunt Rao Gorepara, to the prejudice of Sheeo Rao, the present occupant. The place being surrounded on every side by our own territories, we had been induced to offer our services for its reduction, in preference to allowing Bajee Rao to carry his own military rabble into the neighbourhood. But as yet the Madras Presidency had not found a convenient time for fulfilling this promise; and the court of Poona was always particularly urgent in pressing it, at moments of the greatest inconvenience. The object at the present juncture was evidently to throw obstacles in the way of the formidable assemblage of troops making in the north. Mr. Elphinstone, sensible that our ally had a plausible pretext for complaining of our dilatoriness in this instance, more especially as he was paying to the competitor, whom he favoured and recognised, a compensation of 10,000 rupees a year, suggested to Sir Thomas Hislop the propriety of employing in this service a part of the reserve then collecting about Adoni. The presence of Colonel Munro in the neighbourhood, where he had been sent as commissioner to take charge of the districts lately ceded by the Pêshwa, afforded to the Lieutenant-General the opportunity of availing himself of his services, without embarrassing Brigadier-General Pritzler's operations with the rest of the reserve. Orders were accordingly issued to Colonel Munro to undertake the enterprise; and he was shortly afterwards vested with a separate command of the reserve, and the rank of Brigadier-General, under orders from the Marquess of Hastings. The place was surrendered by Sheeo Rao Gorepara, on Colonel Munro's approach towards the end of October; the British Government agreeing to assign to Sheeo Rao a provision about equal to what Juswunt Rao his competitor had been receiving. The latter, however, becoming involved in the subsequent measures of the Poona Court, Soondoor was ultimately restored to its former occupant.

During the whole of October, Bajee Rao continued to collect troops from all parts, and to call upon his jageerdars to do likewise. The reason assigned for this conduct to Mr. Elphinstone, at the first conference to which he was admitted, which however did not take place before the 14th of October, was his desire to co-operate in the objects of the present campaign to the utmost extent of his means. This pretence was too shallow to disguise his real designs, which were manifested by his altered conduct towards the jageerdars, to all of whom he was now studiously attentive, exerting himself with great address in gaining their attachment. Even Rasteea, whose family had been entirely ruined not long before, and Appa Dussaee Nipaneekur, a third of whose jageer had lately been confiscated, together with the Vinshoorkur, who had himself much to expect from our success in Hindoostan, were completely won over by this conduct. The Pêshwa's intention of heading the hostile league against our supremacy was evident from numberless other circumstances; particularly from the discovery of several profligate efforts to seduce the sepoys of the brigade, as well as those of Major Ford's battalions, to desert their colours. The native officers and men of the regular corps were generally proof against his solicitations, and acquainted their officers with the attempts made to tamper with them. But in Major Ford's battalions there was a larger proportion of Mahrattas, and it was natural enough that these should be won over on such an occasion.

Towards the latter end of October, there was an immense collection of Mahratta troops at Poona, the jageerdars having exerted themselves to bring forward all they could muster, and the prince himself having made extensive levies. Gokla was the adviser and principal commander in this crisis. The Mahrattas fixed their several encampments close round the cantonment of the brigade, the site of which had been chosen judiciously enough with a view to the defence of the city against external attack; but it was particularly open to surprise, and otherwise much exposed, when threatened by an enemy both within and without. In proportion as the accumulation of the Mahratta soldiery on every side became greater, the situation of the brigade grew more and more alarming. Each corps as it came in encroached upon the ground of its cantonment, and the horsemen rode blustering and prancing about, in the manner usual with Indian troops when their designs are hostile. Colonel Burr, the officer in command at Poona, had a strong brigade of three battalions; but the European regiment had not yet joined from Bombay, nor was it expected till the 2d of November. Mr. Elphinstone, though fully aware of the Pêshwa's determination to push matters to an open rupture, was nevertheless very unwilling to be the first to resort to measures of actual or apparent hostility. He therefore refrained from authorising the brigade to take up a stronger position, until it became obviously unsafe to allow of its remaining longer in the present one. He had remonstrated, but to no purpose, against the concentration of troops at the capital, and against the temper they displayed; for Bajee Rao distinctly refused to send away any part of his force. On the 31st of October, appearances were so menacing, that the Resident resolved to move the brigade to Kirkee, where the ground was peculiarly advantageous. The stores were consequently sent off on that day, and the brigade followed on the next. Letters had in the mean time been despatched, to expedite the arrival of the European detachment, which also, by a forced march, came into Kirkee on the 1st of November.

A brief description of the ground about Poona will be necessary to the clear understanding of the ensuing operations. The city of Poona * is situated on the right bank of the Moota-Moola River, which runs from west to east, taking its name from two streams which unite to the north-west of the town. Just at the point of confluence stood the British Residency, separated from the city by the Moota, while the Moola came down with a sweep from the north. This latter river was fordable opposite to the Residency; and about a mile up the stream there was a good bridge over it, above which the river took a semicircular reach to the north. At the western extremity of the semicircle lies the village of Kirkee, between which and the river to the east is an admirable position for a brigade to occupy, protected by the river in the rear and on the left, and supported on the right flank by the village. The original cantonment was on the right bank of the Moota-Moola, to the east of the city, and close upon it, so that both the city and the Moota lay between the brigade and the Residency. By moving the troops to Kirkee, the Residency lay on the contrary between them and the enemy, forming an advanced position towards the city. Major Ford's battalions were cantoned at Dhapoora, a few miles distant to the west.

* Vide plan at the head of this chapter.

After the removal of the troops to Kirkee, nothing but war was talked of. Moro Dikshut, who seems to have conceived an attachment to Major Ford very uncommon between Europeans and natives, sent for that officer, and endeavoured to persuade him to accept his protection and assurance of safety. His master, he said, was bent upon an open rupture, and expected that the greater part of our native troops would come over to him, or at all events, that the numbers he had collected must overwhelm the brigade. He advised Major Ford, therefore, as a friend, to consult his own safety in such an extremity: adding, moreover, that he had exerted himself to the utmost to dissuade his prince from the course he was pursuing, but to no purpose, the counsels of Gokla and of the war party having prevailed; that a sense of duty would oblige him to side against us, though much against his inclination; and that he was desirous of manifesting his friendship for Major Ford, by providing for his personal security. When this officer explained what he considered his own duty to require of him in such circumstances, and expressed his resolution to abide the result, whatever it might be, Moro Dikshut took a very affectionate leave, commending his family to the Major's care, if the event should be adverse to the cause he had espoused, and assuring him of every personal attention and assistance that he could bestow in the opposite case.

Brigadier-General Smith had proceeded northwards towards Byzapoor, on the borders of Kandêsh, early in the month of October; and his absence, by depriving the brigade at Poona of the support it usually derived from the vicinity of the main body at Seroor, which lies about thirty miles only to the north-west of the capital, naturally raised the hopes and courage of the enemy. On hearing of the hostile indications at Poona, a light battalion was ordered back to Seroor; and, towards the end of October, the Brigadier-General himself concentrated his force at a place called Phool-Tamba, on the Godaveree. He had arranged with Mr. Elphinstone, that, if he did not hear daily from Poona, he was to consider the communication as cut off, and immediately to march to the south. But, unless in the last extremity, his force was not to be diverted from the part assigned to it in the general operations towards Hindoostan.

After the movement of the brigade to Kirkee, every day produced more decisive symptoms of approaching hostilities. An officer on his way to Bombay was attacked and plundered, and escaped with difficulty, severely wounded. This occurred only two miles from Poona; where the Mahrattas were continually riding round the cantonment, and abusing our men and officers as they lay at their posts. The Resident, therefore, thought it advisable to increase the strength of his force as much as possible, by calling in the light battalion that had been ordered back to Seroor, together with a corps of 1000 auxiliary horse, that had been forming there under Lieutenant Swanston. Still, however, he resolved to remain at the Residency to the latest moment, in order not to be the first to declare war, or to assume the appearance of hostility. The light battalion left Seroor on the 5th of November, and moved half way to Poona. The news of its approach was conveyed to Bajee Rao in the forenoon of the 5th; and his army was immediately put in motion. A battalion of Gokla's at the same time moved round to the west, and took up a position directly between the Residency and the brigade at Kirkee, with the intention of cutting off the communication between the two. Mr. Elphinstone sent to demand the reason of this hostile proceeding, and of the general movement of the troops. Upon this, an intimate at the palace of the Pêshwa, named Wittojee Naeek, came on his part to say, that intelligence had been received of troops being on their way to Poona, as well from Seroor as from General Smith's army; that Bajee Rao had twice before been the dupe of his own irresolution, but was now determined to be beforehand in his demands. These were explained to be, that the Europeans lately arrived at Poona should be sent back to Bombay; that the brigade should be reduced to its usual strength, and be cantoned at such place as Bajee Rao might select. To these demands a categorical and immediate answer was required, on the tenor of which the question of peace or war would depend. Mr. Elphinstone replied, that he could not admit his Highness' right to make any such demands: at all events, it was out of his power to grant them, the extent of the force to be stationed at Poona having been fixed by superior authority. With respect to the categorical answer required, he could only say, that, if his Highness joined his army, he should proceed to the brigade; and if his Highness' troops advanced towards the brigade, they would assuredly be attacked: for, though he was most anxious to avoid a rupture, he did not fear the issue. Wittojee Naeek returned with this reply. He was no sooner gone, than the Pêshwa, either upon a preconcerted signal, or more probably without waiting the answer, mounted his horse, and joined his army at the Parbutee Hill, which lies a little to the south-west of Poona. His troops immediately advanced on the Residency. Mr. Elphinstone and the gentlemen attached to his suite had barely time to mount their horses, and retire by the ford of the Moola, under cover of the Resident's honorary guard, ere the enemy arrived and took possession of the houses, from which there had not been time to remove a single article. The whole were plundered, and afterwards burnt; whereby much valuable property was destroyed, and, amongst other things, all Mr. Elphinstone's books and papers, a loss more irreparable than all the rest. The Resident's party made good its retreat along the left bank of the Moola, skirmishing with some horse that followed, and under the fire of Gokla's battalion from the opposite side of the river. At the bridge they crossed and joined the brigade, which had previously turned out and advanced from Kirkee at Mr. Elphinstone's requisition, as soon as the hostile approach of the enemy had been observed.

The position at Kirkee was admirably adapted to purposes of defence; but it had been concerted between the Resident and Colonel Burr, that the brigade should advance and fight its battle in the plain between Kirkee and the city. The plan was highly judicious; for it was uncertain how far the fidelity of the sepoys had been proof against the late attempts to seduce them, and it was desirable, therefore, to risk something for the sake of inspiring them with additional confidence in themselves and their cause; whereas, to coop them up in a defensive position, exposed to the taunts and insults of the Mahratta cavalry, would have had a most disheartening effect, and must have operated to increase the number of desertions, by giving to the enemy the advantage of the show of superiority. As it was, 70 men went over from Major Ford's battalion, and were followed after the action by 150 from the irregular horse, notwithstanding the success of the day. Besides the above reason, the enemy were well provided with artillery, which would have enabled them to give great annoyance to the position, and to wear out the spirits of the men by a succession of casualties, and the fatigue of continual alerts from day to day, before General Smith should arrive, which at the shortest could not be in less time than a week. Moreover, although the Mahrattas were at present in the confidence of a great numerical superiority, an advance to the attack, in despite of their numbers, would confound them by its boldness, and contribute to raise the spirits of our own people. At the same time, if we could obtain but a partial success in the plain, it would completely dishearten the enemy, and prevent his afterwards attempting any thing against the position; an object, which was well worth some risk on our part.

Wherefore, leaving the head-quarters at the post of Kirkee, in charge of part of the 2d-6th Bombay native infantry, Colonel Burr advanced with the remainder of his force, consisting of the Bombay European regiment, under Major Wilson, the 2d-1st and 1st-7th Bombay native infantry. His line was formed with the Europeans in the centre, the 2d-1st to the right, and the 1st-7th on the left. A detachment of the battalion left in Kirkee, together with the Resident's escort, which had joined along with himself during the advance, were held in reserve to keep in check any parties of horse that might get round the flanks of the line. In this order, the brigade marched into action. Major Ford, who, with his two battalions, occupied a separate cantonment at Dhapoora, a short distance to the west, marched in immediately to take his share in the danger; but the Vinshore jageerdar had been posted with a large body of horse to intercept him; so that he was obliged to fight his way to the ground in squares, and did not reach the right of the line till the troops were hotly engaged.

The fighting commenced a few minutes after Mr. Elphinstone had joined the brigade by the Kirkee bridge. The enemy showed immense bodies of horse on our front, and opened a heavy cannonade from many guns, but chiefly from a distance. The fire was returned from the four 6-pounders of the brigade, two of which were placed on each flank of the Europeans. In the mean time, the Mahrattas attempted to push bodies of horse round our flanks, in which manœuvre they partly succeeded. A spirited charge was then made in close column by one of Gokla's battalions, raised and commanded by Major Pinto, a Portuguese. It was directed against the left of our line, where the 1st-7th was posted. The battalion was driven back after a short contest, with the loss of its immediate commander and many men: but the 1st-7th, in its eagerness to follow up the success, for the purpose of capturing the guns of the repulsed battalion, became separated from the general line of the brigade. Gokla, perceiving this, ordered down a body of his best horse to charge it while yet in the confusion of the pursuit. Moro Dikshut also led a party of horse, under his command, to the charge at the same time. Our battalion was in considerable danger, the horse having got round both its flanks; but Colonel Burr, hastening to the post with a part of the European regiment, while the two guns on its left were served with great effect, was enabled to restore the day, bring back the battalion into line, and afterwards form it *en-potence* (at right angles with the line), in order to check any further ill consequence from the enemy's out-flanking us. Major Ford had by this time brought up his battalions on the right, which, being formed in square, had a similar effect on that flank.

In the above charge, Moro Dikshut was killed by a grape-shot from the guns on the left of the Europeans, which struck him after he had led on his party into the space intervening between the 1st-7th and the rest of the line. He fell, respected by both parties. He had been stimulated to extraordinary exertion on this day, by an insinuation made in the presence of his prince, apparently with his countenance, that his general opposition to a rupture with the English was the result of personal cowardice. This taunt induced him to solicit the honour of carrying the *Juree Putka*, or standard of the Mahratta empire, in the fight; it was under his charge when he fell.

Except in the above instance, the Mahrattas never came to close quarters. They continued, however, to fire on our line as it advanced, occasioning some further casualties, but keeping always at a respectful distance. At night-fall, the troops returned to Kirkee, and were not afterwards molested. Our loss in this action was, 18 killed and 57 wounded; amongst the latter was Lieutenant Falconer, of the 2d-1st Bombay native infantry. The enemy left about 500 on the field. The light battalion and irregular horse came in from Seroor without opposition, on the morning of the following day; and Bajee Rao, though he drew up his troops in order of battle, refrained from giving us further molestation, but encamped his army on the ground of the old cantonment.

No sooner was the die cast, than the Mahrattas proceeded to give a ferocious character to their hostility, in order to widen the breach, and prevent any speedy reconciliation. Two officers, Captain Vaughan and his brother, who happened to be travelling with a small escort, were surrounded at Tulleegâm, on the Bombay road; and, having been induced to surrender by the offer of quarter, were both inhumanly hanged. The Pêshwa afterwards disavowed altogether this act of barbarity; and it is probable enough that he had no share in the transaction. Ensign Ennis of the Bombay engineers, who was taking a survey about 50 miles from Poona, was likewise intercepted and shot by Bheels. Two other officers, Lieutenants Morieson and Hunter, of the Madras cavalry, were marching towards Poona, from the Nizam's dominions, utterly unconscious of the rupture, until they came within 20 miles of the city. Gokla then sent out a party of Arabs to bring them in. On the first alarm, they took post in a Choultree, and made a resolute defence with the havildar's party they had for escort; but were at last overpowered, and carried prisoners into Poona. Their lives were spared; but they were sent immediately under a guard to the Konkan, and shifted from fort to fort, until re-captured three months afterwards at Wusota. So close was their confinement, that the bursting of a shell over their prison gave the first intimation of approaching deliverance, while the besiegers were equally in ignorance of their fate. The feeling of exasperation, with which the Mahrattas entered into the war, was yet more strongly evinced by their conduct to the women and dependents of the brigade, whom they found in and about the old cantonment. Most of these were mutilated, and sent into Kirkee in that state; and many were put to death with studied cruelty.

While this was passing at Poona, General Smith, finding the communication intercepted, was already on his way to the south. On the 8th of November he arrived at Ahmednugurh, having yet been little harassed on the march. Between this place and Seroor, parties of cavalry kept hovering about him; but it was not till he had passed the latter place likewise, that the enemy gave him any serious annoyance. He had no regular cavalry with him, the 2d of the Madras establishment not having yet joined. The only horse with the division were about 500 of the auxiliaries, lately raised under the treaty of Poona, commanded by Captain Spiller. The Mahrattas appeared in such numbers, as to surround the Brigadier-General on every side; and, though there was some skirmishing between them and Captain Spiller, in the course of which the latter succeeded in dispersing a much larger body than his own, and was wounded on the occasion, still the enemy found an opportunity of breaking in upon the line of march and carrying off a part of the baggage.

On the 13th, the division arrived at Poona; and the next day was fixed for the attack of the Pêshwa's camp. It was delayed, however, in consequence of some doubts entertained, respecting the practicability of fording the river at the place intended. On the morning of the 16th, Colonel Milne, of the King's 65th, was sent with a strong brigade to ford the Moota-Moola, a little below the old cantonment, in order to occupy a village on the east of the enemy's position, whence an attack was to be made at daybreak next morning, while General Smith advanced against his left. The Pêshwa's army turned out to oppose the passage of the river; but it was effected in good order, under a heavy cannonade, which was answered from eight guns attached to Colonel Milne's force. Our loss in this affair was about 60 men and an officer. Colonel Milne then took up his ground for the night on the enemy's right flank. Before daylight next morning, the combined attack was commenced as agreed upon; but the camp was found deserted, the enemy having retired quietly in the night, leaving his tents standing. His rear-guard moved off as General Smith approached, and was cannonaded from a distance. He carried away all his guns, except one of enormous size, called Maha-Kalee, which was too unwieldy for speedy transport, though mounted on a carriage that made it serviceable in the previous cannonade. The city surrendered in the course of the day, and was occupied by our troops, who were with difficulty prevented by General Smith's exertions from committing excesses, in revenge for what their families had suffered from the hands of the Mahrattas. On the 19th, General Smith prepared for the pursuit of Bajee Rao, having been joined on the preceding day by the 2d Madras cavalry, under Lieutenant-Colonel Colebrooke. On the same day, a detachment was sent out to capture the enemy's artillery, which was ascertained to have been left with a considerable part of his baggage in a position under cover of the fort of Singurh. The enterprise was conducted by Captain Turner of the light battalion, and was completely successful: eighteen guns, with all their tumbrils and ammunition, and a large quantity of baggage, fell into our hands on this occasion.

The flight of the Pêshwa and General Smith's unremitting pursuit were productive of nothing of importance during the remainder of the month of November, nor indeed until the commencement of the new year. Wherefore, instead of proceeding with the narrative of operations in this quarter, it will be more perspicuous to relate here the occurrences at Nâgpoor and in Hindoostan, during the two last months of 1817.

Pending the discussions with Bajee Rao, which ended in the treaty of Poona concluded in June, Appa Saheb lent himself openly to the intrigues and counsels of those, who wished him to make common cause with the Pêshwa. On hearing of his submission, the Nâgpoor Raja began to have some personal apprehension of the consequences of the display of such a bias, and accordingly thought it necessary to put on the appearance of a line of conduct directly the reverse. Nerayun Rao was ostensibly reinstated in favour, and occasionally employed in communications with the British Resident. In the course of July, the discussions respecting the reform of the contingent were likewise brought to a settlement; the Bhoosla agreeing to a proposition, that certain of his jageerdars should furnish a definite number of their best horse, none to be paid at a lower rate than 20 rupees, and the whole to be under one well-paid commandant, with two British officers to be attached to the contingent, empowered to inspect and to exercise a general superintendance.

In this favourable disposition the Raja continued till the end of October; indeed, on the 21st of that month, Mr. Jenkins wrote, that although his Highness was still in active communication with Poona, he, the Resident, did not anticipate a change of conduct for the worse. But no sooner were the hostile designs of Bajee Rao towards the English made known unequivocally at Nâgpoor, than he came at once to the resolution of making common cause with the head of the Mahratta nation. Towards the middle of November this change became manifest, and, in consequence, the Resident requested, that a brigade of Colonel Adams's division might be halted to the south of the Nerbudda, and hold itself in readiness to detach a battalion with three troops of cavalry to reinforce the brigade at Nâgpoor, which had suffered much from sickness. Things remained in this posture for some time, Appa Saheb continuing his military preparations. The news of the result of the action at Poona on the 5th of November occasioned no remission of these hostile demonstrations; nor was any stronger effect produced by the subsequent intelligence of General Smith's arrival at that city, with the main body of the subsidiary force. Appa Saheb, however, long hesitated as to the course he should pursue; giving ear alternately to the counsels of those who urged his adherence to the British alliance, and of those who stimulated him to the opposite line of policy, and represented it as an act of imperative duty to aid in the restoration of the Mahratta empire to its pristine splendor and power. His inclination shifted from one side to the other, according to the prevalence of sober judgment and the cooler calculations of prudence and experience, or of the delusion of his imagination by the phantom of ideal greatness, presented to his mind as the sure result of daring enterprise, by the young and thoughtless among his courtiers, at moments when his brain was already intoxicated with the deleterious fumes of the *hooka*. In the public communications between the Raja and the Resident, there was never a word that betrayed any inimical feeling; on the contrary, the Mahratta *Moonshee* attached to the Residency was sent for on the first arrival of intelligence of the Pêshwa's defection, and, in his presence, Appa Saheb inveighed in the strongest terms against the treachery and want of faith evinced by Bajee Rao, in his conduct towards the English at Poona.

On the night of the 24th of November, Mr. Jenkins received a note from Ramchundur Wâgh, informing him that a *Khilât*, (dress of honour), had arrived for the Raja from Poona, and that his Highness intended next day to go in state to his camp, in order to be formally invested with it, and to assume the *Juree Putka* or golden streamer, the emblem of high command in the Mahratta armies, which, with the title of *Senaputtee*, general, had been conferred on him by the Pêshwa. Mr. Jenkins was invited to assist at the ceremony; but he remonstrated against the acceptance of the *Khilât* or of any titles from a power now at open war with the British, and refused to give the sanction of his presence to such an act. Remonstrance was however of no avail: Appa Saheb went in state to his army on the 25th, and was formally invested with the *Khilât* and other insignia. His troops immediately took up positions very threatening to the safety of the Residency; and the indications of approaching hostility were so strong, as to induce Mr. Jenkins to call in the brigade from its cantonment about three miles westward of the city, and to post it in the best attitude for defence of the Residency against any sudden attack. This was done on the evening of the 25th of November. Throughout the 26th, the symptoms of an intended attack grew stronger every hour. The Raja's infantry and large masses of cavalry, in bodies called *goles*, of various strength and number, began to show themselves on all sides; and every gun that could be got ready was wheeled out of the arsenal and brought to bear directly upon some part of our position. But there was yet no official message or communication from the Raja. The best defensive dispositions were made, that the nature of the ground and the limited time would allow. The force at Nâgpoor consisted of two Madras battalions of native infantry, the 1st-20th and 1st-24th, both reduced considerably by sickness. There were also two companies forming the Resident's escort, three troops of the 6th Bengal cavalry, and a detachment of the Madras artillery with four six-pounders. Lieutenant-Colonel Scott of the 1st-24th commanded the whole; and the following was his plan of defence*.

The Residency lies to the west of the city of Nâgpoor, and is separated from it by a small ridge running north and south, having two hills at its extremities, called the Seetabuldee hills, about 330 yards apart. That to the north was the higher,

* Vide Plate fronting the title of Chapter VII. and plan at the head of this chapter.

though much the smaller of the two; upon it were posted 300 men of the 24th native infantry, with one of the six-pounders, under the command of Captain Sadler. The 20th and the escort were stationed on the larger hill with the rest of the 24th and of the artillery; and the three troops of cavalry in the grounds of the Residency, together with some light infantry to keep off the hovering parties of the enemy's horse, but under orders not to advance into the plain against them. The women and valuables were lodged at the Residency.

At sunset of the 26th of November, as our picquets were placing, they were fired upon by the Raja's Arab infantry. Immediately afterwards, his artillery opened on the position, and was answered by ours from the hills. Our men were much exposed, particularly those on the smaller hill, the summit of which was not broad enough for the brow to afford any protection. There was also a *bazar* to the north-east of this hill, that approached close to its foot; here the Raja's Arab infantry were posted, and kept up a very galling fire from under cover of the huts and houses, which cut up our people most severely. The firing did not cease with the daylight, but continued with little intermission till about two o'clock of the morning, by which time we had sustained a heavy loss, particularly on the smaller hill, where some assaults had been attempted that were repulsed with great difficulty. Captain Sadler, the officer in command there, was killed; and Captain Charlesworth likewise, the next in command, was wounded in the defence of this important point.

After two o'clock there was an intermission of the enemy's fire for some hours, with only now and then an occasional shot. Our troops availed themselves of the opportunity to strengthen their position and make up fresh cartridges. This was an awful moment for those, who were at leisure to calculate upon the prospects of the morrow. It was evident, that what had passed was only the prelude of a more serious contest, when day should reappear. We had already suffered much; and if the attack were renewed with tolerable perseverance by a constant succession of troops, it was quite manifest that our battalions, however well they might behave, must in the end be overpowered. The numbers of the assailants would allow, and, indeed, suggest this mode of acting; and this seemed to be their design, as far as could be judged from their previous conduct.

From the unavoidable haste with which the position on the Seetabuldee hills had been occupied, as well as the want of entrenching tools in sufficient abundance, no artificial defences had been added to the natural strength of the ground. This omission was now remedied in the best manner the time would allow, by placing along the exposed brow of the hills, especially of the smaller one, sacks of flour and wheat, and any thing else capable of affording cover to the men. It was also deemed proper to confine the defence of the latter to the summit, many men having been lost from being placed in exposed situations on the declivity. The men of the 24th were also relieved early in the morning by a detachment from the 20th, and by the escort, to whom was entrusted the defence of this important post, the key of the whole position.

At daybreak, the fire recommenced with more fury than before, additional guns having been brought to bear during the night. The enemy fought too with increasing confidence, and closed upon us during the forenoon. The Arabs in the Raja's service were particularly conspicuous for their courage and resolution; and to them the assault of the smaller hill had been allotted. *Goles* of horse also showed themselves to the west and north, as well as to the south of the residency grounds, so as to oblige Captain Fitzgerald, who commanded the cavalry, to retire further within them, in order to prevent any sudden *coup-de-main* in that quarter.

About ten o'clock in the morning, the accidental explosion of a tumbril on the smaller hill created some confusion, as was natural from the confined space occupied by the detachment, and did so much injury to the screw of its gun, as to render it for some minutes unserviceable. The Arabs saw their opportunity, and rushed forward with loud cries to storm the hill. Our men were disconcerted, and the smallness of the total force having made it impossible to hold a support in readiness for such an extremity, the hill was carried before the gun and the wounded could be brought off: the latter were all put to the sword. The Arabs immediately turned the gun against our post on the larger hill, and with it and two more guns of their own which they brought up, opened a most destructive fire on the whole of our remaining position. The first shot from the captured gun killed two officers, Doctor Neven the surgeon, and Lieutenant Clarke of the 20th; the second, a round of grape, was fatal to the resident's first assistant, Mr. George Sotheby *, and totally disabled four men besides. The fire

* At the moment of receiving the wound, Mr. Sotheby was in the act of addressing the men of the escort, who had escaped from the smaller hill, and endeavouring to rally them and revive their spirits. A pistol he had in his girdle was struck on the handle by a grape shot, that forced the muzzle into his body, and inflicted a desperate wound, of which he died in the course of a few hours.

This gentleman was originally of the Bombay civil service, but had been tempted by early ambition to try his fortune in the college of Bengal, where his successful studies obtained him the highest possible distinction, and secured him employment under the Supreme-Government. He thenceforward attached himself to the political line, and his abilities in this department had already been conspicuous on many occasions; nor was there any one of the junior officers of the department, whose reputation stood so deservedly high, or whose services were more justly valued by the Governor-General. He was on the eve of rising to a station that must soon have led to fame and fortune; but after the rugged toils of this from the smaller hill was so destructive, as greatly to distress the troops on the larger, which it completely commanded. The Arabs too, flushed with their late success, were seen advancing in great numbers along the ridge, as if with the design of attacking that remaining point: while the attention of our small party was divided between them on one side, and the main body of the enemy in the plain to the south, who were also closing fast. The prospect was most discouraging; and, to add to the difficulty of the crisis, an alarm had spread amongst the followers and families of the Sepoys, whose lines were to the west of the smaller hill, now occupied by the Arabs; and the shrieks of the women and children contributed not a little to damp the courage of the native troops. They would scarcely have sustained a general assault, which the enemy seemed evidently to meditate.

Just at this critical moment, the spirits of all were raised to the highest pitch of enthusiasm, by observing a most successful and unexpected charge of the cavalry upon an immense *gole* of the enemy's horse. Captain Fitzgerald had kept himself in reserve within the residency grounds, until the enemy, accumulating on all sides, and closing every instant more and

laborious career had been surmounted, was unfortunately thus cut off, just on the point of reaching the summit of his hopes and expectations. The loss of a man of merit, from whom the state has received good service, is a subject of public regret at all times; but the interest felt is enhanced in a tenfold degree, when the individual is yet the object of public hope, and is suddenly snatched away, ere it has been fully realised. Independently of any private sympathy for the deceased, the death of one so generally known and esteemed as George Sotheby, considering the circumstances under which it occurred, could not have been passed over with the bare mention of his name among the list of the slain. The compiler of this narrative is, however, proud to acknowledge, that this notice is equally a tribute paid to private friendship; for he long enjoyed the intimacy of the deceased, and had personal experience of his worth. He was in his thirtieth year when his death occurred in the manner related.

more, brought at last a couple of light guns to bear upon him, the fire of which occasioned several casualties in his line. Seeing now that the case was one of absolute extremity, he resolved to charge the gole that most immediately threatened him, in order if possible to capture these guns. The residency grounds were bounded on that side by a dry nulla, which the charge had to cross. Captain Fitzgerald himself led the column; and as soon as thirty or forty men had got over, advanced at once upon the enemy. They retired before him as he pushed forwards, until, having passed to some distance beyond the guns, and seeing that the Mahrattas were making a demonstration of surrounding his small party, he commanded a halt. In the mean time, the rest of the cavalry had also crossed the nulla, and followed the advance, but had very judiciously stopped short on reaching the abandoned guns. These were immediately turned upon the enemy by the men of the regiment, all of whom had been trained to the use of artillery, as a part of their ordinary discipline. Their well-directed fire kept the Mahrattas at a distance, while two other guns that had also been brought in advance were similarly captured. The latter were instantly spiked; but the cavalry retired with the former, dragging them back into the residency grounds, and firing as they retreated.

The sight of what was passing on the plain below damped the courage of the assailants, in proportion as it elevated the spirits of our men. The firing was now recommenced from the larger hill with loud huzzas, and every one was watching the opportunity to recover the smaller one from the Arabs. An opportunity was very soon offered by the explosion of a second tumbril on the spot, which created a similar confusion to that which the enemy had lately taken advantage of. The confined space on the hill increased the liability to such accidents. The circumstance was no sooner observed, than a party from the larger hill, headed by several officers, who darted forwards without any particular orders, rushed to the attack, and drove the Arabs from the post at the point of the bayonet, recovering our own gun as well as capturing the two others brought up by the enemy. Amongst the rest, Captain Lloyd of the resident's escort distinguished himself on this occasion, as did Lieutenant Grant, the adjutant of the twenty-fourth, who, though twice wounded, was amongst the foremost of the party, and received a third and mortal wound in the assault. The tide of success had now turned, and Appa Saheb's troops gave way on every side. The Arabs, however, still remained in force about their bazar to the north-east of our position, until a brilliant charge was made upon them by Cornet Smith with a troop of the cavalry, which succeeded in dispersing them, and in capturing two more guns. Our troops now moved down from the hills, and drove the enemy from all the surrounding houses and villages, securing all the guns not previously carried off.

Thus, about noon of the 27th, terminated the most trying contest that our native army had ever been engaged in. Its fatigues and anxieties continued without intermission for eighteen hours. Under Providence, the success of this action must be chiefly attributed to the bottom of the troops, and to the cool decision in the hour of danger which particularly marked the conduct of the officers engaged. The former quality is entirely distinct from any strength of limb or of muscular power requisite to the long endurance of fatigue. It is purely a virtue of the mind, and consists in a buoyant disposition, that never will abandon itself to despair. The natives of India are of themselves rather prone to throw up the game as lost upon the slightest reverse; and the history of its wars, particularly that of the battles of Aurung-Zeeb, affords abundant instances of the ruin of a good cause, by yielding to this habitual despondency. If the character of the native sepoy is so different in our service, it is because he acts rather upon his officer's judgment than his own; and so long as he observes him coolly giving his orders, sees hope in implicit obedience, and never will despair while this ground of confidence remains. The conduct of the British officers engaged at Nâgpoor afforded a triumphant display of that collected judgment under extreme peril, which, to the glory of the nation, is its peculiar characteristic. The well-timed charge of Captain Fitzgerald stands conspicuous amongst the many brilliant exploits achieved in the campaign. It was generally allowed to have given the turn to the tide of success on this day; and, consequently, to have mainly contributed to the salvation of our interests within the Nâgpoor dominions: to say nothing of the effect on public opinion, that would have been felt throughout India, even to Nipâl, had Appa Saheb succeeded in cutting off this brigade.

The number of the combatants on either side was immensely disproportionate. Altogether, on our side, there were not more than from thirteen to fourteen hundred fighting men, including the cavalry and artillery: whereas the Bhoosla Raja had upwards of 10,000 infantry on the field, and at least an equal number of horse. His chief reliance, however, was placed in a body of between 3 and 4000 Arabs, who behaved with great bravery on this, and, indeed, on all subsequent occasions. Our loss in killed and wounded amounted by the returns to 333, being about one-fourth of those engaged, a most unusual proportion for the victorious party. Amongst these were four officers * killed and seven severely wounded, besides Mr. Sotheby above mentioned. The loss on the Raja's side was never precisely ascertained; but it must have been very severe. His

* Captain Sadler and Lieutenant Grant of the 24th Madras native infantry, Lieutenant Clarke of the 20th, and Doctor Neven, assistant surgeon, killed. Captains Charlesworth, Lloyd, and Pew, wounded severely; also Lieutenants Thullier and Bayley, with Cornets Smith and Heansay of the cavalry, and several others slightly.

army was so disheartened after the action, that it could not be persuaded to renew the attack, notwithstanding that a Sepoy of the escort, who deserted immediately after, represented in strong colours the exhausted condition of our troops, and their want of ammunition for many more rounds, in order to excite them to a second trial.

The result of this action proved the wisdom of the resolution of the commanding officer at Poona to advance and meet the enemy, in preference to abiding his attack. At Nâgpoor, indeed, there was no choice; but the much greater hazard of the contest there proves the superior advantage of numbers when acting on the offensive, with the same odds of skill and discipline.

It has been thought necessary to be thus particular in the account of these two affairs, because they formed two of the most glorious triumphs of the war, and because the effect, produced by their issue, gave the Mahrattas a distrust of themselves, highly favourable to the early accomplishment of Lord Hastings's views. Both the Pêshwa and the Bhoosla evidently reckoned with certainty on their ability to overwhelm the small force stationed at their respective capitals, and were astonished to find their utmost means baffled by mere detachments. In proportion as their estimate of their own strength had before been sanguine, they now gave way to despondency; and though Bajee Rao was sensible, that he had too long practised the arts of duplicity, to be admitted to a reconciliation on any terms, that would leave him in the exercise of dominion, he never afterwards attempted any enterprise that showed the smallest confidence in his means, nor ever rose above the character of a heartless and desperate fugitive. Appa Saheb had yet something to hope from the known clemency and moderation of the English. As soon, therefore, as he despaired of the cause he had espoused, he resolved to establish a claim to forgiveness by the promptitude of his submission. Immediately after the action of the 26th and 27th, he sent vakeels to express his sorrow, and to disavow having himself authorised the attack. The Baees, or women of the Raja's family, also interceded for him; but Mr. Jenkins refused to treat at all, while his army continued in force.

Bajee Rao and Appa Saheb have been accused of treachery, as well as of a breach of hospitality and of the laws of nations, in thus attacking the residents, who, in their capacity of ambassadors, might be deemed entitled to a sacred inviolability. There is, however, this palliative to be found for their conduct; that the residents had each of them an army under his direction, expressly designed for his support against the intrigues or violence of the court at which he resided. Thus armed, they of course lost much of the sacred character of heralds. If justice required, as doubtless it did, that they should at least have had the option of retiring unmolested, this option, or something equivalent to it, was afforded to Mr. Elphinstone; and if it was not tendered to Mr. Jenkins, it was merely because, when the matter was discussed in the Raja's council, it was decided to be useless to make an offer, which the attitude he had already assumed showed that the resident had no thought of accepting. With respect to the treachery of secret previous preparation, if we allow to a native power the abstract right of shaking off our alliance under any circumstances, we must concede to him this further step, as indispensable to its exercise. For, as it is an article of all our subsidiary alliances, that a military force shall be stationed at the capital, it is to be presumed, that open preparations for war would always be anticipated, and the design frustrated by the immediate employment of the force against the person of the prince. Wherefore, if there was any treachery in the conduct of these Mahratta chiefs, it was not so much in the manner, as in the act itself of their defection; for it is in the essence of our contracts of alliance, that, although accepted by the native power for the sake probably of some present advantage, or to get rid of some temporary evil of yet harder endurance, the benefit on our side is intended to be permanent; for which purpose, we stipulate for the perpetual continuance of the engagement, and the native power binds itself to this stipulation. Thus, it is as much an act of treachery in our ally to attempt to balk us of our advantage, by shaking us off after having got for himself the benefit stipulated for and contemplated, as it would be on our part to leave him to be in the first instance overwhelmed, after having engaged to assist him out of his difficulties. In this view, the defection of both these princes was decidedly treacherous, inasmuch as both, with a full knowledge of the terms on which alone our aid would be granted, bound themselves personally and voluntarily to adhere to them in perpetuity, and neither had any plea whatever of any default in executing the stipulations on our part, to urge in justification of his breach in the performance of his own part of the engagement.

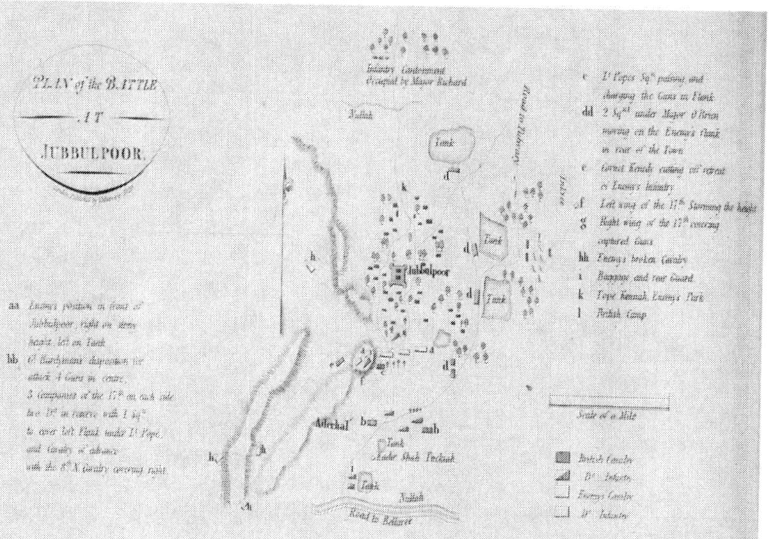
PLAN of the BATTLE
AT
JUBBULPOOR.
Jubbulpoor
Tank
Nullah
Aderhal
Road to Bellaree
Scale of a Mile
British Cavalry
Enemys Cavalry
k Tope Kannah, Enemys Park
l British Camp

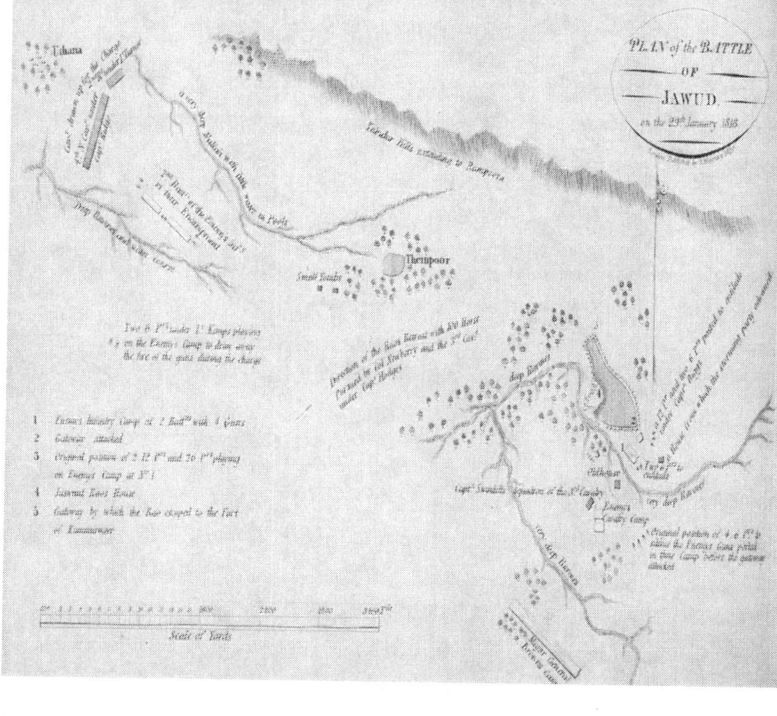
PLAN of the BATTLE
OF
JAWUD,
on the 29th January 1818.
Uthana
Thempoor
Small Tombs
Oldhouse
very deep Ravines
Scale of Yards
1 Enemys Infantry Camp of 2 Batt^ns with 4 Guns
2 Gateway Attacked
4 Jeswunt Raos House

CHAPTER XII.

NÂGPOOR—HINDOOSTAN.

1817, DECEMBER.

Reinforcements to Nâgpoor—Colonel Gahan—Major Pitman—Brigadier-General Doveton—Brigadier-General Hardyman—Terms proposed to the Raja—He temporizes—and surrenders—His camp attacked—and carried—Fort of Nâgpoor occupied by Arabs—besieged and assaulted without success—Arabs capitulate—Reasons for the Raja's reinstation—terms—dissent of Governor-General—retracted—British acquisitions—Reflections—Hindoostan—Pindarees—Suspicious conduct of regular powers—effect on Lord Hastings' plans—Cholera morbus—its virulence—and symptoms—Centre division arrives at Erich—moves back to the Sindh—movements in pursuit of Pindarees—affair at Bicheetal—wife of Kureem captured—Escape through Huraotee—distress—Exploit of a Havildar—Consequent military dispositions.

The Bhoosla Raja's defection and attack on the British Residency did not remain long unpunished. Troops poured into Nâgpoor from every quarter: some in consequence of the provisional requisition of the Resident, others under orders from Sir Thomas Hislop or the Marquess of Hastings himself. The first reinforcement that arrived was that under Lieutenant-Colonel Gahan, which had on the first alarm been ordered down from the valley of the Nerbudda. It consisted of a strong battalion of Bengal infantry, 1st-22d, the remaining three troops of the 6th Bengal cavalry and two gallopers. This detachment arrived on the 29th, and gave entire confidence to the troops in position on the Seetabuldee hills, which till then had been under very considerable apprehension of a second attack, and of the ultimate failure of their stores and ammunition. Mr. Jenkins had on the preceding day agreed to a suspension of arms, at the Raja's request, in order to allow time for this reinforcement to join without molestation; holding out, however, to Appa Saheb, the necessity of disbanding or separating himself from his army, as an indispensable preliminary to a restoration of peace on any terms.

Major Pitman, who brought up the second reinforcement, was at Omraotee on the frontier of Berar, when he received a hasty note despatched by Mr. Jenkins on the night of the 25th, while the issue of the attack was yet doubtful. He immediately forwarded the note to Brigadier-General Doveton, who was then at Jafeerabad, and set off himself with two battalions and a few of the Nizam's reformed cavalry, hastening his march in the hope of arriving at the scene of danger in time to afford relief. He reached Nâgpoor on the 5th of December. Brigadier-General Doveton followed with the whole second division of the army of the Dukhun, and entered that city with the light troops in advance on the 12th of December. The rest of the division came up two days afterwards. On his arrival, he rightly judged the re-establishment of affairs at Nâgpoor to be an object of paramount importance, in comparison with the occupation or probably the reduction of Aseergurh, which was one of the duties originally assigned to him in the general plan of operations. Indeed, it was of the utmost consequence, that the Bhoosla should be crushed as early as possible, in order that other potentates might be deterred by the rapid and exemplary punishment of his defection, from following in the same career.

In addition to the formidable force thus collected at Nâgpoor, the Marquess of Hastings, immediately on hearing of the attack made upon the brigade there stationed, ordered down Brigadier-General Hardyman with the corps of observation under his command, in Rewa. This officer, not receiving the order until the 6th of December, did not reach the neighbourhood until every thing had been already adjusted by General Doveton. His force was, however, of use in reducing Jubulpoor, where it gallantly routed a considerable body of troops opposed to it in the field, and in occupying the Bhoosla territory to the north and in the valley of the Nerbudda; and its further advance was countermanded, to allow of its being so employed. In the mean time, Brigadier-General Doveton, having allowed his troops a day to recover from the fatigue of their long and harassing marches, had proceeded to enforce upon Appa Saheb the acceptance of such terms, as should break his military power, and reduce him for the future to a state of entire dependence on the British Government.

On the morning of the 15th of December, Mr. Jenkins offered to the Raja the following terms of submission, as the only means of saving his army from attack, and himself from absolute ruin. The Raja to acknowledge, that by his defection he had placed his territories at the mercy of the British Government, which was consequently absolved from all ties towards himself, and free to dispose of them at pleasure; to give up all his artillery, leaving it to the discretion of the British authorities to restore such as they might think proper; to disband the Arabs and other mercenary troops, who were to march off in the directions assigned, leaving the city and fort of Nâgpoor to our occupation. Appa Saheb himself was required to come in and reside at the British Residency, as a hostage for the performance of these conditions, and four o'clock of the next morning was fixed as the limit of time for his acceptance of the conditions; by which hour if he did not submit, it was declared, that he would be attacked without further ceremony. He was however given to understand, that, upon accepting the above terms, the former relations would be restored, and no greater sacrifice required, than a territorial cession sufficient to meet the charges of the subsidiary force, and due provision for our future exercise of so much internal control, as might be necessary to secure us against a repetition of similar conduct on the part of the Raja.

Nerayun Pundit, who, since the breaking out of hostilities, had been the constant mediator between Appa Saheb and the British Representative, came several times in the course of the 15th to temporize, and to solicit a longer respite. But Mr. Jenkins insisted on the acceptance of the terms by the next morning at the latest, though he extended the period to seven o'clock. In the evening of the 15th, General Doveton beat to arms and approached the Seetabuldee position, where he bivouacked for the night. At six o'clock in the morning, Nerayun came again to say, that the Arabs and other troops would not allow his master to come in, and that a longer time would be indispensable to settle with them, and to withdraw them from the artillery which was demanded to be given up. The acceptance of the conditions was promised, but a respite of two or three days was solicited. The period allowed for Appa Saheb to come in was now extended till nine A. M.; with the understanding, that, by submission in this particular, he might obtain a farther extension for the execution of the other terms prescribed. When the time expired, nothing had been done. Brigadier-General Doveton accordingly advanced his army in order of battle*, to a position close upon the Raja's camp on the south of the city, from which he had previously determined to make the attack. Appa Saheb now gave way entirely to his personal fears, and, mounting his horse, rode off with his ministers, Nagoopunt and Ramchundur Wâgh, and a few other attendants, straight to the Residency, where he delivered himself up to Mr. Jenkins. Notice was immediately sent to Brigadier-General

* Vide Plan at the head of the preceding chapter.

Doveton, who halted upon receiving the information. The time for the surrender of the artillery and disbanding the army was then brought into discussion; the Resident insisting on the instant execution of the former point, in order to prevent any clandestine removal of the guns, while the Raja pressed for a further delay. It was arranged, that the artillery should be abandoned and the troops withdrawn to a distance by twelve o'clock of the same day; and Ramchundur Wâgh was sent to expedite the requisite arrangements for the purpose. He returned a little before twelve, reporting every thing to be in readiness; whereupon a couple of *hurkaras* were sent to the Brigadier-General, in order that he might detach a party to take possession of the guns said to be so abandoned. On questioning them more closely, General Doveton suspected that some deception was intended; and accordingly, instead of sending a party, he resolved to advance his whole line. He did so by open column of companies from the right of battalions. The guides led him to the arsenal south of the city, where thirty-six guns were found and taken possession of without resistance; a Lascar, however, was on the point of applying the match to one of them, when his arms were seized. The General, leaving Colonel Scott with a brigade from his left in possession of these guns, continued his advance towards the Sukur-Duree gardens, where he knew there were other batteries. The moment that the troops debouched from behind some trees separating the Sukur-Duree from Nâgpoor, a heavy fire was opened upon their front and right flank: no time was therefore lost in forming them into line for the attack. The cavalry and horse artillery on the extreme right, under Colonel Gahan, made a detour round the Sukur-Duree garden, and, after carrying a battery that opposed them in that quarter, came in flank of the main position of the enemy; while Colonel M'Leod's division advanced to the attack in front under a heavy cannonade. The enemy was formed in a retiring angle; and after Colonel M'Leod had carried the right of his position, where his strength of infantry was the greatest, the guns on his left still kept playing on our reserve, under cover chiefly of his cavalry. Colonel Gahan charged and drove them off, continuing the pursuit to some distance; but the guns were not silenced, until stormed shortly afterwards by a party from the reserve. By half-past one, seventy-five guns, mortars, and howitzers of different calibre and descriptions were in our hands. The enemy's camp was also taken, with forty elephants, belonging for the most part to the Raja, and all his camp equipage. The troops had on this occasion to advance upwards of 1000 yards in face of a powerful artillery; consequently the acquisition was not made without loss. Of the Europeans 39, and of the natives 102 were killed or wounded; but fortunately no officer was amongst the number.

Mun-Bhut and Gunput Rao were the Sirdars who instigated this resistance. Treachery on the part of the Raja was not suspected; though it is not improbable that Ramchundur Wâgh may have connived at the subtraction of many of the guns, under the notion, that Brigadier-General Doveton would have been satisfied with the capture of those left at the arsenal. Such a trick is so perfectly consistent with the half-measure policy pursued throughout by Appa Saheb, as to leave it by no means clear, that he did not participate in the guilt of the blood unnecessarily shed on this occasion. But the point was never made the subject of a special investigation.

Mun-Bhut Rao, with the Arab infantry, fled into the city, and occupied the fort, a place of considerable strength, within which were the Raja's palaces and other strong buildings. Two days were spent in endeavouring to persuade them to evacuate it and retire, on which terms they were promised a safe conduct to the Nâgpoor frontier. Their arrears were also paid up in the course of this negotiation; yet in the end they refused to evacuate. The siege of the fort was accordingly commenced. By the 20th, a howitzer battery was erected at the foot of the larger of the Seetabuldee hills, and, on the 21st, the mound of a tank that lay between it and the fort, not 250 yards from the western (Jooma) gate, was seized, for the purpose of being converted into a breaching battery. All the captured guns that were thought to be of sufficient calibre were brought into this position; and though it was soon found, that their fire had little effect in comparison with our own eighteen-pounders, yet on the 23d of December, the gate was considered to be sufficiently injured, to make an assault practicable. Accordingly, a storm was attempted on the morning of the 24th; and four companies of the Bengal battalion, 1st-22d, headed by a company of the Royal Scots, and accompanied by the sappers and miners, advanced to the Jooma gate, in the hope of establishing themselves there, if not of carrying the place. At the same time, Colonel Scott led an attack on the Toolsee-bâgh, a garden on the south of the city, and between it and the river Nâg, while Major Pitman advanced to co-operate with a detachment of the Nizam's infantry. The breached gate was found to be so commanded from inner walls, as to have all the effect of a second intrenchment; and the storming party, after losing many men in attempting to penetrate or establish themselves, was in the end obliged to retire. On this failure, Colonel Scott and Major Pitman were also recalled. Our loss was 90 killed, and 179 wounded. Lieutenant Bell, of the Royal Scots, was amongst the former, and Lieutenants Cameron and Cowell in the number of the latter.

Brigadier-General Doveton now saw, that the place could not be taken without a more sufficient battering train. He therefore resolved to wait the arrival of that attached to his own force from Akola, before he ventured to renew his operations. The Arabs, however, feeling that they had already done enough for their honour, and that, being entirely without hope of support, their ultimate reduction was almost inevitable, resolved to make the best advantage of their successful resistance, by offering to evacuate on terms. They accordingly proposed to march out with their families, baggage, private property, and arms. The proposition was immediately accepted, as time was a principal consideration with us: and the garrison evacuated the fort on the 30th of December, and was escorted beyond the Nâgpoor frontier by a detachment formed for the purpose. Mun-Bhut surrendered himself to the Resident on the same day.

The military operations against the Bhoosla state were thus happily brought to a final conclusion, within little more than a month from the commencement of hostilities by the Raja. Nothing now remained, but to make such a settlement of the Nâgpoor Government, and of the relations of the state with the British, as should give us complete security for the future, and some indemnification also for the past. There were many important considerations involved in the choice of the course to be now adopted, which rendered it desirable that the views of the Governor-General should first be ascertained. But the communication had hitherto been so completely cut off, that no instruction as to the treatment of Appa Saheb, in the event of his submission, had yet been received. The Raja still continued at the Residency; and, as he was impatient to return to the palace, upon which the British flag was now flying, there seemed to be no ground for his further detention. The case, therefore, appeared to require the Resident to act upon his own responsibility, and come to some agreement, or at least lay the foundation for a final settlement without further delay. Mr. Jenkins had seen no cause to be dissatisfied with the conduct of the Raja since he had voluntarily surrendered himself; on the contrary, he regarded the circumstance of the abandonment of so many guns at the arsenal, as well as the subsequent payment of the arrears due to the Arabs as soon as demanded, as clear proofs that he had exerted himself both sincerely and sedulously to execute the conditions demanded of him; so that, although he had not come in within the prescribed time in the first instance, nor surrendered the whole of the guns, nor quietly disbanded the troops, nor given up the city and fort, agreeably to the letter of the stipulations, still, as his personal surrender had been received when he did come in, and as the failure of performance in other respects arose from causes apparently beyond his control, the Resident did not consider his claim to be reinstated, with the limitations and sacrifices he had been led to expect on his submission, to be at all weakened by subsequent events. Yet, while he felt the necessity of permitting the fallen prince to resume his station, he was no less sensible of the impossibility of placing further confidence in one, who had proved himself to be so inveterately addicted to intrigue, and so complete a Mahratta at heart. His military power had fortunately been annihilated; but the resources of the Nâgpoor territory, if left to Appa Saheb's uncontrolled disposal, presented means of further mischief, which there could be little doubt he would avail himself of, unless checked with a strong hand. In preparing the definitive treaty for the Raja's acceptance, Mr. Jenkins, therefore, resolved to assume and act upon the principle, of reducing the head of the Bhoosla state to the condition of a mere pageant, and giving the British Government a control over every branch of internal, as well as of external administration, to the extent of imposing a ministry of its own selection, though composed of native subjects of the Raja. The forts of the country were, according to this plan, to be open to the discretionary introduction of British garrisons; and, for securing the subordination of the capital, the Seetabuldee hills were to be fortified. In fact, we were to have complete military occupation of the whole country; and, after his recent experience of the character of the ruling prince, the Resident could not consider any less security as either solid or permanent. In addition to the powers of general control, territory equal to the full charge of the subsidiary force (about 24 lack rupees) was to be ceded in perpetuity, in lieu of the present annual payment of 7½ lack, which only provided for the extraordinary field charges of the troops. The districts proposed to be demanded were, those held by the Raja, north of the Nerbudda, including Sir-Gooja, Jushpoor, Sohagpoor, and Sumbhulpoor to the east; all the valley to the south of the river, and as far as Chupara, between Jubulpoor and Nâgpoor; together with Mooltaya, Bytool, Gawilgurh, and all the Raja's remaining possessions in Berar.

Mr. Jenkins had drawn up a treaty on the above basis, and was on the point of submitting it to the Raja's acceptance, preparatory to his reinstallation; when, on the 2d of January, he received the instructions issued by the Marquess of Hastings, on first hearing of the defection of the Bhoosla prince. These instructions peremptorily forbad any personal reconciliation whatever, directing the young grandson of Ragoojee, by the daughter married to Gooja Appa, to be placed on the *Guddee*, and affairs to be confided to the conduct of a regency of our own selection. The deposition of Appa Saheb was considered to be indispensable, both as a punishment for his defection at so critical a period, and from a conviction, that he could no longer be trusted even with the semblance of authority. The powerful motives, that had swayed the mind of Mr. Jenkins, were wholly unknown to his Lordship at this time: consequently, when indistinct accounts of the recent occurrences at Nâgpoor, subsequent to the arrival of General Doveton at that city, were received by his Lordship from different quarters, before the official reports of the negotiations came to hand, the vētō against the reinstallation of Appa Saheb was twice repeated, under the supposition of his reiterated default in the performance of his engagements; unless the British Government should have been already too far committed to retract with honour.

In consequence of the receipt of these instructions, Mr. Jenkins delayed to submit to the Raja his own draft of the definitive treaty, substituting a provisional engagement, which stipulated, that he should retain the *guddee* until the pleasure of the Governor-General should be known; but with a proviso for an eventual settlement on the basis above set forth, in case the Marquess of Hastings should confirm his restoration. The Resident confidently expected this confirmation, as soon as all the circumstances should have been made known; and in this he judged rightly. For the Governor-General, on receiving the ample details contained in the official despatches, which, however, were a long time on the road, became sensible of the necessity of replacing Appa Saheb, not so much with a view to the immediate and advantageous settlement of affairs in that quarter, as from respect to the moral obligation to do so, under the circumstances of his surrender. As a matter of policy, it may be right to mention, that the Baees along with the infant grandson of Ragoojee, who was nine or ten years old, and had already the title of Bala-Saheb, had, with Gooja Appa his father, been sent off against their will to Chanda, before General Doveton's arrival. This could not have been prevented at the time; neither would it have been possible to have secured the person of the reigning prince, in the event of the most complete success of our arms, after all the reinforcements had come up. To have proclaimed the boy would, therefore, have only had the effect of occasioning his instant death; after which we should have had a long and harassing war to wage against the actual sovereign, unaided by any party in the state, or any head round which the malcontents might rally.

Convinced by the representation of these difficulties, Lord Hastings in the end approved of the propositions submitted by

Mr. Jenkins, and directed the treaty to be concluded on the basis above described, which was done in the ensuing month of February. However, when the specific cessions demanded came to be discussed, along with the other provisions for the control of the Raja's internal administration, Appa Saheb pressed, with apparent earnestness, that the whole country should be taken under British rule, with a reservation of one-fourth of the revenues for his personal expenses, under a guarantee that this proportion should not fall short of fifteen lack rupees. For such an income, he offered to forswear his independence and abandon the cares of government altogether, and to range himself in the same class with the Nuwabs of the Carnatic and of Bengal. But the offer being saddled with other expensive provisions for creditors and relations of the Raja, and the possession of the country by the British Government being on other grounds not desirable, it was not thought fit to entertain it. By the arrangement actually concluded, we obtained the cession of territory that stood in the Bhoosla accounts as yielding a net revenue of 2,247,200 rupees, after deducting alienations and demands of all kinds. The ceded country was fertile, and, with the exception of the jungul tract south of Behar, well watered by the Nerbudda and its tributary streams. Through the exertions of the troops commanded by General Hardyman, who defeated the Sooba of Jubulpoor * in a brilliant affair on the 19th of December, and of the reserve brigade of the subsidiary force under Lieutenant-Colonel M'Morine, which was equally successful against Sudoo-Baba of Sirinugurh on the 15th of January, the whole had been brought under subjection before the end of the latter month, except the forts of Chouragurh and Mundela; and the considerable resources they afforded were made available to the operations of the current season.

* Vide plan at the head of this chapter.

It is impossible to close the account of this portion of the transactions at Nâgpoor, without remarking on the extreme weakness and irresolution betrayed throughout by Appa Saheb. He might perhaps be excused for not concerting the time of his defection with the Pêshwa, so that both attacks should have been made the same day; for the character of Bajee Rao warranted the precaution of waiting to see him actually committed, before his ally should stir a step. But, after the resolution to join the confederacy was once formed, and after collecting an overwhelming force, which he assured himself must overpower the brigade at Nâgpoor, his long hesitation before the attack was authorised, his disavowal of it after the failure, and his paltry attempt to throw on Mun-Bhut the whole responsibility, in the hope thus to escape himself, were acts of the most decided pusillanimity. He never seems to have known his own mind from first to last, but betrayed the greatest weakness and want of judgment, in so soon abandoning the cause he had espoused, before it was by any means desperate; and particularly in not renewing the attack after the first repulse, when he knew our troops must be exhausted, instead of remaining idle at Nâgpoor, till the arrival of General Doveton with an overpowering force, without making any effort whatever to obstruct his march, or to cut off either of the detachments which preceded him. He must have felt, and indeed was explicitly told, that he could be admitted to no reconciliation that would leave him political independence or the reality of power: but sovereignty on any terms, though but a mere shadow, was too dearly prized in possession, to allow him fairly to commit it to the hazardous chance of a protracted struggle for the substance. No country was ever better adapted to desultory warfare than the Bhoosla territory; the whole is a continued tract of mountains, ravines, and junguls, forming altogether as difficult a theatre of war as any in existence. Subsequent experience has proved the facility, with which, had he retired with his army unbroken, he might have prolonged the contest indefinitely, and, by giving occupation to a large proportion of our military force, have prevented that concentration of means for the destruction of his confederate, the Pêshwa, which was afterwards so successfully directed to that object. However, there can be no doubt, that both must have fallen in the end; but a great difference might have been made in the time, the charge, and the trouble, it would have cost us to effect our purpose. It was the peculiar merit of Lord Hastings' plan of operations, to have placed such means at command, as should make the cause of the Mahrattas desperate under any combination of circumstances; and the further we trace the detail of events in their order of occurrence, the more reason shall we find to admire the forecast, which so disposed those means, that not one adverse circumstance or occasion of danger arose, without its remedy and corrective being found ready at hand. This will be particularly observable as we proceed with the narrative of the transactions on the side of Hindoostan, to which quarter it is time again to turn our attention.

The march of the three divisions of Malcolm, Adams, and Marshall to Tullain, Bairsea, and Basouda, and the advance of the last named to Seronj, had completely driven the Pindarees out of their haunts in Malwa by the end of November. As above related, the *durras* of Kureem and Wâsil Mahommed retreated northward by Nya-Seraee on the main road to Gwalior; while Cheetoo moved off in a westerly direction, as well to avail himself of the support he expected from the army of Holkar, which was already assembled in force, as to fall back on the position of Juswunt Rao Bhâo, one of Sindheea's commanders, from whom he had obtained assurances of protection and of a refuge for his family in the strong fort of * Kumulner.

* Vide plate at the head of Chapter XV.

The disposition of Holkar's military began at this time to assume a decidedly hostile character. The march of the main body of the Pindarees towards Gwalior, and the uniform conduct of Sindheea's captains, as well as the reluctance of the chief himself to execute the conditions of the treaty of concert he had lately signed under compulsion, seemed to indicate a similar bias in that durbar. It was also doubtful, whether Ameer Khan would ratify the engagements of his agent at Dehlee. Connecting all these appearances, therefore, with the open resort of the Pêshwa and of the Bhoosla to arms, there was certainly ground to apprehend the worst from the aspect of affairs at the close of the month of November. The Goorkhas of Nipâl too were collecting their forces, and known to be in close communication with the powers of Hindoostan; so that the slightest reverse, in the temper of men's minds at the time, would soon have been magnified into a disaster, capable of involving the whole of India in one general combustion. The success at Nâgpoor, however, confounded all their calculations, and operated powerfully to destroy the vain illusions of the ill disposed. Ameer Khan ratified the treaty of his agent on the first receipt of the intelligence; communicating to Sir David Ochterlony the circumstances of the battle, and using many expressions of wonder and admiration at the conduct of the troops engaged, with whose numbers he was perfectly acquainted. But the spirit which had been excited was not every where so soon allayed; and in Hindoostan, as well as in the Dukhun, there were moments, when the firmness and decision of those entrusted with the chief direction of affairs were distinctly called forth into action. The sudden development of the extent of combination, which had been organizing against us, might have induced many to contract their views, in proportion to the increasing cloud of difficulties; but had a contrary effect upon the mind of the Governor-General. To his eye, these crude attempts to thwart his plans presented but the means of establishing the settlement he designed for India upon a broader and more solid foundation: so just and so unbounded was his reliance on the machinery he had prepared for the accomplishment of his purpose.

Unlooked for circumstances, however, combined to put his Lordship's fortitude to the test. Having by his advance to the Sindh enforced upon Sindheea the acceptance of the treaty of concert, he was in the middle of November moving leisurely with the centre division to take up such a position, as might be calculated to connect the object of keeping that chief in awe, with the interception of the Pindarees, should they attempt to penetrate by the north or east; when his army was afflicted with a pestilence as violent and destructive, as any recorded in the pages of history. The malady, from some similarity in its principal features to that previously known by medical men under the title of the *cholera morbus*, has usually been designated by this appellation. It was, however, decidedly epidemic, and, like all similar visitations of nature, its source is matter of pure conjecture, though its progress has been distinctly traced. It was first observed in the Delta of the Ganges about the middle of the rainy season of 1817; and, from the early part of September, its ravages were felt at Calcutta, where for a long time it destroyed upwards of 200 persons daily. Spreading thence up the course of the Ganges and its tributary waters, it reached the camp of Brigadier-General Hardyman about the beginning of October; but as it was pitched in a healthy country, and his force consisted of but one European and one native battalion with a regiment of cavalry, its destructive effects, though serious, were not particularly marked, in comparison with what had previously been felt in its progress thither. Continuing westward, however, it fell with extraordinary violence upon the army commanded by Lord Hastings in person, which it overtook on the commencement of its march eastward from the Sindh on the 14th of November. The year was one of scarcity, and grain had been collected for the troops and camp followers with extreme difficulty, and of course of very inferior quality. That part of Bundelkhund, where the division was encamped when the disease first showed itself was, moreover, low and notoriously unhealthy; besides which, except when obtained from running streams, the water was generally indifferent. The time of the year too was precisely that, at which the heat of the day is most strongly contrasted with the cold of the night. All these circumstances, superadded to the crowded state of the camp of so large an army, gave to the epidemic, when it did break out, a degree of violence much exceeding what it had manifested in other parts of the country. For about ten days, that it raged with particular fury, the whole camp was a hospital*, and the deaths in this short period amounted, according to the nearest estimate that could be made, to a tenth of the whole number collected, Europeans and natives. Fighting men and camp followers were alike affected; but the latter, being generally worse clothed and fed, suffered in a greater proportion. Of the Europeans there were fewer cases of seizure; but those which occurred were seldom otherwise than fatal, and usually so within a few hours. The camp continued for some days to move eastward, in the hope of finding a better climate, as soon as it should reach the Betwa; but each day of march many dead and dying were abandoned on the route, and many more fell down on the road, for whom it was impossible to furnish the means of transport, though the utmost possible

* The narrator himself lost seven men and a *moonshee* in about four days, besides twelve others who were sick and unserviceable for a month, out of an establishment of fifty-three; and others of the staff were equal sufferers. The fighting men filled the whole of the hospitals in the first two days; and for servants and followers every man's tent was his only receptacle, and himself the only doctor.

provision had been made by the previous distribution of carts and elephants for the accommodation of the sick. Such indeed was the general distress, that, so long as the epidemic raged, even the healthy were broken in spirit, and incapable of labour or fatigue; while the bazars and public establishments were deserted, and the whole efficiency of this fine army was, for the time, apparently destroyed.

The symptoms of the disease may be described in few words. Its approach was indicated by a giddiness that came on suddenly and without warning, attended with an immediate and total prostration of strength; insomuch, that men fell from their horses in the line of march, and were unable afterwards to rise from the ground, though perfectly well when they had started in the morning. A nausea succeeded, with purging and vomiting, so violent as to defy the power of medicine. Laudanum was generally given at this stage in large quantities; but the stomach would retain nothing, throwing up a peculiar green or whitish fluid. After this, the patient was seized with cramps and coldness from the extremities upwards, even to the parts about the heart. In the midst of his agonies, he felt a burning thirst, and called incessantly for cold water, but vomited it the instant it was given. This lasted from 24 to 48 hours, and the person affected either died under its severity, or was left in a state of such extreme debility, that the utmost power of medicine availed nothing. The cure was very rare when these spasmodic affections came on with any degree of violence. It was observed of this malady, that neither the voice, nor the power of swallowing, nor the intellect, were ever lost while life remained; also, that after death the bodies had a peculiar smell, which was immediately perceptible at some distance. Medical men have never yet discovered wherein the disease lay; much less have they found any probable cure. Laudanum or opium to allay the irritation within, and calomel, the universal specific of India, with stimulants when the patient is about to sink from exhaustion, form the most approved, if not the general practice. The medical art has gone no further.

Towards the end of November, the Governor-General had reached a healthy station at Erich on the Betwa, and the epidemic had visibly expended its virulence. The camp was, however, still crowded with convalescents, when the march of the Pindarees towards Gwalior threatened to call for the active exertions of the centre division, and the personal appearance of its noble commander upon the scene of operations.

It has before been mentioned, that one detachment had been sent from this division under Major Cumming, to cover the civil station of Bundelkhund. This had subsequently been pushed forward as far south as Tearee, while a second detachment, chiefly of cavalry, under Colonel Philpot of His Majesty's 24th dragoons, was in the course of November stationed at Burwa-Sâgur, so as completely to connect the centre division at Erich, with that of General Marshall, then moving on Seronj. But, as soon as it was ascertained that the durras of Kureem, and of Wâsil Mahommed, had decamped to the northward, Lord Hastings ordered the detachment from Burwa-Sâgur to move through Dutteea, across the Sindh, to cut them off from Gwalior; and, at the same time, seeing reason to suspect the fidelity of his ally to his new engagements, he again marched upon the Sindh, from his station near Erich, calling in the detachment from Tearee. This movement had the double object of giving a support to Colonel Philpot, and more effectually overawing the councils of the Gwalior durbar. His Lordship reached Soonaree, which is only 30 miles S. S. E. of Gwalior, on the 11th of December, where his unexpected appearance had the desired effect. Sindheea was alarmed, and the Pindarees halted in consternation in the junguls and broken ground about Shahabad, not knowing what course to pursue, or whither to direct their march. Despairing of aid from Gwalior, they could not retrace their steps; for General Marshall, though he had not been able to make all the progress expected, had nevertheless reached Nya Seraee on the 12th of December, while Colonel Adams was with his force at Googul Chupra on the Parbutee; both of which points were particularly well adapted to intercept their return southward. To force the passes of Huraotee to the S. W., or those of the Chumbul towards Jypoor, seemed the only modes of escape now left to the fugitives: but the state of the river, and a variety of precautions, which had been taken to strengthen the principal passes in the latter quarter, by troops from Agra and from General Donkin's division, rendered the passage of the Chumbul, lower than Huraotee, wholly impracticable. Sir David Ochterlony had also arrived with the reserve in the neighbourhood of Jypoor, and was prepared to support this line of defence. Again, with respect to escaping by Huraotee, the country there was in the hands of the Raj-Rana Zalim Singh, manager for the Raja of Kota, who was now in strict alliance with us. Immediately upon the conclusion of the treaty with Sindheea, Captain Tod had been ordered from Gwalior, where he was acting assistant to the Resident, in order to cement a closer union with this chieftain; and he had not only been successful in this object, having obtained from the Raj-Rana the blocking up of all the passes through his dominions, but had further induced him to place a contingent at the disposal of the British authorities, which had for some time been in the field. General Donkin also, with the right division, arrived at Boondee on the 10th of December; and hearing from Captain Tod of the situation of the Pindarees about Shahabad, was now in full march eastward to cut them off, in case of any effort to escape in that direction.

On the 13th of December, General Marshall made a move

towards Shahabad, where he was informed the united durras still remained encumbered with their baggage and families. At the same time Colonel Adams crossed the Parbutee, and took the same direction, to co-operate with the above movement. General Marshall arrived in the afternoon of the 14th at the Lodwana Ghât, one of those leading into Huraotee, which he found the Pindarees had lately forced, in consequence of the ill conduct of Zalim Singh's troops there posted. Here he was told, that the freebooters were still encamped at Bichee-Tal, a short distance only from the top of the Ghât. Accordingly, he lost no time in pushing forward his advanced guard with all the cavalry, in the hope of giving them a surprise. A party of about 1000 of the best mounted, immediately on perceiving the approach of the advance, presented themselves as if to oppose it; but, instead of abiding a charge, led Colonel Newbery, who commanded the cavalry, into a long pursuit, away from the route by which the rest effected their escape. General Marshall, however, took much baggage that day, notwithstanding that no more than fifty or sixty of the enemy were killed. In the course of his advance next morning, he found the road strewed with loads of grain and other baggage, thrown away in the confusion of the flight. Kureem and Wâsil had moved off westward, intending to cross the Chumbul by the Loharee Ghât, in the hope of being joined by Muhtab Khan, one of Ameer Khan's principal officers, as soon as they should penetrate to Jypoor. That Ghât, however, was guarded by the wing of one of General Donkin's battalions, previously detached for the purpose; and the General himself, after crossing the Chumbul on the 13th, was now in full march towards Burôd, which lay in the direct line of their retreat by this route. The Pindarees did not hear of General Donkin's approach, until he had surprised their advanced guard, in a night bivouac, about four miles north-east of Burôd, capturing the wife of Kureem Khan, and all his state elephants, kettle-drums, standards, and other insignia of command. The main body of the two durras was then only six miles distant; but, on finding themselves intercepted, they instantly called a council of the leaders, when it was agreed, that, burning their tents and abandoning their baggage, all but the *élite* or fighting men should disperse, every one free to seek his own fortune. The two chiefs, with less than 4000, all well mounted, went off in the utmost haste to the south; and passing to the left of Colonel Adams' division, while he was manœuvring on the right bank of the Parbutee, made good their passage through Zalim Singh's territory, although Colonel Adams, immediately on hearing of their flight that way, detached his cavalry under Major Clarke in pursuit. Of those left behind, many were cut up by the different divisions, some in attempting the Loharee Ghât, and the remainder by the villagers, who now regarded their destruction as certain, and no longer hesitated to retaliate on them the cruelties they had so often suffered at their hands. So complete was the despondency of these once formidable hordes, and so hopeless their present situation, that the appearance of the smallest party of our Sipahees was enough to make a large body of them throw every thing away and disperse. Availing himself of this feeling, on the night of the 23d of December, an Havildar, with only thirty-four men of Captain Tod's escort, ventured to attack a very considerable body, as it lay encamped in a part of Zalim Singh's territories. The whole galloped off on the first volley, deserting their camels, and even many of their horses; but when the morning dawned soon after, and they saw the smallness of the party, they rallied, and showed a disposition to dispute the prize. The Havildar, however, manœuvring as if he was merely the advance guard of a larger force, put them a second time to flight: nor did they venture again to turn. Khooshal Koonwar, a Sirdar of note, was the commander of the routed party. The Havildar secured a large booty, and gained great credit by the enterprise.

The object having been thus accomplished in this quarter, Major-General Marshall was ordered to return with the head-quarters of his division to Seronj, in order to be at hand to prevent any broken parties of the marauders from re-appearing in their previous haunts, as well as to hinder other powers from establishing their jurisdiction in the territory whence they had just been expelled, unless with the express authority of the Governor-General or Sir Thomas Hislop. The scene of operations, as far as concerned the Pindarees, was now entirely confined to Mewur, in which direction Chetoo had originally retired, and whither the remains of Kureem's and Wâsil's durras had directed their flight.

A new plan of operations was forthwith devised, in order to surround them similarly in this quarter. Colonel Adams moved down upon Gungrar to hem them in on the east; while General Donkin, recrossing the Chumbul, proceeded to take post at Shahpoora, westward of the Bunas, so as to inclose them on the north. The Marquess of Hastings also despatched Major-General Brown from the centre division at Soonaree, with a light force, composed of the 3d native cavalry dromedary corps, one troop of horse-artillery, and some companies of light infantry; which, after being reinforced by a regiment of cavalry*, some irregular horse, and a battalion from Major-General Marshall's army, was directed to march by the line of Shahabad, and to the southward of Huraotee, so as to be available to the north of Colonel Adams, in case its services should be required in that direction. In the mean time, the divisions from the Dukhun,

* 4th native cavalry, and 2d-1st native infantry.

under Generals Sir Thomas Hislop and Sir John Malcolm, as well as the army from Guzerât under Sir William Keirr, had become available in the same quarter. But, before we follow up the operations against the Pindarees, it will be necessary to relate the other more important transactions, in which the two divisions from the Dukhun had just been involved with the army of Holkar.

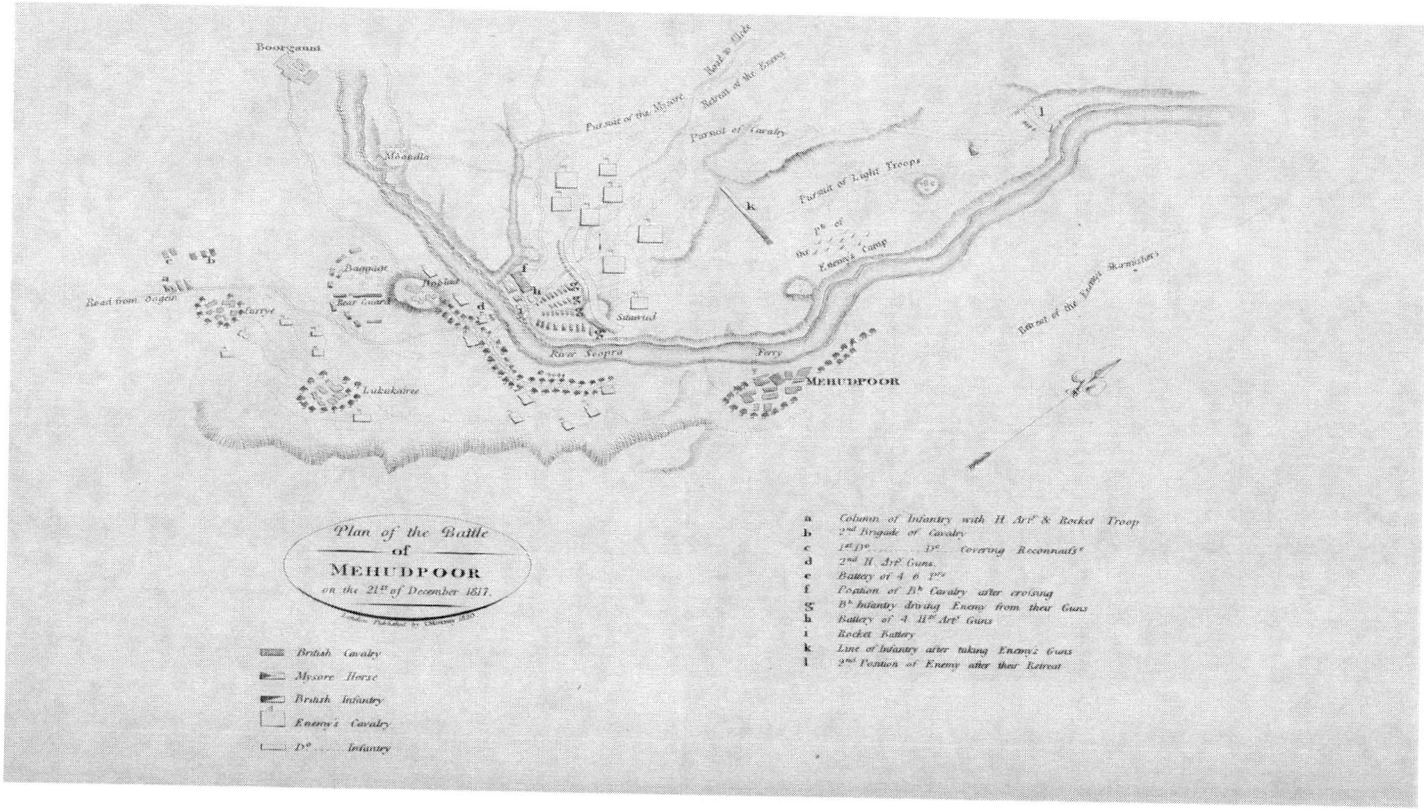
Boorgaum
Road to Alote
Retreat of the Enemy
Pursuit of the Mysore
Pursuit of Cavalry
Moondla
Pursuit of Light Troops
Enemy's Camp
Baggage
Road from Oogein
Rear Guard
Dooblai
Sauvrud
River Seopra
Ferry
MEHUDPOOR
Lukakairee
Retreat of the Enemy's Skirmishers
Plan of the Battle of MEHUDPOOR on the 21st of December 1817.
British Cavalry
Mysore Horse
British Infantry
Enemy's Cavalry
D° ...... Infantry
a Column of Infantry with H. Art^y & Rocket Troop
b 2nd Brigade of Cavalry
c 1st D° .... D° Covering Reconnaiss^e
d 2nd H. Art^y Guns.
e Battery of 4 6 P^rs
f Position of B^h Cavalry after crossing
g B^h Infantry driving Enemy from their Guns
h Battery of 4 H^se Art^y Guns
i Rocket Battery
k Line of Infantry after taking Enemy's Guns
l 2nd Position of Enemy after their Retreat

CHAPTER XIII.

HOLKAR—HINDOOSTAN.

1817-18. DECEMBER, JANUARY, FEBRUARY.

Brigadier-General Malcolm pursues Cheetoo—meets the army of Holkar—Falls back on Oojein—overtures from that durbar—Effect of Pêshwa's defection—army advances—Junction of the divisions of Malcolm and Hislop—negotiation tried—Regent put to death—hostilities—Battle of Mehudpoor—Junction of the Guzerat division—Terms offered—Treaty of Mundisôr—affair of Rampoora—Effect on Sindheea—Juswunt Rao Bhao—affair of Jawud—Kumulnèr and other forts taken—Final settlement in that quarter—Pindarees expelled from Mewur—surprised at Kotree—further pursuit—Submission of Namdar Khan—Wâsil Mahommed—Kureem and his son—how disposed of—Cheetoo.

It has been mentioned in the preceding chapters, that Sir John Malcolm, with the third division of the army of the Dukhun, arrived at Tullain on the 26th of November. Here being informed of Cheetoo's flight to the west, and that Kureem and Wâsil had taken the northward route, he resolved to move in pursuit of the former, and proceeded by Sarungpoor to Agur. But the motions of the army of Holkar having latterly been very suspicious, it was arranged between the Brigadier-General and Colonel Adams, that the latter should move westward also as far as Rajgurh-patan, to afford his support in case of necessity. Sir John Malcolm arrived at Agur on the 4th of December, and from this point opened a communication with Captain Tod at Kota, whose information confirmed the reports of his own intelligencers, representing the intentions of Holkar, or at least those of his army, to be decidedly hostile. The reception of Cheetoo, whose camp was pitched close to that of Holkar, and who was himself admitted to an audience before he set off to deposit his family with Juswunt Rao Bhâo in Kumulnèr, was a sufficient proof of the sentiments of the ruling party at this durbar. Sir John Malcolm, therefore, having in the interim heard that Sir Thomas Hislop was on his return to Oojein, resolved to fall back upon that *appui*, and to let Colonel Adams advance to the north, in co-operation with the division of General Marshall, which was on the point of moving from Seronj. It will be necessary to give some explanation of the conduct of Holkar's administration at this juncture.

It will be recollected, that it formed part of Lord Hastings' general plan, to conclude with this durbar a treaty of concert similar to that effected with Sindheea; with the difference, however, of detaching Ameer Khan from his dependency upon the chief, and procuring the acknowledgment of his independent sovereignty over such districts as might be in his actual possession. In conformity with this plan, a letter had been addressed to the Regency of Holkar by the Resident at Dehlee, at the same time that negotiations were opened with Sindheea and Ameer Khan, inviting it to send a confidential agent to Dehlee to treat, and intimating the terms on which it was the Governor-General's wish to form a closer connexion with his durbar. For a long time no answer was returned to this communication; but on the 15th of November Mr. Metcalfe received an overture from the Regent, Toolsee-Baee, offering to place herself and the young Mulhar Rao under the protection of the British Government. This overture, though conveyed with much secrecy, came either from the ministers of the day, Gunput Rao and Tanteea Jog, or at least with their knowledge and concurrence. Accordingly, on Captain Tod's being sent to Kota, he was instructed to open a communication through the ministers;

and as it was supposed to be the Baee's principal object in making the offer, to rid herself and her ward of the influence of Ameer Khan and the rebellious commanders of his infantry, General Donkin was apprised beforehand of the probability that the Baee might need the active aid of a British force; and this had been one of the objects of his advance up the left bank of the Chumbul.

Soon afterwards, however, the news of the Pêshwa's defection spread abroad, and the first impulse of the sirdars of Holkar was to march immediately to the south, in order to rally round the legitimate head of the Mahratta nation. The intention to move in that direction was soon publicly announced; but it was at first supposed to be a feint on the part of the Baee and her ministry, who, finding it impossible to control the soldiery, were thought to have taken this step with a view to deceive them by the appearance of a cordial unison of sentiment. But the sirdars were not to be so deceived; and suspecting that the ministry was intriguing underhand with the English, resolved upon its removal from office. On the 24th of November, Tanteea Jog was accused in open durbar of a conspiracy to betray the principality to the English; and he was accordingly stripped of his office and placed in close confinement. Gunput Rao was left nominally in the chief conduct of affairs; but the real power fell into the hands of the Patan sirdars, at the head of whom was Ghufoor Khan, the avowed agent of Ameer Khan, and Ramdeen, one of the most considerable of the infantry officers. The march from Rampoora was commenced very soon afterwards; and it was resolved to move by Indrok on Mehudpoor, and thence by Indore across the Nerbudda by the ford of Choolee-Muheshwur. Every effort was made to collect the dispersed infantry of Holkar's establishment; and, before the 28th, fourteen additional battalions under Roshun-Beg and Roshun-Khan had joined on the line of march.

Things were in this state in the camp of Mulhar Rao, when Cheetoo formed a junction with it, and the near approach of Sir John Malcolm brought it more directly into contact with the British armies. The mutinous troops were kept together by the promise of being paid their arrears on arriving at Indore, and the hopes of all were buoyed up by the expectation of a liberal supply of money from the coffers of Bajee Rao, as soon as they should have crossed the Nerbudda: assurances to this effect had been received from Poona but a few days before, so that it was no time to expect any favourable disposition towards ourselves, nor indeed was the soldiery inclined to pay much attention to the remonstrances addressed to the sirdars by Sir John Malcolm, in consequence of their reception of Cheetoo, or to the efforts of that officer to persuade them to relinquish the design of espousing the cause of the Pêshwa. The sirdars themselves, however, were liberal of their professions, and answered the letters both of Sir John Malcolm and of the resident at Dehlee with general protestations of their desire to maintain the existing relations of amity. The march to the south was nevertheless continued: all ranks, particularly the regent-princess, expressing the most enthusiastic devotion to the cause of the Mahratta sovereign. Seeing, therefore, to what issue matters were fast verging, Sir John Malcolm, as above mentioned, fell back upon Oojein, in order to effect a junction with the division of Sir Thomas Hislop.

The two divisions met on the 12th of December, and, after a halt of two days at Oojein, advanced on the 14th towards the camp of Holkar, for the purpose of giving effect to the negotiation. A draft of treaty was prepared, similar in most of the terms to that concluded with Sindheea, and was proffered to the acceptance of the durbar. Its reception was at first outwardly favourable; and, to carry on the deception as long as possible, a confidential agent was sent to treat and discuss the several articles. Things continued in this uncertain state for some days, the two armies lying all the while within fourteen miles of each other; that of Holkar being at Mehudpoor, while Sir Thomas Hislop was at Punbehar, a little to the north of Oojein. On the 17th of December, the mutinous spirit of the Patan sirdars openly gained the preponderance; and, distrusting the designs of Gunput Rao and the Regent Baee, whom they still suspected of a secret design to throw themselves upon British protection, they seized and confined both, and broke off all further communication with Sir John Malcolm. It was the general feeling of the sirdars, that if the court were to accede to the terms proposed, they would themselves lose all personal consideration; and there was little difficulty in persuading the troops, that such a measure would necessarily deprive them for ever of their means of livelihood. In this feeling, it was unanimously resolved to offer battle to the English, in preference to accepting the terms; and, with a view to prevent any future intrigues from interfering with the resolution, the regent, Toolsee Baee, was carried down by night to the banks of the Soopra, and there put to death by order of Ghufoor Khan and the Patans.

The ascendancy of the war faction was immediately apparent in the attacks made upon our foraging parties, from which cattle were daily carried off, not without some loss of lives. On the 20th of December, Sir Thomas Hislop, thinking thereby to curb this spirit of hostility, advanced to within seven miles of Holkar's camp; but that very day a picquet of Mysore horse was attacked by a party of about 200 of Holkar's Barabaee horse, under circumstances which showed that they were not actuated by any motive of plunder. It was accordingly resolved to enforce immediate submission to the terms proposed to the acceptance of the durbar, or to bring on a general action without further delay.

On the morning of the 21st of December, the British army again advanced; but its march was more openly opposed by bodies of Holkar's horse, which appeared on every side. A letter had been written over night to invite the durbar to submission, and another to the agent employed to negotiate, to know why communication had been so abruptly broken off. To both of these answers were received on the march: the reply to the former contained mere general assurances; but that of the negotiator explained more fully, that the sirdars were bent upon abiding the result of an action. Sir Thomas Hislop, therefore, no longer hesitated as to the course to be pursued.

On approaching Mehudpoor*, the enemy were discovered drawn up in line on the opposite bank of the Soopra, as if they intended to dispute the passage of that river by the most practicable ford, which lay a little above their position, that is to say, to the south of the town. A *reconnoissance* was immediately made by Lieutenant-Colonel Blacker, the quarter-master-general, who ascertained that there was ground on the opposite side of the river and within its bed for the troops to form upon after the passage, where they would be completely sheltered from the fire of the enemy's artillery by the brow of the overhanging bank. He likewise observed, that on ascending the bank the men would only have to advance 300 yards before they reached the enemy's guns. Upon this report, it was determined to attack in front by the ford, notwithstanding the obvious disadvantages of the ground, in preference to manœuvring so as to turn the position, which would have required a long detour and much time, while any appearance of hesitation could not fail to produce a very prejudicial effect. The enemy's right was protected by a deep ravine, and his left by a slight bend of the river, and a deserted village called Sitawud, not far from its

* Vide plan at the head of this chapter.

bank. The ground on which the British army had to form itself after crossing the ford, was within the two horns of this position; the enemy's line retiring a little in the centre to make the most advantage of it. Sir Thomas Hislop placed the baggage in a village on the right bank called Doolait, under protection of the rear guard and a few Mysore horse; and then, while Sir John Malcolm with the cavalry drove off the hovering parties of the enemy's horse, a few light troops were pushed across the ford, followed by fourteen guns of the horse artillery and a troop of rocketers. The passage was effected without much difficulty, although the enemy brought up some guns to bear on the ford. The horse artillery immediately opened a battery on the enemy's line, while the rest of the army crossed to the low ground under cover of the bank, in order there to form for the attack. The enemy were so superior in artillery, that in a short time the whole of our guns were disabled. Four guns of the foot artillery were, however, opened with good effect, from a position they had taken on the opposite side of the river, a little nearer Mehudpoor, whence they enfiladed the left of the enemy's line, which had been advanced between the village of Sitawud and the river, in order to open with more effect on the ford.

By the time the horse artillery were nearly silenced, the British army had passed the ford, and was formed for the attack. The first brigade, composed of the flank companies of H. M.'s royal Scots and the Madras European regiment, with the second battalion of the Madras 14th native infantry, the whole under Lieutenant-Colonel R. Scott, was destined to the attack of the enemy's left. The light brigade, consisting of the rifle corps, with the Palam-cotta and Trichinopoly light infantry, the whole under Major Brown, formed the centre; and the second brigade, composed of the 2nd-6th Madras native infantry and the Nizam's battalions under Captain Hare, formed the left of our infantry line. The cavalry were directed to operate against the enemy's right, where the ground was most favourable for this arm. The main attack, however, was entrusted to the first brigade, where the enemy was strongest in artillery, and the distance to be passed under his fire the longest. Sir John Malcolm solicited permission to lead this attack, which was granted; and in the same manner Lieutenant-Colonel M'Gregor Murray, deputy adjutant-general to the King's forces, obtained leave to head the detachment of the royal Scots, which had precedence in it. These dispositions were no sooner completed, than the attack was commenced. The enemy's artillery was extremely numerous and well served, so that our loss was very severe, particularly in the first and in the light brigade, which latter being in the centre, was exposed to the cross fire of the whole line. The troops, however, advanced with great steadiness, the Europeans * in particular reserving their fire and trusting to the bayonet alone. Holkar's artillerymen stood to their guns till they were bayonetted; but his infantry battalions gave way as soon as the guns were carried.

Meanwhile, the cavalry had turned the enemy's right, and driving off the horse who opposed them, made a dreadful slaughter of the broken infantry. Holkar's camp was directly opposite to Mehudpoor, a little to the north of the field of battle. This, with all the artillery, were soon in our hands; but on the pursuit being continued, the fugitives attempted to rally, and got together some guns to cover their retreat across a ford about four miles lower down the river than Mehudpoor.

* Sir John Malcolm observing a Sepoy battalion stop and fire in its advance, turned round to the men and said, "My lads, there is little use in that; I think, we "had better give them the cold iron." Whereupon he was answered with characteristic bluntness from the ranks; "Yes, your honour, I think we had;" and the line advanced with shouldered arms in high glee, notwithstanding the destructive fire then playing upon it.

Upon this, Sir Thomas Hislop ordered his line to be again formed; but the guns were soon taken, and the feeble resistance offered at this point overpowered by the rapid advance of Sir John Malcolm with the cavalry and a light detachment. Our camp was formed upon the field of battle, while Sir John Malcolm continued the pursuit across the river with the regular cavalry, and Captain Grant with the Mysore horse moved down the left bank. The enemy's flight was supposed to be directed northwards towards Rampoora. An immense booty fell into the hands of the Mysore horse. Eight elephants and some hundred camels were brought in chiefly by them. The camp itself was found deserted when entered by the regular army: sixty-three guns were, however, captured, and the total destruction of so many disorderly battalions was a yet more important consequence of the success of this day.

Our loss was severe, amounting to 174 killed and 604 wounded; among the former were three officers, Lieutenants M'Leod, Colman, and Glen; amongst the latter, no less than thirty-five, whereof eight were of the rifle corps alone *.

* Names of officers severely wounded:

Quarter-Master Griffin, horse artillery.
Lieutenant Campbell, royals.
Lieutenant Hancome, European regiment (since dead).
Captain Norton, Lieutenants Gwynne, Shahanan, Drake, Calder, Castment, Gem, } rifle corps.
Lieutenant Jones, Palamcotta light infantry.
Major Bowen, Lieutenant Palmer, } Trichinopoly ditto.
Lieutenant Gibbings, quarter-master-general's department.
Lieutenant Lyon, brigade-major of cavalry.

Besides other officers slightly wounded.

Sir Thomas Hislop resolved to remain himself a week at Mehudpoor, and to establish a hospital and depôt there; while Sir John Malcolm continued the pursuit with a light division from his army, and followed up the victory. One of the principal reasons of this delay was, to allow of the junction of the Bombay army from Guzerât, which arrived at Rutlam on the 24th of December. This army had also been directed to move on Oojein, and, according to the original plan of operations, would have been in time to have taken part in the battle of Mehudpoor, had not its march been arrested by an order of recal addressed to Major-General Sir William Keir by the Bombay Government, immediately on hearing of the defection of the Bhoosla. This event, it seems, was so totally unexpected at that Presidency, that in the uncertainty how far the appearance of fidelity kept up at Brodera could be trusted, the Governor in council felt alarmed at the idea of the Guzerât force being so far removed from the territory of his Government, and wished to retain it for the protection of Surat and the Gykwar state from the secret or open attempts of Bajee Rao. The Marquess of Hastings was by no means pleased at this diversion of the Guzerât army from the part assigned to it in his original plan; and no sooner heard of it, than he called upon the Bombay Government to rectify the error without delay. In the interim, however, the strong representations addressed to Sir William Keir by Sir Thomas Hislop, showing the necessity of his advance into Hindoostan, had induced that officer to resume his forward march after a short retrogade, before he received the positive order to that effect, addressed to him by the Marquess of Hastings in person; and he had from Rutlam furnished a light reinforcement to Sir John Malcolm, which joined at Kurdla on the 27th of December. On the 30th, the Guzerât army effected a junction with the head-quarters of the army of the Dukhun, and the united force then advanced upon Mundisôr in support of Sir John Malcolm, who had already reached that point.

There was, however, little further to be done in this quarter, except to receive the submission of the Holkar, whose power had been completely broken by the defeat of the 21st, and who, finding retreat cut off by our divisions on every side, had no longer the means of resistance or evasion. The negotiation was opened by Ghufoor Khan, who sent the agent that had conducted the previous negotiations, to make inquiries about a son-in-law left wounded on the field of battle. This opportunity was taken to forward the most humble assurances of the present altered sentiments of the leading men of the durbar. Tanteea Jog had already been released from confinement and restored to office; and Sir John Malcolm, in his reply to the above unofficial communication, caused it to be suggested, that the durbar could adopt no fitter course than to depute that minister immediately to the camp of Sir Thomas Hislop, to tender the submissions of the court, and conclude a treaty on the best terms he could obtain. In conformity with this intimation, Tanteea Jog came into Sir John Malcolm's camp at Mundisôr on the 1st of January.

By this time, the Brigadier-General had received the instructions framed by the Marquess of Hastings in the contemplation of a rupture, and prescribing the terms on which the Holkar's submission was to be accepted and his authority reestablished. He accordingly entered at once upon the negotiation. The terms proposed were, that Mulhar Rao Holkar should place himself and his dominions under British protection; that he should confirm the engagement already concluded with Ameer Khan, and renounce all sovereignty over the lands guaranteed to that chieftain; the four pergunnas of Puchpuhar, Deeg, Gungrar, and Ahoor, which Zalim Singh of Kota had for some years rented, to be ceded to the British in perpetuity, to enable them to recompense the useful services of the Raj-Rana; also, all territories possessed by Holkar north of the Boondee hills or south of the Sâtpoora range, including the fort of Sindwa in the latter, with a glacis, to be ceded to us, together with all claims for tribute on the Rajpoot princes. The state to be placed on the footing of other powers connected with us in subsidiary alliances, and its contingent to be fixed at 3000 horse. The Governor-General's plan for settling the factious differences that for so many years had distracted this durbar was to invest Ghufoor Khan, the avowed head of the Patan interest, with an hereditary jageer to be held of Holkar in perpetuity under our guarantee. It was thought that this measure would satisfy the expectations of that party, and probably tend to separate it for ever from the intrigues of the durbar; and it was hoped the lands known to be already in Ghufoor Khan's possession would prove an ample provision. It was not known to his Lordship, when these instructions were issued, that Ghufoor Khan was suspected of being the principal instigator of the murder of Toolsee Baee; else in all probability a different arrangement would have been devised. As it was, however, Sir John Malcolm executed his instructions to the letter, and effected all these objects after a short negotiation, in which Tanteea Jog insisted principally on three points: first, the extent of the cession for the benefit of Zalim Singh, which he wished to limit to two instead of four pergunnas; secondly, the arrears due on account of the past year's tribute from the Rajpoots, for which he solicited our guarantee; and thirdly, the retention of the forts of Chandore and Umba, with some villages in Kandêsh and the Dukhun. Sir John Malcolm distinctly refused to give up either of the above points, but promised to submit a request on behalf of Mulhao Rao, that some hereditary civil rights in several of the villages in the Dukhun should be reserved to the family, after and although the sovereignty should be ceded to us. The treaty was signed and executed on the 6th of January, in conformity with the original draft. The jageer secured to Ghufoor Khan, under its stipulations, included the pergunnas of Sunjeet, Mulhar-gurh, Tal Moondawur, Joura, and Buród, with the Peeplouda tribute: and the condition of tenure was the military service of 600 select horse, the number to be liable to increase on the eventual improvement of the jageer. The ratification of the Governor-General was affixed on the 17th of January 1818; and at the same time Sir John Malcolm was authorised to make an advance of five lack rupees on the revenues of Koonch, one of the pergunnas of Holkar not included amongst the cessions, but bordering on our own territory of Bundelkhund. An arrangement had been made some years before with this durbar, by which we had undertaken the collection of its revenues, and annually paid them from the Dehlee treasury. The pergunna having been assigned to a sister of Mulhar Rao, its cession was not insisted upon; and the sum advanced upon it was necessary to the peaceable settlement of his government in its new relations.

Immediately on the conclusion of the above treaty, Mulhar Rao came in, with Gunput Rao, Ghufoor Khan, and his principal Sirdars, and placed himself under the protection of the British army. Tanteea Jog was vested with the principal administration of the public affairs, the prince being a youth of about twelve years of age. Gunput Rao, who held the high office of hereditary dewan, was reduced to the exercise of a mere nominal authority.

An occasion very soon occurred, to call forth the active exercise of our protective engagements. Roshun Beg and Roshun Khan, two principal officers of the infantry destroyed at Mehudpoor, had, with a few hundred men, the poor remnant of their fourteen battalions, fled to Rampoora; where, hearing of the submission of their chief, they exhibited symptoms of discontent, and acted as if they meant to set up for themselves. Sir Thomas Hislop, sensible of the necessity of vigorously suppressing the first symptoms of such a disposition, was about to direct the force under Colonel Adams, still posted at Gungrar, to the punishment of these refractory leaders: but hearing, in the mean time, of the arrival of General Brown, with the detachment from Lord Hastings' camp, at Sorel, in the direct line of Rampoora, thought it most convenient to use its services for this object. General Brown, with his usual activity, hastened forthwith to the spot; and, appearing before Rampoora on the 10th of January, immediately made his dispositions to carry the place by assault, notwithstanding that it was surrounded by fortifications of some strength, and well capable of defence. About 400 of the infantry collected by the Roshuns were put to the sword in the town, and some horse, who fled in the opposite direction, were also cut up by the cavalry of our detachment, which had been sent round to intercept their escape. The two leaders themselves got clear off, but several other principal Sirdars were killed or taken prisoners. After this successful enterprize, the settlement of this territory proceeded with the utmost tranquillity under the superintendance of Sir John Malcolm and Major Agnew, which latter had been appointed by the Governor-General to act temporarily as Resident at that court.

Thus was peace re-established with the second of the three principal Mahratta powers, who had risen in arms to oppose the execution of his Lordship's plans. The immediate effect of so sudden an annihilation of the power of Holkar was apparent in the altered conduct of the Gwalior durbar, which from this time forward resigned itself to the most perfect acquiescence in every arrangement, indicated by the British Resident as the wish of the Governor-General. Juswunt Rao Bhâo, too, the most turbulent of Sindheea's Sirdars, became somewhat more tractable; and, dismissing Cheetoo with his durra, which had remained for some time in his neighbourhood, received Captain Caulfield, the officer appointed by Lord Hastings to act with his division, under the stipulations of the treaty of Gwalior, with every assurance of deference to his Lordship's commands. But these professions were soon found to be deceitful; for it was ascertained, that he was at the same time giving underhand the utmost protection in his power to the leaders and their banditti, by admitting them into his ranks, or concealing them in his different forts and villages. A body of 500 Pindarees, under Fazil Khan, were declared by Juswunt Rao to be a part of his regular establishment; and he went so far as to request a protection for them, in case they should fall in with any of the divisions of our army. Captain Caulfield granted the desired protection provisionally, until he should have ascertained the wishes of the Governor-General in respect to this party; but, in the interim, Sir William Keir, who had been despatched by Sir Thomas Hislop in pursuit of Cheetoo, was led by his hurkaras to the village where Fazil Khan had been reported to be quartered, under information that a large party of Cheetoo's durra were there harboured. Upon the first appearance of the British troops, numbers of armed horsemen were seen to gallop forth from the opposite side of the village, which confirming the previous information, he ordered the cavalry to give chase to the fugitives, and immediately attacked the village. It was carried in a few minutes, and many Pindarees and others had been put to death, before the head man had time to produce Captain Caulfield's protection, upon sight of which instant orders were issued to stop the pillage. This was not effected without resorting to the extreme measure of hanging a sepoy caught in the fact; but the circumstances induced Sir William Keir to institute an inquiry upon the spot, when it was indisputably proved, both by the confessions of many of the prisoners and by other evidence, that the major part of the horsemen found in the village had but very recently parted from the durra of Cheetoo, there to seek an asylum. This was one of many instances of Juswunt Rao's unwarrantable conduct. He harboured Bheekoo Seyud of Kureem's durra, the very Sirdar who had led the expedition into Guntoor in 1815, in a yet more barefaced manner; suffering him to come within his camp, and pitch his tents within a short distance of that of Captain Caulfield: and, although the man was clearly identified, and Captain Caulfield made the most earnest demands for his arrest or expulsion, he could procure no redress.

The Marquess of Hastings, being apprised of this conduct, sent instructions on the 24th of January, authorising Juswunt Rao to be proceeded against as a public enemy, pursuant to the conditions of the Gwalior treaty, unless he should in the intermediate space have adopted a different course of conduct. The detachment of General Brown was directed to give effect to these instructions; but, before the arrival of the orders, matters had already been brought by this force to the issue of the sword with the refractory chieftain.

On General Brown's approach to Jawud, Captain Caulfield renewed his remonstrances, but still without producing any change in the conduct of Juswunt Rao. Accordingly, on the 28th of January, after having in vain waited the expiration of the period prescribed for compliance with his demand of the surrender of the harboured Pindarees, Captain Caulfield retired from Juswunt Rao's camp to that of the General; and on the morning of the next day, having intelligence that arrangements were making secretly to remove the Pindarees to some place of safety, suggested the sending round a squadron of our regular cavalry to counteract this intention, by occupying the road through which they must pass. In performing this duty, the squadron was fired at both from the town and camp*; where-

* Vide plan at the head of Chapter XII.

upon the General ordered out his whole line, and determined on the immediate assault of all Juswunt Rao's posts. The 3d cavalry, under Captain Hodges, were ordered down with the horse artillery to the support of Captain Swindell, who commanded the squadron that had been fired upon. This force was immediately led by Colonel Newbery, the brigadier of cavalry, to the attack of one of Juswunt Rao's camps, which lay on the south of the town: it was soon carried. General Brown determined to follow up his success against the town itself; and blowing open the gate with a twelve-pounder of the horse artillery, while the rest of the guns were employed in taking off the defences, the Major-General caused the place to be stormed by the 1st-1st, under Major Bellingham, and by the dromedary corps, which was dismounted for the purpose, and led by Lieutenant Patton, the only officer wounded in the whole affair. Captain Ridge, with the 4th cavalry, and a party of Rohilla horse, had in the mean time been sent round the town, under the guidance of Lieutenant Franklin of the quarter-master-general's department, to attack another camp to the north-west, in which a large portion of Juswunt Rao's force was cantoned. There were in this encampment six guns and two battalions, besides horse. Captain Ridge came upon them in a quarter, whence he was exposed to the fire from the town as well as that of the troops in the camp. Leaving the town to the General, whose attack had by this time commenced on the opposite gateway, he charged at once into the camp, dispersed and cut up the battalions, and captured all the six guns. The Rohilla horse were led on this occasion by Lieutenant Turner, and behaved with as much spirit and steadiness as the regular cavalry. The result was complete success in every quarter, without a single check. Juswunt Rao himself owed his escape to the fleetness of his horse, and got off with very few attendants.

As soon as information was received of matters having been

brought to this issue, General Donkin, who was still at Shahpoora, was ordered down to occupy the possessions of Juswunt Rao Bhâo in Oodeepoor, and particularly the forts and districts of Kumulnèr, Rypoor, and Ramnagurh, three recent usurpations from the Rana, who had a few days only before placed himself under our protection. The acquisition of these fortresses was effected by the middle of February, the garrisons agreeing to evacuate on receiving their arrears, which in no instance exceeded 4000 rupees. Kumulnèr * is one of the strongest hill forts in India, and there it was that the Pindarees had been desirous of depositing their families and baggage during this campaign. It was now restored to the Rana of Oodeepoor, along with the other recent usurpations. Jawud and Neemuch, two of Sindheea's pergunnas assigned to Juswunt Rao, were likewise seized by us, and held for some time, but afterwards restored to the chief, in order to enable him to make a peaceable settlement with a man, who had otherwise sufficient influence to give trouble. It had been distinctly intimated to him, at the time of concluding the treaty of Gwalior, that, in the event of any of his Sirdars requiring chastisement for infractions of the articles, the acquisitions made from them would be retained by us as a remuneration for the trouble of inflicting it. Wherefore this attack of Juswunt Rao and seizure of his territories gave little umbrage, and occasioned no discussions with the durbar.

It is now time to notice the further operations against the Pindarees, after the remnant of the durras of Kureem and Wâsil Mahommed had effected their escape through Huraotee to Mewur, where they had hoped to share the promised protection of Juswunt Rao Bhâo. Early in January, Colonel Adams had taken up a position at Gungrar, and General Donkin another to the north of Mewur, while General Brown was advancing

* Vide plate at the head of Chapter XV.

towards Rampoora. Upon the conclusion of the treaty with Holkar, Major-General Sir William Keir was immediately despatched with his fresh division in a north-westerly direction from Mundisôr, to operate against Cheetoo, or any other of the Pindaree chiefs of whom he might receive intelligence. The durra of the former was partially cut up in the neighbourhood of Satoolla; and several were taken in villages, where they had singly or in small parties sought protection. Sir Thomas Hislop remained in the mean time at Mundisôr, a centrical point, well calculated for the general direction of affairs in this quarter. Harassed by the activity of Sir William Keir's pursuit, the marauders resolved to endeavour to retrace their steps to their haunts in Malwa and in the valley of the Nerbudda. Cheetoo succeeded in baffling every effort made to overtake him, and effected his object, by penetrating through a most difficult country to the south of Mewur. He re-appeared near Dhar, where a very high range of hills sends forth the streams which form the Mhye, a considerable river, emptying itself into the Gulf of Kambay. In this march he was obliged to disencumber himself of his baggage, and lost many of his horses; while Sir William Keir, being unable to follow by the same route, made a circuit by the open plain beyond the sources of that river, and then moved southward up the Chumbul in the same direction.

The wreck of Kureem's durra, under Namdar-Khan,—for both Kureem and his son had been left behind in a jungul in the flight through Huraotee,—had rejoined Wâsil Mahommed; and both were driven, by the operations just described, to attempt, in common with Cheetoo, a return towards Malwa and the Nerbudda. After having rounded the camp of Sir Thomas Hislop at Mundisôr, they were proceeding easterly, with the confidence of no other British force being in their neighbourhood; when, after crossing the Chumbul, they bivouacked on the 12th of January, at a small village named Kotree, on the

Kalee-Sindh. By good fortune, Colonel Adams was still lying at Gungrar, within a few miles of their bivouac. He detached the 5th Bengal cavalry to give them, if possible, a night surprise. Major Clarke, who commanded this regiment, fell in with their encampment about an hour before daylight of the 13th, and found them either in such security, or so worn down by continued fatigue, that they evidently had no intelligence whatever of his approach, when he was within sight of their fires. Perceiving that he was quite undiscovered, he resolved to wait until the first appearance of dawn, that their flight might not be aided by the cover of darkness. On the first blush of day, he divided his force, ordering three troops under Lieutenant Kennedy to attack in front, while with the other three he made a detour himself round the village, to come upon them in the direction their flight would obviously take on the first alarm of danger. The manœuvre was most masterly; and the loss of the durras in this affair was greater than they had sustained in any previous attack, not excepting that of the year before, when surprised by Major Lushington in the Dukhun. The whole body was completely dispersed, and many leaders of note left dead on the field.

Soon after this success, Colonel Adams having ascertained that the freebooters had entirely evacuated Mewur, with the intention of returning into Malwa, hastened after them without delay, and sent notice of this movement to General Marshall, who had for some time been in the neighbourhood of Bairsea and Seronj expecting this event. On their march, the Pindarees were several times severely handled by detachments from the divisions of Adams and Marshall, and in the end harassed to such a degree, as to be unable longer to keep their followers together.

It would be uninteresting to follow the track of these miserable fugitives with further minuteness. Such was the extremity of their distress, that Colonel Adams, judging them to be now ripe for unqualified submission, caused an intimation to be conveyed to them through the Nuwab of Bhopâl, that, if they were willing to throw themselves entirely on the mercy of the British Government, surrendering their arms and horses, the Sirdars might expect a livelihood in some part of our provinces remote from their old haunts, and the lives of their followers would be spared. Namdar Khan was the first to avail himself of this intimation. He delivered himself up to Colonel Adams on the 3d of February at Deorajpoor in the Bhopâl territory, with all his yet remaining followers, which were no more than eighty-seven. He required no other terms than a bare assurance that he should not be sent to Europe or Calcutta: on receiving which he surrendered without further stipulation. Others came in daily by twos or threes; and all reported that Wâsil Mahommed was in equal distress, and ready to avail himself of the same proffer of pardon. He had penetrated further to the east; but soon after fled for refuge to Gwalior, where Sindheea, though from a point of honour he at first refused to seize and deliver him up, when the Resident discovered the place of his concealment, and demanded his seizure and surrender, was ultimately obliged to do so, at the express requisition of the Governor-General *. The rest, for the most part, followed the example of Namdar Khan. Kureem it appeared was alone in concealment at Jawud, when the place was stormed by General Brown. He escaped with extreme difficulty on foot, and lived for some time in the neighbouring junguls; but, after a variety of risks and adventures, finding the restoration of his affairs utterly hopeless, he surrendered himself

* Sindheea, on being told by the Resident that Wâsil Mahommed was concealed in his camp, replied, that he had his leave to arrest the fugitive, but was required to do so himself, and that in broad day, that all India might see that an enemy of the British Government could nowhere find an asylum.

to Sir John Malcolm on the 15th of February. His son, Shuhamut Khan, with Ruttun Koonwur, a noted leader of luhburs, and about 200 followers, were still lurking in the junguls and mountains of Huraotee and Boondee, when Zalim Singh of Kota conveyed to them the assurance of life, and induced them to yield on the same terms as had been granted to Namdar Khan. Kureem Khan was settled with his family on an estate purchased for him in the Gôrukpoor district, of the value of about 1000 rupees a month. Wâsil Mahommed was on his seizure kept in strict *surveillance* at Ghazeepoor; but continued evidently restless, and refused to send for his family, or to take measures to settle himself in the manner desired by the British Government. At the close of the following rains he attempted an escape, having by some means or other procured relays of horses to be laid to carry him beyond our frontier; but being detected in the act of getting out of the house in which he resided, he destroyed himself by taking poison.

Thus were the two durras of Kureem and Wâsil Mahommed annihilated. Cheetoo, though he had suffered much in detail, had hitherto avoided a rencounter with any of the British corps in the field. But, on the 25th of January, he was heard of at Kurnôd by Colonel Heath, who commanded the garrison and post of Hindia. A party was immediately sent out, which beat up his bivouac in the night, and utterly dispersed the remnant of his durra. The Bheels and Ghasseas were encouraged to plunder and destroy the fugitives, a commission they zealously executed. After this, Cheetoo wandered about Malwa a short time with about 200 followers; and seeing his affairs to be nearly desperate, endeavoured, through the Nuwab of Bhopâl, to make terms for himself, in conjunction with his remaining adherents. For this purpose, he suddenly entered the Nuwab's camp; but when he learned that Nuzur Mahommed had nothing to offer, beyond a slender personal maintenance in some distant part of Hindoostan, while he demanded a jageer in Malwa, and the entertainment of himself with his men in the British service, he decamped as suddenly as he had come. While he staid, his horses were constantly saddled, and the men slept with the bridles in their hands, ready to fly instantly, in case of an attempt to seize them. Preparations were making for the purpose the very night he went off; but he was too much on his guard, and too much alive to suspicion, to allow them to be completed. He was instantly pursued by the Nuwab's people; and General Malcolm also sent out parties to take him, which distressed him so much, that Rajun left him, and made his submission. Mahommed Punah, his son, was likewise made prisoner. Yet he subsequently found his way into Kandêsh and the Dukhun, and made common cause with the Arabs and chiefs of the Pêshwa's routed army, with whom he became assimilated, receiving occasional protection from the Killadar of the fortress of Aseergurh. His durra was completely destroyed, and his followers almost entirely deserted him *.

* Vide infra, Chap. 18.

CHAPTER XIV.

POONA.

1817-18, NOVEMBER TO APRIL.

Pêshwa's flight and pursuit—is cut off from the north—returns to the south—affair at Koragâon—resolute defence of Captain Staunton—repulse of the enemy—remarks—flight of Bajee Rao continued—Brigadier-General Pritzler's pursuit—Bajee Rao turns north—met by General Smith, and pursued up the Kishna—new distribution of British force—Suttara taken—plans of Governor-General in respect to Pêshwa and Suttara Raja—reasons and reflections—instructions issued—Suttara Raja proclaimed—General Smith pursues Bajee Rao—comes up with him at Ashtee—Gokla slain—Suttara's family captured—notice respecting Gokla—Pêshwa's distress—capture of his forts—desertion of his Jageerdars—joined by Gunput Rao and Ram Deen—flight to the northward.

It is now time to revert to the transactions of the war with Bajee Rao in the Dukhun. For the purpose of preserving the continuity of the narrative of occurrences in other quarters, we have reserved these for separate notice, there having as yet been no such direct connexion between the operations on the two opposite sides of India, as to require the relation to be interwoven.

After his defeat at Poona on the 16th of November, the Pêshwa fled southward towards his strong holds in the vicinity of Suttara. It was at first believed, that he intended to shut himself up in some one of them, there to abide a siege. It appeared, however, that he had no such design, the recent fall of Hatras having shaken the confidence of all the native chieftains in their fortified places. His march to the south had no other object, than to effect a junction with a party sent before to carry off the family* of the Raja of Suttara from Wusota. Fearing to trust a race of so much political importance to the safe keeping of even the strongest of his forts, he resolved to carry the principal members of the family along with him, in order to prevent the possibility of their falling into our hands, or being set up by us in opposition to his own authority.

Towards the end of November, Brigadier-General Smith, having completed his arrangements for the occupation and eventual defence of Poona, set off in pursuit of the fugitive prince. On the morning of the 29th, he forced the passage of the Sâlpa-Ghât, leading to the high land in which the Kishna takes its rise. Gokla, with a body of 5000 of the Pêshwa's best horse, had, since the 22d, been continually hovering about the Brigadier-General's line of march, for the purpose of taking advantage of the least confusion. It would have been far too harassing a duty for the single regiment of cavalry and few irregulars attached to the division, to have attempted to keep at a distance an enemy that never ventured to stand a charge. However, by occasionally masking a galloper gun, and employing Shrapnell shells, the General was enabled to make the service of Gokla's horse rather too perilous for a continuance. On the day of his forcing the Sâlpa-Ghât, the nature of the ground gave an opportunity of opening the battery of a whole troop of horse-artillery in this manner, and with such effect, that for some days afterwards, indeed, until the 6th of December, the hovering clouds of horsemen completely disappeared. Bajee Rao himself usually kept at the distance of two long marches in advance.

Nothing of interest occurred in this very long and arduous pursuit: it will be sufficient, therefore, to notice the line of the

* Vide Forbes' Oriental Memoirs.

enemy's flight. Passing Suttara, he went as far south as Poosa Saolee (Possessolee.) From this point, either to avoid falling in with Brigadier-General Pritzler, who was advancing with the reserve from the ceded districts, or having no object in remaining to the south of the capital after the junction of the Suttara Raja's family, and naturally wishing to be joined by the support he expected from Hindoostan, he made a few long marches eastward, as far as Pundurpoor; and thence getting round Brigadier-General Smith, marched rapidly in a north-westerly direction, and, passing half-way between Poona and Seroor, moved northward as far as Wuttoor, on the direct road to Nassick. Here he was joined by Trimbukjee Dainglia, who brought with him a considerable reinforcement of horse and foot, raised in Kandêsh, or invited down from Hindoostan into the service. General Smith followed close at his rear, arriving at Pundurpoor on the 8th of December, the second day only after Bajee Rao had left it. As soon as the Pêshwa had passed clear of Poona, the Brigadier-general moved to the old cantonment of Seroor, and, after recruiting his cattle, resumed the pursuit on the 22d of December. Keeping now greatly to the east of the enemy's route, he entered the valley of the Godaveree, by the Nimba-Deora Ghât, in the hope thus to intercept his retreat northward: for the Pêshwa, finding himself less pressed, had loitered some days at Wuttoor, and in the neighbourhood of the strong fort of Jooneer. He was still in vicinity of that place on the 26th of December, when his active pursuer had already advanced to Hunwuntgâon, yet further northward than himself. He then attempted to continue his march towards Nassick; but General Smith was gaining fast upon him from the east, and he had scarcely descended the Ghât to the valley of the Peeree, on the 27th, when he heard that the Brigadier-general had already passed Sungumner, and was in full march to intercept his flight. Finding it now impossible to prosecute his march to the north without taking a more westerly route, he moved first to Kootool; but then fearing to be entangled with his cavalry in the difficult country in the immediate neighbourhood of the western ghâts, he determined to give up the intention of continuing his flight in that direction, and, re-ascending the table-land he had quitted only the day before, returned to Wuttoor, on the 28th of December, and thence hastened his flight in a southerly course on the direct road to Poona. This gave occasion to one of the most memorable actions, that has ever been fought in India.

Colonel Burr, the officer left in command at Poona, hearing of the Pêshwa's advance by the direct road to that city, and not being sufficiently aware of the manœuvres that had forced him into this line of retreat, and the closeness of the pursuers in his rear, thought an attack upon the capital was meditated. He accordingly solicited a reinforcement of a battalion from Seroor, the better to be prepared for defence. The following is an accurate account of what befel the reinforcement forwarded at his request.

The detachment consisted of a detail of Madras artillery, with two six-pounders, the 2d-1st Bombay native infantry, about 500 strong, and 300 auxiliary horse, the whole under Captain Staunton of the Bombay establishment, who commanded the battalion. It began its march from Seroor for Poona, at eight p. m. on the 31st of December, and at ten next morning reached the heights overlooking Koragâon, about half way to the city; when the whole of the Pêshwa's army, estimated at 20,000 horse and several thousand infantry, were discovered on the plain to the south of the Bheema. Captain Staunton found his march to Poona thus intercepted, and himself in great danger of being cut off. In order to avoid the exposure of the plain, which would have given an immense advantage to the Mahratta cavalry, he advanced hastily to seize the village of

Koragâon, before it should be occupied by the enemy's infantry. On perceiving his intention, they made for the same point, and Captain Staunton succeeded in part only; for half the village, and several of the strongest positions, remained in the hands of the enemy, who manned the whole of their portion with Arabs, whom he found it impossible to dislodge, notwithstanding several attempts for the purpose. A most desperate struggle now commenced between this mere handful of men, and the whole of the Mahratta army, which fought under the stimulus of the presence of the Prince himself, who personally witnessed the action from an adjoining height.

The enemy also had but two guns, but his infantry outnumbered ours in the proportion of more than ten to one, and the majority were Arabs*, a race whose determined courage, or rather desperation of boldness, had frequently been experienced in former wars, and was perhaps never more conspicuous than at Nâgpoor, and in this affair. The Arab infantry had also the support of immense clouds of cavalry, before whom the few horse that accompanied the battalion dared not show themselves; indeed, Captain Swanston, who commanded those auxiliaries, was wounded early in the day.

The contest continued until after sunset, and was a series of obstinate attacks and defences of such posts, as the situation of the houses and circumjacent buildings afforded. In actions of this nature, the advantage of having fresh troops to bring up is every thing, and this the enemy possessed and availed himself

* It may be proper to mention, as a proof of the estimation, in which the Arabs are held as soldiers by the native powers, the rate of pay they received in the Pêshwa's army, in comparison with natives of other countries.

Arabs, natives of Arabia - -	15 rupees a month.
Their descendants born in the country	10 ditto.
Hindoostanees, (the same as our sepoys)	8 ditto.
Mahrattas and Dukhunees - -	6 ditto.

of to the utmost degree; while Captain Staunton had scarcely sufficient for the defence of the ground he occupied, much less any men to spare for a reserve, or for the occasional relief of his different posts. The attack commenced a little before noon, and was not discontinued till nine in the evening, during the whole of which time our men remained without refreshment, and, what was of more consequence, no water was to be had in that part of the village in their possession. In the evening its situation was peculiarly critical. Lieutenant Chisholm, the officer of artillery, with most of his men, had been killed at a post near a pagoda in the village, against which the Arabs principally directed their efforts. At the same time, the exertions that the European officers had been called upon to make, in heading repeated charges, had so reduced their number, that, of the whole, three only remained undisabled, Captain Staunton himself, Lieutenant Jones, and Assistant-Surgeon Wylie, the two latter nearly exhausted. The Arabs at this time charged and obtained possession of the gun at the pagoda, round which many of our wounded were lying; among the rest, Assistant-Surgeon Wingate of the artillery, Captain Swanston, and Lieutenant Connellan, were there, all in a helpless state. The Arabs immediately commenced a massacre of the wounded, and the mutilation of the bodies of the deceased. Dr. Wingate was the first victim to their cruelty; he was literally hacked to pieces, as was the body of the deceased artillery officer. But they did not long enjoy the triumph; for the three remaining officers, immediately upon the loss of the gun, although themselves almost exhausted, and their men fainting from want of water, exerted themselves to bring them on to a final charge. On this occasion Lieutenant Patterson, who had been wounded and lodged in a place of safety, appeared again at the head of his men, and continued to exert the little strength he had left, until he received a second wound, which utterly disabled him, and in the end proved mortal. The charge fortunately was successful, and was executed with such judicious celerity and spirit, that it saved the lives of Captain Swanston and Lieutenant Connellan, both of whom were in the Arabs' hands, and having just witnessed the massacre and mutilation of their comrades, were expecting a like fate to themselves. Every man of the Arabs, who had penetrated to the pagoda, was bayoneted without mercy, and from this time the enemy relaxed much in the vigour of his attacks. As it grew dark, the men were enabled to procure a supply of water, which was the only refreshment they received for the whole day and night. By nine p. m. the enemy was driven out of the positions he had till then held in the village, and the rest of the night was passed by the detachment without molestation, but under the alarming anticipation of a renewed attack with fresh troops on the ensuing morning, and the certainty of their ammunition failing in that case after a few rounds. At daybreak it was found, that although the Mahratta army still hovered about the village, it was not disposed to renew the attack. The day was, however, passed under arms, and without any opportunity of procuring a supply of provisions. On the night of the 2nd of January, Captain Staunton, despairing of being able to effect his march on Poona, prepared to move back to Seroor. Wherefore, sacrificing much of his baggage in order to provide the means of transporting his numerous wounded, he commenced his march in the dark, and reached Seroor by nine next morning, bringing back not only his guns, but likewise all his wounded.

Brigadier-General Smith himself arrived at Koragâon with all his division in the course of the 3rd of January. But Bajee Rao had previously decamped, and continuing his flight to the southward, had on the same day ascended the Boor-Ghat beyond Poona, passing a second time within twenty miles of the capital. The approach of General Smith had obliged him to allow the battalion to march back to Seroor without further molestation.

The extraordinary obstinacy of Captain Staunton's defence against such overwhelming numbers, and his ultimate success in driving off the enemy, are amongst the most surprising exploits that our Indian army has ever achieved. There were but six * officers and two assistant-surgeons with the detachment; but the latter felt themselves called upon for exertions altogether out of their profession, and frequently lent the influence of their example, in leading the Sepoys to the charge of the bayonet, and inspiring them with that confidence of success, which the ascendancy of the European character never fails to produce. Our loss in the affair was three officers killed and two wounded out of the eight engaged. In the artillery the loss of men was most severe, twelve being killed and eight wounded, out of a detail for two six-pounders only. Of the battalion, 50 killed and 105 wounded. It may be worth while to compare the loss suffered on this occasion with that of other hard contested actions, in order to enable us to form a just estimate of the degree of credit to which the troops were entitled for their exertion and endurance in this memorable defence. At the battle of Mehudpoor, the rifle corps suffered undoubtedly a more severe loss in officers, and, of the men, there were no less than 130 killed and wounded, which, as the corps was weak, is

* Names of the officers:

Captain Staunton, commanding.
Lieutenant-Adjutant Patterson, died of his wounds.
Lieutenant Connellan, wounded.
Lieutenant Jones, doing duty.
Assistant-Surgeon Wingate, killed.
Lieutenant Chisholm, artillery, killed.
Assistant-Surgeon Wylie, artillery.
Lieutenant Swanston, auxiliary horse, wounded.

nearly an equal proportion: but this was one regiment of an army, and had it been cut off to a man, the victory might still have been gained by the rest of the troops: no analogy can be drawn between the behaviour of a battalion executing part of a combined movement, even though it should bear a disproportionate share of the brunt of the action, and the conduct of one that has to fight by itself, without support or hope, except from its own exertions. The Nâgpoor affair, where the whole of the troops were actively engaged, and nearly in an equal degree, is probably that which, in its circumstances, was most similar to the affair of Koragâon. The duration and obstinacy of the attack in both cases; the description of troops engaged; the partial success and ultimate discomfiture of the Arabs, are all so many points of resemblance between the two; and many more might be pointed out. At Nâgpoor, however, the general loss was nearly equal to that of the Bombay battalion, while that of the 1st-24th* alone amounted to 149 killed and wounded, which is only six short of the loss of Captain Staunton, although the proportionate number of combatants was rather in favour of the latter. On the whole, therefore, the contest may be considered to have been nearly as severe in one case as in the other, and in each the alternative of victory or ignominious death was presented to the combatants, which may account for the perseverance and resolute valour evinced on both occasions. But the discouraging circumstances under which the Bombay battalion fought, having to take up its ground hastily after a long and fatiguing march, and being forced to fight without food or refreshment, and without water, give to its efforts a character of

* This distinguished battalion was originally the 1st-1st; but in consequence of its concern in the mutiny of Vellore, it had been degraded from the highest to the lowest place in the numerical scale of the native corps. Its behaviour at Nâgpoor and general good conduct has since obtained the restoration of its former rank and number.

desperate and deliberate gallantry, much beyond what the most distinguished corps on any other occasion of the war had displayed, as indeed was universally acknowledged. To testify the sense entertained by the Supreme-Government of the conduct of Captain Staunton in this affair, the Marquess of Hastings nominated him an honorary aide-de-camp, and subsequently conferred on him the command of the fortress of Ahmednugurh, when formed into a regular garrison. The government has further ordered the erection of a public monument at Koragâon to the memory of those who fell.

After this repulse, Bajee Rao a second time ascended the table land, whence the Kishna takes its rise, and continued his flight south-eastward through Poosa-Saolee to Merich. In the mean time, Brigadier-General Pritzler, who, on the first rise of Bajee Rao in arms, had been summoned to take part in the operations against him, had advanced with part of the reserve by the route of Bejapoor, and was between Peergâon and Pundurpoor on the Bheema, when he heard of the Mahratta army being in full march to the south. He immediately moved westward, with a view to intercept them; but finding the enemy had already ascended the Ghâts, followed in the same direction, and passed the Salpa-Ghât on the 6th of January. On the next day he fell in with his rear guard, and pressed it with his cavalry under Major Doveton, by which means about sixty or seventy of the Mahrattas were killed. The Brigadier-General continued the pursuit, following them close at the heels to Poosa-Saolee and Merich, and thence crossing the Kishna after them by the ford of Erroor a little lower down the river. It was given out in the Pêshwa's army and through the country it traversed, that he meditated the invasion of Mysore and our own ceded districts. With this view he went as far south as Gokâk on the Gutpurba, and endeavoured to open a correspondence with the Raja of Mysore: failing in this, however, and hearing that the country on the other side of the Gutpurba had been armed against him by the exertions and popularity of Brigadier-General Munro; and, moreover, finding that the same indefatigable officer had collected the scattered and inconsiderable force of regular troops at his disposal, and was already prepared to oppose his further progress to the south, he resolved on the 15th of January to retrace his steps, and from Gokâk turned eastward, and recrossing the Kishna at Gulgula, diverged thence to the west, and marched by Hutanee on Merich, thus circumventing General Pritzler's division, in the same manner as he had done that of General Smith in his first flight to the south. But in this he did not succeed without being hard pressed by his pursuers, and particularly in the turn he made to the east. On the 17th of January, Brigadier-General Pritzler's cavalry had a smart brush with a part of the Mahratta army, and occasioned it very considerable loss. General Pritzler was stronger in this arm than General Smith had been, having two squadrons of the 22nd dragoons, besides the 7th native cavalry: but the enemy could never be brought to stand a charge, and it was only by means of galloper guns, or by breaking our line in pursuit, that they could be materially injured: and the latter could rarely be hazarded in the face of such disproportionate numbers.

While General Pritzler was tracking the Pêshwa's flight in the manner above mentioned, General Smith, having again recruited his division at Seroor, prepared to move likewise to the south with the major part of his force lightly equipped, in order to act against the enemy as circumstances might enable him. He started from Seroor on the 8th of January with this intention, leaving a part of his force, under Lieutenant-Colonel Boles, to follow with the stores and heavy guns. On the 12th of January he was near Fultun, and thence directed his march on Malwullee, pursuing a southerly course. On the 21st of January he heard of the enemy having wheeled round General Pritzler's division, and of his being in full march on Merich from Hutanee. General Smith was at the time not far from Hingungâon, whence he immediately moved on Merich to take up the pursuit. On the 22nd he arrived at Oogar on the Kishna, a little above the town, where he learnt that the fugitive Pêshwa had encamped only the day before. From this point Bajee Rao, crossing the Kishna, made a feint of descending into the Konkan by the Amba-Ghât, but soon giving up that design, continued his flight up the right bank, while General Smith followed on the opposite side, hoping by this means to prevent any escape to the east. The pursuit was very close; yet the enemy was enabled, by a rapid march from Suttara on the 28th of January, to cross the river and clear the Salpa-Ghât with the loss of only part of his rear guard, which was intercepted in the defiles. On moving forward, however, towards the Boor-Ghât, he was met and cannonaded by the detachment under Colonel Boles, and in the end fled eastward through Fultun to Pundurpoor, and afterwards to Solapoor, where he hoped to gain possession of the treasures of his old minister Suda-Sheeo-Bhâo-Mankishur, who had died but a few months before.

Here he halted, and was left for some days unmolested, while General Smith, finding himself in the neighbourhood, resolved to call up his heavy guns and employ them in reducing Suttara, still the nominal capital of the Mahratta empire. Besides the *eclat* and political importance that would necessarily result from the capture of this celebrated fortress, the Brigadier-General had other motives for undertaking the enterprise. He was desirous of effecting a junction with General Pritzler, who was still considerably in his rear, and of then making a new disposition of the troops composing the two divisions, by forming all the cavalry and light troops of both into an active corps for the pursuit of Bajee Rao, while the heavy artillery and a sufficient force for sieges and similar operations was left to reduce the many strong places in the country south of the capital. This most politic and judicious plan was adopted at the suggestion of Mr. Elphinstone, and it would have been earlier put in practice, had not the hope of coming up with the Pêshwa's army carried off General Pritzler in another direction, and prevented his having the necessary communication with General Smith. The mere pursuit of the fugitive prince from place to place, without wresting from him the occupancy of the country, had proved to be productive of little benefit hitherto, and seemed moreover likely to be spun out to an indefinite length, unless prosecuted on a very different plan. Whereas, on the contrary, by employing the troops according to the new and improved military arrangement, it was not improbable, that rather than submit quietly to the loss of his fortified places, the enemy would risk a general action, which was exactly what we most desired. Resolving to act upon this principle, General Smith waited the junction of the reserve division, which was coming up with a convoy, an encumbrance it had not been able to rid itself of during the whole line of pursuit, and employed the interval in laying siege to Suttara. The place surrendered the same day that the Brigadier-General appeared before it, the garrison offering to evacuate, the moment the mortar battery was brought to play with effect. It was taken possession of next morning, the 11th of February; but instead of hoisting the British flag on the walls, the standard of Sevagee again floated over the ramparts of this his ancient seat, while Mr. Elphinstone took the occasion of publishing a manifesto to the Mahratta nation, declaring it to be the intention of the British Government to restore the Suttara family to an independent sovereignty, and to punish the long continued treachery and ultimate defection of Bajee Rao, by the perpetual exclusion of his dynasty from all authority or concern in the affairs of the

Mahratta empire, and by the assumption to itself of all his territorial possessions.

This course of policy was taken under orders from the Governor-General, which were not issued without very mature consideration of the question. On the first occurrence of the rupture, the Resident at Poona had addressed to the Marquess of Hastings a solicitation for special instructions, respecting the conduct to be observed in the event of Bajee Rao's capture on submission, and generally upon the question, whether the present prince was to be reinstated upon any terms in any portion of the dominions of his family. In case of its being resolved to restore him to some share of nominal authority, Mr. Elphinstone submitted a plan for imposing such complete restraint upon all his actions, as he hoped would afford a sufficient safeguard against any future ill effects from his ambition and rooted fondness for intrigue. He proposed, however, at all events, to curtail his means effectually, as well by requiring compensation for the charges of the war, as by the demand of the arrears of the pension paid to Umrit Rao under the agreement made with that chief by the Duke of Wellington on his first advance to Poona; besides insisting on the cession of a territory, to be conferred on that prince in lieu of the pension for the future. The policy of setting up Umrit Rao himself, as well as that of placing Chimnajee, the brother of Bajee Rao, on the Guddee, were at the same time brought under consideration, in case the deposition of the present Pêshwa should be determined on. In submitting these points, the Resident did not express any preference of one plan above another, conceiving the choice to lie peculiarly in the judgment of the Governor-General; and the Marquess of Hastings, whose closest attention had already been turned to the subject, decided in favour of the total expulsion of Bajee Rao from the Dukhun, the perpetual exclusion of his family from any share of influence or dominion, and the annihilation of the Pêshwa's name and authority for ever.

These were certainly strong measures, and may at first sight carry the appearance of harshness. But he considered them to be warranted by the uniform conduct of our insidious ally for the four preceding years; and both the manner in which he had placed himself at the head of the confederation against the British power, and the critical time he had chosen to set the example of defection, demanded that his treatment should be a warning example to the nations of India, and an awful lesson on the consequences of incurring the full measure of our just indignation. The mere removal of the individual from the seat of imperial sway, for the purpose of elevating either Chimnajee, or Umrit Rao, or any other member of the same family, would have had the effect of impressing the minds of other princes with the idea, that the personal chastisement of the individual was to be the extreme consequence of the most implacable and persevering hostility; while the dignities and advantages of sovereignty, nominal at least, if not real, would still, under any circumstances of provocation, be left to descend in the uninterrupted line of hereditary succession. But how many men are there, that would set wealth, rank, and even life at hazard, in a desperate grasp at personal or political advancement, however precarious or remote, who yet would hesitate to set on the same cast the fortunes of an entire family, and the extinction in perpetuity of an ancient and illustrious house! There can be no doubt that Bajee Rao and his advisers never acted under the belief that they were putting so much at stake: they had misconceived the motives, by which the British Government had all along been actuated; construing its signal moderation as a mark of politic prudence and fear. Arguing from the aid we had afforded in establishing the authority of the Pêshwa, as well as from the uniform desire we had testified to keep on good terms with his government, that its maintenance in the existing form was indispensable to the stability and duration of our system, they were led into the presumptuous hope of succeeding, by menace and opposition, in exacting an equivalent for this imaginary benefit, and reckoned with confidence upon being always able to save themselves by a timely accommodation, however justly or deeply they might incur our resentment by the display of a rancorous animosity. The Prince himself had, since his defection, made several overtures for this purpose, and was not a little surprised to find them uniformly rejected, or answered by a declaration, that nothing short of unconditional submission could be listened to, or more than life be guaranteed. It was observed, that the recollection of the negotiations and disasters which attended our first connexion with the Pêshwas, when the Bombay Government espoused the desperate cause of the father of Bajee Rao, had far too much influence on the counsels of this durbar, and had from the first infused a most ambitious and arrogant spirit. The Marquess of Hastings had hoped, that the humiliations imposed by the treaty of Poona, concluded in the preceding June, would have subdued or abated this spirit; but a contrary effect had followed; and there seemed now to be no choice left to the British Government, but for ever to annihilate the state of things that had first generated it, and to show that it could itself occupy the guddee of Poona, and direct its control over the chiefs of the Mahratta nation to the maintenance of public tranquillity, with yet more efficiency than it had been possessed of, since the first Bajee Rao and Balajee united the Mahratta race for the devastation of the rest of India.

These were the principal motives, that fixed the Marquess of Hastings in the resolution to annihilate the authority and name of Pêshwa; and, with the reservation above noticed for the Suttara family, to assume the whole authority and dominion into the hands of the British nation. In December, he issued his instructions to this effect, constituting Mr. Elphinstone commissioner with full powers for the execution of his plan. The Jageerdars, who had heretofore held of the Pêshwa, were to be admitted to hold on the same terms of the British Government, unless they should engage in active hostility against us, or delay the period of their submission for too long a period. The lands of Gokla were directed to be immediately resumed; and it was to be a part of any arrangement that might be made, that his person, together with that of such other chiefs as were equally active in the same cause, should be lodged in safe custody. It was likewise to be an article, that the parties concerned in the hanging of the two Vaughans should be given up for execution. The Raja of Suttara was to be established in a territorial possession, to be held either as a dependant Jageer, or as a distinct sovereignty, under stipulations securing the supremacy of the British Government. The declared object of this part of the plan was, to conciliate the Mahrattas to the new order of things, and establish a counterpoise to the remaining influence of the Pêshwa's Brahminical administration. The mode, and form, and amount of the provision, were left to Mr. Elphinstone's discretion, so that the object might be most securely attained. The above, with a territorial reservation for the settlement of a Jageer upon Chimna Appa, formed the outline of the plan devised by the Marquess of Hastings: in prosecution of which, immediately upon the capture of Suttara, the Mahratta flag was again hoisted on its walls, in the manner above mentioned, and a proclamation issued, inviting the Mahrattas to rally round their rightful hereditary sovereign, for whom it was declared, that Suttara and the adjacent territories would be reserved as an independent dominion under British protection. In this form Mr. Elphinstone thought the establishment of the Suttara Raja would be effected with most advantage under existing circumstances; and the early submission of several jageerdars, who were eager to establish a prior claim to the honours and advantages of the restored dynasty, attested the policy of the measure. Events occurred within a very few days after the fall of Suttara that materially forwarded the completion of these arrangements.

After the capture of that fortress, Brigadier-General Smith, in concert with Brigadier-General Pritzler, formed a light division in the manner proposed, with which, on the 13th of February, he moved to the eastward on the route to Pundurpoor. Arriving at Yellapoor, on the 19th, he heard that Bajee Rao had left Solapoor, where he had remained during the operations against Suttara, and was on his march due west. Hoping, therefore, to fall in with him about Pundurpoor, the Brigadier-General made a night march on that point, but heard in the morning that he had gone off to the northward, and was at Kurkumbh, totally unconscious of the vicinity of a British force. Upon this intelligence he crossed the Bheema at Keroulee, and pushed on with all his cavalry and horse-artillery, in the hope of coming up with the enemy. At half-past eight in the morning, he had the gratification of hearing the state kettledrums of the Pêshwa beat in preparation for a march, which had been hastily resolved upon, in consequence of information of General Smith's approach having just got the start of him. The British troops were concealed by the brow of a hill from the enemy's view, until the cavalry appeared on the ridge drawn up in battle array. Gokla now, seeing that it would be impossible for the Pêshwa's army to escape without sacrificing nearly all its baggage, took the resolution to risk an action, in the hope of saving it. General Smith had with him the 2d and 7th regiments of Madras light cavalry, and two squadrons of his Majesty's 22d dragoons. He had also a troop of horse artillery, but the ground was too rugged to expect much benefit from this arm. Some of the guns were, however, brought up by the exertions and zeal of Captain Pierce, so as to have opened with effect; but the Brigadier-General, observing the enemy disposed to stand a cavalry charge, resolved to bring the matter to this issue in preference. He accordingly advanced in three columns, the dragoons forming the centre. The enemy was formed on the other side of a difficult ravine at the foot of the hill, which our troops had to pass before they could reach him. On forming line, the 7th cavalry, which was on the right wing, came soonest upon the ravine, and, getting in some degree entangled in it, Gokla took the opportunity of pushing a body of horse beyond its right flank, and even into its rear, which, coupled with a demonstration of simultaneous attack in front, created some confusion in the 7th regiment. But Major Davies, who commanded the detachment of the 22d dragoons, immediately ordered a troop to fall back and scour the rear; and the commandant of the 2d regiment also adopted the same precaution. By this means, the body that had succeeded in getting to the rear were completely dispersed. A *gole*, led by Gokla, was charged by the troop of dragoons in the most gallant manner, on which occasion that distinguished chief was himself slain. He died bravely, having wounded several of our men with his own hand before he fell, and amongst the rest Lieutenant Warrand, of the 22d dragoons, the first who attacked him. The death of Gokla left the enemy without a head: for Bajee Rao had already gone off with his personal guard and attendants, deserting his palanquin, and mounting a horse for the purpose as soon as the battle commenced. From this moment there was no longer any appearance of order in the resistance opposed. Our cavalry, particularly the dragoons, charged successively several masses of the enemy's horse, until the dragoons penetrated to their camp and baggage, the whole of which, after a slight resistance, fell into their hands. The person and family of the Suttara Raja were found there and secured, and were by no means the least important prize obtained on this occasion. The family consisted of the Raja, Noor Nerayun, a young man about twenty years of age, his two brothers, and mother. There were also 12 elephants and 57 camels taken. Our loss was very trifling, being only one officer, Lieutenant Warrand, and 19 men, wounded. The Brigadier-General was himself surrounded, and received a slight wound on the head, at the time when Gokla and his party had penetrated to the rear; but this accident did not prevent his continuing to direct in person the operations of the day. Besides Gokla, the enemy lost another sirdar, Moro Punt Aptee; but the death of the former in particular, and the capture of the Suttara family, gave peculiar importance to the battle fought at Ashtee, on the 20th of February. Bapoo Gokla was reputed a good officer; he was one of the sirdars who accompanied the Duke of Wellington throughout his campaigns in the Dukhun, during the Mahratta war, and was then well esteemed for his services and general character, insomuch as to be particularly recommended to the favour of the Pêshwa's government on the close of that war, besides deriving other substantial advantages from the General's good opinion. He had subsequently been yet more deeply indebted to the favour of the British government, which more than once interfered to secure his possessions from his master's rapacity, at a time when the latter was stimulated by private pique*, as well as by avarice, to aim at his ruin. These benefits

* The Pêshwa's animosity was long irreconcileable, in consequence of Gokla's refusing to suffer his wife to visit at the palace, where she could not have gone without dishonour; such was the sensuality that prevailed there. Gokla yielded the point, when the prospect of guiding the counsels of the state was opened to him; and "was generally known to have owed his former disgrace and subsequent favour to his tardy acquiescence in the dishonour of his family."—*Elphinstone's Despatches.*

were of course forgotten, as soon as ambition and the desire of restoring the Mahratta empire to its ancient splendour became the ruling passions of his soul. Since 1814, he had uniformly been the adviser of the most decided hostility, and the avowed head of the war faction. When Bajee Rao conceived the project of rising against the British power, he found it convenient to court Gokla, and subsequently at different times added largely to his military fiefs, besides giving him a command in his immediate and personal troops. His post, since the rupture, had been always in the rear guard, or wherever else there was most danger; and his master's confidence was unbounded and well merited. After his death, the Pêshwa himself directed the movements and operations of the Mahratta army, there being no other chief on whom he could place equal reliance.

The routed host fled northwards, towards Kopergâon and Kandêsh, their numbers now thinned daily by desertion. The capture of Suttara and of its Raja, added to the distress and precipitation of the flight, made even the most sanguine of the Mahrattas themselves regard the cause of their chief as altogether desperate. The daily fall of some one or other of his southern forts before Brigadier-General Pritzler confirmed this impression. On the 20th of February, that officer appeared before Singurh, which capitulated on the 2d of March. He thence proceeded to the attack of the two contiguous forts of Viziergurh and Poorundur, which were also taken after two days' cannonade and bombardment. This occurred on the 15th of March. The garrisons amounted to 1136, while in Singurh there were upwards of 1300, whereof 300 were Arabs. After the fall of these two of the Pêshwa's strongest holds, Wundun-Chundur, Nundgaree, Wyruntgurh, Kurnalgurh, Pandoogurh, and Kelinga, surrendered as soon as the army appeared before them; the two last-mentioned only having waited for the batteries to open. After these successes, Brigadier-General Pritzler prepared himself, on the 31st of March, to proceed against Wusota, reckoned the strongest of all the forts in these parts, and in the repair and improvement of which large sums had recently been lavished. Châkun, a place on the north-west of Poona, had previously been reduced by Colonel Deacon, who was bringing up a reinforcement from Berar. Colonel Prother, who had been despatched with an armament from the Bombay Presidency into the southern Konkan, was equally successful. In the course of January and the commencement of February, Kurnala, Bopâlgurh, Kotillagurh, Oochitgurh, and Sungurh surrendered successively to this officer. The fort of Pâlee, which commanded the Ghât of that name, was also reduced after a short resistance. The sea-port of Sevandroog had been taken some time before, by a force equipped for the purpose, from Fort Victoria, or Bankoot. In addition to the above captures, General Munro, having completely occupied the country to the south as far as the Malpurba, and driven out the officers placed there by Bajee Rao or Gokla, had proceeded against Badamee, a place famous for its long resistance to Nana Furnavees, who had attacked it with all his means. It soon yielded to General Munro, and Bhagulkote in the same neighbourhood fell very shortly after. All these forts were no doubt ill defended; but their garrisons felt themselves wholly without hope of support, and, therefore, were impressed with an early conviction that the cause was hopeless, and could be but little advanced by their best exertions. They were also strangers to the effect of shells thrown with precision; and there being no protection against this artillery within the forts, the defenders were soon disheartened by its destructive effect, and our divisions, aware of the nature of the service, were well provided with this arm.

This uninterrupted chain of success induced many of the principal jageerdars of the Mahratta empire to make their terms with Mr. Elphinstone. The Putwurdhuns were the first to desert the standard of Bajee Rao. The Prithee-Nidhee and Punt-Suchem, the two chief officers of the Suttara family, sent to offer their submission immediately on the publication of the manifesto; others followed every day; insomuch, that in the southern portion of his dominions the influence and hold of the country, possessed by the Pêshwa, were fast passing away. He was, however, reinforced in his flight to the north by the junction of Ramdeen, with part of Holkar's broken infantry. Gunput Rao, with the remnant of the army of Appa Saheb, had previously joined, at the time Bajee Rao was loitering between Pundurpoor and Solapoor. The troops he brought were chiefly horse, who, after their defeat by General Doveton, were successfully conducted through the Nizam's dominions by that leader, notwithstanding the various attempts to intercept their march made by different detachments of our troops, as well as of those of the Nizam.

The flight of Bajee Rao northward towards Hindoostan brought him into contact with divisions of our army, different from those with which he had been hitherto engaged; and his operations also became thenceforward connected with the transactions of the other durbars. With a view, therefore, to perspicuity of arrangement, it will be proper to bring up the relation of events in Hindoostan and at Nâgpoor to the same period.

S.E. VIEW of the FORT of KUMULNÉR.

TALNÉR

CHAPTER XV.

HINDOOSTAN—KANDÊSH.

1818. FEBRUARY, MARCH.

Holkar—Ameer Khan—his crafty conduct—guns obtained—Troops disbanded—takes refuge in Kota—Patans taken into British service—Policy of the measure—Proceedings of Sir David Ochterlony—Troops in the field in February—exchanges with Sindheea proposed—Lord Hastings quits the field with the centre division—Sâgur—its reduction ordered—Reasons—Terms offered to Bunaeek Rao—and accepted—Dhamonee reduced—Mundela stormed—New distribution of the forces—Sir Thomas Hislop's return—Soandwara reduced—Sindwa occupied—Resistance at Talnêr—and storm—Loss of officers—Garrison put to the sword—Killadar hanged—Sir Thomas Hislop in communication with Brigadier-General Doveton.

To return to Hindoostan; we have seen already, that, before the close of the month of January, the bond of union, that kept together the turbulent bands attached to the standard of the Holkar family, had been completely dissolved. Their collective strength had been irretrievably broken at Mehudpoor, while the example of Rampoora and of Jawud had seriously impressed on the sirdars individually the necessity of conforming to the new order of things, which it was the design of the Marquess of Hastings to introduce. Ameer Khan had all along been sensible of this necessity; but his subordinate sirdars were by no means satisfied with the terms he had procured, the advantages of which were entirely personal to himself. It appeared indeed, that the Patan chief had not scrupled to deceive his associates in arms, causing the agent he employed at Dehlee to forward accounts of the negotiation in progress there, much more favourable to their interests than the truth warranted. This deceit was continued, even at the conference held by appointment between himself and Sir David Ochterlony on the 18th of December, for the express purpose of exchanging the mutual ratification. A number of additional stipulations were then brought forward, as having been agreed to by Mr. Metcalfe at Dehlee; amongst others, the promise of a jageer to his son Vizier Mahommed, and of similar grants to other sirdars. In proof of these having been agreed to, the above letters were produced, bearing the seal of Nerunjun Lal, his Dehlee agent, who was himself called into Sir David's presence to make an oral declaration to the same effect. Fortunately, the Major-General was well acquainted with the Patan character; and, having been furnished with correct information of all that had passed at Dehlee by Mr. Metcalfe himself, at once declared his disbelief of the whole, stating that he had come to receive the ratification of the engagement actually signed; and, as he knew nothing of any further concessions, must insist on an explicit answer, whether the chief was prepared to ratify that engagement or not. This peremptory demand had the effect of procuring the delivery next day of the ratified engagement, by the terms of which there can be little doubt that Ameer Khan was from the first prepared to abide, though the total insubordination of his army, and the independence of the sirdars possessed of influence or command in it, had obliged him to practise the above deceit, in order to amuse and feed them with delusive hopes, while he was making separate terms for himself.

After the ratification, Ameer Khan came into Sir David Ochterlony's camp, and took up his quarters there for some time, until he should succeed in persuading his mutinous officers to disband and deliver up their guns. It is to be observed, that each brigade of infantry, with its equipments, was considered as the especial property of some one sirdar, who derived his profit from the sale or hire of its services, or the share of its plunder and exactions. The motive that led so many of them to rally round the standard of Ameer Khan was, the want of regular employment elsewhere, and the idea that his talents for command promised to afford, in the spoils he would put them in the way of sharing, a better livelihood than could be elsewhere obtained. Many of the brigades were undoubtedly of Ameer Khan's own raising, but more than half had been raised by others; and he had bound himself to disband the whole, and deliver up their artillery, with only five lack of rupees in hand to effect the business. It may easily be imagined, that, in order to satisfy the greedy wants of an army so composed as his, which had been living as it were from hand to mouth for several years past, and was now called upon to surrender the very means of subsistence, and to abandon for ever the inveterate habits of military licence, no distribution of those very limited means at Ameer Khan's command could make them suffice. The sirdars and troops consequently remained for some time sullen and dissatisfied, and the brigades would not give up their artillery, notwithstanding the most earnest endeavours on the part of the chief to obtain their compliance. But the Marquess of Hastings had never expected to wring from them these implements of trade, by any other motive than the strong and immediate influence of fear. The destruction of Holkar's infantry at Mehudpoor, whose case they felt to be exactly their own, and the judicious advance of Sir David Ochterlony with the reserve to a position * directly between the two principal divisions of the Patan army, those of Muhtab Khan and of Raja Bahadhur, had at last the desired effect; and the artillery of both were procured in the course of January.

* The Major-General was already in the neighbourhood; and he made this movement on the pretence of greater convenience of forage: nor were the Patan sirdars aware of the commanding nature of the position, until it was actually taken up.

Other sirdars continued refractory for some time longer; particularly Jumsheed Khan, whose guns were not obtained until the end of March, and were then yielded on compulsion only, and in consequence of the threat of immediate attack by a detachment sent for the purpose.

It was a yet more difficult task to procure the quiet dispersion of the Patan soldiery, than to obtain the surrender of their guns. Ameer Khan exerted himself with equal zeal to effect this, as indeed every other part of his agreement, but for a long time with little success. His soldiers had before them the prospect of absolute starvation, if they abandoned their present livelihood and habits; while the money at the chief's disposal, however fairly distributed, afforded no compensation to the individuals for so great a sacrifice. The well known address of Sir David Ochterlony, brought in aid of Ameer Khan's exertions, was scarcely equal to the task of inducing so many armed men to return quietly to their respective homes, notwithstanding the awe inspired by his position, and by the efficiency of the army under his command. And Ameer Khan was so beset by the discontented rabble thus turned adrift, who depicted to him in glowing colours the hardships and disgrace of their present situation, that, after trying every means in his power to allay the ferment, and practising in vain all manner of deceit, he found it necessary at last to retire with precipitation to Sheergurh, a fort in Zalim Singh's territory, until this feeling of irritation should in some degree have subsided. His son had already arrived at Dehlee as a hostage; and the sincerity of the chief's individual efforts and intentions was never doubted for a moment, notwithstanding the suddenness of this flight and his notorious want of integrity *.

* Amongst other modes of avoiding the present importunity of his troops, he gave many of the sirdars drafts on the Resident at Dehlee, which he must have known would not be honoured, as he had already overdrawn the amount stipulated. He drew in this way for nine lack beyond his credit.

The difficulty of completing this part of the Governor-General's plan for the final settlement of Rajpootana had been distinctly foreseen; and Major-General Sir David Ochterlony, to whom the execution was entrusted, had been empowered, in case it should be found indispensable to adopt such a means of allaying that discontent, which would unavoidably be excited, as a temporary expedient to entertain a portion of the most efficient of Ameer Khan's troops in British pay, under such regulations, as would best adapt them to our system of discipline and organization. Acting upon this authority, the Major-General, in the course of February, made the tender of British service to eight of the best Patan battalions and to about 3000 horse. The former, after pensioning off the native officers above the rank of soobadar, and thinning the ranks by the strictest scrutiny into the character, age, and general qualifications of the men, were formed into four battalions for the provincial duty, of which two were sent to the Dehlee territory, and the other two retained for similar service in Rajpootana, under the conduct of British officers appointed to command them. These battalions were found extremely serviceable; and, in the existing demand for troops in every quarter, the arrangement was attended with essential benefit. The horse were formed into bodies called *resalas*, of 500 each; and, as the very best only were taken, they also rendered good service; while, the arrangement being merely temporary, and recruiting disallowed, the expense is continually decreasing.

It was a most important point of the original plan, not hastily to drive to despair the whole swarm of military adventurers, by depriving them suddenly and entirely of their habitual means of subsistence; but to destroy those only, whose habits or ambition prevented their conforming to our system of rule, and so to hold the balance between the hopes and fears of the rest, as to render them instrumental to the establishment of order, and content with the offer of a moderate and regular provision. It was partly with this view, that the stipulation for an auxiliary force had been introduced into the treaty of Gwalior, to open a field of employment to many of the unsettled characters, who must else have been turned loose upon society, and allure them with the assurance of fixed and regular pay under British guarantee. The same policy had dictated the large extension of irregular levies on our own establishment, and the formation of the auxiliary contingent at Poona before the commencement of operations.

No fitter agent could have been chosen, for the practical application of these principles to the settlement of affairs with the army of the Patan chief, than Sir David Ochterlony himself. By his consummate address and judicious arrangements, the whole affair was completely settled before the end of February, by which time all the sirdars had submitted, with the exception of Jumsheed Khan and one or two subordinate officers, who vainly hoped, by holding out to the last, to advance instead of impairing their interests. Notwithstanding the natural turbulence of the Patan character, all the divisions, not even excepting those who last submitted, were restrained from any kind of violence in the interim; so that, in fact, the destruction of this predatory association, which seemed more likely than those of the Pindarees to require a great display of our military strength, was brought about wholly by negotiation, aided by the awe that our attitude of preparation was calculated to inspire. The merit of this early and entire success is due principally to Sir David Ochterlony's personal skill and judgment, which met with the Governor-General's uniform approbation, and to the imposing force of the division placed under his command, which consisted of two very strong brigades of regular infantry, with a regiment of cavalry, and two corps (1000 each) of native horse, raised and embodied by Colonel Skinner. Besides these, the contingents of the military chiefs, to whom lands had been assigned on our western frontier on the settlement of 1805-6, were for the most part attached to the reserve division, when called out to take a part in the present operations; by which means its numerical strength was more than doubled.

The concentration and advance of the reserve had been connected with the further object of carrying into effect the arrangements intended to be made with the Rajpoot chiefs. The greater part of these were in train long before the close of the month of January; but the mention of them has been purposely omitted, that the narrative of the events and military transactions might not be interrupted by the constant recurrence to measures of a purely political nature. As these all formed part of a general system of permanent pacification, it was thought more convenient to reserve them for separate mention, when the result of the whole operations and the nature of the final settlement of our Indian empire came to be explained. It will be sufficient, therefore, to mention in this place, that, with the exception of Jypoor, the counsels of which evinced their usual indecision and imbecility, all the Rajpoot states entered readily into the terms and propositions offered for their acceptance: nor was there one that did not show the utmost eagerness in the promotion of the Governor-General's views, for the restoration of order in that part of India, occupied by their dominions.

The Marquess of Hastings, seeing every thing to be in a train of easy adjustment with the Rajpoot princes, and feeling equally confident respecting the settlement with Ameer Khan and the Patans, the detail of which had been left to Sir David Ochterlony, thought himself at liberty, by the beginning of February, to relax a little the military attitude he had assumed on the side of Hindoostan. He accordingly resolved upon a new distribution of the force there collected, in order, if possible, before the close of the season, to secure every remaining object.

The predatory power of the Pindarees had by this time been completely destroyed. Of the routed bands of Holkar, some had rallied again round that chief, whose government having fallen into the hands of Tanteea Jog, and being aided by the advice and exertions of Sir John Malcolm and the British representative at the durbar, was fast assuming a regular shape. Many more had been destroyed piecemeal at Rampoora and elsewhere; while all, who still remained in arms, had fled into the Dukhun, and were gathering round the banners of Bajee Rao, who alone still kept the field, and maintained the cause of opposition and disorder. On the 1st of February, the British force actually in the field to the north of the Nerbudda was thus disposed. The reserve division, under Sir David Ochterlony, in the neighbourhood of Jypoor: the centre division, under Lord Hastings' personal command, still posted on the banks of the Sindh: the right division, that of Major-General Donkin, was proceeding to take possession of Kumulnèr and the usurpations of Juswunt Rao in Mewur: of the left division, part was with General Marshall about Seronj and Bairsea, and of the remainder, a quota had been furnished to the force with Major-General Brown, who was still in the vicinity of Jawud, and two battalions had joined his Lordship's head-quarters, under Brigadier-General Watson.

Of the army of the Dukhun, the divisions of Sir Thomas Hislop and Sir John Malcolm were still near Mundisôr, while Lieutenant-Colonel Adams was in the Bhopâl territory, employed in receiving the submission of the Pindaree chiefs. The Guzerât army, after a long pursuit of Cheetoo's durra, was now halted in the neighbourhood of Indore, to receive its further destination according to circumstances. Besides the above, a corps of observation was still posted on the southern frontier of Behar, under Brigadier-General Toone; and Brigadier-General Hardyman with his corps occupied Jubulpoor.

The present humility of Sindheea, as evinced by the readiness with which, since the destruction of Holkar's army, he had forwarded the levy and equipment of the auxiliary horse stipulated in the treaty of Gwalior, and more recently by the indifference he had manifested at the attack on Juswunt Rao Bhâo, satisfied the Marquess of Hastings, that it was no longer necessary for the army under his personal command to occupy the forward position it had assumed to awe the counsels of this durbar. It was accordingly resolved to break up the centre division of the grand army, and march the greater part of it back to its cantonments within the Company's provinces, whereby an important saving of expense would be effected. However, before this measure was carried into execution, it was thought right to open to that durbar the ulterior views of the British Government, and to sound its disposition in respect to them. The principal remaining points, which it was the wish of the Governor-General to obtain, were—the cession of Ajimeer to ourselves, in order perpetually to exclude the Mahratta influence from that part of Rajpootana; the transfer of Islamnugurh to Bhopâl, with a view to a similar exclusion from that quarter; and, lastly, the cession in perpetuity of all the Maha-Raja's claims on the Boondee principality, as well as of lands obtained from time to time in lieu of such claims. As an equivalent for these sacrifices, the Marquess of Hastings was prepared to offer the lands of the Vinshorekur (except the portion already given to Bhopâl), together with those of other late tributaries of the Pêshwa similarly circumstanced, and the tributes and personal rights of that Prince in Hindoostan, which had been assigned to us by the recent treaty of Poona. The Vinshorekur's lands had become justly forfeit, in consequence of his continued adherence to Bajee Rao, since his defection. The value of the equivalent about to be offered considerably exceeded that of the cessions intended to be demanded; besides which, Sindheea relied upon our bounty for the restitution of Jawud, and the territory lately resumed from Juswunt Rao Bhâo; so that there was little reason to expect any serious opposition on his part to the arrangement. Yet it was impossible to estimate beforehand with any degree of certainty, what sensation the demand of a permanent cession would make on a Mahratta court. His Lordship accordingly resolved to ascertain this beyond a doubt, before he should relinquish the attitude, which had given him such advantages in the past negotiations. For this purpose, before finally quitting the banks of the Sindh, the Marquess of Hastings caused a proposal for the above exchanges to be submitted to the Gwalior durbar.

Finding it to be well received, his Lordship did not think it necessary to wait the complete execution of the arrangement; but on the 13th of February commenced his homeward march to our own provinces, having for some days previously moved gradually along the right bank of the Sindh from Sonaree and Oochar down to Beercha, which lies but a few miles above Seanda, the point on which he had first moved in the November preceding, to enforce the signature of the treaty. Of the troops composing the centre division, the Europeans for the most part returned to the cantonment of Cawnpoor; while the native infantry were so disposed along the Bundelkhund and Etâwa frontier, as to be capable of immediate reunion, in case any appearances in the court or army of Dowlut Rao Sindheea should require their second advance. A brigade, of three strong battalions, however, with the 7th native cavalry, and the heavy train, which had purposely been attached to this division, were sent, under the command of Brigadier-General Watson, to reinforce the troops under Major-General Marshall, which it was determined to employ in the reduction of the territory of Sâgur, with a view to its permanent annexation to the British dominions.

The right of paramount sovereignty over this territory formed part of our acquisitions, by virtue of the late treaty of Poona; and it will be recollected, that, in assertion of that right, Bunaeek Rao, the occupant, had been called upon in the September preceding, either to fulfil the terms, on which the fief was held of the Poona state, by furnishing the quota of 666 horse, and paying the tribute of one lack of rupees to the British Government, or to agree to an advantageous money commutation, offered to be taken in lieu of that contingent. The letter containing the offer of commutation was answered evasively; the more positive demand of the fulfilment of the original terms, which was accompanied by a notice that General Marshall was already advancing against the Pindarees, and a requisition, that the quota of 666 horse should join his division, and co-operate on the service, was equally disregarded: besides which, instead of receiving assistance in the procurement of its supplies, the left division experienced every sort of impediment, and was uniformly treated as an enemy in the Sâgur territory. As a further proof of Bunaeek Rao's infatuation, no effort had subsequently been made to calm our just resentment, notwithstanding the favourable turn of affairs in every quarter. Neither had he offered a rupee of the tribute due, or the service of a single horseman. Under these circumstances, the Marquess of Hastings resolved to regard the occupant of Sâgur as a feudatory, who had incurred the forfeiture of his fief; more especially as there was evidence forthcoming of his correspondence with the Pindarees since the commencement of operations against them, and of his attachment to the cause of the Pêshwa. Wherefore, no sooner did the state of affairs in Hindoostan permit the allotment of a sufficient force to this object, than the reduction of this province was resolved upon. Accordingly, in the middle of February, Major-General Marshall was ordered to proceed against the capital of the principality, so soon as he should be joined by the battering-train and reinforcement sent to him for this purpose from the centre division.

The following were the modified terms, to which submission within three days was now to be peremptorily demanded. The present government to be displaced, and the territory transferred to the administration of British agents; the revenue actually realised to be allotted as follows:

Tribute to the British Government - - -	S^s. R^s.	100,000
Commutation for military service, with 666 horse - -		159,840
Total payment to the British Government - -	S^s. R^s.	259,840

This, together with 10 per cent. on the gross assets, for the expense of administering the affairs of the province, to be the primary charge on the total receipts *. After defraying which, the revenues to be next charged with a stipend of two lack and a half, as a provision for the maintenance of Bunaeek Rao, and the Bhaych, widow of the former possessor, in whose name Bunaeek administered the country; any excess of the revenues beyond this, to be allotted to the hereditary proprietor of the territory, that is to say, to Nana Govind Rao, the holder of Jaloun, who had already made his separate terms for the portion of the family dominions in his own possession. It was, however, to be distinctly explained, that if any improvement should be effected in the revenues of Sâgur proper, in consequence of our management, beyond the estimate of their former product, taken at 698,000 rupees, the same was to be the exclusive profit of the Company. The extreme limit of the stipend to the Nana of Jaloun was therefore 118,360 rupees, being the total surplus above the forementioned charges, in case the whole of that estimate and no more should be realized.

In obedience to these instructions, Major-General Marshall, reinforced by Brigadier-General Watson, appeared before Sâgur,

* This ratio was assumed, on an estimate of the past revenues of Sâgur and its dependencies, at 698,000 rupees.

on the 8th of March. Bunaeek Rao was now convinced of his danger, and resolved upon submission. The capital of Sâgur was accordingly surrendered on the 11th of March; and the other forts and territories were quietly taken possession of in the course of the month. General Marshall's force then proceeded against Dhamonee, a fortified town belonging to the Raja of Nâgpoor, situated to the north of the Nerbudda, and thus comprised within the late cessions of Appa Saheb, though the Killadar and garrison refused to comply with the order for its evacuation. The General appeared before the place on the 17th of March, and tendered the payment to the garrison of their arrears, as far as 10,000 rupees, on the condition of immediate evacuation. The garrison demanded the full arrears of two years and a half, declaring that, for the whole of that period, they had received no pay whatever. As this amount greatly exceeded what the Major-General thought himself authorised to offer, the town was immediately invested, and batteries having been raised within breaching distance, the garrison surrendered as prisoners of war, on the 24th of March; when the Killadar and principal officers were in the first instance dealt with as rebels, and sentenced to confinement in different forts, but subsequently pardoned and released.

The division was now directed to effect the reduction of Mundela, on the Nerbudda, which had in like manner resisted Appa Saheb's public order for its surrender. The main difficulty here was to bring up the heavy artillery through the roads and passes that led to the town. This being at last effected, two batteries were raised, and opened their fire on the 26th of April. The ground was so well chosen, and the fire so accurate, that the besieged were driven entirely from the angle of the wall attacked. Lieutenant Pickersgill, of the Quarter-Master-General's department, observing this, approached the spot in the afternoon, and ascertained by close inspection, both that the breach was practicable, and the wall abandoned. On receipt of his report in the trenches, a storm was immediately resolved on. It was led by Brigadier-General Watson himself; and, after some fighting in the streets, the town was carried. Of the garrison, part escaped into the fort, but the rest were either cut up in the streets, or, in attempting to escape by an opposite gate, were attacked and cut to pieces by the cavalry, previously posted to complete the investment on that side. The fort surrendered at discretion next morning, the Killadar having been taken during the night, while endeavouring to cross the river in a boat. The Marquess of Hastings had ordered him to be dealt with severely, not only for his rebellion in resisting the order of evacuation, but likewise and specially, because he had attempted to circumvent and cut off Major O'Brien, the officer who had been despatched with a mere escort to present it. He was accordingly tried for his life by a drum-head court martial; but acquitted, on exhibiting proof that he had the private orders of Appa Saheb not to deliver up the place. Another active partisan, of the name of Nathooram, was similarly tried and acquitted. Although this did not occur until the end of April, it is here introduced by anticipation, in order to complete the notice of General Marshall's operations for the season.

Before proceeding further, it will be necessary to explain the part assigned, under the new distribution of February, to the other divisions of the British armies then in activity on the side of Hindoostan. Major-General Donkin's, or the right division of the grand army, was ordered to be broken up as soon as it should have succeeded in occupying Juswunt Rao's possessions in Mewur. The European portion of the troops composing it, (8th dragoons, his Majesty's 14th foot, and the artillery), were ordered back to the cantonment of Meeruth: from the native troops, a reinforcement was to be furnished to Sir David Ochterlony. The detachment, which had been sent in advance from Lord Hastings', the centre, division, under the command of Major-General Brown, was, immediately after the affair of Jawud, likewise made available for the purpose of strengthening the force to be left in Rajpootana, which it was determined to put in a most efficient state, for the completion of the settlement of that quarter. This reinforcement afforded the means of forming an additional brigade of infantry, which, together with a regiment of cavalry, and a complement of the other arms, it was intended to station at Holkar's capital, for the defence and protection of that chief's remaining dominions. Lieutenant-Colonel Ludlow was appointed to the subordinate command of this corps, which, after the execution of the service, was to be annexed to the division of Sir David Ochterlony. Such was the new distribution of the troops, that had been brought into the field on the side of Hindoostan. The whole arrangement was ordered and carried into execution by the Marquess of Hastings, by the middle of February; and, at the same time, the two corps of observation to the east were recalled from their advanced position. Of the native troops composing the latter, a competent force for the occupation of Jubulpoor was detached by Brigadier-General Hardyman, and left under the command of Major O'Brien; while the troops requisite for the military occupation and settlement of the Jungul tract to the south of Behar, lately ceded by the Bhoosla Raja, were furnished from the corps of Brigadier-General Toone. Major Roughsedge commanded the detachment employed on this latter duty, and by his means Sirgooja, Jushpoor, Sohagpoor, and Sumbhulpoor, were quietly annexed to our dominions, though the wildness of the country, and of the native tribes that inhabit it, rendered its peaceable settlement a work of time and attention.

Of the three divisions of the army of the Dukhun, still in the field to the north of the Nerbudda, that under the personal command of Sir Thomas Hislop, and the 5th, commanded by Lieutenant-Colonel Adams, were directed to return forthwith to aid in the early restoration of the affairs of the Dukhun. Colonel Adams was ordered to proceed in the first instance upon Chouragurh, a fort in the northern extremity of the Mohadeo hills, which, like Dhamonee and Mundela, had refused to obey the orders of surrender forwarded for the purpose from Nâgpoor. We shall come presently to the detail of the operations of this force. Sir Thomas Hislop was ordered to conduct back his division by the route of the Sindwaa Ghât and Kandêsh, so as to admit of their immediate employment in the reduction of Bajee Rao's possessions in that province, and in the occupation of the recent cessions of Holkar within it. The country was remarkably strong by nature, and was besides full of fortresses and Arab colonies, that promised no inconsiderable trouble and impediment in the way of its quiet settlement. It had at first been resolved to employ the head-quarter division of the Madras army, in co-operation with that of Brigadier-General Doveton, in the reduction of Aseergurh; but the evident importance of early reducing the strong holds of Kandêsh, and of making further means available against Bajee Rao, who still kept the field in formidable force, prevailed with his Lordship to give the above plan the preference, leaving Aseergurh until such time, as our armies might be less extensively employed in other directions.

It was further suggested to Sir Thomas Hislop, that, as the objects, with a view to which the several subsidiary forces had been formed into divisions of the same army, and placed under his own personal command as general in chief, had now been entirely accomplished, by the dispersion of the Pindarees and the destruction of the military power of Holkar's predatory adherents, there was no longer any occasion for continuing the same organization of the troops under the general control of a commander-in-chief: and, as the subsidiary forces of the Nizam and Bhoosla might conveniently be replaced on their former footing, under the direction of the Residents at the respective durbars, who had special and immediate instructions from Lord Hastings, there was little necessity for the Lieutenant-General's further presence in the field. The Poona subsidiary force, which temporarily formed the third division of the army of the Dukhun, had previously been separated from that army, and placed again at Mr. Elphinstone's disposal, in the same manner as before Sir Thomas Hislop took the field in person; and, as the services in other quarters would now become equally insulated, the motives, which had suggested the measure in one case, were obviously applicable to the other forces of the same description. The army of the Dukhun was accordingly ordered to be broken up without delay. The Marquess' present plan was, to direct Brigadier-General Doveton to prosecute the operations in Kandêsh, the settlement of which province, as well as of the rest of Bajee Rao's dominions in the Dukhun, was subjected to Mr. Elphinstone's general control and superintendance; and to distribute the troops composing the division of Sir Thomas Hislop in the reinforcement, as well as of the corps to be so employed, as of the other corps at present acting against Bajee Rao, the regulation and disposition of which had equally devolved on Mr. Elphinstone as commissioner. Of course, however, the Lieutenant-General was to be at liberty to retain any corps he might prefer, for his personal escort during his return to his immediate command at the presidency of Fort St. George.

The above orders and instructions were issued by the Marquess of Hastings on the 2d of February. By the middle of the month, the head-quarter division of the army of the Dukhun commenced its southward march by the route of Indore and Muheshwur. Brigadier-General Malcolm retained the Madras troops attached to his division, the corps of Bengal troops allotted for the protection of Holkar's dominions not having yet been organized. He was also desirous of employing a military force for the reduction of Soandwara*, a province lying west of Malwa, the natural difficulties of which encouraged its inhabitants to persevere in the predatory habits they had been bred to, notwithstanding the change of system proclaimed on the establishment of our influence in those parts. The early repression of the smallest indication of a marauding spirit was of course an essential object; and in this view the enterprize was promptly undertaken. In addition to the troops of his own division, Sir John Malcolm also retained for this service a strong brigade of infantry, and a battering-train from the Guzerât army, which, under the recent military arrangements, the Marquess of Hastings had ordered back to the Gykwar's dominions. Of these elements, a field force was soon formed, which, after the junction of the troops of Zalim Singh of Kota, and those of Holkar's present government, penetrated into the country. The capture of a few strong holds, which were carried with great spirit, completely effected the business before the end of March. The troops of Holkar and of Zalim Singh† co-operated with the utmost alacrity, and did good service on all occasions. Indeed, it was by no means the least gratifying circumstance in the accomplishment of the object contemplated in this expedition, to observe the promptitude and good will with which our new allies come forward with their contingents to aid the enterprize. The spirit they displayed afforded the most satisfactory test of the policy whereon the new system was founded, and the best

* A tract extending from Aggur to the Chumbul east and west, and from near Bhanpoora to Oojein north and south. In this tract, the freebooters mustered near 2000 horse. Lalgurh was their principal hold.

† Meerab Khan, his general, particularly distinguished himself in the attack of the village and fortress of Nareilla, which he stormed, though the breach was hardly practicable, and took, with the loss of 200 of his troops, and several officers of rank.

security for the solidity and permanence of the arrangements either made or in progress.

Pending the settlement of Soandwara, Sir Thomas Hislop was on his way to the Dukhun as abovementioned. Having crossed the Nerbudda at Mundlisôr, a little above Muheshwur, he moved direct to the Sindwa Ghât, where he arrived on the 22d of February. The fort was surrendered on the 23d, agreeably to the orders to that purport, brought from Holkar's court. A battalion was left to garrison it and overawe the country between the Sâtpoora range and the Nerbudda; and Sir Thomas Hislop continued his march to the south. On the 27th of February, he reached the post of Talnèr*, commanding the ford over the Taptee, and one of the places ceded by Holkar under the late treaty of Mundisôr, the orders for the surrender of which were in Sir Thomas Hislop's possession. It had been reported that the Killadar intended to refuse compliance; and, on the approach of a party of our troops, a fire was opened upon them. The Killadar was warned, that, if he continued to resist the order of his master, he would be dealt with as a rebel; but this produced no abatement of the fire from the walls. The Petta, or open town, was accordingly occupied; and the artillery of the division, consisting of ten six-pounders, with two five and a half inch howitzers, was opened from a position it afforded about 300 yards distant from the fort. The fire was directed chiefly at the defences, and was briskly answered by matchlocks from the wall. In the evening, it was resolved to attempt to force the gate of the place; for which purpose, two six-pounders were carried up to the outer gate by the flank companies of the Royal Scots and the European regiment, the whole led by Major Gordon, accompanied by Lieutenant-Colonel M'Gregor

* Vide plate at the head of this chapter.

Murray, Lieutenant-Colonel Conway, and other officers of the staff. On reaching the first gate, it was discovered that the fire during the day had so injured the wall beside it, that the men got through without finding it necessary to blow it open. Wherefore, leaving the guns on the outside, the storming party pushed on to the second gate, which was found open. At the third gate they were met by the Killadar, who came out by the wicket along with some *buneeas*, native merchants, and proffered his surrender to Colonel Conway. The third and fourth gates were then opened, and the party advanced along with the Killadar to the fifth, which led into the body of the place. This was found closed, and the garrison from within demanded terms, and expressed their dissatisfaction. After a very short parley, in which they were distinctly summoned to surrender at discretion, the wicket-gate was opened from within, and Lieutenant-Colonel Murray and Major Gordon, with three other officers, entered, followed by about ten or twelve grenadiers.

In the mean time, the Arabs of the garrison, probably distrusting the intention of the British towards themselves, and seeing every thing on the point of being lost, worked themselves up to a frenzy of desperation; and either resolving to sell their lives as dearly as possible, or hoping yet to be able to save the place, made a sudden attack with swords, spears and knives on the few who had already entered the wicket. Major Gordon and Captain M'Gregor were presently killed. Lieutenant-Colonel Murray received several wounds, and was at last cut down and disabled, as were the other two officers who had accompanied him, Lieutenants Chanwal and M'Gregor: most of the foremost grenadiers were also killed or wounded. However, as those who entered first had maintained their ground, others crowded through the wicket to their support; and, in the end, the Arabs were driven to seek shelter in the circumjacent houses. The guns were also brought up after blowing open the outer gate, upon which the place was soon carried, and the garrison, in number about 300, were put to the sword. The Killadar was executed on the spot, on the twofold charge of original resistance to the order of his sovereign and supposed implication in the treachery of the garrison. The example was highly useful, and no doubt influenced the subsequent surrender of the much stronger forts of Gâlna, Chandore, and other places, immediately on the presentation of the orders by the several detachments sent to occupy them. The total loss on the part of the British was seven officers and eighteen men killed and wounded. The death of Major Gordon was the subject of universal regret, as he deservedly enjoyed the highest estimation of his brother soldiers, as well as of the government he served.

Leaving a garrison to occupy Talnèr, the Lieutenant-General crossed the Taptee, and advanced by Umulnèr to Pahrola, where he came into communication with Brigadier-General Doveton, then posted at Outrân. This officer, having already completed the settlement of affairs at Nâgpoor, had returned westward by Ellichpoor in the course of January, expecting orders to proceed against Aseergurh; but, on the abandonment of the intention of reducing that fortress in the current season, he had been ordered to direct his march upon the point of Kandêsh-Ootrân, on the Gyrna. Sir Thomas Hislop now ordered him to move up the Gyrna to Bâl, following himself the course of the Boaree, and sending a detachment to receive the surrender of Gâlna. No resistance was attempted; and this, with several other of Holkar's possessions in the neighbourhood, was quietly occupied by the troops of the two divisions.

While these divisions were thus employed in Kandêsh, Sir Thomas Hislop received intelligence that Bajee Rao had penetrated the Ghâts separating that province from the valley of the Godaveree: whereupon he immediately hastened to the south, ordering Brigadier-General Doveton to move on a parallel line in the same direction, in the hope of being able to intercept him before he should be apprized of their approach. It will be convenient, however, to relate the intermediate occurrences at the court of Nâgpoor, before we return to trace the motions of the fugitive Pêshwa, and the further operations against him.

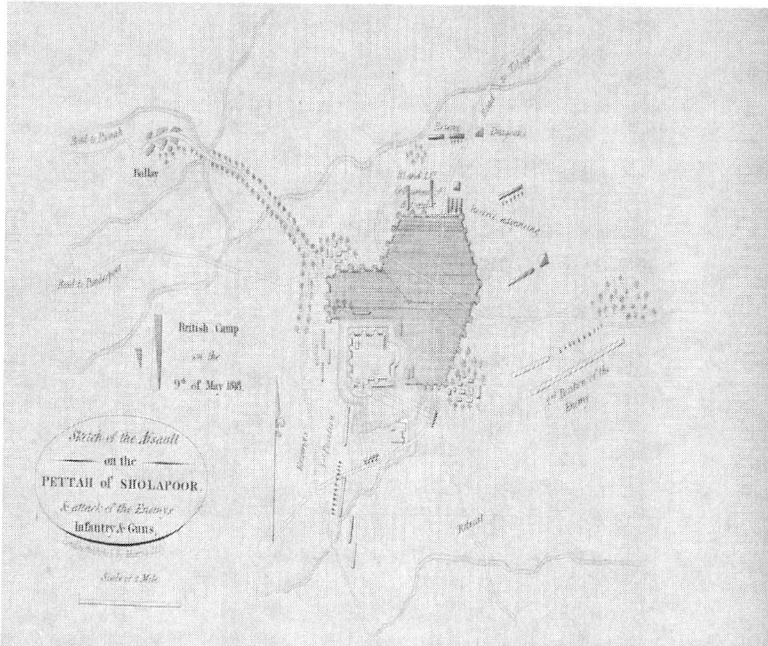

British Camp on the 9th of May 1818
Sketch of the Assault on the PETTAH of SHOLAPOOR & attack of the Enemys Infantry & Guns

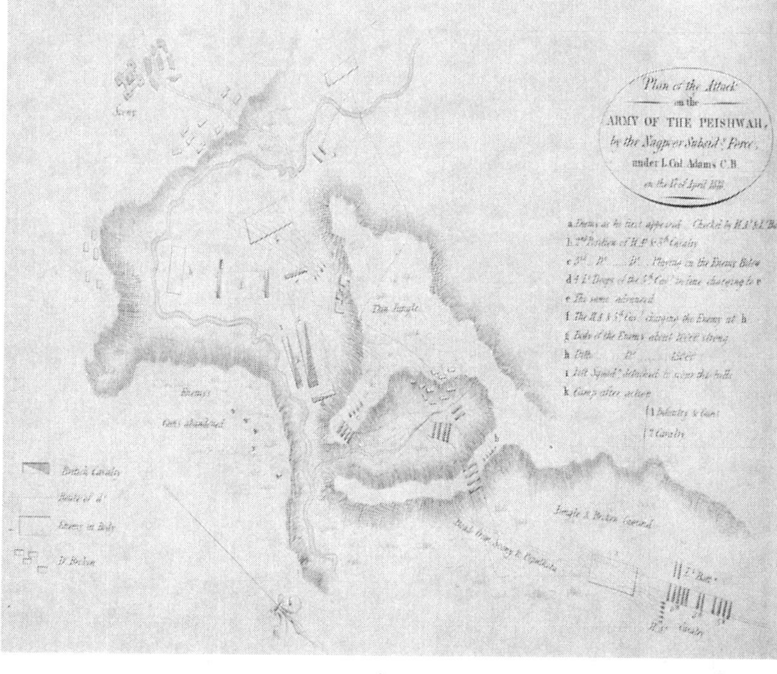

Plan of the Attack on the ARMY OF THE PEISHWAH, by the Nagpoor Subsid.y Force, under L.Col. Adams C.B.

CHAPTER XVI.

NÂGPOOR—DUKHUN.

1818, FEBRUARY TO MAY.

Nâgpoor—ministry of restored Raja—his fresh intrigues and early treachery—Resident's suspicions and measures—Governor-General's first instructions—Detection of the plots—arrest of Raja and his ministers—Bajee Rao applied to by Bhoosla for aid—consequent proceedings—marches eastward—eludes Sir Thomas Hislop's division—Army of the Dukhun broken up—progress of Bajee Rao—Brigadier-General Smith co-operates with Brigadier-General Doveton—Lieutenant-Colonel Adams—repulse of Gunput Rao—Lieutenant-Colonel Adams at Hingunghât—waits for other divisions, and advances—route of Soonee—pursuit by Brigadier-General Doveton—dispersion of Mahratta army—detention and submission of sirdars—Wusota invested and captured—new distribution of the forces—capture of other forts—affair of Solapoor—Chanda invested—its surrender.

The affairs of Nâgpoor have been passed over in silence, since Appa Saheb's return to the palace of the Bhooslas, under an arrangement confirmed by the Marquess of Hastings, as mentioned in the 12th Chapter. This occurred in the course of January, the date of the Raja's return being the 9th of that month.

It will be recollected, that, when Appa Saheb made his submission, the principal channel of communication between him and the Resident was Nerayun Pundit, one of the negotiators of the original subsidiary alliance. This man was rewarded for the share he had in that transaction, and for his former tried fidelity to the British Government, by being immediately invested with the second place in the administration, under the name of Pêshkar. Nagoo Punt, however, the other negotiator of the alliance, a man more deep in Appa Saheb's confidence, was retained as dewan; and Ramchundur Wâgh, who had also submitted, together with his master, on the 16th of December, was not displaced, though known to have been an active instigator of the late hostilities. This man had been included in the indemnity for the past, by an express stipulation with Nerayun, before Appa Saheb could be induced to come in; and Mr. Jenkins, willing to regard the fact of his surrender along with his master, as a sufficient indication of his altered sentiments, not only showed towards him no displeasure at the part he had lately taken, but allowed him to retain his offices and influence in the court.

The European reader will scarcely believe it possible, that, after submitting to be reinstated in the Guddee of Nâgpoor by the mediation of the British Resident, at the sacrifice of his army and political independence, Appa Saheb should again have entered into treasonable plots against the power, which had thus restored him. It would seem, however, that no sooner was the personal danger gone by, than he began to be ashamed of the weakness that had urged him to throw up a cause by no means desperate; and, sensible that he had acted more from fear than judgment, he could scarcely divest himself of the idea of his having been betrayed into the step, by what he now deemed to be Nerayun's interested exaggerations of the danger. Ashamed and mortified at the folly and cowardice of the course he had taken, he thought only of repairing the error, as soon as he should recover the means; and by way of ensuring success, not only agreed with apparent readiness to the terms proposed, but proffered more than was asked, in the hope of regaining our confidence, and thereby masking his future conduct and designs.

So rapid was this change of sentiments in the Raja, that, even while yet in our power, and living at the Residency, nay, at the very moment of subscribing to the terms which were to be the price of his restoration, was he practising the deception, by which he hoped to retrieve his affairs and renew our embarrassments. In the interval between the attack on the Residency and the arrival of Brigadier-General Doveton, secret orders had been issued to the several Goand and other jungul and mountain Rajas, to call out their followers, and offer every annoyance in their power to the British authorities, especially to cut off detachments in charge of convoys, and prevent the country from furnishing supplies to the different armies in the field. Appa Saheb and his ministers, while negotiating the terms of the treaty, perceiving, from the omission of any stipulation for the recal of these orders, that Mr. Jenkins had then no notice or suspicion of them, resolved to allow them to take effect, though perfectly aware, as they afterwards acknowledged, that the consequence of not recalling them would be, to raise the whole country in arms, not only against us, but against any government that might act under our sanction. This deception was continued in the measures taken to prevent the due execution of the treaty after its signature. It was ascertained, that the Killadars of Mundela and Chouragurh had from the first received private instructions not to surrender to the public orders which should be presented. The commander at Dhamonee * also pleaded the receipt of similar instructions, which order, to be effectual, must have preceded the signing of the treaty, or at least have followed so closely, as to be sure of anticipating the public sum-

* The private orders to Dhamonee were in these words: "Jysa Dekho, wysakuro;" "As you see, so do:" meaning, as the Killadar naturally interpreted them, "Resist, if you think yourself able."

mons; which shows the early commencement of the plot. In prosecution of the same designs, orders were issued on the 18th of January, nine days only after the Raja returned to his palace, for the Killadar of Chanda to recruit, and particularly to enlist Arabs. It was moreover subsequently ascertained, that, along with Gunput Rao, who carried off with him the remnant of the army defeated by Brigadier-General Doveton, an agent of the name of Sukha-Ram had been sent directly from Appa Saheb, carrying with him one of the seals of state in token of his mission, to convey the Raja's earnest request for immediate assistance towards throwing off the British yoke. The issue of this part of the intrigue will presently be mentioned, when we come to relate what was passing in the camp of Bajee Rao.

The first suspicion entertained by Mr. Jenkins of the existence of these designs was excited by the obstinate refusal of the Killadars and garrisons to evacuate Mundela and Chouragurh, notwithstanding the liberal offer of all arrears; for the rejection of which it was impossible to assign an adequate motive, without supposing them to have other resources or the assurance of other support in the back ground. Indeed, the Killadar of Chouragurh asserted the receipt of private orders of a contrary purport, in reply to the summons sent to him by Lieutenant-Colonel M'Morin. Coupling this obstinacy of the Killadars and the reasons so publicly assigned for it with some appearances of a similar nature in the behaviour of the Prince himself since his restoration, Mr. Jenkins thought it necessary to take measures for ascertaining the truth or falsehood of the reports in circulation, and for watching the agents of the several parties, and endeavouring to intercept some of their confidential despatches. It was particularly an object to discover, whether the intrigues were confined to the ministry and inferior departments, or originated with the Raja himself. There was certainly ample ground to suspect Appa Saheb; for it had been observed, that, although he had since his return to the palace shut himself up in his own apartments, professing to be indifferent to all state concerns, still he was evidently discontented, and never saw Nerayun Pundit without reproaching him as the cause of his present degradation. At the same time it was known, that he had frequent private conferences with Nagoo Punt and Ramchundur, the purport of which was studiously concealed from their colleagues in administration, and from the Resident. His participation in whatever intrigues were on foot was also inferable from his general character and conduct; besides which, on more than one occasion, suspicion was excited by Nagoo Punt's mode of conducting the internal branch of the administration, particularly by some measures he took to favour the interests of those proscribed in consequence of their continued disobedience. When Mr. Jenkins preferred a complaint against him to Appa Saheb, the Raja pledged himself for the dewan's fidelity, and would listen to no argument tending to impeach it; thus evidently identifying himself with the measures of the favourite. But the circumstance, which threw the strongest personal suspicion upon Appa Saheb, was, the discovery that, instead of bringing his treasures back to Nâgpoor along with the women of his family, he had issued secret orders to have the greater part conveyed back to Chanda and other forts, and even what was brought into the town was not openly deposited in the palace, but given out in trust with great secrecy and care.

Influenced by these suspicions, Mr. Jenkins first set a watch upon a man named Govind Pundit, whom he knew to be the agent at court on behalf of Nathoo-Ram, an officer who had been commissioned to expedite the surrender of Mundela. On the 4th of March, having intelligence that a letter was on its way from him to Nathoo-Ram, in the hands of a confidential messenger, he caused the bearer of it to be seized, and thus obtained possession of it. The letter gave circumstantial details of what had passed at some conferences with Nagoo Punt, and Ramchundur, to which Govind had been admitted, and afforded abundant evidence of those ministers having instigated the refusal to surrender Mundela. Upon this, Mr. Jenkins caused Govind Punt to be arrested and examined; and being apprehensive of an attempt on the part of Appa Saheb to depart secretly, redoubled his vigilance, and, under the pretence of an improved police regulation, ordered every possible precaution to be taken to prevent any one from quitting the town by night. Though the suspicions were strong, nothing further had yet attached to Appa Saheb himself; when a private letter of the date of the 6th of March, was addressed by Mr. Jenkins to the Governor-General, pressing for early instructions for his guidance. He was answered in the same spirit by Mr. Adam, the Governor-General's secretary, that, without direct proof against the Raja, he was only to act against the ministers; but that he would be justified in taking the most vigorous measures to obtain the removal of such dangerous counsellors, as Nagoo Punt and Ramchundur had now proved themselves to be, and the exclusion from the durbar of others of the same stamp. In the mean time, however, reports poured in from every quarter of applications by Appa Saheb to Bajee Rao for assistance, and of the hostile advance of Gunput Rao with succours. Mr. Jenkins, therefore, redoubled his efforts to penetrate the mystery. Having ascertained that two agents were about to be despatched by Ramchundur to Bajee Rao, one a confidential *chitnavees* (secretary) of Ramchundur himself, the other a *bareedar* (private servant) of the Raja, caused them to be seized just on the point of setting off. Before this strong measure, he had contrived to procure from the chitnavees an acknowledgment of the nature of his errand, which was made in a place where he could be overheard, and to a supposed friend, who was in reality a spy set to win his confidence. Atma-Ram (so was the secretary named) destroyed a paper he had about him as soon as he found himself betrayed; but it was discovered that this paper contained a few words in the Prince's own hand-writing, which were to give the assurance of his being a true messenger. Next morning, when Appa Saheb was informed of the arrest of the courier, he expressed the utmost anxiety to know if any paper had been found upon him, and seemed much relieved, at learning that none was actually forthcoming. This occurred on the 14th of March; and at the same time arrived the positive intelligence of Gunput Rao being in full march to Nâgpoor, while it was confidently reported, that the Pêshwa was himself following with his whole army, and had already passed the frontier of the Nizam's dominions in his way. Previous accounts had reported him to have moved in an easterly direction after evading the pursuit of Sir Thomas Hislop, so as to render such an intention extremely probable. It was rumoured also, that the Raja was on the eve of flying to Chanda to meet him.

The Pêshwa's detachment of Gunput Rao with reinforcements, and movement with his main army in a direction to support that chief, was so strong a confirmation of the truth of the designs said to be in agitation at Nâgpoor, as, even without positive proof and on mere suspicion, would have justified the most vigorous precautionary measures. More decisive evidence had, however, been obtained by the seizure of Atma-Ram and his companion, evidence going directly to implicate the Raja himself. Feeling, therefore, that, should the Bhoosla prince escape and join Bajee Rao, all that had been done to establish order in the Nâgpoor dominions would be undone again in a moment, and being now armed with more convincing testimony, the Resident resolved to wait no longer for instructions, but to act upon his own responsibility, and take the only step, which could effectually secure the British interests intrusted to his charge against the impending danger. Up to this time he had confined himself to measures of precaution and inquiry; but the knowledge of these, and of the arrest of the couriers, was calculated to precipitate the crisis with the Raja, and to urge him to immediate flight, as the only means of avoiding the consequences of detection. Thus, it was impossible to delay for another moment the necessary measures of prevention, however anxious he might have been to receive the instructions of the higher powers, before he took so decided a step.

Accordingly, having determined immediately to place the Raja under close arrest, he sent notice of this intention over night to Buka Baee, whom the reader will remember to have been before mentioned, as the favourite wife of the deceased Ragoojee, and at all times attached to the party opposed to the reigning Raja. In the morning of the 15th of March, he despatched a note to Appa Saheb, informing him that doubts had arisen, which made it absolutely necessary that he should come and remain at the Residency till they were cleared up, representing strongly the utter impossibility of resistance, and the prudence of immediate compliance, without rendering it necessary to resort to forcible measures. Buka Baee in vain exerted her influence to induce the Raja to attend to this very peremptory summons: whereupon, Mr. Jenkins being determined to enforce it, sent a party of Sepoys unarmed, under the conduct of Captain Brown, 22d Bengal native infantry, and Dr. Gordon, the Resident's assistant, who succeeded in effecting the arrest, and fortunately without the necessity of entering the apartments reserved for the women. Nagoo Punt and Ramchundur Wâgh were in like manner seized, and all three brought to the Residency, and placed under separate guards. They in some measure confessed their participation in the plot, particularly Nagoo Punt, who accused his master of being the cause of his ruin by his incurable love of intrigue, and made it his principal request, that, if doomed to imprisonment, he might be separately confined.

The confessions of the Raja and of his ministers were quite unnecessary to convince the world of their criminality. Proofs multiplied from every quarter immediately after their apprehension; while the daily advance of Bajee Rao, and the gradual development of the intrigues that had been passing between him and the Bhoosla, satisfied every one of the necessity of the Resident's precautionary measures. Amongst other articles of accusation, that transpired in the course of the inquiries instituted on this occasion, the circumstances of the murder of Pursajee first came to light on the day before the arrest. Indeed, one of Mr. Jenkins' motives for holding the Raja in close confinement was, the idea, that Lord Hastings might perhaps desire so heavy an accusation to be brought to trial, in order to visit the crime with the merited punishment, in the event of the charge being clearly established.

In this posture affairs remained at Nâgpoor, while the Resident awaited the Governor-General's instructions as to the steps to be next adopted. And here we will for the present leave them, turning aside to notice the circumstances of Bajee Rao's advance into this territory, and the events to which it led.

We have already followed Gunput Rao to the time of his junction with Bajee Rao, at the head of the broken horse of the Nâgpoor army. The junction took place in the neighbourhood of Tambaornee, before Bajee Rao's retreat on Solapoor, whither Gunput Rao accompanied him, and was afterwards present at the battle of Ashtee. Naroo Sukha-ram, the agent beforementioned, had followed in the train of this Sirdar, and delivered the errand from his master, soliciting aid: and the course to be adopted in consequence was under consideration, when Bajee

Rao's army was surprised on the 20th of February. In the flight, Bajee Rao had scarcely got as far north as Purinda, when two *hoojras* (confidential messengers) arrived also from Nâgpoor, pressing for the early adoption of some plan for the Raja's relief. On their heels followed two other similar messengers, who repeated Appa Saheb's earnest entreaty for assistance, bringing a letter in his own hand-writing to confirm the veracity of their verbal statement. The despatch was brief and simple: "Sumana Meer to Gungana Dobeeya—Assist me in any way you can." The names are those of two holy men, famous in Mahratta legends for the assistance they mutually rendered each other in extremity. These messengers Bajee Rao carried along with him, and continued his flight northward to Newasa, whence he endeavoured without success to expel a garrison of Sebundees left by Colonel Deacon in his way to the south-west. From Newasa he directed his flight north-west to Kopergâon, crossing the Godaveree at Phool-tamba. Finding the heat of the pursuit somewhat abated, he took the opportunity of visiting Nassick, and then proceeded to Warner near Chandore, where he effected the before-mentioned junction with Ramdeen, who had brought with him some Pindaree horse, and a portion of the routed infantry of Holkar. Hence the Nâgpoor messengers were at length despatched with a written answer to the Bhoosla, the contents of which never transpired; but there can be no doubt it conveyed an assurance of immediate help. This was on the 2d of March; and Gunput Rao and Sukha-ram at the same time solicited an advance of money, and leave to depart for Nâgpoor, stating that preparations for war had been making at Chanda, that a force under Chundojee Bhoosla was at Bhandaree, and that they had certain information of the hill people having risen in arms, as well as of Mundela and Chouragurh having been put into a condition to stand a siege. With a small advance of money and troops, they engaged to raise a general insurrection, as soon as they should reach the Bhoosla territory; and strongly recommended the Pêshwa to proceed himself in the same direction by the route of Kandêsh and Boorhanpoor. Bajee Rao, though he seemed to listen favourably to this advice, could not be brought to give a distinct or immediate answer, but desired Gunput Rao to wait a few days for his determination. He then skirted the Ghâts into Kandêsh, collecting information as he went, as to the practicability of the plan, and the disposition of the several British divisions. At Unkye he first learnt Sir Thomas Hislop's arrival in Kandêsh, and near approach in a direction to intercept completely the route by Boorhanpoor; whereupon he fled with the utmost precipitation across the Godaveree at Kopergâon, and as far south as Assee on the Peeree. Thence again, fearing to fall in with the division of Brigadier-General Smith in its advance from the south, he turned off due east, and continued his march in that direction. The suggestion of Gunput Rao was now openly adopted, and this chief sent forward by a parallel, but different route from that pursued by the main body, which passed the Nizam's frontier, and crossed the Godaveree at Ruk-husbun to the south of Jâlna, with the evident and avowed intention of entering the dominions of the Bhoosla state.

On the 11th of March, Sir Thomas Hislop ascended from Kandêsh to the plain of the Godaveree, and made one or two ineffectual efforts to come up with the enemy; but, finding that he had escaped by the superior rapidity of his marches, first to the south and then to the east, the Lieutenant-General resolved, without further delay, to carry into effect the orders he had received from Lord Hastings. The several corps forming the head-quarter division were accordingly distributed amongst the other forces in the field; and, on the 31st of March, the final orders were issued from Lassoor for breaking up the army of the Dukhun. Sir Thomas Hislop himself, with the whole general staff of the army, prepared for his return to the Madras presidency with a slight escort of cavalry and infantry; and subsequently, in order to avoid the inconvenience of diverting so large a force as would be necessary to form an efficient escort, from the more important object of contributing to the settlement of the country, he resolved to proceed from Poona to Bombay, and thence round by sea to Madras, leaving all his escort at Mr. Elphinstone's disposal, along with the other troops in the field.

In the meantime, Bajee Rao was hastening his flight from his own dominions in the direction of Chanda. His march was marked with cruelties and excesses of the most wanton kind, which, indeed, were mostly attributed to the professional plunderers brought down by Ram-Deen from Hindoostan; for the Mahrattas had hitherto shown some moderation and forbearance in their passage through the country. During the retreat, great pains were taken to mislead the pursuers. The Pêshwa himself always gave out the line of march for the day, withholding every morning from all his officers the next place of halting, until his standard and treasure elephants had actually moved forward. Brigadier-General Smith had not urged the northward pursuit of Bajee Rao after the action at Ashtee on the 20th of February; thinking it necessary first to escort the Raja of Suttara, to receive his formal investiture by Mr. Elphinstone. This occasioned a few days respite; after which the light division, under the Brigadier-General, again proceeded to the north, and having halted to refresh at Seroor, left that place to prosecute the pursuit on the 10th of March. Hearing at this point of Bajee Rao's march eastward, the Brigadier-General moved towards Jâlna, in order to concert a combined plan of pursuit with the division of Brigadier-General Doveton, who had by this time received his reinforcements from Sir Thomas Hislop, and reached that position. Brigadier-General Doveton, who was the junior officer, resolved to march himself upon Basum, and thence along the

Ghâts into Berar, as far as Kurinja, in the hope of, by that means, effectually cutting off the Mahratta army from the north; and suggested to Brigadier-General Smith the advantage of his moving along the line of the Godaveree, at such a distance from the river, as should prevent the enemy from turning his right without crossing, which the difficulty of the fords gave him little chance of effecting, or of getting off to the southward again, without laying himself open to attack.

The van of the Mahratta army, after having traversed the Nizam's dominions from west to east without resistance, appeared on the banks of the Wurda on the first or second of April, at a point near Woonee, a little above the confluence of this river with the Payn Gunga. In this quarter, however, he found his plans wholly disconcerted by the preparations made for his reception. It will be recollected, that, after receiving the submission of Namdar Khan and other Pindaree leaders, the division of Lieutenant-Colonel Adams had been ordered to return from Hindoostan to its original station in the valley of the Nerbudda, there to prepare for the reduction of the fort of Chouragurh, the Killadar of which had been repeatedly summoned by Lieutenant-Colonel M'Morine without effect. The beginning of March was passed by Colonel Adams in making ready for the attack of this place, and in procuring from General Marshall a reinforcement of heavy guns for the purpose, the two in the depôt at Hoshungabad having suffered a little in their carriages. While yet engaged in these preparations, the events above detailed were passing at Nâgpoor, and Mr. Jenkins, having reason to believe that * Chanda was to be the destined rallying point of resistance, even before it was certain that the Pêshwa was on his way thither, directed Lieutenant-Colonel Adams' particular attention to the importance of summoning, and eventually reducing it before the close of the season, and therefore recom-

* Vide plate.

mended his leaving Chouragurh for the present, in order to make Chanda his first object, in case there should not be time for the reduction of both before the setting in of the rains. It was further suggested, that General Marshall's force might be advantageously employed against Chouragurh as well as Mundela, immediately after the taking of Dhamonee, on which service it was then employed; and this arrangement was afterwards ordered by the Marquess of Hastings to be carried into execution, as we have before incidentally noticed in the preceding chapter.

These discussions respecting the importance of reducing Chanda had prepared Lieutenant-Colonel Adams for an early summons to the southward, before the receipt of positive intelligence, that Bajee Rao was on his way towards the same point. Wherefore, on the first advice of the probability of this event, he began to move by forced marches upon Nâgpoor, carrying with him the 5th Bengal cavalry, his horse-artillery, and a brigade of infantry, and leaving Major Popham with a detachment to bring up by easy stages the two eighteen-pounders, forming the whole heavy train at his command. Mr. Jenkins had previously summoned a detachment of the 8th Bengal cavalry from Jubulpoor to strengthen his force in that arm; and further, on learning that Chanda was the point for which the troops from the westward were making, Lieutenant-Colonel Scott had been despatched with the greater part of the force then at Nâgpoor, in the hope of his being able to cut off the enemy from any communication with that strong fortress, and hold him in check until the arrival of Colonel Adams with the main body. Colonel Scott reached Wuroda, or Wuroona, about fifteen miles from Chanda, on the 3d of April. Here he fell in with the van of the Mahrattas, under Gunput Rao, and drove it back across the Wurda, though with the trifling loss of ten or twelve only; for the rencounter was quite unexpected by the enemy, who fled with precipitation on the first appearance of the British force. Thus stopped short in his advance, and at the same time apprized of the arrest of Appa Saheb and the little hope of support within the Bhoosla territory, Bajee Rao continued for some days irresolute, shifting his ground between the Wurda and the Payn-Gunga, but not daring to cross the former river. After the affair at Wuroda, Lieutenant-Colonel Scott proceeded to Chanda, hoping to succeed in investing the place, or at least to cut off all communication from without; but he found the fortifications so extensive, that with his small force, consisting of only one weak brigade of infantry and the 6th Bengal cavalry, it was impossible for him to cover it entirely. Lieutenant-Colonel Adams in the mean time, having made arrangements for the defence of Nâgpoor, hastened his march to Hingun-Ghât, which he selected as the most appropriate point, both to cover the Bhoosla capital and to support Lieutenant-Colonel Scott in case of emergency. He reached Hingun-Ghât on the 6th of April, and found that Bajee Rao was still on the other side of the Wurda, undetermined what course now to pursue. Lieutenant-Colonel Scott had left Nâgpoor in such haste, that he had come away with insufficient supplies; and, as the country about Chanda was found to be wholly destitute of the means of support, he felt himself under the necessity of soliciting from Lieutenant-Colonel Adams a part of his stores, which was instantly forwarded; but Colonel Adams thought it advisable in consequence to wait the arrival of a fresh supply from Nâgpoor, before he embarked any further in a service, that promised to draw him into a long pursuit through an impoverished country, and away from his own resources. By good fortune, the delay was every way advantageous, as it would enable Brigadier-General Doveton to reach the desired position to the north-west of the enemy, while Brigadier-General Smith approached to cut him off from the southward. With the three divisions thus closing in upon him from opposite sides, it seemed utterly impossible he should escape. Halting therefore at Hingun-Ghât, the Lieutenant-Colonel exerted himself to procure intelligence of every motion of the enemy; and, ascertaining that he still loitered about Pundur-Koura and Woonee without attempting any thing, forbore for the present to disquiet him or beat up his quarters. On the 11th of April, Lieutenant-Colonel Scott was called in from Chanda, in contemplation of an eventual attack; and, on the information that Bajee Rao had on the 13th ventured across the Wurda, at a place called Poona, a little way up the river, Colonel Adams on the 14th made a westward movement on Alumdoho, which had the effect of immediately driving him back. Brigadier-General Doveton had on the same day reached Doodgâon on the Aran, fifty miles only to the north-west of Pundur-Koura, whence he had written to Lieutenant-Colonel Adams, that he should march by long stages directly on Pundur-Koura, so as to reach the latter place on the 17th; and it was reckoned, that, by that time, Brigadier-General Smith would be sufficiently advanced along the line of the Godaveree to intercept any retreat to the south. In the course of the 16th, Colonel Adams received the letter conveying this intelligence; and learning from his own scouts that Bajee Rao was within a forced march to the south-east of his position at Alumdoho, resolved to march the same evening, in the hope of either falling upon his encampment, or driving him back upon the division of Brigadier-General Doveton, on its advance to Pundur-Koura. At eight in the evening, the Lieutenant-Colonel began his march; and, on the morning of the 17th of April, arrived at Peepul-Kôt, where the Pêshwa had been encamped the preceding day. It was here found, that he had gone off to Soonee, a village said to be six coss further to the south-west.

Upon this, not yet despairing to overtake the fugitives, he called up the cavalry and horse-artillery, together with a light infantry battalion, and resolved to push forward with this force to Soonee, leaving the rest of the troops to follow more at leisure. Colonel Adams had with him the entire 5th and 6th and a squadron of the 8th Bengal cavalry, a brigade of the Madras European horse-artillery, and a troop of the native corps of the same arm from the Bengal establishment. The light battalion was composed of the light companies of the several corps originally attached to the 5th division of the army of the Dukhun, on its formation in the preceding October. With this force he hastened his march upon Soonee. On approaching the village, he found that Bajee Rao, whom his own advance had driven to the south-west, had just discovered himself to be in full march on Brigadier-General Doveton's line, which on the same day was marching to Pundur-Koura, only twelve miles south of Soonee. In the anxiety to avoid this new danger, he had again taken a northerly route, and was making off with all despatch along the very road, by which Colonel Adams was approaching. The advance guard of the two armies met about five miles from Soonee*; when Lieutenant-Colonel Adams, guessing, from the number of elephants and standards, that Bajee Rao was present in person, immediately put the head of his column, consisting of the 5th native cavalry and horse-artillery, into a gallop, and drove the enemy back in confusion for some miles. The course of the road led to the brow of a rising ground, whence, in the valley beneath, and on the opposite declivity, the main body of the Mahratta army was discovered in great confusion. The horse-artillery opened their fire with admirable effect upon them in this disorganised state, while the cavalry formed, and charging into the valley, in a short time completely cleared it.

* Vide plate at the head of this Chapter.

The Lieutenant-Colonel, who led the charge himself, had by this time left the rest of his troops considerably in the rear: undismayed, however, by the numbers of the enemy, he determined to follow up his success with the single regiment he had with him. Wherefore, detaching one squadron to scour the rising ground on his right, he continued a hot pursuit with the two others, tracking the fugitives up the valley which took a turn to the left of the road, until he reached another elevation overlooking a second valley watered by the same stream that runs by Soonee. The Mahrattas were here seen collected in greater numbers than before: the horse-artillery again opened upon them with great effect, while Colonel Adams formed the two squadrons with him into line, and, charging a second time, drove every thing before him. At the further end of this second valley, two large bodies of the enemy's horse were drawn up, as if prepared to stand their ground. The first of these, however, dispersed quickly, on receiving the fire of the horse-artillery, and on finding its flank threatened by the squadron that had been sent to scour the elevated ground on our right. The other body, which was posted on our left, was then driven off by a change of front and rapid advance in that direction. The enemy was thenceforth seen only in broken detachments, flying through the surrounding jungul in complete rout. Five guns, the only ones he had with him, were captured in this action: three elephants and 200 camels also fell into our hands. The elephants were of those which always preceded Bajee Rao's line of march, and on which his treasure was usually laden; but no more than 11,000 rupees in cash was found upon them, the rest having been made away with in the confusion. The Prince himself escaped with difficulty, by mounting a horse and galloping away on the first appearance of the British troops. One of his palanquins was taken, and proved to have been perforated by a round shot; from its appearance, it was conjectured to have been the same in which he had just been riding. The British loss was only two wounded, the enemy never having stood a charge; whereas, in the pursuit, and particularly by the fire of the horse-artillery, upwards of 1000 of the enemy were left dead on the field. Particular credit was due to the officers and men of both corps of horse-artillery. Captain Rodbeer, of the Bengal native corps, had joined Colonel Adams at Alumdoho but eight hours before the march was commenced on the evening of the 16th; yet he was up with the foremost of the cavalry, notwithstanding the length of the march and pursuit, as was likewise Lieutenant Poggenpohl, a very distinguished officer of the Madras artillery. Indeed, it was mainly in reliance upon his strength in this arm, that Colonel Adams ventured so far in advance of his main body, with only a single regiment of cavalry (5th), being determined to make the affair as decisive as possible, though at some risk, and aware that every moment afforded for escape would detract from the importance of the result. The rest of the cavalry, owing to some misapprehension on the part of Colonel Gahan, its commander, did not join until after the enemy had entirely disappeared. The troops were then encamped on the field of battle, after a continued march of upwards of thirty miles, and waited the coming up of their supplies, before the pursuit could be further prosecuted.

Brigadier-General Doveton arrived at Pundur Koura, on the morning of the very day on which this action was fought; and, being only 12 miles distant, was not long in hearing of the success of the other division. The concurring reports of all his scouts having represented the line of the Pêshwa's flight to be to the southward of west, the Brigadier-General resolved to push forward and give chase in that direction. Consequently, he divided his force into two bodies; one of which he led himself, and of the other he gave the command to Captain Grant, of the Mysore horse, with whom, besides his own corps, he detached for the purpose two squadrons of regular cavalry, two gallopers, and two light companies of infantry. In this manner the Mahratta army was followed at the heels for five successive days, during all which time it suffered the extreme of distress from famine and fatigue, the British officers making only occasional halts for the indispensable refreshment of their men and horses.

The routed Pêshwa was found to have taken a direction south-westerly, as far as Oomer-Kher, and thence due westward, by Kullumpoor, to Boree. At this place, or in the way to it, disheartened at their uniform ill success, and broken down by long privations, nearly two-thirds of his remaining adherents left his standard, with the intention of returning quietly to their homes. Brigadier-General Doveton pursued without halting, as far as Oomer-Kher, and then made a move rather to the north, in order to procure supplies from Basum. Thence he continued the pursuit as far west as Pepree beyond Jâlna, which he reached on the 3d of May. Here, however, he had the mortification to discover, that he was following a detached party led by chiefs of inferior note, while the Pêshwa himself had turned off from Boree northwards, with the design of crossing the Taptee, and penetrating if possible into Hindoostan.

Of the countless host that had followed his fortunes to the Wurda, there now remained with him no more than 8 or 10,000 at the utmost. All the Sirdars deserted after the affair of Soonee, except Trimbukjee, Ram-deen, the Vinshorekur, (Balooba), and the widow, with some of the troops, of Gokla. This dispersion of the several Sirdars with their followers in so many different directions rendered it very difficult to determine with precision the exact line of the prince's flight. The party, that Brigadier-General Doveton pursued so far to the westward, proved to be led not by himself but by Madhoo Rasteea and Appa Dhunderee, Bajee Rao's father-in-law. The

Brigadier-General no sooner discovered his error, than he left them to continue their route unmolested; and both made good their way to Kandèsh, and sent their submissions thence to Mr. Elphinstone. In the same manner Appa Dussaee, with Chimnajee Nerayun, Bajee Rao's own brother, separated themselves entirely from his standard at Boree, and fled directly to the south-west, crossing the Godaveree at Nander. Esajee Punt, a Gokla nearly connected with the chief slain at Ashtee, and Wittoba Naeek, the same man who had delivered the declaration of war to the Resident at Poona, fled also in a south-west direction with another remnant of the fugitives. The pursuit of these parties was taken up by Brigadier-General Smith, who was at Nermul, when the affair of Soonee took place, and, hearing of the total dispersion of the Mahratta army, started in pursuit, on the 22d of April. Appa Dussaee and Chimnajee surrendered to a detachment sent out by the Brigadier-General, under Captain Davies, of the Nizam's reformed horse, and were by that officer conducted to Ahmednugurh, where they consented to abide the orders of Mr. Elphinstone. The other party was pursued by another detachment from the same division, under Major Cunningham, as far as Pundurpoor, whence their chiefs also sent in their submission.

In the interim, Brigadier-General Pritzler, whom we left preparing for the attack of Wusota, appeared before that place and closely invested it, on the 31st of March. Such, however, were the natural difficulties of the ground, that the heavy guns could not be brought into battery until the 5th of April. The fort itself, though nature and art had done their utmost to strengthen it in other respects, was commanded by a neighbouring hill, called Old Wusota, which was accordingly chosen as the position for the breaching batteries. Such was the effect with which they opened, that the Killadar stood out but one day's fire, and surrendered the place on the 6th of April. The remainder of the Raja of Suttara's family was found here, and the Killadar declared that he had received orders from his master to put the whole of them to death, sooner than allow them to fall into the hands of the British. These orders he found an obvious interest in neglecting, in the present depressed condition of Bajee Rao's fortunes. Lieutenants Morrieson and Hunter, whose capture at the commencement of the war was before noticed, were also found immured in the dungeons of this fort. Valuables belonging to the Suttara family, estimated to amount to near three lack rupees, were likewise captured: for these, however, the troops were allowed a compensation, in order to admit of their restoration to the Raja. On the reduction of Wusota, the force under Brigadier-General Pritzler was broken up; the corps of it drawn from the reserve, after being reinforced by a Bombay battalion, were sent to meet Brigadier-General Munro*, who was advancing from the south to attack the infantry and guns that Bajee Rao had left behind at Solapoor. The remainder proceeded against the strong holds on the north of Poona. Brigadier-General Pritzler in person led back the troops of the reserve, and received on his route the submission of all the forts along the line of the Kishna, none of which offered the slightest resistance. Major Eldridge, of the Bombay European regiment, commanding the troops detached to the north, obtained possession, in the course of April, of Sheeoneer, or Jooneer, which had been evacuated, and of all the other forts south of the range that separates the sources of the

* Brigadier-General Munro was not strong enough without this reinforcement, and though repeated requests had been addressed to the Madras Government, not a single company was allowed to join him from within our provinces in that quarter: indeed, the march of a reinforcement, which the commanding officer took upon himself to furnish, was specially countermanded from the Presidency, on the plea of its being required to guard our own frontier; as if the destruction of the enemy were not its best possible defence.

Bheema from those of the Godaveree. Lieutenant-Colonel M'Dowal, in the mean time, with a detachment from Brigadier-General Doveton's division, reduced the important forts of Unkye, Rajdeho, Dhoorup, and Trimbuk, which gave to us the entire command of the valley of the Godaveree, and a ready entrance into Kandêsh. Captain Briggs, who had been placed in the political charge of the British interests in this quarter, in subordination to Mr. Elphinstone, the supreme commissioner, now resolved to employ the force of Lieutenant-Colonel M'Dowal, though consisting of only 1100 firelocks, in the reduction of the Pêshwa's remaining possessions in Kandêsh, from which object the pursuit of Bajee Rao had necessarily diverted the Brigadier-General. The influence already possessed there, from the occupation of all Holkar's late cessions, gave us advantages that led Captain Briggs to hope for success, notwithstanding his very inadequate means; and the event justified the correctness of his calculations, although a temporary check was experienced at Malugâon, as will presently be mentioned.

Meanwhile, Brigadier-General Munro, having advanced with the available portion of the reserve under his command, and effected a junction with Brigadier-General Pritzler, cleared the south country of several detached marauding parties, driving them before him till he reached Solapoor*, on the 9th of May. He there found the main body of Bajee Rao's infantry, with eleven guns of his field train, encamped under the walls, and the fort and town strongly garrisoned with Arabs. On the morning of the 10th, the Brigadier-General marched with all his brigades of infantry but one to the north side of the place; and forming them into two columns with a reserve, advanced for the purpose of carrying the *petta* by escalade. Besides the

* Vide plate at the head of this Chapter.

fort, there was an inner and an outer petta; the latter of these was soon in our possession, and a lodgement was also effected in the wall of the inner petta close to the fort. However, while this operation was going on within, Gunput Rao Panre, the commandant of the infantry of the garrison, brought a party round to the east of the fort, and unexpectedly opened five guns on the troops left in reserve with the artillery, consisting of six flank companies. The fire was answered, though not silenced, by ours: but, after carrying the petta, Lieutenant-Colonel Dalrymple, the commanding officer of artillery, and the only field officer with the reserve, perceiving the enemy to be in the act of retiring his guns, led the companies of the reserve to the charge. In his advance he was reinforced by Lieutenant-Colonel Newal from the petta, and succeeded in capturing three of the guns, and driving the enemy back with considerable loss of men. Partial firing continued in the petta; nor did the action cease till 4 p. m., at which time Brigadier-General Munro, observing the infantry to be moving off in small parties from the camp adjoining to the fort, ordered Brigadier-General Pritzler in pursuit, with the cavalry attached to his force, consisting of not more than three troops of the 22d dragoons, and about 400 irregulars. At the head of this small force, Brigadier-General Pritzler came up with the enemy a few miles from the town, and found him marching in pretty close column. The gallopers were opened, and one troop detached to the right, and another to the left, with orders to charge. The column was completely penetrated and broken, the dragoon officers judiciously restraining their men from using their pistols, until this first object had been fully accomplished. The infantry was then cut up in detail by the dragoons and irregulars, a duty in which the latter troops are in general particularly alert. The greater part of the fugitives threw away their arms and escaped;

but considerable havoc was made amongst the Arabs, who disdained to secure their flight by such means. Gunput Rao had already been wounded in the attack on the reserve, and Veetul Punt, the second in command, killed on the same occasion. But Major de Pinto, a Portuguese officer, who had raised some battalions for Gokla, and had been actively engaged at Kirkee, was slain in this pursuit, together with more than 800 of the fugitives. The fort of Solapoor surrendered on the 15th of May, after one day's bombardment; and with it all Bajee Rao's remaining artillery fell into our hands, while the previous destruction of his infantry left his cause entirely destitute of adherents within his late dominions, except in the garrisons of a few remaining forts in Kandêsh. Of Brigadier-General Munro's division, 97 were killed and wounded in the course of these operations. The capture of 37 guns on the surrender of the place, most of them in very serviceable condition, affords a fair criterion of the importance of the success, and the credit due to those who conducted the enterprise.

While Bajee Rao was thus hunted down, and his country reduced by the several British divisions and detachments in the field, Lieutenant-Colonel Adams, having ascertained that the direction of the flight from Soonee was due west, and that Brigadier-Generals Doveton and Smith were both hotly engaged in the pursuit, resolved to lose no time in moving the force under his command towards Chanda, in order to summon that important fortress. He accordingly called up the two eighteen-pounders, which had been directed to follow him from Hôshungabad: and, having obtained another of the Nizam's from Major Pitman at Umraotee, proceeded with this weak train, and set himself down before Chanda on the 9th of May. The poisoning of the wells on his approach indicated the Killadar's determination to hold out to the last extremity; nevertheless, the Lieutenant-Colonel forwarded a letter, containing the most moderate proposals, offering to the garrison permission to march out with all their private property and arms, and only requiring them to account for the treasure and public property, which he was instructed to hold in deposit for the successor of Appa Saheb. The Killadar not only sent no reply, but detained the bearer of Colonel Adams' letter, seemingly in full confidence of his ability to resist. The place was so extensive, that the whole of the 10th and 11th was occupied in reconnoitring* and fixing upon the point of attack. Good ground for the breaching battery was, however, found in a *nulla* about 250 yards to the south-east of the place. On the 13th, therefore, the British camp was moved from the north-west angle to the south of the fort, and a battery of light guns made to play upon this face, in order to divert the enemy's attention from the main attack. This object was completely attained; and the place having been invested at the same time to the north and west, the garrison, though it amounted to upwards of 3000 men, was kept in a state of constant alarm and uncertainty, and obliged to spread itself over the whole extent of the defences, instead of being concentrated on the single point of importance. The breaching battery opened on the morning of the 19th of April, from the ground originally selected for it. Before evening the breach was perfectly practicable; but the great extent of the works, and number of the garrison, made the Lieutenant-Colonel averse to a night assault. Major Goreham, who commanded the artillery, undertook to prevent the garrison from throwing up any retrenchment or other defence behind the breach during the

* A random shot from the last gun that was fired at the reconnoitring party unfortunately killed Surgeon Anderson, a valuable and much esteemed officer of the Bengal medical establishment.

night; and the morning of next day, the 20th, was fixed for the storm. Lieutenant-Colonel Scott, of the 1st-1st Madras, the next in command to Colonel Adams, volunteered to lead the attack, and the utmost ardour and confidence were shown by the troops. Two squadrons of the 5th native cavalry consented to dismount, and act with the light infantry battalion as a reserve. The place was carried in the course of the day, with the loss of 11 killed and 51 wounded on our part, while, of the enemy, Gungadeen the Killadar was killed, with at least 500 of the garrison. No British officer was amongst the slain; but Major Goreham, a most valuable officer of the Madras artillery, who had directed the operations of this arm during the siege, died of fatigue in the course of the day, and Captains Charlesworth and Watson, of the 1st-1st Madras, were wounded severely; as were also Lieutenant Fell, of the Bengal Pioneers, and Lieutenant Casement, of the 1st-19th Bengal native infantry. Two other officers were also wounded, but very slightly. The storm of Chanda closed the campaign for this season in the Bhoosla territory. Chouragurh had already been evacuated on the approach of Brigadier-General Watson, who was detached against it by Major-General Marshall, immediately after the capture of Mundela.

The division of Lieutenant-Colonel Adams had now completed the object of its destination to the southward. As it was quietly returning to the cantonment at Hôshungabad, it was, however, attacked by the same fatal disorder, which, in the preceding November, had thinned the ranks of the centre division of the Bengal army. In a few days the casualties far exceeded what the troops had suffered in the whole course of those military operations, in which they had borne so active a part. The symptoms and effects of the disease were precisely similar to those already described, when we had occasion before to mention it, and there is no need again to dwell upon them. Major-General Marshall's division also had experienced the destructive ravages of the pestilence in the course of the operations against Mundela; and no part of India, from the hills of Nipâl to Cape Comorin, escaped this dreadful visitation.

CHAPTER XVII.

NÂGPOOR—PÊSHWA, &c.

1818. MAY, JUNE, JULY.

Appa Saheb's exile—and escape—consequent measures—Bajee Rao's designs—frustrated—He sends an agent to Sir John Malcolm—is surrounded—negotiates—terms offered—intentions of Governor-General—approach of Brigadier-General Doveton—arrested—Bajee Rao submits—terms—objections—Reflections—Dispersion of Bajee Rao's army—Trimbukjee seized—Arabs refractory—General submission of the country—Review of Mr. Elphinstone's proceedings—their effect on the several classes of the population—cultivating—religious—military—commercial—Arabs of Kandêsh—their expulsion resolved—Siege of Malugâon—vigorous sally—repulsed—Assault fails—Reinforcements—bombardment—explosion of magazine—surrender of the place—mistake in the terms—Close of the campaign.

Pending the operations that terminated in the rout of Soonee, Appa Saheb was held in close confinement at the Nâgpoor Residency, along with his two confidential ministers, Nagoo Punt and Ramchundur Wâgh. The military defence of the capital, in the expected event of the Pêshwa's approach, was the object which at this time engrossed all the attention of the Resident. No sooner was he relieved from apprehension for the capital by the successful issue of this affair, and the consequent dispersion of the Mahratta army, than he selected from the troops at Nâgpoor a strong escort, for the conveyance of his prisoners to a place of greater security within our own immediate provinces. A communication of the Governor-

General's wishes in this respect had reached the Resident, accompanied by an intimation, that an old palace of the Moghul's, within the fort of Allahabad, was every way the place best fitted for the ex-Raja's accommodation and safe custody. Accordingly, on the 3d of May, Appa Saheb, with his two ministers, was conveyed from Nâgpoor, under charge of a wing of the 22d Bengal native infantry, and three troops of the 8th native cavalry, the whole under the conduct of Captain Browne of the 22d, the same officer, whose judgment had been conspicuous in the previous arrest of the Raja in his palace. Arrangements had been made to provide a fresh escort to take charge of the prisoners from Jubulpoor onwards; and, on the 12th of May, Captain Browne's detachment arrived at Bychore, one march only from that place. In the interim, however, the captive Prince had not been idle. It is conjectured, that, by the agency of a Brahmin, who accompanied the party from Nâgpoor for the first few marches, then left them, on some pretext or other, to make his arrangements, and afterwards rejoined on the 12th, a few of the Sepoys of the 22d Bengal native infantry were seduced from their duty; and that, partly by representation of the merit and glory of the act of assisting a Hindoo of the race of Sevagee in his distress, but chiefly by the profuse distribution of bribes, a conspiracy was formed amongst them to aid in effecting the ex-Raja's escape. Accordingly, about two o'clock in the morning of the 13th, a Sepoy's dress was introduced into the tent: Appa Saheb, thus accoutred, joined the guard; and, under semblance of a relief, marched without interruption completely out of the camp. Relays of horses were in readiness to carry him to a distance before the alarm should be given; and, as every precaution was taken to prevent an early discovery, he succeeded in getting clear off. Six Sepoys of the regiment deserted along with the prisoner, carrying with them their arms and accoutrements;

and a few others followed the example in the course of the succeeding week. Indeed, it appeared, from circumstances which came out before the court-martial appointed for the trial of Captain Browne for neglect in suffering this escape, that several other men of the corps were deeply implicated in the conspiracy; and there was reason to suspect even a Soobadar to have been corrupted. Besides the Sepoys, Appa Saheb took with him only two of his personal attendants. He had left Nâgpoor with upwards of a hundred in different capacities, most of whom were allowed unlimited access at all hours; and, as it was a part of Captain Browne's instructions, to treat his prisoners with the utmost consideration that was consistent with their safe custody, he had not thought it necessary to restrict this intercourse, or to have an European officer on guard night and day over the deposed Raja: though, considering the character and importance of the prisoner, he ought perhaps to have taken that precaution.

Every thing in the tent was left in its usual place, insomuch, that the two servants, whose duty it was to handrub (*shampoe*) Appa Saheb as he slept, continued to perform the same office to the cushions of his bed; and, when the guard was changed at four in the morning, the native officer, who, according to Captain Browne's standing orders, looked into the tent to ascertain the presence of the Raja, seeing them so engaged, was satisfied, and entertained not the least suspicion of his evasion. However, as soon as the escape was discovered, Captain Browne sent off parties of cavalry in every direction, and despatched expresses to Brigadier-General Watson and Lieutenant-Colonel M'Morine, then engaged in the act of taking possession of Chouragurh, which was evacuated on the very same day. Information was also sent to Major O'Brien, the commandant at Jubulpoor, and to all the civil authorities. But it was found impossible to trace the flight of Appa Saheb in time to seize him, notwithstanding the utmost exertion of despatch and vigilance in every quarter.

Ere long it was ascertained, that he had fled in the first instance to Heraee, a place about forty miles south-west of Rychore, and thence to the Mohadeo hills, where he was harboured and concealed by the Goands, and particularly by one Chyn-Shah, a Raja of considerable influence among them. By the close of the rains, he was enabled to collect round his standard a few followers from the wreck of Bajee Rao's army, and from among the fugitive Árabs driven out of Kandêsh. With this band he gave considerable trouble in the ensuing season: nor has the consequent disturbance of that part of the country yet been remedied, or the rising in his favour been entirely subdued to this day*. He has, however, for some months been confined to the hills, and reduced to the greatest straits; and his partisans have been decidedly worsted, wherever they have ventured to show themselves. But of this more hereafter.

The government of Nâgpoor, immediately on hearing of the escape, authorised the offer of a reward of a lack of rupees in cash and a jageer of 10,000 rupees a year in land for the re-apprehension of the fugitive. The reward in ready money was afterwards doubled; and it was for some time hoped, that the notoriously venal disposition of the Goands would have induced them to violate the rights of hospitality; but in the end these hopes proved in this instance fallacious, and the whole force of Lieutenant-Colonel Adams was consequently obliged to take the field in two bodies, one occupied in watching the passes into the Mohadeo hills, while the other is still employed in hunting him down within their range. Neither Nagoo Punt nor Ramchundur Wâgh were parties to the escape; but both were safely conveyed to Jubulpoor, and thence forwarded to

* February, 1819.

Allahabad, the place of their original destination. The escape of Appa Saheb at this juncture was particularly unfortunate, as it gave a new head to the turbulent and factious, whose minds might else have been reconciled to submission, if not by the example of their neighbours, at least by the total want of organisation and of union, that must have followed the loss of every leader of note and personal influence.

Bajee Rao had himself been reduced to extremity by the battle of Soonee, and was on the eve of throwing up the game. We have mentioned, that from Boree he turned northwards, directing his flight towards Hindoostan, in despair of being able to gain any thing by returning towards his late dominions. The faint reed, on which he now leant his hopes, was the idea, that, in the event of his reaching the territory of Doulut Rao Sindheea, he might, either through that chief's mediation secure advantageous terms of reconciliation with the British, or, by drawing him into his measures, obtain the necessary accession of strength, without which all further struggle was utterly hopeless. The reputation of Sindheea's military power had always stood pre-eminent among the Mahratta states; and, as he alone had survived the general crash of the late events, it was not unnatural for the fugitive head of the nation to look to it as a resource in his present desperate condition. Submission, however, was at this moment the primary object of his desire; and, in token of his humiliation, he despatched agents both to Mr. Jenkins at Nâgpoor and to the commissioner at Poona, to intimate his readiness to tender his personal surrender. Meanwhile, having crossed the Taptee on the 5th of May, just below its confluence with the Poona, he proceeded down the valley as far as Chupara, with a view to penetrate into Hindoostan by the Sindwa Ghât and Indore. At Chupara he discovered that this route was altogether closed against him by our possession of Sindwa, as well as by the judicious precautions already taken by

Sir John Malcolm for defence of the line of the Nerbudda from Hindia downwards to Muheshwur. Equally baffled in this attempt, as he had been in his former design of reaching the Bhoosla dominions, he sent forward an agent to Sir John Malcolm, retiring himself eastward towards Boorhanpoor, in order to wait the result of his mission. It appeared as if he intended, in case of failure, to shut himself up in Aseergurh as his place of final refuge, or explore a more easterly route to Hindoostan, should any one seem to be practicable.

Every exertion had been made to provide against the possibility and danger of his penetrating to the north, and to overwhelm the adherents that still clung to his fortunes. There was fortunately at Hindia, besides the usual guard of that important post, a strong detachment of infantry, having under its escort the guns taken at Mehudpoor, and the hospital establishment and convalescent left there by Sir Thomas Hislop, and now on their way to the Dukhun. The presence of these troops afforded the means of forming a force of sufficient strength to advance upon Bajee Rao from the north-east, and either attack him on that side, or at least effectually shut up the Ghâts of the Sâtpoora range. Brigadier-General Malcolm also prepared to advance in person, with what troops he could collect, from the neighbourhood of Indore to the north-west, while Brigadier-General Doveton was known to be approaching from the southward. Hence it seemed more than probable, that the enemy would be again hemmed in, and give the opportunity of another affair as important as that of Soonee. Eastward of Hindia, the defence of the Nerbudda was confided to Brigadier-General Watson, who, after occupying Chouragurh, and affording Lieutenant-Colonel M'Morine a reinforcement to assist in the pursuit of Appa Saheb, had retired to Sâgur with the greater part of his force, in conformity with orders received direct from the Marquess of Hastings for his occupation of that post. In anticipation of the possibility of Bajee Rao's success in getting to the northward, before the above precaution should be in a sufficient state of forwardness to cut him off entirely from this line of retreat, the Marquess of Hastings, on the first alarm, had instructed Sir David Ochterlony to be in readiness to throw his force between the enemy and Gwalior, and in that case to take upon himself the personal and supreme direction of all the operations. Such were the accumulated means, with which, if necessary, it was determined to crush the expiring efforts of the fugitive Pêshwa. That Prince, however, distracted at the operations that he saw about to close upon him on every side, remained irresolutely hovering about Aseergurh, where he was visited by Sindheea's Killadar, Juswunt Rao Lar, who, during the whole of his stay in the neighbourhood, participated in all his counsels, and rendered every assistance in his power. Indeed, the reliance upon this resource and upon the shelter of the fortress in case of need, appears to have been a principal motive of his delay at Dhôlcôt in that vicinity.

While Bajee Rao was thus wasting his time in indecision, and allowing the British forces to draw a net completely round him, Anund Rao Juswunt, the agent who had been sent to Sir John Malcolm, reached the camp of that officer at Mow, a few miles from Indore, late in the night of the 16th of May. The letter he brought from his master contained an appeal to the generosity of the British Government, and a spice of adulation to the general himself, whom, in a strain of Asiatic compliment, he protested he had been looking out for on every side, as one of his oldest and best friends *, in order to solicit him to become

* In the subsequent conference between the General and Bajee Rao, the latter urgently appealed to the long friendship between them; stating that, of his three oldest and best friends, Colonel Close was dead and General Wellesley in a distant land, and the only one now left him was Sir John himself. That officer's great experience of Indian politics and long intercourse with the native princes had indeed

the instrument of peace and reconciliation with the British. Particular allusion was made to the liberality, with which conquests heretofore made from Holkar and Sindheea had been restored without equivalent or reason; with an evident insinuation, that a similar degree of generosity in his own instance was expected or hoped to result from his choice of this channel of reconciliation.

Sir John Malcolm resolved at once to convert this communication, which really differed little in substance from what Mr. Elphinstone had been in the habit of receiving from the outset of the campaign, into a negotiation for surrender upon terms. The vakeel accordingly, finding the General in this mind, pressed him earnestly to advance to a personal conference with his master, for the purpose of discussing the terms and receiving his submission. This, however, was refused; but Sir John's first and second political assistants, Lieutenants Low and M'Dowall, were despatched along with Anund Rao, bearing the General's reply; and Lieutenant Low was instructed, if possible, to open a negotiation on the following basis: first, Bajee Rao to renounce all sovereignty in the Dukhun for himself and family for ever; secondly, not to return thither on any terms; thirdly, the surrender of Trimbukjee and all persons concerned in the hanging of the two Vaughans at Tulligâm on the first breaking out of the war. In the event of the Pêshwa's agreeing to these preliminaries, Lieutenant Low was to insist upon his immediately separating himself from Ram-Deen and other proscribed rebels or Pindarees that might be with his army, and advancing to meet the Brigadier-General, who, in such case, engaged to be the medium of an adjustment with the British Government, on

recommended him to their particular confidence, and made them look up to him for protection in their time of need. Of this feeling the best proof is to be found in the number of chiefs that surrendered to him, besides the Pêshwa: amongst others, Kureem, Rajun, Kander-Buksh, &c.

the basis of personal security to the prince himself, and a liberal maintenance at such holy city, as he might select for his future residence. Protection from the attack of Brigadier-General Doveton, or any of the other divisions that threatened him, was not to be granted, except on compliance with the requisition to advance in the direction prescribed.

Sir John Malcolm, had in due course, been furnished with a copy of the Governor-General's instructions to Mr. Elphinstone, which had put him in possession of the outline of his Lordship's intentions with regard to the personal treatment of Bajee Rao, in case of his being reduced to surrender himself unconditionally; and the terms, which Lieutenant Low was directed to offer, were framed upon those instructions. Conceiving himself to be acting according to their spirit, the General did not think it necessary to wait the result of a reference for special orders in the present instance: nor indeed would the distance from his Lordship's quarters at Gôrukpoor have allowed of such a reference. The Marquess of Hastings, however, immediately on hearing of the step taken by Sir John Malcolm, could not avoid expressing his apprehension, that the deputation of an officer for the avowed purpose of negotiation would have the effect of cramping the military operations of the several divisions, which it was particularly desirable to leave as free as possible to the last. It was evident that Bajee Rao could have but one motive of desire to submit, viz. the desperate posture of his affairs. Another rencontre with any of our divisions must necessarily complete his ruin; consequently, any thing that embarrassed the military movements, besides impeding the grand object of annihilating the military power of the Mahratta sovereign, promised to give him a further advantage in the negotiation also, as it must create an impression, that the basis of treaty was not that of an individual resorting to us for personal safety upon any terms that he could get, but a bargain, founded upon views of a mutuality of interest; in other words, a compromise, in which he was to receive value for his forbearance to exert his remaining means of mischief and annoyance. His Lordship particularly deprecated this construction being put upon the measure by other powers: nor did he feel less anxiety, lest the government should be committed in respect to the place of the captive's future residence, wishing to have this left to his own selection, as well as the fixation of the amount of the stipend for the chief's permanent establishment, which he declared his intention of limiting to two lack rupees per annum. Instructions to this effect were issued from Gôrukpoor, whither the Governor-General had retired on the breaking up of the centre division of the grand army. As had been apprehended, the letter containing them did not reach Sir John Malcolm until every thing was concluded; but the event of Lieutenant Low's deputation proved the correctness of his Lordship's anticipation of its effect upon the military operations; while the deviation from his wishes, in respect to the other points, showed that his anxiety was not without sufficient grounds.

The Lieutenant proceeded on the 18th of May, in company with Anund Rao Juswunt, and reached Mundlisôr on the next day. He was here overtaken by fresh orders from the Brigadier-General (who had on the night of the 18th received advice of the escape of Appa Saheb), in obedience to which the Lieutenant stopped short himself, and sent forwards a Soobadar of the Madras cavalry, by name Seyed Husein Ulee, whom Sir John Malcolm had selected for his native aid-de-camp, and another native, together with the vakeels. The latter were made acquainted with the conditions on which their master was expected to advance and meet Sir John Malcolm; and the Lieutenant himself followed by easy stages, expecting that, by the time he arrived in the neighbourhood, the mind of the prince would be prepared by their representations for submission. Bajee Rao had all this while remained at Dhôlkôt, five miles north of Aseergurh, where every day his alarm increased at the approach of Brigadier-General Doveton from the south. On the 25th of May, this officer arrived at Boorhanpoor, and was on the point of equipping a light force for the immediate attack of the enemy, when he received a letter from Lieutenant Low, dated the 23d of May, giving him the first intimation of the mission and of its result being still in suspense. Although the letter contained no positive request to suspend his further operations, yet Brigadier-General Doveton could not but see the desire of the negotiator, that time should be allowed to Bajee Rao: indeed it was mentioned, that Colonel Smith intended to halt at Bhekungâon to the north-west, until apprized of the result. The Brigadier-General accordingly deemed it right to remain at Boorhanpoor for the same purpose. In the mean time, Bajee Rao, though still undecided as to the acceptance of the conditions, was most earnest in the expression of his anxiety for the arrest of Brigadier-General Doveton's advance. This Seyed Husein Ulee reported to Lieutenant Low, who, upon his arrival at Bhekungâon on the 25th, inclosed to the Soobadar an absolute requisition on the Brigadier-General to delay his advance conditionally, in case Bajee Rao should have made a movement, however short, in the direction indicated. The Soobadar was not himself in Bajee Rao's camp when he received this despatch, but forwarded the letter with two troopers, to whom he gave similar directions. The Brigadier-General having previously upon his own judgment resolved to wait the result, the receipt of any absolute requisition became a matter of no importance; but it might have been otherwise.

Up to the 30th of May, Bajee Rao continued in his position at Dhôlkôt, still equally irresolute. In the interim, however, Sir John Malcolm had brought down the force he had collected at Indore as far as Bhekungâon, where he found Lieutenant Low, together with the Pêshwa's vakeels, who had come the day before to press him to proceed to their master's camp, which he accordingly did by the order of the Brigadier-General. The troops from Hindia also had advanced to Peeplouda, while Brigadier-General Doveton still occupied Boorhanpoor. Being now, therefore, completely surrounded, Bajee Rao, on the 31st of May, sent Balooba, dewan of the Vinshore Kur, to Sir John Malcolm, and agreed to a personal conference on the following day, at Kiree, a village on the plain about half a mile from the Ghât of that name in the Sâtpoora range. The meeting took place according to this appointment, at 5 p. m. of the 1st of June, Bajee Rao having come to Kiree for the purpose with all his family, and an escort of about 2500 horse and foot. In the conference that ensued, Sir John Malcolm recapitulated the terms that had before been communicated, and pressed the immediate surrender of Trimbukjee: but this was asserted to be impossible, as that chief had a separate camp of his own, and was in too great strength. Sir John then declared his intention to attack him forthwith, whereupon Bajee Rao replied he was welcome for his part, using the expression, "*Mobarùk*," "Success attend you." He subsequently, however, solicited time to recal some of his own people from Trimbukjee's camp, a favour that was perhaps incautiously granted, and thus most probably the opportunity was taken of warning Trimbukjee of his danger: for the attempt, when subsequently made, proved abortive. The conference lasted till 10 p. m. when the Pêshwa re-ascended the Ghât, where he had some guns placed to protect his retreat; all the neighbouring passes were lined with his Arab infantry. Sir John Malcolm retired to his tent, and the same night prepared a written note of the conditions, and forwarded it the next morning to Bajee Rao. They differed little from those before tendered by Lieutenant

Low, except in the omission of the article for the surrender of Trimbukjee. It was insisted, however, that his Highness should proceed to Hindoostan without the delay of a day, and come to the British camp for the purpose within 24 hours. At the same time, Sir John Malcolm took upon himself to guarantee, that the annual allowance to be assigned for the future maintenance of his Highness should not fall short of eight lack rupees per annum; and the written paper further declared, that if his Highness, by prompt and full performance of the terms, should evince his entire confidence in the British Government, his requests in favour of jageerdars and adherents, who had been ruined by their fidelity to his cause, should meet with liberal consideration; also, that his representations in favour of Brahmins and religious establishments founded or supported by his family, should be treated with attention. This article was subsequently explained, in respect to the jageerdars, to mean, that they should be received upon the same terms as had been accorded by Mr. Elphinstone to those who had tendered their submission after the rout of Soonee; viz. to retain any lands which belonged to their families in absolute property; but lose those they held by *surunjamee*, tenure of military service. In order to enforce compliance, or, in case of refusal, to proceed to attack the enemy's position, Brigadier-General Doveton was requested by letter to interpose, if possible, between his camp and Aseergurh, whither the Pêshwa had before conveyed a great part of his remaining valuables. Lieutenant-Colonel Russell was also ordered to advance from his position at Bhoorgâon, and combine with that officer in an attack upon Trimbukjee.

At length, upon these conditions, after a fruitless attempt at further procrastination*, Bajee Rao joined the camp of Sir

* "It would fill a volume to detail the particulars of all the intrigues which "occurred. I have never witnessed a scene in which every shade of the Indian

John Malcolm, on the 3d of June, at 11 a. m. The engagement, although not exactly according with his Lordship's views, was nevertheless confirmed and ratified by the Marquess of Hastings; and Bithoor, a place of Hindoo pilgrimage, distant a few miles only from the large cantonment of Cawnpoor, was subsequently fixed upon for the residence of the deposed and exiled prince.

The principal objection to this arrangement was, the extent of the personal allowance promised to his Highness, amounting to no less than 100,000*l.* a year for life. This was far beyond the probable amount of his personal expenditure in retirement, and it was feared might leave a surplus applicable to purposes of intrigue and mischief. Sir John Malcolm had been guided in the fixation of the stipend, by a recollection of the amount enjoyed by Umrit Rao, under the arrangement made with that chief, by the now Duke of Wellington. He thought there would be some insult, both to the prince and the feelings of the Mahratta nation, in offering less to one, who had so long sat upon the guddee as his birthright, than was enjoyed, as the price of abdication, by a claimant by mere adoption. The cases, however, seemed to admit of little analogy; for Umrit Rao was a chief of powerful influence and numerous adherents, brought

" character was more strongly displayed. It is honourable to Balouba, the " Vinshorekur jageerdar, to the Purunder chief, and the manager of the in- " terests of the Gokla family, who committed their cause to him, that, though " they professed themselves hopeless of success, and, convinced by my arguments, " that their master had no choice but submission, they took care to make me " understand, when I informed them that their only claim to consideration rested " on the success of their influence in promoting this measure, that, though they " would use every means of persuasion and remonstrance to effect this end, harsh- " ness or coercion they would never resort to. The vakeel of the Vinshorekur " said, that his master's family had served that of the Pêshwa for five generations, " and had always spoken boldly to them; but added, that now that fate, *Bukht*, " was on him, he must be silent: even unmerited reproaches had been and must " remain unanswered."—*Malcolm's Despatches.*

over in critical times, and at the outset of a war of doubtful issue. And, even in his case, the extent of the stipend had enabled the chief to entertain a large retinue, and create an influence of most pernicious tendency, necessary as the purchase may have been to the success of the operations of that period. Experience, therefore, was against entrusting similar means to the discretion of chiefs so circumstanced: and the ex-Péshwa's proneness to intrigue was too notorious to admit of the hope, that, if possessed of the means, he would forbear to employ them.

Independently, however, of all considerations of tenderness towards the feelings of this fallen head of the Mahrattas, and of the policy of conciliating the good-will of his late subjects, by indulgent and liberal treatment of their deposed monarch, considerations most apt to work upon the generous spirit of a British soldier, there were other reasons of no little weight, which had helped to guide the conduct of Sir John Malcolm in this very delicate business. The remnant of the Mahratta army arrived in the neighbourhood of Aseergurh, in a most exhausted condition; but the supplies received from that fortress, and the halt of several days in the vicinity, had recruited both men and cattle, and put them in a condition to renew their flight with their usual rapidity, which might again have baffled the pursuit of regular troops. Besides, the Killadar of Aseergurh had already afforded shelter to the remaining baggage and valuables of Bajee Rao; and his conduct, in furnishing him with guns and other stores, had shown his readiness to receive his fugitive prince within the cover of his walls, in case of extremity. The near approach of the rainy season, and the absence of the small battery train attached to Brigadier-General Doveton's division, which had been recently sent to Lieutenant-Colonel M'Dowal, and was now employed before Malugâon, made it impossible to undertake the siege this season; and even to invest it so closely as to prevent his personal entrance or exit, was, in the opinion of the most experienced officers, impracticable during the rains. The recent escape of Appa Saheb, who has not yet been retaken, had shown the difficulty of tracing a fugitive, however illustrious or important, in this wild and rugged tract, and amongst a friendly population. But the principal motives of desire for the immediate possession of the person of the Pêshwa were, the saving of the great additional expense that must have been incurred by the protraction even of desultory warfare, and the speedy restoration of general tranquillity, by removing the ostensible cause and the leader of tumult and disorder. The whole country was still infested by the broken remnants of the Pindaree durras, and the dispersed Arab and other mercenaries, whom the late changes had turned loose upon the world. Already had they begun to flock from all parts towards the standard of the prince, who still possessed the hereditary respect and affections of the Mahratta nation; and it was impossible to say how far the uncertain issue of protracted hostility might work upon the unsettled minds of the different chiefs, or to calculate the full effect of any casual check or disaster. In justice to one of the most distinguished officers that our Indian service can boast of, these reasons and motives should be duly weighed; and it is but fair to add, that nothing has yet occurred to impeach or call into question the policy of the arrangement effected by his agency.

Whatever opinion may be entertained of the terms granted, or the manner of accomplishing the end, no one ever for a moment doubted the advantages resulting from the actual possession of the ex-Pêshwa's person. The effect produced on the minds of the native population, by his progress in the character of an exile through Malwa, so lately the territory of his nominal dependents and feudatories, is hardly to be described. It appeared to make the same impression upon high and low, and was considered by all as the consummation of the national downfall, and the final dissolution of the Mahratta Confederacy, beyond hope of renovation. Nor was the generosity of the victors the least imposing part of the scene. The strong only can afford to be merciful and generous; and what greater proof could be offered of the power and magnanimity of the British nation, than the quiet march of the vanquished prince to the place of his honourable retreat, escorted by his still remaining adherents, and treated with every attention due to fallen greatness?

Bajee Rao joined the British camp with a force of from 4 to 5000 horse, and about 3000 infantry, of whom 1200 were Arabs, whose numbers were afterwards increased to near 2000, by the juncture of detached parties left to guard the passes in the hills. The Vinshorekur and the widow of Gokla resolved to accompany their late master to Hindoostan. The remainder of his vassals either deserted him immediately upon his submission, or fell off one by one in the course of his march to the Nerbudda, whither he had proceeded in company with General Malcolm's division, and escorted by a large body of Mahrattas and Arabs, whom he seemed for some time unwilling to dismiss, as if still fondly clinging to the shadow of departed power. The General, though not altogether satisfied with the continued presence of this lawless soldiery, was loath to disturb by harsh interference the last moments of intercourse between a fallen Prince and his yet faithful adherents; and experience led him to expect, that their numbers would gradually diminish on the march. It was not long before the mutinous spirit of these disorderly retainers, and their tumultuous demands for their arrears of pay, compelled the ex-Pêshwa to resort to the protection and friendly mediation of the British commander, whose firmness and conciliatory justice soon relieved him from danger, and dismissed them equally grateful for his clemency and content with his award. From the banks of the Nerbudda, the captive proceeded with a train reduced to little more than 600 horse and 200 infantry, every day more reconciled to his condition, and more inclined to regard his protector with deference and confidence.

Ram-Deen, who had since the peace of Mundisôr deserted the standard of the Holkar, under which he had borne a principal command, and joined the Pêshwa with the wreck of his army, submitted at the same time, upon a promise of pardon for his rebellion. Trimbukjee also was very solicitous to obtain terms; but found the Brigadier-General inflexible in demanding his surrender as a prisoner, with a bare stipulation that his life should be spared, and some prospect of ultimate pardon at some future period, when tranquillity should have been completely restored. On these terms he refused to submit. Brigadier-General Doveton had on the 3d of June sent out a detachment to attack his camp; but, as it had marched by a route leading under the walls of Aseergurh, and the Killadar, though written to, refused a free passage, and opened his fire on the troops as they approached, the attack by that route was abandoned; and, before arrangements could be made to assail him by another road, he had disappeared with his followers.

Thus was the war in this quarter brought to a happy termination; for neither Trimbukjee nor any other of the sirdars attempted again to rally the dispersed forces of Bajee Rao, or longer to keep the field. A few Arabs, however, went off to the eastward in quest of Appa Saheb, and in their way* pos-

* On the 18th of July, Captain Sparkes, then at Rytoor, heard of some Arabs having entered his district; when, immediately collecting his detachments, he set off in quest of them. His force consisted of but 107 fighting men of the 2d-10th Bengal native infantry. On the 20th, near Mooltaya, he fell in with about 1500 Arabs and a body of horse, who surrounded him on all sides as soon as the action

sessed themselves of Mooltaya, and overpowered a detachment of two companies gallantly led against them by Captain Sparkes, the officer in civil charge of the district. The residue of the Mahratta host returned quietly to their homes; among the rest Trimbukjee, who for some time endeavoured to secrete himself in the villages lately subject to his influence; but Mr. Elphinstone succeeded in effecting his seizure in the course of the following month, when he was remanded to Tannah, the place of his former confinement, and has since been ordered round to Bengal, where it is proposed to confine him in the fort of Chunar. To inflict capital punishment on him was deemed an act of unjust rigour, as the escape was no aggravation * of the original offence, for which he had only been sentenced to imprisonment for life. Besides, the subsequent conduct of his then master had afforded pretty strong evidence of his participation in the Sastree's murder.

Throughout the whole of the late dominions of Bajee Rao, there was henceforward not one of his officers, who ventured to keep the field in opposition to the British authority. The last vestige of open hostility had been destroyed in the affair of

commenced. Nevertheless, he made good for several hours a position he took up in haste, repelling three different charges of the enemy. At last, having driven them back a fourth time, he was following to secure a better position about fifty yards off, when he was shot dead. The Soobadar who succeeded to the command, for there was no other European officer present, met the same fate immediately after; when the whole detachment was cut to pieces, with the exception of nine men only, who were behind in charge of the baggage. A strong body of troops was immediately sent down from Hôshungabad by Lieutenant-Colonel Adams, the advanced guard of which, under Lieutenant Ker of the 7th cavalry, a very promising officer, who has since fallen a victim to the climate, enticed the Arabs from the fortified town by a judicious feint, and then turning upon them, made them suffer severely. They were soon afterwards driven out of the district, and confined to the inaccessible parts of the Mohadeo hills.

* The laws of England treat it as such; but they are at variance in this particular with justice and common sense.

Solapoor. Neither was there, by the close of May, a single fortified place that still held out, excepting a few strong holds in Kandêsh, obstinately defended by the Arab garrisons. Rygurh, where Bajee Rao had placed his wife for safety, surrendered to Lieutenant-Colonel Prother in the course of that month. The wife was treated with every possible consideration, and allowed one of the palaces of the deposed Prince for her residence, until an opportunity offered of sending her to rejoin her husband at his place of exile.

The rapidity and apparent ease, with which the British rule was established over a country of so much natural strength and difficulty, as that composing the late dominion of the Pêshwas, must excite astonishment in European readers; more especially when the inimical spirit, testified by all ranks at the opening of the war, is taken into the account. Some of the causes, which had produced this important revolution in the minds of the natives of India, have already been hinted at in the relation of the different events as they occurred, and the mode in which they were turned to advantage. It may be useful, however, to give in this place a general summary of the course of policy pursued by Mr. Elphinstone throughout the transactions we have now brought to a close, in order that the merit of his services may be more justly estimated.

At the time when Bajee Rao's concealed enmity broke forth into an open rupture, there was scarcely an individual from one end of his dominions to the other, that did not confidently reckon upon our being driven entirely out of the country. Even our warmest well-wishers apprehended the probability of this result: consequently, either from hope or from fear, every one assumed the appearance of hostility. The two affairs of Poona, though they had helped to confirm the confidence of our own troops, were not sufficiently decisive to destroy the impression so universally entertained of our relative inferiority.

The two succeeding months passed without yielding any more decisive occurrence; and, though Bajee Rao was all the while little better than a fugitive, still, as that character accorded well enough with the policy and military habits of the Mahrattas, and as the enemy had suffered no material loss, our superiority in the field was scarcely yet admitted.

While this feeling was still prevalent, Mr. Elphinstone received instructions to occupy the whole of Bajee Rao's dominions on behalf of the British authorities, and found himself nominated sole commissioner for the execution of this bold measure. Brigadier-General Munro, who had already begun to operate against the southern territories of the Pêshwa, was anxious to expedite the avowal of the intentions of the British Government, thinking the assurance of never again experiencing the tyranny of Mahratta misrule would be of the best consequence. And doubtless, in that part of the country adjoining to our own frontier, where the people were in the habit of comparing their relative condition under the two governments, and were familiarised to the estimate of their relative strength, the step would have been attended with great advantage. Mr. Elphinstone, however, feared that our power was not yet sufficiently known and respected in the other and more remote quarters of Bajee Rao's dominions; and that, before the population should have good cause to anticipate our ultimate success in the war, the national spirit would probably but take fire at the arrogant presumption of an open declaration of the design to assume the whole sovereignty to ourselves.

Impressed with this conviction, he determined to observe the utmost secrecy, until time and the march of events should have worked a revolution in the prevailing sentiment towards us. The first indication of our real views was exhibited on the fall of Suttara, when Mr. Elphinstone issued the manifesto noticed in the progress of the narrative; but the commissioner, in order more accurately to mark the effect that should be produced by this avowal of our intentions upon the minds of the Mahratta population, at first circulated his *exposé* with great caution, and affected to make the communication a matter of individual confidence. Even after the capture of that fortress, doubt as to the result of the war was still the prevalent feeling, and the explanation of our views was consequently listened to with comparative indifference. The Mahratta Prince was still much too powerful for any class to divest itself of apprehension of the consequences of declaring against him, the more especially as he had already made several severe examples.

His defeat at Ashtee, accompanied as that disaster was by the death of Gokla, his only military commander of repute, and followed by the deliverance of the Suttara family, produced at once the desired change in the popular mind. The Pêshwa's approximate downfal was now universally predicted, and all not actively embarked with him looked upon his power as already extinct. The desire of his favour and the fear of his resentment were thenceforward alike discarded; and what was to follow on the establishment of our ascendancy, became the natural object of public curiosity. The manifesto was now sought for and read with avidity: copies were made and circulated by the natives of every class; and the declarations and assurances it contained became the general topic of conversation. This was exactly the disposition that the commissioner had desired to see excited; and he resolved to allow it full swing, in the confidence, that the terms of his *exposé* were calculated to satisfy all ranks of life, and that his own reputation, and that of the government he served, would prevent the least doubt being entertained of its sincerity. The immunities held out gave contentment to every one, and the resolution to submit was cheerfully and promptly embraced. The rapidity of our subsequent successes was at once the cause and the effect of the rapid diffusion of this sense of security, and of the conduct naturally resulting from it.

Borne along by the impulse thus excited, the British influence and authority spread over the land with magical celerity. Applications to be received within the pale of our dominion came pouring in faster than civil officers could be provided for the administration of the districts that sued for our sway, and long before the means of military protection could be furnished from our inadequate regular establishments. The most impregnable holds opened their gates as we have already seen, and not unfrequently before they were summoned: nor could the casual possessors urge any claim to consideration for the early surrender, since the submission was so general. It was the commissioner's peculiar merit to have taken advantage of the precise moment, when the tide of popular feeling, which flowed strong against him at the opening of the campaign, had expended its force, and to have made such use of the reflux, as to have arrived at the point of his hopes before it had again reached the flood. It will be necessary to trace more minutely the effect of the commissioner's measures on the several classes of Mahratta society, all of which he ultimately succeeded in reconciling to the new form of government.

In India, the terms rent and revenue are so nearly synonimous, that the distinction of payers and receivers of revenue affords a pretty complete classification of the mass of population. The former class throughout the Pêshwa's dominions, though Hindoos by race and in religious tenets, were very partially of the Mahratta nation; and having experienced that most odious form of fiscal extortion, the farming system under the administration of Brahmins* and Mahrattas, needed only the assurance

* It has frequently been remarked, that a Hindoo is always a more avaricious and pitiless extortioner than a Moosulman. Great subtleness, unwearied patience, and a never satiated desire of accumulation, distinguish the Hindoo all over India;

of future protection to throw off at once the yoke under which they groaned. To change it for any that promised to be lighter, was to them a most desirable occurrence. Mr. Elphinstone's proclamation gave them the guarantee of a direct resort on all occasions to British officers, the promise of remissions of tribute on account of military ravage, of protection and equal justice for the future, and, what was a greater boon than all, a guarantee that they should never again be delivered over to Mahratta pillage or extortion. The effect of these assurances was perceptible in the immediate change of demeanor in the cultivating class, who had no sooner lost all apprehension from the vengeance of Bajee Rao than they withheld the revenue from his delegates, expelled his officers, and voluntarily brought the rents and produce of their villages and towns into the British treasuries.

To give confidence and contentment to the payers of revenue, was perhaps the easiest part of the commissioner's duties. It was a far more difficult task, to procure a recognition of the new order of things from those, who enjoyed the benefits of the existing system—men of large hopes and expectations, whose wealth, influence, and education, placed superior means of obstruction at their disposal. The receivers of revenue or rent were of two classes; the religious, which, under the Brahminical government of the Peshwas, had engrossed vast possessions, considerably increased of late by the superstitious personal character of the Prince; and the military and official, at the head of which stood the jageerdars and ancient Mahratta families.

To conciliate the religious orders was a very material object. Accordingly, the commissioner's manifesto expressly set forth the murder of Gungadhur Sastree, a Brahmin of the highest

while there is a love of ease and a heedlessness of the future, which give a libera cast to the character of the Moosulman. The latter also is fond of popularity, and frequently regards name beyond wealth.

caste, as the original cause of the breach that had taken place between the British Government and the Mahratta sovereign; and held out a distinct assurance, that all existing establishments for religious purposes should be maintained, and all endowments, grants, or assignments made before the war, be held inviolate. To increase the effect of these public professions, Mr. Elphinstone took the earliest opportunity, after the battle of Ashtee, to repair in person to Wye, a place of high repute for Hindoo sanctity, whither the principal Brahmins and several moderate men, who desired to stand aloof from the contest, were known to have retired. There he convoked a general assembly, and repeated verbally before them the assurances contained in his *exposé*, so as to leave all minds satisfied of the sincerity of the intentions of the British Government towards them, and content with the concessions to the interest of the religious orders. A similar meeting was afterwards convened for the same purpose at Poona; and both there and at Wye presents were distributed with a liberality, which was intended as some sort of compensation to the class for the loss of that indiscriminate bounty, with which the Pêshwas were wont to lavish gifts and largesses at festivals and on other occasions of rejoicing. The present expense of this measure was doubtless considerable; but it produced a favourable disposition, or at least served to stifle the jealousy of a powerful body, whose neutrality more than repaid the sacrifice.

The military and official class, which can hardly be considered separately in a Mahratta community, in the shape of jageers and military tenures, had appropriated upwards of one half of the ordinary revenue of the whole territory. It yet remained to reconcile this important body to the new order of things.

The re-establishment of the Suttara Raja, in the very seat of the ancient power and splendour of his race, was well adapted to reconcile the older Mahratta families to the annihilation of the more recent title and authority of Pêshwa. It had the further effect of rendering the cause of Bajee Rao rather a personal than a national one; more especially as the commissioner's manifesto contained the promise to all, who might submit within two months of its date*, of enjoying in perpetuity, under British guarantee, whatever lands they might at the time be possessed of. Hence the great families saw, that they had themselves nothing at stake, so they did but stand aloof or withdraw from the scene of action, while Bajee Rao on one hand and the British on the other were contending for the mastery. Besides, there were amongst the jageerdars many, who were indebted to the very guarantee now proffered for what they actually held, and none but what were well able to appreciate the value of the offer, and to set the superior security of property it afforded in comparison with the capricious duration of a despot's favor. To these motives are to be referred the frequent submissions of the great families, that we have had occasion to record as having been tendered immediately after the battle of Ashtee. The fear of forfeiting their lands to the victors then began to exceed their apprehension of Bajee Rao's vengeance, and quickened the determination of the generality. But the indigent of the military class were not to be won over by the same motives; for they had nothing to lose. Many of the old families too, from pride or from principle, resolved still to share the fortunes of their prince. Wherefore, until the spirit of military adventure should have been subdued by a more lively fear than had yet been created, nothing could be hoped, while every thing was to be apprehended from the jealousy, with which it was natural the new order of things should be regarded by those, who suffered in the change. This object was fortunately accomplished to the utmost extent that could be desired, by the result of the two affairs of Soonee and Solapoor. The fugitives from both returned

* 12th of February. The term expired five days before the rout of Soonee.

humbled to their homes, and showed in all their acts, that their minds were prepared for ever to abandon their calling with all its ambitious hopes and vicissitudes, or to be content with the moderate provision allotted to those who accepted employment in our Sebundee establishment. As an act of policy, the levies of men for this force were carried to a considerable extent, in order to furnish the means of livelihood to many that must else have been left wholly destitute. Nor, indeed, could their services have been well dispensed with; for the regular army was unequal even to furnish garrisons for the forts reduced, much less was it in a condition to provide detachments for the duties of internal administration. By denouncing and rigorously enforcing the penalty of instant military execution to all persons guilty of plundering on their return, and at the same time declaring every one's home to be a secure retreat to such as sought it with peaceable intentions, the late dominions of the Pêshwa were, immediately on their subjugation, preserved in as perfect tranquillity, as in a season of profound peace. No small credit is due for the complete attainment of this object, considering the vast influx of military rabble, that followed the rout of the Mahratta army at Soonee, and the distressed circumstances in which all returned from the field. Previous orders had been issued to note the names of all the runagates, but to leave them unmolested, unless guilty of excess; and proclamation had been made to the same effect. Thus, for their own security, it became a matter of scrupulous caution with the fugitives, to avoid rendering themselves obnoxious to the penalty. It deserves to be recorded, that a comparison of the excesses, which followed the dissolution of the Pêshwa's tumultuary host, with those incident to a large and sudden reduction of the troops of an European state, on the conclusion of a peace or other similar occasion, would even have exhibited a result in favour of the Indian executive.

Such were the measures adopted for the reclamation of the military classes; and their minds had been so impressed with awe, as well by the forecast of arrangement with which they had found themselves encountered at every step, as by the astonishing successes obtained from them by mere handfuls of disciplined troops, that, even before the knowledge of Bajee Rao's personal submission, the most sanguine and presumptuous had become sensible of the impotence of their utmost efforts, and were well prepared to take the law from our dictation.

Of the mercantile class, as forming a distinct interest and a constituent part of the population of Bajee Rao's dominions, we have taken no account, because in fact the *buneeas* of India, though many of them absolutely rolling in wealth, are rather a despised caste, little remarkable for public spirit on any occasion, occupied in the exclusive pursuit of sordid and selfish gain, possessed of no influence beyond the walls of the populous towns, and even there generally subservient to the government of the passing hour. The security of property and of public credit, universally attendant on the introduction of the British authority, probably made them rather wish for our establishment, and secured their limited good offices in our favour: but Bajee Rao also had a strong party amongst them; as indeed might any one else have had, who possessed but the means of purchasing their services.

These details of Mr. Elphinstone's general plan for the settlement of the conquered dominions of the Pêshwa, have a very partial application to the province of Kandêsh. The greater part of this district had been usurped by Arab colonists, who could hardly be expected to be influenced by the motives of submission, that had operated so extensively upon the Mahratta inhabitants. Fortunately, the Arabs had proved tyrants in the exercise of their usurped authority, and the body of the people were consequently desirous of shaking them off; at the same time, they were not sufficiently numerous to hope successfully to cope single handed with the British power. The condition of submission offered to them by our policy was, however, nothing short of retransportation to their native wilds of Arabia; and, as this involved the sacrifice at once of all their past acquisitions, and of all their future prospects, the intrusive race was driven to desperation, and resolved to defend their possession to the last. The Arabs of Kandêsh were undoubtedly no better than lawless buccaneers, equally incapable of regular military discipline, or of systematic political subordination; their expulsion was, therefore, a matter of absolute necessity. Accordingly, Captain Briggs, when he commenced the work of reducing the province, declared by proclamation, that such were the only terms, upon which the military of the Arab nation could be allowed to capitulate. He offered, however, that the British Government should be at the expense of their transport back to Arabia, and of discharging any actual arrears of pay.

With these views towards the intrusive Arabs, though guided in respect to the rest of the population by the principles so successfully acted upon by Mr. Elphinstone, the subjugation of Kandêsh was undertaken about the middle of May. As the divisions of Brigadier-Generals Doveton and Smith were then both employed in the pursuit of Bajee Rao, Lieutenant-Colonel M'Dowal's force of about 1100 firelocks, and the garrisons of Talnér and Sindwa, were the only regular troops immediately applicable to the service. The Arabs had concentrated their force at Malugâon, a fort of more than ordinary strength; and Captain Briggs, conceiving that he had established an understanding with part of the garrison through Raja Bahadhur, late jageerdar of the place, until its forcible occupation by the Arabs, who now held him in a kind of thraldom, resolved to make his first attack upon this point. On the 15th of May, Lieutenant-Colonel M'Dowal approached within five miles of Malugâon;

Raja Bahadhur now represented, that the Arabs in the fort were well disposed, and desired the aid of our troops to overawe those in the Petta, for which purpose he pointed out a position between the two for the detachment to occupy. Captain Briggs was inclined to place confidence in these professions of the Raja; but Lieutenant-Colonel M'Dowal suggested, that, before taking up so hazardous a position, the fidelity of the garrison in the fort should be put to the test, by demanding the admission of a few companies of our troops. The demand was made and rejected with scorn, as was also the offer of arrears, together with an advance for subsistence until such time as the Arabs might reach their native country. Indeed, it was soon found, that preparations had been made for a most obstinate defence, and that the siege would require the utmost exertion of courage as well as science to ensure success.

The engineers broke ground at night-fall on the 18th of May, Lieutenant-Colonel M'Dowal having disposed two-thirds of his force in working and covering parties, in the hope of completing two batteries in the course of the night. The arrangements for this purpose were, however, no sooner completed, than a vigorous sally was made from the fort. Malugâon is situated on the Moosee, just above its confluence with the Gyrna. The ground chosen by the engineers was on the opposite bank of the Moosee, and Lieutenant-Colonel M'Dowal gave orders to his covering parties, not to fire a shot until the enemy should have crossed the river. Immediately, therefore, that the firing began, Colonel M'Dowal, perceiving the determined nature of the attack, ordered down the whole of the troops that remained in camp to support the covering parties. Major Andrews, with a few men of the Madras European regiment, was the first to arrive on the scene of action. He found the Arabs within twenty paces of the working party, driving our advanced posts in before them. He was fortunate in being able to check their further progress, and ultimately to rally the covering parties and drive the enemy back with considerable loss: the Major, however, himself received a shot through the shoulder; while Lieutenant Davis, the senior engineer, who hastened forward on the alarm with a party from the trenches, was shot dead by the Arabs in their retreat. In him the service lost one of the most distinguished officers of the Madras establishment: though young in rank, he had seen more desperate service than had fallen to the lot of most colonels*. The besiegers had altogether twenty-one killed and wounded by this sally, chiefly of the European regiment. Notwithstanding this attempt to interrupt their operations, the work was completed according to the original intention; and, in the course of the night, two batteries were thrown up within 500 yards of the fort.

However, after this sample of the opposition he was to expect, Lieutenant-Colonel M'Dowal summoned to his aid every reinforcement he could procure, and thus collected from different quarters about 600 more infantry, and 500 irregular horse from Hindoostan, who had joined before the 23d of May. By the 28th of the month, the breach in the curtain of the fort appeared to be practicable, and the defence, as well of the rampart as of a *fausse-braye* at its foot, seemed for the most part to be destroyed. At the same time, Lieutenant-Colonel M'Dowal found his ammunition on the point of failing, which determined him to try the chance of an assault. The exact nature of the defences of the ditch and those of the covered way beyond it were not known; but all that was visible above the glacis had been levelled by our fire. Under these circumstances, a few

* He had accompanied Lieutenant-Colonel Gillespie into the fort of Vellore during the mutiny there, and was particularly distinguished for the cool intrepidity, with which from the top of the gateway he let fall a plummet, to ascertain the exact situation of the fastening, in order to be sure of the direction of his fire, when the galloper should arrive with which it was intended to blow open the gate.

remaining shells, that had been especially reserved to the last for this purpose, were thrown in to clear the breach, and the troops advanced to the assault at daybreak on the 29th of May. They were led by the surviving engineer officer, Ensign Nattes, followed by a party of sappers and miners, each carrying a bundle of wet grass to fill up the ditch if necessary. On arriving at the verge of the outwork beyond the ditch, it was found, that the rubbish of a low wall that had stood there had carefully been removed, and that beyond it the Arabs had dug a trench so deep, that it was impossible to descend from the glacis. Ensign Nattes was killed on its verge, while in the act of pronouncing the word "impracticable." The troops were, however, unwilling to desist; but Lieutenant-Colonel M'Dowal, finding that the breach had further been cut off from the works on either side, and that loopholed traverses had been erected to bear right upon it from within, while the trench above described made the attempt to pass forward hopeless, recalled the storming party, but not till Major Greenhill, the officer in command, and three other officers, had been wounded, and the engineer abovementioned killed. A simultaneous attack, made on the Petta by a party led by Lieutenant-Colonel Matthew Stewart, was completely successful, the place being carried sword in hand.

Upon this failure, Lieutenant-Colonel M'Dowal, having expended all his ammunition, and being determined nevertheless not to move from before the place till its fall, turned the siege into a blockade, and solicited further reinforcements, especially of artillery, from all quarters.

Brigadier-General Smith had by this time returned to Seroor, with the greater part of the light force he had carried eastward in pursuit of Bajee Rao. He immediately ordered off an additional train and a fresh supply of stores from the depôt at Ahmednugurh, accompanied by a strong reinforcement of Europeans, and a native battalion under the command of Major

Watson. The convoy arrived on the 9th of June, up to which date little had been done since the failure of the assault, except that three mines had been commenced from the Petta; but, as the fort was built on a rock foundation, that plan of attack was abandoned. By the 11th of June, a battery of five heavy mortars and four howitzers was completed, and opened its fire at daybreak. The besiegers had discovered the situation of the principal magazine; and, in the course of the day, upwards of 300 shells were thrown principally in that direction, by which means it was at length fired, and exploded with a tremendous crash, blowing about thirty feet of the curtain outwards into the ditch, and at the same destroying and wounding many of the garrison.

The Arabs now found their situation hopeless. Fearing that a longer resistance would bring on them a similar fate to what their comrades had met with at Talnér, they sent two jemadars on the morning of the 12th of June, to ask on what terms they would be admitted to surrender. Lieutenant-Colonel M'Dowal replied, at discretion, for other terms could not now be granted. The jemadars returned; and, on the morning of the 13th, Ubdool Kadur, the principal of the Arab chiefs, came out and declared, that the garrison were prepared to surrender at discretion, but urgently solicited a written assurance that their lives should be spared. These freebooters had no accurate conception of the meaning attached, by the usages of European warfare, to the term surrender at discretion; and the recent occurrence at Talnér had made them yet more suspicious and distrustful than before. Lieutenant-Colonel M'Dowal, therefore, out of consideration for this feeling, declared his readiness to give the written assurance of their lives being safe; and, in order further to encourage them, engaged that they should be well treated. By some mistake, however, the Mahratta Moonshee, who received orders to write a letter to this effect, used expressions capable of a much more extensive interpretation than was intended; promising to do "whatever was most advantageous for the garrison; that letters should be written regarding the pay; that the British Government should be at the expense of feeding and recovering the sick; and that the Arabs should not want any thing till they reached the places where they wished to go:" this latter expression being a mistake for "where it was intended to send them." Ubdool Kadur, having obtained this written paper, marched out on the morning of the 14th with the survivors of the garrison, 300 Arabs and about sixty Hindoostanees, when the whole laid down their arms on the glacis, and surrendered themselves prisoners of war. The Lieutenant-Colonel now wished to transfer his prisoners to the political agent, Captain Briggs, with a view to their transportation back to their native country; but that officer, conceiving the terms of the written letter not to warrant such treatment of the garrison, declined to take charge of them. Colonel M'Dowal declared the letter to have conveyed a mere assurance of clemency after compliance with his terms, which were, surrrender at discretion; that, consequently, it ought not and was never intended to limit the right of disposing of the prisoners according to the original conditions. The point was, however, referred to Mr. Elphinstone, who determined to allow the Arabs the utmost advantage they could be entitled to, by the most favourable construction of the terms of the letter; and, as there was a kind of a promise of good offices for the recovery of the pay due to the garrison, as well as an expression admitting of a construction, that they were to go where they wished, he ordered the whole arrears to be paid up to them from the Government treasury, and that they should immediately be released, and furnished with a safe conduct, and money to supply their wants, till they reached any place they might prefer to retire to.

The capture of Malugâon was the last operation of any consequence in the territories of Bajee Rao. The rest of Kandêsh submitted with little resistance; and the disposition of troops for the maintenance of order, and for the immediate punishment of any insurrectionary attempt or other interruption of the public tranquillity, became the only remaining requisite for the complete settlement of the country. The province of Kandêsh continued, however, for some time to be the scene of more disturbance, than was experienced in other parts of the Pêshwa's late dominions; which was partly owing to the clashing of the various Mahratta authorities anterior to the establishment of our influence, which had brought the province to the lowest possible pitch of disorganisation, and partly to Sindheea's continued retention of his former interest within it. But an arrangement is now in progress, by which it is hoped to remedy this latter inconvenience.

CHAPTER XVIII.

GENERAL RESULT.

Objects of this chapter—political result—Dukhun—Suttara Raja—Bhoosla—Nizam—Hindoostan—Holkar—Nuwab of Bhopâl—Ameer Khan—Ghufoor Khan—Reflections—Rajpoot princes—Kota—peculiarity in the treaty—Joudhpoor—Oodeepoor—Captain Tod's arrangements—convention of Thakoors—and constitution fixed—Boondee—Bhikaneer—Jesulmeer—Jypoor—indecision—treaty concluded—State of Jypoor—plan for its settlement—Raja's death—New military posts in Hindoostan—Sindheea—His present condition—external relations—internal government—how remedied—Auxiliary horse—Fate of sirdars—Baptiste—Bapoo Sindheea—Effect of their ruin—Probable issue—General reflections—Financial result—character of Indian revenue—Financial condition in 1814—in subsequent years—Result up to 1818—Home supplies—Value of territorial acquisitions—Comparative view—Home territorial charges explained—General reflections.

We have now arrived at the close of the narrative of the important military transactions, that occupied the season of 1817-18. But the account, which it has thus been attempted to give of what passed in that eventful season, would obviously be incomplete, were it to end here, without entering upon the more difficult, though necessary task, of presenting a summary of the political state, that has resulted to India from the widely extended operations above described; nor is it to be expected, that the public of England will rest satisfied, without a short statement of the financial advantages, that have accrued to the nation from the successful exertions of its Indian servants. To bring these two important subjects distinctly under view will be the business of this concluding chapter.

Before we notice the general outlines of the new political condition, in which India has been left by the events of the campaign, it will be necessary shortly to recapitulate, in the first place, the arrangements made with the greater powers, with whom the course of affairs successively embroiled us, and afterwards to take a similar notice of the minor transactions of a political nature, which have been purposely reserved to be brought together in one view, on the eve of the termination of our narrative.

The whole of the Pêshwa's late dominions are now incorporated with the former conquests of the British nation, excepting that part allotted to form a dependent sovereignty for the Raja of Suttara. The territory assigned for that purpose lies within the following limits: the great range of western Ghâts on the west, the Warner and Kishna rivers to the south, the Neera and Bheema to the north, and the frontier of the Nizam's dominions to the east. Of this territory, lands to the value of about 17 lack rupees per annum are still held in Jageer by the old feudatories of the Pêshwa, whose allegiance and obligations of service have been transferred to the British Government. The net resources of the Raja, therefore, cannot be regarded as beyond 15 or 16 lack, a revenue, which is far too little to confer much political influence or consideration. The chief claim of the Raja to be dealt with as a distinct political interest must arise from the recollection, still fondly cherished by the Mahrattas, of the former splendour of the family, and from the respect, which long custom may still attach to its offices and employments, notwithstanding the inadequate and economical scale of its establishment under the present system.

The personal character of the Raja, Noor Nerayun, is represented to be not deficient in natural acuteness, though, from youth and the defects of education, utterly devoid of all substantial knowledge, and as ignorant of business and of the world, as well versed in the outward forms and ceremonials of royalty. The country designed for his principality was in the first instance occupied directly by the British authorities, and Captain Grant was appointed by Mr. Elphinstone to superintend its administration, on the same principles as were observed throughout the territory permanently assumed to ourselves. This arrangement will continue until the country becomes more tranquil and settled; when the transfer will be made by degrees, according as the Raja's character and competence for such a trust may unfold themselves, and justify the reposal of such a confidence in him. In the mean time, the revenues are carefully brought to the account of the Suttara Government; nor do the British authorities interfere with the domestic concerns of the Raja, or his disposal of the surplus after defraying the charges of management, and of some indispensable establishments.

Such is the character of the state, that now occupies, in the political horizon, the space so lately filled by the mischievous court of Bajee Rao. The Mahratta families undoubtedly still look up in some degree to the Suttara Raja as their legitimate and hereditary superior; but their entire independence of the family has been secured, by transferring the obligations of allegiance exclusively to the British Government. The Rajas of Suttara will, therefore, henceforward find in them rivals rather than subjects, and must eventually and rapidly sink into the rank of equals, notwithstanding the broad line of nominal distinction, that must always separate this from the rest of the Mahratta families, in the scale of rank and importance. The motives of hope and fear, the only props by which a claim of real superiority could be sustained, are not amongst the instruments of power left at the Raja's disposal.

Next to the settlement of the affairs of the Poona state, the arrangement made with the Bhoosla is the object most worthy of consideration. The extensive sacrifices demanded of this state, upon Appa Saheb's restoration to the guddee, left to the Bhoosla little more than half of the resources he possessed before the war; and, in the internal administration of the residue, our right of direct control was made a matter of special stipulation. Upon the discovery of Appa Saheb's continued infidelity, his person was secured, and his deposition became an act of necessity. The Bhoosla state may be regarded as having been then placed at our feet a second time; nor was there any thing to prevent the Governor-General from moulding it to whatever shape might best accord with his views, to the extent even of occupying the whole for his own nation, had he been so minded. The state was, however, already sufficiently reduced for the completion of his plans, and the Marquess of Hastings, in confirming the deposition of our faithless ally, directed his successor to be seated on the guddee, without alteration of the terms, upon which Appa Saheb had been reinstated in the preceding January. His subsequent escape during his conveyance to Allahabad made no change in this determination; and, instead of delaying its execution, rendered it the more necessary to use despatch, in giving a settled form to the government, which it had been resolved to establish in his stead.

The Marquess of Hastings issued his final orders to this effect on the 18th of June; and they were carried completely into execution before the close of the month. The reader will have anticipated, that the grandson of Ragoojee Bhoosla was destined for the succession; and he was accordingly placed upon the guddee by the name of Bajee Rao Bhoosla. Buka Baee was constituted regent during the new Raja's minority, and Nerayun Pundit placed at the head of the ministry. This man was recommended by his fidelity, rather than his talents or fitness in other respects: indeed, it was soon found, that he had neither the influence nor the habits of business necessary to conduct the public affairs in the present circumstances of difficulty; and the impossibility of finding, amongst the more respectable of the old officers of the Nâgpoor Government, persons fitted by capacity and experience for the executive duties of the administration, led Mr. Jenkins to depart from the original plan; and, while the present embarrassments lasted, to employ British officers in the principal departments of the state. Over these he exercised himself a general control and supervision, though in the Raja's name. The arrangement was sanctioned provisionally by the Governor-General; but the Resident was directed to bear in mind the eventual revertence of the administration to the native authorities, and to frame all his acts with reference to that transfer. It will readily be imagined, that this anomalous form of government was not without its inconveniences; nor would it have been adopted, had the court of Nâgpoor yielded proper materials for the formation of a respectable native ministry, whose fidelity could be relied on. However, with the view of gratifying the family of the young Raja, and giving every practicable weight and respectability to the new government, Goojaba Dada, a relation of the Bhoosla, of whom mention has before been made, and who had all along been attached to the party of Buka Baee, was called down from Allahabad, whither he had retired to avoid the jealousy of Appa Saheb, and joined with Nerayun Pundit in the nominal administration. By this means, an efficient executive was established, which was too sensible of its dependence on the support of the British, not to co-operate heartily in the measures taken for preserving the tranquillity of the country, and in the efforts made to prevent the contagious example of insurrection, set by the Goânds of the Mohadeo hills, from spreading to other parts of the territory, equally wild and difficult of access. Nevertheless, the influence of Appa Saheb succeeded in raising the hill country to the east of Nâgpoor, and a partial rising was likewise effected in other quarters during the season of the rains. At Kumpta, and in the Lanjhee hills, an insurrection was organised by a man of the name of Chimna Potêl, little inferior in importance to that of the Mohadeo range. But some British detachments took the field from Nâgpoor, in August, notwithstanding the severity of the rainy season; and, by a series of well-combined operations, this rebellious disposition was put down before the close of September. The service was one of infinite suffering from fatigue, exposure, and unhealthiness of the climate; and there were several very brilliant exploits performed in the course of it. By the return of the cold season, resistance was confined to that portion of the hilly tract, in which Appa Saheb had first taken refuge; and intelligence has just arrived of his expulsion thence towards Aseergurh, the capture* of which strong hold, if he there should seek an asylum, will soon bring the war to an end. Yet it must not be concealed, that the whole territory of this state is still, and must long continue, in a very unsettled

* Appa Saheb did take refuge there, and the place was consequently invested about the middle of March. The Killadar, Juswunt Rao Lar, surrendered at discretion on the 9th of April; but Appa Saheb had escaped in disguise before the investiture was complete. Cheetoo was killed by a tiger in the adjoining junguls, in which he sought concealment, on being refused admittance into the fort. The particulars of this tragical death may perhaps be interesting. It appears, that Cheetoo and his son accompanied the ex-Raja in his flight from the hills; but, on their presenting themselves at the gate of Aseer, the Killadar consented to admit Appa Saheb alone, desiring the Pindarees to wait a few days. The vicinity of the fort afforded no protection to the rejected fugitives from the British detachments approaching in pursuit. The father and son consequently separated; and Cheetoo on horseback and unaccompanied, dashed through a dangerous jungul, in the hope of effecting his escape. Some days afterwards his horse was found grazing near the margin of the forest; upon him, his furniture, a bag of 250 rupees in coin, several seal rings, and some documents containing promises of reward from the ex-Raja, for services

condition; and it will require much moderation and vigilance in the executive, as well as the frequent display of our military strength, to establish a settled government in this part of the late Mahratta empire.

In order to rivet more firmly the dependence of the Nâgpoor state, the Governor-General resolved to reduce its military establishment to the lowest possible scale; and to put the contingent, that was to be the sole efficient force on its establishment, upon the footing which had been found so beneficial in the Nizam's dominions; viz. placing both horse and foot under the command and direction of British officers. The contingent was fixed at two battalions of infantry, and 3000 horse; the former to consist of natives of Hindoostan, armed, clothed, and disciplined like our regular sepoys: the horse to be raised in the country; and it was hoped, that, by leaving this field of employment open to the military class, a considerable portion would become reconciled to the new order of things. By these arrangements, the Bhoosla Raja has been reduced to a condition scarcely superior to that of the reinstated Raja of Suttara. Both princes owe their elevation to the British arms; both are young, and incapable of public business. At present, the government is virtually conducted by the British Resident, and his subordinate agents; and measures have been taken for

which Cheetoo might perform in support of his cause against the British Government. Search was immediately made for the Pindara; the track of a tiger was observed; it was followed, and some articles of dress picked up all clotted with blood. A little further on, scattered fragments of the bones of the robber, and soon afterwards the head entire, the features of which were recognised to be those of Cheetoo.

Thus perished the late formidable chief of 20,000 horse—the savage man, by his brother savage of the wilderness! an incident worthy of the brush of Salvator Rosa, and the pen of a Byron. Mahommed Punna, the son, was taken soon after leaving the gate of Aseer: a competent sum was presented to him for the interment of his father's mangled remains.

the avowed purpose of perpetuating the political dependence of both. If there be security for the public tranquillity of this district in any system, we may, therefore, surely place confidence in one, which has established our direct authority over one half of the country, and invested us with all the real power and influence over the other. The public may already be congratulated on the successful trial of this system in the territories of the Poona state; and, but for the disturbance that has necessarily resulted from Appa Saheb's being still at large, a similar degree of quiet might have been enjoyed by the subjects of the Bhoosla.

With the other powers of the Dukhun, the political relations of the British have remained unaltered. With the Nizam's Government there has never arisen a subject of discussion, since the confinement of the refractory princes in Golkonda. The power of this state is daily settling more and more in the hands of the British party, at the head of which is Raja Chundoo Lâl; while the apathy of the Nizam himself is gradually increasing. The territories of this prince are as ill governed as any portion of India, scarcely even excepting those of Doulut Rao Sindheea; and although the efficiency, which the introduction of British officers has given to its military establishments, has doubtless contributed to the maintenance of public order, it has yet afforded a very inadequate remedy for the gross abuses and corruptions of the civil administration, in respect to which the British Government has, through motives of delicacy, abstained from all direct control or interference.

So much for the Dukhun. We must now turn our attention to the political changes effected on the side of Hindoostan, and the grounds, on which it is confidently hoped, that the annihilation of the habits of predatory adventure will follow, as a natural result of our late operations in that quarter.

Northward of the Nerbudda, the country which had so long

been a prey to military despotism, or rather license and anarchy, has now been parcelled out among a number of chiefs, of whom all but Sindheea hold their lands of the British Government, under the direct obligation either of feudatory or of tributary dependence. Even the proud court of the Holkar has fallen to this condition; for the contingent of 3000 horse, that it has stipulated to maintain from its remaining resources, and to hold perpetually at our disposal, can be regarded in no other light than as a feudal obligation, although the treaty of alliance with this court is nominally of a subsidiary kind. It is true, we have on our part engaged to furnish military protection to the remaining territories of the family against any hostile attempt; but, in requital for this protective engagement, we have obtained in perpetuity the cessions in the Dukhun, and those to the north of the Boondee hills, together with the assignment of all the Rajpoot tributes enjoyed by the Holkar. Nor are we tied down to the maintenance of any definite force for the purpose, or to the occupation of any specified position. The obligation is, therefore, in effect no other than that of protection by the superior lord to his feudatories; and the court of the Holkar has little pretensions to a higher political rank. In point of resources, the state has been so dismembered by the allotment to Ameer Khan, the guaranteed Jageer of Ghufoor Khan, and the absolute cessions to ourselves and to our stanch allies of Kota and Boondee, that 20 lack may be assumed as the very utmost revenue remaining to Mulhar Rao. The court has been induced to abandon the martial custom of residing in a camp, and to fix upon Indore for its future seat of government. The territory, though still greatly interwoven with that of Sindheea, is fast recovering under the orderly government of Tanteea Jog, backed by the weight and influence of the British Resident and of Sir John Malcolm, who still continues invested with the general political superintendence of affairs in that quarter of

India. The treaty of Mundisôr, concluded by Sir John Malcolm with Tanteea Jog on the 16th of January, and ratified by the Marquess of Hastings on the 17th of that month, is the basis on which the present relations of this court are founded; and, except in the subsequent arbitration of some disputed points with Sindheea, and in the adjustment of the frontier towards Boondee, with some few other matters of inferior importance, that treaty has sufficed for the tranquil settlement of its affairs.

Next to the Holkar, the most considerable military chief, under the late settlement, is the Nuwab of Bhopâl. It has been mentioned, that, before the troops crossed the Nerbudda in the month of November, the Nuwab signed a preliminary engagement, binding himself to the conditions, on which the Governor-General had signified his consent to admit his father within the circle of protection; and that, during the whole operations, he furnished the contingent required of him, and heartily exerted himself in the cause. As a reward for the cordiality displayed by the Nuwab, the Punj-Muhal of Ashta Ichawar, &c. along with some other lands parcel of the Vinshorekur's forfeited jageer, and whence the Pindarees had expelled his people, were, on their final dislodgement, annexed to Bhopâl, whose boundary was by this addition advanced westward as far as the Kalee Sindh. A part of Shujawulpoor was subsequently added, and Islamnagurh was obtained from Sindheea in his favour by the way of negotiation. The principality was thus placed on a most respectable footing. The definitive engagement, which permanently fixed the relations of the Nuwab, was concluded at Bhopâl on the 26th of January 1818, and ratified by the Governor-General on the 8th of March following. The contingent he stipulates to furnish is limited to 600 horse, and 400 foot; a low proportion in reference to the resources of the state, but so fixed expressly to favour the Nuwab. As a more substantial mark of consideration, the obligation of paying tribute, in return for the protection we have engaged to afford, is waived in this instance, notwithstanding that the eventual payment of 125,000 rupees on this account was an item of the preliminary agreement, concluded with Lieutenant-Colonel Adams and Sir John Malcolm in November. Besides, the entire occupation of the Sâgur territory has rendered it expedient to station the military force, required to awe this neighbourhood, within the frontiers of that province; by which arrangement Nuzur Mahommed is relieved from the obligation of furnishing a cantonment, and surrendering a fort to be converted into a depôt for a stationary British force within his territory, which had also been a part of his original contract.

Ameer Khan, notwithstanding the consideration he before enjoyed as the head of the Patan military, occupies now a rank secondary to the Bhopâl Nuwab. His possessions are so scattered and disconnected, that it will be long before any thing like order can be introduced into his affairs, even after he shall be relieved from his pecuniary difficulties, and from the continued importunity of his hungry troops and followers. He holds Seronj in Malwa, and Tonk on the Banas, which may be considered as his two principal possessions; but there is scarcely a district of Rajpootana, or of the country east of the Chumbul, in which he has not some fort or assignment of lands, or some pending claim. The removal of all his thanas, or military posts, to hold in check the country he had usurped, was the first result of the treaties concluded with Jypoor and Joudhpoor. Yet he still holds some places previously obtained from those Rajas by the Holkar, and by that chief assigned to him; for the terms of his engagement with the British Government secure to him all lands which he held by grant from the Holkar, his former master, and deprive him of such only as were the fruits of his own unauthorized predatory career. He advanced a claim to the lands guaranteed in Jageer to Ghufoor Khan, alleging that chief to have been merely an agent or manager, set over them on his behalf; nor is it by any means improbable, that such may have been the origin of Ghufoor Khan's title; but as, in the late settlement with the Holkar, the present condition of Ghufoor Khan had introduced the stipulations for his benefit, it was not deemed advisable to be over scrupulous in tracing the origin of his title; and the Governor-General's award rejected the claim: nor would his Lordship permit the feudal allegiance, due by Ghufoor Khan, to be transferred from the Holkar to the Patan, as solicited by Ameer Khan. However, as one step towards the consolidation of this chief's possessions, Rampoora, which had been ceded by the Holkar to ourselves, has been conferred upon him, and it is further in contemplation to invest his son with a Jageer.

There was an obvious advantage in raising the Bhopâl Nuwab and these two Patan adventurers to consideration in this particular part of India, in order that they might form a counterpoise to the preponderating influence of the Hindoos, who otherwise would have been sole masters of the whole country. No doubt, there exists at present very little community of feeling between the Mahrattas and the Rajpoots; for, though both are equally of the Hindoo faith, and of the Khutree caste, they have for generations been at war with each other, and the memory of past injuries will for a long time survive the establishment of outward tranquillity. Still, as there is this common bond of union, it will not be thought an act of needless precaution to guard against the possibility of revolution, however faint or remote. It must be recollected, that these same Rajpoots were the means of leading the Mahratta to the gates of Dehlee; and their union with the Hindoos of the Dukhun it was, that drove the Moosulmans to seek the foreign aid of the Abdalees, and thus brought on the crisis, that, by their mutual destruction at

Paneeput, opened the door for a few skilful Europeans, to raise upon their ruins the fabric of that power, which now holds them all in equal thraldom.

Reserving the still unadjusted relations with Sindheea to our latest notice, we shall now proceed to detail the respective arrangements with the several Rajpoot princes.

In point of rank, the Oodeepoor Rana is entitled to the first place in our consideration, as being the descendant of the family that opposed the Emperor Akbur in the field. All the other Rajpoots regard him with the deference of acknowledged inferiority, even those that owe him no allegiance. Under our new system, however, each Raja was to be recognised as distinct from the rest, and the condition of all to be that of protected independence. It will, therefore, be most convenient to observe the order, in which the several arrangements were concluded.

It was to Mr. Metcalfe, the Resident at Dehlee, that the Governor-General intrusted the execution of his plans in relation to the Rajpoot states; and the reader has already been apprized, that, at the commencement of the campaign, he addressed a circular letter to them all, calling upon them to send agents with full powers to Dehlee, if they wished to participate in the advantages of the league about to be formed. None of them failed to send a plenipotentiary, for all were anxious to be relieved from their existing burthens and oppressions, more especially those resulting from the laxity of the Mahratta management. In those where the government was exercised with any efficiency and order, there was no difficulty experienced in settling the terms of the alliance to be formed with the British. To them it was proposed, that any tribute, demandable under a fixed agreement with a Mahratta or a Patan chief, should be paid directly into the British treasury at Dehlee, leaving us to account for it to the party to whom it might be due. This was accompanied with a tender of protection against external attack, on the usual condition of abstaining from constructing new relations with other powers, and submitting to our arbitration of all external disputes.

The first to conclude a treaty upon this basis, was Zalim Singh Raj-Rana, or manager, of Kota, whose agent at Dehlee signed the engagement on the 26th of December, which was ratified by the Marquess of Hastings on the 6th of January following. The tribute, which this chief owed to the Mahrattas, was three lacks, reduced by admitted allowances and deductions to 257,600 rupees of the country (Goman-shahee), equal to 244,720 rupees Dehlee currency. To this were to be added 19,997 rupees Dehlee currency, due from the relations of the family, under the designation of the seven kotrees or houses; so that altogether the tribute of Kota payable at Dehlee amounted to 264,717 rupees Dehlee currency. It will not be necessary to state the particular stipulations of the protective alliance concluded with Zalim Singh, as they corresponded with those of similar engagements with the other chiefs of this class. There was, however, a peculiarity in the engagement so characteristic of the Rajpoot character, that it ought not to be omitted. The Raja of Kota is still living; but Zalim has long held him in strict *surveillance*, and in fact a prisoner in the fort of Gagroon, while he himself sways with a vigorous hand the whole power of the state. Conformably to the principle of regarding occupancy as the rule of right, the Marquess of Hastings was prepared to have concluded the treaty for Kota directly with Zalim Singh, without reference to the legitimate but captive Raja, and to have guaranteed the succession to his heirs; but the Raj-Rana himself would not hear of such a proceeding; and accordingly, at his own suggestion, the treaty has been made with the Raja Kishwur Singh, to whom and his heirs the Raj is guaranteed, but with a reservation of the powers of administration to Zalim Singh and his heirs for ever, under the title of Dewan.

Zalim, as well after the ratification, as during the negotiation of the treaty, proved a useful ally against the Pindarees, and was rewarded for his zeal by the acquisition in personal sovereignty of four pergunnas he had farmed of the Holkar, and by a very favourable consideration in the arrangements subsequently made with Sindheea, to whom he owed tribute for Shahabad, and arrears of rent for some other places held in farm of that prince.

The second in order of the Rajpoot princes to sign his engagements with the British Government, was Raja Man-Singh of Joudhpoor. This prince had suffered severely from the irregular exactions of the Patans, though the Sindheea was the only power to whom he owed legitimate allegiance or tribute. The nominal amount due to that durbar was 180,000 rupees per annum, but the allowed deductions reduced it to little more than the half, viz. 97,000 rupees Dehlee currency, at which rate it was therefore fixed by the treaty. But it appeared afterwards, that a jagheer of 11,000 rupees had been reserved as a personal gratification to the British negotiator; which, though of course declined by the individual, was subsequently thrown into the scale, and swelled the amount of tribute to 108,000 rupees. The ejection of all thanas, recently placed in the country by Ameer Khan, was the first advantage reaped by the Raja from his new connexion. His signature was delivered at Dehlee on the 6th of January; and, in addition to the above tribute, the Raja engaged to furnish a contingent of 1500 horse.

Of all the Rajpoot princes, the Rana of Oodeepoor had suffered most from the usurpations of rebellious subjects, as well as from the oppressions of the Mahrattas and Patans. Indeed, he had lost nearly the whole of his dominions, and the money exactions of his oppressors were limited only by the extent of his means. His chief minister came early from Oodeepoor to settle the terms, on which his master was to be liberated from the misery of his present situation; and, on the 16th of January, an arrangement was concluded with this state, by the terms of which four annas in the rupee, that is to say, one quarter of the total revenue that might be realized, was agreed to be paid into the British treasury for the first five years; after which period, six annas, or three-eighths, was to be the proportion. The same rate of three-eighths was promised upon all new acquisitions or ancient possessions recovered by our means in the intervening period. In return, we engaged to lend the aid of our influence towards restoring the Rana's affairs, which, what with external ravage, and the internal usurpations of his dependents, were now at the lowest ebb. The expulsion of the Pindarees and of Duleel Khan, a Patan, who had for some months been devastating the Oodeepoor territory, was amongst the first advantages resulting to the Rana from the alliance with the British; and, before the end of January, the affair with Sindheea's commandant of Jawud placed at our disposal further means of befriending this state.

With a view more effectually to assist in the restoration of order to the affairs of this principality, Captain Tod, who had first been deputed to Kota to superintend the exertions of Zalim Singh against the Pindarees, and had since been employed in adjusting the affairs of Boondee, was ordered to proceed to Oodeepoor; and, to add to the importance of his mission and increase his influence, he was made the instrument for bestowing on the Rana the fort of Kumulnèr, and other late acquisitions from Juswunt Rao Bhâo. A more judicious selection of an agent could not have been made, for Captain Tod had made the character and history of the Rajpoots his peculiar study, and was consequently well qualified to execute the task assigned him. He found the Rana in the lowest degree of indigence, and at the mercy of a few designing miscreants about his person; while the Thakoors, or feudatories, of the state maintained themselves in perfect independence, and were their master's most formidable enemies. At Captain Tod's suggestion, and under his safe conduct, a general assembly of the Thakoors was convened, for the settlement of the future constitution of the principality. After some days' debate and unavailing discussion about immaterial points, Captain Tod, perceiving that, if left to themselves, they would come to no decision whatever, resolved himself to draw up a charter of rights, and induce the Raja to submit it for their consideration and eventual adoption. The sixteen principal Thakoors were accordingly assembled at noon on the 4th of May, when the Raja laid the plan before them; and, after a debate that lasted without intermission until three in the morning of the 5th, the following articles were agreed to, and the paper containing them signed by all present.

Art. 1. Provided, that all usurpations made by individuals upon the Rana, or upon one another, since the Sumbut year 1822 (A. D. 1766), should be mutually restored.

Art. 2. No Thakoor to continue to levy the impost known by the name of *Rahwaree Bhoom*, a kind of black mail levied as an immunity from plunder.

Art. 3. The *Dhan Biswa*, or rateable impost upon the produce of agriculture, to be the exclusive property of the Rana's government, and to be levied by no other authority.

Art. 4. The Thakoors renounce all predatory habits, and engage to harbour or protect no thieves, but to encourage trade, and leave all caravans unmolested. (This was a proviso that had become most necessary).

Art. 5. The Thakoors engage to attend on the durbar at Oodeepoor in rotation for four periods, each of three months, with their respective military followers, in order to give strength and respectability to the executive government.

Art. 6. At the Dussera of each year, a general meeting of the Thakoors to be convened for the settlement of all public affairs of magnitude; the meeting to commence ten days before the Dussera, and not to last more than twenty days after it: but extraordinary meetings to be held on extraordinary emergencies.

Art. 7. The immediate feudatories of the prince bound to render immediate service, according to the terms by which they might respectively hold.

Art. 8. All exactions, mutual violence, and fines on dependents to cease, and every one to be regulated in his conduct by the new order of things to be established.

Art. 9. The Thakoors bound to confirm what Ajeet-Singh, the Dehlee negotiator, had agreed to.

Art. 10. The Rana vested with the executive authority, for the enforcement of obedience to the new constitution to be established.

The articles of the above settlement have been given at length, both because they are in their nature curious, and because the arrangement promises to be productive of permanent good. It has given a right direction to the national spirit, and rendered the classes most interested themselves the instruments of the introduction of the new constitution. And this work they have, in fact, since undertaken with alacrity, under the impression, that they are labouring for the restoration of the good old times of the recorded prosperity and power of Oodeepoor. The Marquess of Hastings entirely approved of the above plan of settlement; and, in order to relieve the present exigencies of the Rana, and place the executive authority of the country on the footing necessary to ensure respect and obedience to its orders, he authorized an advance of money for present exigencies, to the extent of one or even two lack of rupees, in full confidence, that, on the establishment of order, the natural fertility of the country would make so rapid an improvement of its resources, as to afford the means of speedy repayment. Captain Tod still remains at Oodeepoor, charged with the superintendance of the settlement of affairs in that quarter; and the utmost benefit has already resulted from the system introduced at his suggestion. Should it eventually succeed, as there is every reason to hope it will, he will be recorded as having been the first to introduce among the natives of India the true principles of limited and constitutional authority; or at least to call again into action those principles, which, if they ever were known and practised at any former period of their history, have lain dormant so long, as to be well nigh obliterated. Perhaps in some future age, when the genius of Britain shall no longer lord it over the prostrate realms of Asia, this germ of liberal institutions of internal polity may be referred to as the commencement of a happier era in these ample regions, as the first lesson of self-government, which we shall have taught to the now slavish minds of the Hindoo race, and which may have afterwards led to the gradual diffusion of political liberty and moral improvement.

The Raja of Boondee followed next in order, and signed the arrangement proposed for his acceptance on the 10th of February. His net annual tribute, payable to the Mahrattas, amounted to 80,000 rupees: but this chief had established a claim on the gratitude of the British Government, by the fidelity and hospitality, with which he assisted Colonel Monson in his disastrous retreat in 1804. The rupture with Holkar fortunately afforded the means of bestowing a substantial proof of our grateful recognition of his good offices on that occasion: not only were all Holkar's acquisitions from the Raja recovered for him, but, in addition, the above tribute was released in perpetuity, and moreover, the restitution of Sindheea's encroachments and possessions within the Raja's frontier was obtained for him by negotiation. The town of Patun was also an object of the Raja's strong desire, and he was indulged in the hope of being gratified upon some future occasion. But his loss of this place was of too old a date to allow us to call upon the Mahrattas gratuitously to resign possession; while, as it lay below the Boondee range, the third share enjoyed by Holkar did not fall within the cessions of the treaty of Mundisôr. This third has since been acquired for the Raja by compromise; and, should an opportunity offer, the share of Sindheea will probably be also obtained, in the ultimate arrangement with that chief.

The Raja of Bhikaneer within the desert was the next Rajpoot prince that came into the league. The treaty with him was signed on the 13th of March. The suppression of the practice of pillage, the restoration of property plundered within his territory, the obligation of paying for such British as he might require, and of rendering military aid according to his means upon our requisition, were the terms of this chief's admission within the pale of protection. He had never paid tribute, and consequently no claim was now set up on that score. The Raja of Jesulmeer was soon after received upon the like terms; as was Raja Kuluan Singh of Kishengurh in the neighbourhood of Ajemeer, a chief of minor consideration, who had also never been subjected to tribute. Arrangements with the Rajas of Doongurpoor, Purtabgurh, and other chiefs of inconsiderable note and resources, situated to the south of Mewur, and on the frontiers of Guzerât and Malwa, were concluded under the direction of Sir John Malcolm, who had the general superintendance of political affairs in that quarter.

The alliance formed with Jypoor remains to be mentioned. Though nearest in geographical position to Dehlee, this state was the last to send negotiators; and, when they did at length arrive, they proved the most difficult to treat with. Jypoor, like Oodeepoor, owed no tribute either to Mahrattas or to Patans; but its losses from the ravages and usurpations of the latter, and from the system of depredation and anarchy pursued by its dependant Thakoors, were indefinite in extent; and the remuneration demanded for the relief, by our means, from evils so grievous, was fixed on a scale high in proportion. The negotiation ultimately fell into the same hands, as had conducted the conference of 1816; but the personal indecision of the Raja was such, that the negotiators did not make their appearance at Dehlee until the middle of February; and probably even a further delay would have been experienced, had not the Raja begun to take alarm at the engagement concluded with Ameer Khan, and had not this apprehension been quickened by the approach of Sir David Ochterlony to his capital, and by a show of making terms with some of his feudatories, which threatened to detach them for ever from their allegiance. Fearing now to be left completely in the lurch, the principal people of the court were despatched to Dehlee in all haste, along with the deputation appointed to negotiate; and, after much discussion, the terms were at length agreed upon, though the treaty was not actually signed until the 2d of April. The amount of tribute was the main difficulty: fifteen lack, with remissions for the first few years, was the rate demanded by Mr. Metcalfe, as in the former negotiation of 1816. To this, however, the envoys would not agree, and tendered in lieu no more than two lack and a half. In the end, the tribute was fixed as follows: for the first year nothing; four lack for the second; five lack for the third; six, seven, and eight lack for the three next successive years; after which eight lack to be the permanent amount, liable to be increased by five-sixteenths on any excess in the revenues of the state, beyond the estimated product of forty lack rupees. The territory is large, and its resources are confidently expected to yield, under good management, not less than eighty lack; so that the agents of the Raja will have gained little, by their refusal of the fixed sum originally demanded.

To restore order to the affairs of Jypoor, was a matter of infinite difficulty. The aristocratical faction of Manjee Das had been dismissed in the preceding July, for presuming to put to death one of the Raja's favourites. Manjee Das was himself struck by the Raja in open durbar for the act, and afterwards placed in confinement. Since then, the Prince had been surrounded by none but favourites and low dependants, amongst whom the intriguing Cheetoor Bhoj was the only man of ability, and he was a partizan of the Patan interest. In this plight Sir David Ochterlony found the court, when he went to visit the Raja in May; and, on that occasion, two favourite menials, one a eunuch, were pointed out to him as being, in conjunction with Cheetoor Bhoj, the Raja's principal ministers. The General found, that attempts had already been made to lavish on these creatures some of the first acquisitions resulting from the removal of the Thanas of Ameer Khan. He also discovered, that the Raja himself was a complete slave to the most odious vices; while the greediness and corruption of the favourites were the object of universal execration. Under these circumstances, it was deemed a necessary preliminary to any attempt to settle the affairs of this Raj, to summon a meeting of the Thakoors, similar to that which had been convened with so much judgment and good effect at Oodeepoor, in order to adjust their relations with the Raja, and establish some principles for the guidance of their future conduct. The Thakoors of Jypoor were, however, superior both in number and in relative power to those of the other Rajpoot states; insomuch as to require the exertion of military force against several, who, trusting to the great natural strength of their fortresses, presumed to oppose the arrangements effected under our mediation. The holders of Kooshalgurh and of Madhoorajpoor, or Madhoogurh, were amongst the refractory; but their strong holds were reduced without much trouble, though the latter had baffled the repeated attacks of Ameer Khan for the last two years.

The settlement of Jypoor is still in progress, under the superintendance of Major-General Sir David Ochterlony, who has lately been appointed to the Residency* of Dehlee. The Raja died in December 1818, before the settlement had been finally concluded; and the succession is now in dispute between Man-Singh, a posthumous and alleged spurious son of the late Raja's uncle, and a distant relation of the Narwar branch of the family, placed on the Juddee in the most hurried manner, and at an immature age, by Mohun-Ram, the eunuch minister before mentioned. All parties, however, agree in leaving the matter to the award of the British Government; and it will be one of the first blessings attendant on the establishment of its influence in this quarter, to effect a constitutional determination of this important question of right, instead of leaving it to the doubtful issue of a civil war, the immediate consequence of which must be, to give a free rein to the tumultuous spirit of the Thakoors, and annihilate all executive control throughout the territory of the state.

The relations established with the Holkar, with the Patans, of which race is the Nuwab of Bhopâl, and with the Rajpoot states, form nearly the whole of what has been done to fix the political dependance of the portion of Hindoostan not included within the arrangements of 1805-6. Divisions of the British army have been stationed in the positions most likely to give efficiency to the system thus introduced. Ajimeer, an acquisition from Sindheea, received in exchange for the Vinshorekur's lands on the Sindh and elsewhere, has been retained in our immediate occupation, for the especial purpose of being formed into a military post and depôt. Another new station has been fixed at Sâgur; and Mow, near Indore, has been chosen for the cantonment of the force attached to the Holkar court. Some

* Mr. Metcalfe has been called down to fill the office of Political Secretary, vacant in consequence of Mr. Adams's promotion to Council.

time must necessarily elapse, before all the claims of the several chiefs upon their respective dependents, or upon each other, can be finally arranged, if indeed they can ever be completely so; but the grand object of the campaign has been attained, by transferring all such disputes and jarring interests from the arbitrement of the sword, heretofore the sole umpire, to that of negotiation.

To a superficial observer, indeed, the apparently unaltered condition of Sindheea will occur, as presenting an insuperable obstacle to the final pacification of India; but those, who look more closely into the relations newly established, will see, that the condition of this Mahratta chieftain has undergone a very material change from what it was before the war. The first and most essential point of variation is, that he now stands single in political independence. Surrounded now on every side, by either avowed tributaries, or dependents upon our protection, he is quite as completely shackled in his external policy, as if bound by sealed contract to abstain from all dealings with his neighbours, except through our medium. Has he a claim to advance on any one of his neighbours? he dares not use the means he possesses of enforcing it; for, in so doing, he would infallibly commit an aggression on a protected ally of the British power, which, be the pretension ever so well founded, would nevertheless be resented as an act of insult and direct hostility to its authority. He has no alternative, therefore, but to lay his claim before it in the way of argument, to solicit its mediation, and abide by its award. Indeed, this effect of the extension of the British influence on all sides of him has been already experienced. Between Holkar and Sindheea there were many points in dispute, which the British Government has for some time been occupied in adjusting; and there are others still pending, for the decision of which the Gwalior Durbar is looking to the same umpirage. In like manner, we have been, and must continue to be, the arbiters between Sindheea and Zalim Singh of Kota, with whom his Durbar has very intricate relations: so also with Boondee and other states; for there is not a single prince or chief of acknowledged territorial jurisdiction within the whole circuit of India, with whom this court is free to pursue an independent line of policy.

Wherefore, as far as regards the external policy of the Durbar of Gwalior, it is scarcely possible, that any obstacle to the permanence of the desired tranquillity should arise out of the nominal independence in which it has been left. The anarchy of its internal administration might have proved a much more fruitful source of embarrassment to our plans and arrangements for the maintenance of public peace, had not a corrective been provided for this evil also, though its operation will necessarily be but slow. Upon this subject, a little further explanation will be indispensable.

The want of order, that was generally found to prevail whereever the influence of Doulut Rao Sindheea extended, was owing, partly to the nature of his military establishment and the laxity of the subordination of its officers to the government, and of the men to their officers, and partly to the partial kind of success, that attended its tumultuary operations. After gaining possession of a fort or a district, the prior occupant was commonly left to prey upon the country with what followers he could collect or keep together; while the harassing and dangerous service of hunting down those, who had thereby been reduced to desperate courses, was by no means congenial to the habits or temper of a Mahratta army. The career of Jysingh, after he had lost his district of Ragoogurh and the other strong-holds he possessed, was a fair specimen of the mischief thus occasioned. Madhoo Singh, the expelled Raja of Narwar, was another instance. Both turned captains of predatory bands, which Sindheea had no prospect whatever of being able to suppress, without a total change in his system. It was evident, that, so long as his military commanders were thus licensed themselves to commit excesses without control, in the manner they had practised heretofore, or, by their acts, to bring into existence bands of desperadoes, with no other means of maintenance than the habit of general spoliation, little approximation could be made to the establishment of universal tranquillity. The stipulations of the treaty of Gwalior will be found to contain very effectual provisions against the continuance of this evil. It will be recollected, that it was one of the articles, that British officers should be stationed with each of Sindheea's divisions, to supervise their movements; and it was left to the Governor-General to assign the positions they should respectively occupy. The object of this arrangement was, to enable us either to control the military commanders, or to bring matters at once to issue with them, if they should be so inclined. That the plan had the desired effect, the affair at Jawud is a convincing proof. There was, however, a further stipulation in the treaty, that 5000 horse should be maintained in an efficient state, and placed under the command of British officers, with our guarantee for their pay; towards securing which, Sindheea's stipend, his Rajpoot tributes, and the lands about Aseergurh and Hindia were ceded for three years, by way of indemnity for the expense. To this well-paid and well-officered force the Governor-General looked for clearing the country of all depredators by profession; and the means proved not only adequate to that end, but Sindheea has derived so much personal benefit from its disciplined exertions, that it has already become necessary to him. It has, indeed, been of the most essential service, in overawing the license of his military commanders, and enforcing the executive authority of the Durbar; on which account it is still kept afoot under British officers, though the suppression of the Pindarees, the ostensible object of its original formation, has been for some time completed.

Sindheea has always been equally anxious with ourselves, to put down the lawless independence of his Sirdars; and no sooner had the occurrences of the war checked that ambitious spirit, which is the common characteristic of all the Mahrattas, and by which he was inspired like the rest at the commencement of our military operations, than he gave into the contrary impulse, and determined to profit by the occasion to extend his personal power, and reduce or get rid of the soldiers of fortune in his service, who were in reality so many thorns in his side.

Circumstances favoured his views in this matter. Colonel Baptiste, the commander of his most effective force, took alarm at the signature of the treaty of Gwalior; and, even before Major Bunce, the officer appointed by Lord Hastings to reside with his division, could reach his principal cantonment at Buhadhurgurh, he had hastened to the capital, as was mentioned above, with only a few attendants, to ascertain, and, if possible, to participate in the immediate councils of the Durbar. There he was in the first instance well received, and dignified with a higher military grade; but no sooner had the battle of Mehudpoor confirmed Sindheea in the resolution to keep well with the English at all hazards, than he threw off the mask towards Baptiste, had both himself and his son placed in strict confinement, and demanded of him to account for the revenues of the lands assigned for the pay of his troops, and to make good all arrears. At the same time, care was taken to hold out Baptiste to the indignation of the mutinous soldiery, as the man who had defrauded them, and appropriated to himself the treasures, from which only their dues could be satisfied; and another commander was appointed to the troops left at Buhadhurgurh, over the heads of Baptiste's lieutenants there. By his intrigues, a counter interest was established, but not without mutual violence; and the auxiliary force under British officers was, in the end, made use of to awe both parties into submission. Thus was the dangerous power of Baptiste annihilated. He was himself put to the torture * (not for the first time), in the hope of extorting a confession of his secret hoards. All his territorial assignments have been resumed; and nothing remains to him now but Sheeopoor, which his family still hold with a garrison, and whither he supplicates in vain to be allowed to retire.

Juswunt Rao Bhâo, by his own violence, relieved the Durbar from the necessity of compassing his ruin by similar duplicity: but there can be little doubt, that the principal motive to reconcile Sindheea to the cession of Ajimeer, in exchange for our offer of lands of equivalent value in Malwa and upon the Sindh, was, the jealousy he secretly entertained against his relation Bapoo Sindheea, whose main strength lay thereabouts. Bapoo surrendered the place agreeably to the orders presented; but not without showing much ill-will, and probably more from ocular proof of the irresistible nature of our preparations to take it by force, in case of resistance, than from any respect to the order of his nominal master. As the result of these proceedings and events, it will be taken for granted, that what little organization before existed in the military establishment of Doulut Rao must now, upon the indiscriminate ruin of the superior commanders, have been utterly dissolved. Indeed, the natural consequence has been, the utter extinction of whatever military strength this state, on its former footing, may be thought to have possessed; while the broken troops, having now the Durbar only to look to for their arrears, have crowded into Gwalior, and, by their clamorous demands, increased the financial difficulties of their master; insomuch, that, were it not for the presence of the auxiliary force under British officers, which ensures him a certain degree of respect, Sindheea would have every thing to

* Once before tow had been tied round his fingers, oiled, and set fire to, in order to extort some confession of concealed treasure.

fear personally from their importunity and discontent. There is nothing this Prince for his own part more earnestly desires, than to rid himself of the whole rabble, by disbanding them at once; but for this he has neither money nor credit to borrow upon: nor does there exist within his own dominions sufficient wealth for the purpose. In this extremity, it would seem, that he has but the choice of two courses; either to throw himself into the hands of the rich bankers of the upper provinces of the British territory, who are able enough to assist him, but have refused to come forward without the security of our guarantee; or to solicit aid direct from the British Government. But, in either case, whether our bare guarantee be required, or the money be paid from our treasury, he is aware that he must submit to the sacrifice of a territorial security, and to the humiliation of throwing himself on our mediation to effect a settlement; and to this point matters appear to be fast converging.

Gokul Paruk, the Gwalior minister for so many years, has proceeded on a pilgrimage to Mutra, within the British provinces, whence he shows no disposition to return, notwithstanding the solicitations of the Durbar, which still hopes to obtain the requisite funds through his means. As the supply for the discharge of the importunate military is an indispensable preliminary to the succession of any other to the office, the appointment of a new ministry will probably form part of the arrangement resulting from an appeal to our influence. Every thing, however, is still in suspense, and it will be some time before the quiet settlement of this state can be finally completed. It is satisfactory to reflect, that this is the only political object remaining to be accomplished, in order to affirm the indisputable predominance of the British power, and its right of overt control throughout the whole of Hindoostan and of the Peninsula.

There are, perhaps, who will say, granted that this object be gained to the full extent of your wishes; what permanent good is expected to follow from its attainment? The answer is short and plain: a twofold benefit is anticipated; first, to the natives of India; secondly, to the fabric of the British power. In respect to the former, the primary consequence of the establishment of the new system of political relations must be, the complete deliverance of a portion of Hindoostan and of the Dukhun, comprehending a space of nearly 40 square* geographical degrees, from the most destructive form of military violence. The total annihilation of the Pindarees, and other predatory associations, would alone have been sufficient for the purpose; but the finishing hand has been put to that useful and necessary work, by erecting a barrier against all manner of usurpation from henceforward, whether by mere adventurers and soldiers of fortune, or by one legitimate chief upon his less powerful neighbour. A solid and permanent form of government, good or bad, will have been set over all this vast space, which, for half a century, has been the area of continued anarchy and devastation: such a government, as will secure its subjects at least from all external violence; and the example of the territory, occupied by the Bundela chiefs, and by the Seikhs, to say nothing of the Mysore dominions, is abundantly sufficient to show, that this alone will ensure the revival of agriculture and commerce, and restore the tract to a condition of high, if not of complete prosperity. The first step is always the most difficult to make: give but the impulse requisite to set the machine of improvement once in motion, and its own progressive power and tendency will of itself effect the rest, unless counteracted by the active opposition of unthrifty military

* The term, though not strictly correct, is expressive enough; and, as the boundaries on either side are not sufficiently definite to allow a correct estimate of the number of square miles, this mode of estimating the extent must stand for the present.

despotism, like to that which has just been subverted. This first step will have been secured, by the universal establishment of regular authority, and by the measures adopted for the maintenance of order and tranquillity in every quarter. For thus much those, under whose administration this advance has been effected, will at any rate have a claim upon the lasting gratitude of this great family of the human race.

To the British interests in India, there will result from the new order of things, first, a perpetual immunity from the hostile ravage of our immediate provinces; an evil, against the recurrence of which we could never have had any security, so long as this ample portion of India had been suffered to remain a hot-bed for the engendering of the instruments of rapine and disorder, and a place of refuge in defeat, or an asylum for the harvest of successful spoliation. The consolidation of the various parts under one uniform system, if that system afford but the prospect of sufficient stability, which experience leads us to discover in the recent arrangements, will leave us no ground of internal alarm; while it advances the external frontier of the British dominions to the natural barriers of India, the sea, the Humachul, the sandy deserts of the Indus, and the impenetrable forests and mountains on the east. These barriers are assailable at very few points; and the security they will afford from outward violence, cannot but give additional vigour to any effort that may be requisite, whether for the maintenance of internal order, or the resistance of foreign aggression, through any one of the few avenues of approach. In the latter event, there will be no enemy within to fear: the compact with each of the protected states will be sufficient to secure its fidelity and zeal in the common cause, against the occurrence of any but the most serious disaster; and, in the utter absence of any military power within the barrier, to threaten the integrity of an unguarded frontier, except such as would be available along with our own against every invader, the strength that could be thrown forward to meet such an intruder would be almost unlimited; and faulty, indeed, must the government be, if, with such means at its disposal, it should risk the bare possibility of disaster. In short, nothing more is wanting, than the lapse of time for the present generation to forget their past habits, and for a new one to grow up in the daily contemplation of the order and tranquillity, which it is now our comparatively easy task to establish and maintain. The population will soon be weaned of the habits of warfare and violence, and stimulated to the cultivation of the arts of peace, by the sense of security, and the hope of enjoyment; and there is little doubt, that the system now introduced will speedily acquire a degree of consistency, which no internal combination, or effort of external hostility, will be able to shake or endanger.

The struggle we have just terminated is, however, the more important and worthy of attention, because it promises to be the last we shall have to maintain with the native powers. Henceforward, we can have no enemies, but such as may be called into being by our own neglect or misgovernment, or by the distraction of our own councils. Against the two former sources of danger, we ought to be continually on the watch. In respect to the last, we ought fervently to pray, that India may never be the scene of British dissension or party animosity; but that, if any should unfortunately arise, it may be referred to the arbitration of the mother country.

Nor is the additional stability of our political grandeur and ascendancy the sole advantage, that has resulted from the late extension of alliances and territorial limits: there are further benefits of a financial nature, that remain to be brought to account; but which the subject of Indian finance is too little understood to enter upon, without some preliminary explanation.

The British public are doubtless aware of the marked difference between India and the other colonial dependencies

3 M

of the empire, arising from the constant retention in the hands of the government for the time being of the property in the soil, instead of its being parcelled out amongst a gentry tenacious of their rights, in the manner observable in Europe, or becoming the prize of the first occupant, as is necessarily practised in the first colonization of a desert tract. Thus the nation holds its Indian revenue as a property, instead of deriving it from the subjects in trust for the duties of management. Nearly three-fourths * of the whole revenue, realized from our Indian territories, is derived in this way from the land: so that the dominion, possessed by the nation in that country, may be likened to a large plantation; and the question of finance resolves itself into one of cultivation, in the mode best calculated to raise a surplus for the proprietor. With this idea constantly before us, we will proceed with the inquiry, what financial benefits have resulted, or may be expected to result, from the recent operations?

The year of the Marquess of Hastings' arrival in India was considered as a remarkably productive one. The establishments were then on the peace footing, and every branch of revenue was in that year more than usually prolific. We shall commence, therefore, by showing what was the state of this national concern on the 30th of April, 1814, the close of that official year; and then trace consecutively downwards the financial effect of each year's exertion, until the close of the season of 1817-18, beyond which the accounts have not yet been made up: we

* The remaining fourth is composed of various items. The customs, with an excise on spirits and one or two other articles, are heir looms of the former governments; the stamp duty being the only direct impost, which has originated with the British. In Bengal, the monopoly of salt for home consumption, and of opium for the China market, are two great sources of profit, and occasion the large comparative surplus of that presidency. The Mogul Government drew a revenue from the former by means of transit duties, the aggression of individuals on which brought on the rupture with Kâsim Ulee. The opium monopoly was established in the same time of violence by the agency of contractors.

shall then, however, give upon estimate the prospects for the future. It is a singular coincidence, that the period either of war or of warlike preparation, takes its commencement in the same year with the operation of the financial provisions of the act, renewing the charter of the Honourable Company. We shall presently have to notice those provisions more particularly.

The accounts made up for the year ending in April, 1814, showed the Indian receipts for the 12 months to have been no less than 15,03,76,201 * sicca rupees. The expense of Indian management, however, amounted to 13,58,43,011 sicca rupees; so that the net proceeds of the national concern were only 1,453,3,190 sicca rupees, about one million, eight hundred thousand pounds. This was a tribute capable of specific transfer to the exchequer of the parent state from the produce of its Indian concern, after defraying every expense of administration in the country. As to what became of this surplus†, that is a matter foreign to the present object. Suffice it to say, that there were home demands within the year, and those too for the expense of territorial management, which absorbed the whole; but of this more hereafter.

The Indian debt consists of two items. There is always a floating debt of deposits and out-standing demands, included in the annual accounts, though there be assets to meet it fully or in part. This debt is subject to no interest, and is entered with

* These sums may be converted into pounds sterling, by dividing by eight; but the numeration by sicca rupees is observed throughout, because it is that of the accounts of the Supreme Indian Government: 2*s.* 6*d.* is an assumed value for the sicca rupee, being about the medium rate of exchange with England. A Calcutta sicca rupee contains troy grains 175,927, which, compared with the standard shilling, equals 2·566. 100 Spanish dollars are coined into 210½ sicca rupees; but, private bullion being subject to a seignorage duty, the mint produce is, sicca rupees 206⅐. This calculation is made upon the old standard of 62 shillings to the lb. of silver.

† There was actually furnished to England in that year a sum of 1,48,59,957 sicca rupees.

this distinction. On the 30th of April, 1814, the out-standing demand, bearing no interest, was 3,09,46,564 sicca rupees. The more immediate debt of India, viz. that on which interest was payable, stood on the same date at 23,15,86,634 sicca rupees, 23 crore 15 lack, or about 29 millions of pounds sterling. To preserve the mode of illustration adopted above, this may be regarded as a mortgage on the revenues of the plantation, the amount having been raised and expended by the Indian executive in making the purchase for the nation; and it is after allowing for the interest of this mortgage debt amongst the current charges of the year, that the above surplus is exhibited. Such was the financial condition of India during the first year of the Marquess of Hastings' administration. In 1814-15, the Nipâlese war commenced; and the exigencies of that war, added to the expense of preparation against the Pindarees and Mahrattas, made a considerable alteration in the products of both that and the following year. The revenue also fell somewhat short of the product in 1813-14, being only 14,69,84,106 sicca rupees, in 1814-15; and 14,66,86,106 sicca rupees, in 1815-16. The surplus beyond the charges of Indian management was consequently reduced to 1,18,54,412 sicca rupees in the former, and 35,77,488 sicca rupees in the latter year. The usual supplies were, however, furnished to England without material abatement, notwithstanding the reduction of surplus, the Marquess of Hastings having procured funds for his military operations, by the loan of two crore of rupees from the Nuwab Vizier at Lucknâo. In 1816-17, the same military attitude was maintained; insomuch, that the disbursements nearly equalled the charges of 1815-16; but the revenue was unusually productive, being made to yield no less than 15,44,08,916 sicca rupees; hence, notwithstanding that the scale of charge was about 80 lack, a million of pounds sterling, beyond the rate of the peace establishment of 1813-14, there was still a surplus on the management of 1,09,37,238 sicca rupees.

We now come to the great and final effort of 1817-18, the funds for which had been accumulating in the Indian treasury in the preceding years. For, although the supplies to England had annually exceeded the amount of the Indian surplus, still the resources, derived from loans and occasional remittances of bullion from Europe, had more than compensated for the deficiency. Thus the means in hand, which, at the beginning of 1814-15, amounted to 4,70,75,293 sicca rupees, had been increased to the enormous amount of 6,55,99,156 sicca rupees, upwards of eight millions of pounds sterling, lying in the several treasuries of the government, and consisting almost entirely of coin or bullion. The revenues of 1817-18 were fortunately even more productive than those of the preceding year, having advanced to 15,68,71,060 sicca rupees; so that, although the extra charges of the effort of this season exceeded by nearly 80 lack, a million of pounds sterling, those of the two previous years of preparation, and amounted to 15,27,00,957 sicca rupees, there was nevertheless an actual surplus on the Indian management of 41,70,103 sicca rupees. It needed, however, a crore more to make up the supply expected in England from the Indian treasury; and, as there was a certainty, that the year immediately succeeding that of the grand effort must also be one of extraordinary expenditure, it was not considered safe to part with so large a portion of the sum in hand in the several treasuries. Accordingly, it was proposed to raise near 60 lack more by loan, and measures were taken with that view. An unlooked for supply of near 30 lack, beyond what was expected from England, enabled the Indian Government to preserve, for the eventual service of the year 1818-19, a balance in hand, reduced by only 35 lack from the rate of the preceding year; there being on the 30th of April, 1818, a total of 6,20,76,946 sicca rupees in the treasuries.

In the current year, 1818-19, the new resources acquired by the campaign will come distinctly into account. But the winding up of the war charges may, and indeed must, swell the expenditure of the season; and the impossibility of immediately placing every establishment on the permanent scale, designed for the approaching period of tranquillity, will preclude the expectation of a result so favourable, as we may hope to see annually recur at no distant date. The accounts have not yet been prepared; the expense of the operations can, therefore, only be calculated with certainty up to the 30th of April, 1818; and the portion of charge remaining to be provided for in the current year of revenue, must be left to swell the estimate of current expenditure. We shall first show the extent of the pecuniary sacrifice made, to effect the introduction of the new system of relations, up to the 30th of April, 1818; to which date the accounts have been already brought up.

It has been mentioned, that the Marquess of Hastings raised the funds, which enabled him to enter upon the extensive scale of operations which he adopted, without trenching materially on the annual remittance expected at home from India, by loans raised in India within the period. The debt account ought, therefore, to show the additional encumbrance brought upon the country by the execution of these measures. It will be found, that, in the course of the four years, between April, 1814, and April, 1818, there was debt incurred in India to the extent of 3,43,73,932 sicca rupees, three crore and 43 lack, about four millions and a half of pounds sterling. Two crore of this was obtained by the Marquess of Hastings from the Nuwab Vizier, and 56 lack more came into our hands in consequence of the death of the Begum of Fizabad, his Highness' grandmother. This princess had, during her lifetime, and in order to secure her property from confiscation, made a will bequeathing the whole to the British Government, on the condition of being allowed to bestow, in the way of legacies, perpetual pensions equal to the interest at six per cent; an arrangement, which, having been previously guaranteed, was punctually executed on her death in 1815-16. Of the three crore and forty-three lack, therefore, the public revenue was called upon to furnish no more than about ninety lack.

Of the debt raised from the Nuwab Vizier, one crore of rupees was cancelled in consideration of territorial cessions, in the manner above mentioned in the narrative: by which means, the real increase of the debt was still further reduced from three crore and forty-three lack, to two * crore and forty-eight lack. But it will be recollected, that the balances in hand of that date exceeded those of April 1814; so that, although, by the debt account, there will be a deterioration of two crore and forty-eight lack, the amount of the still unexpended balance ought further to be deducted, in the estimate of the actual cost previous to the date in question. The difference of the balances of the two periods was no less than 1,50,01,653 sicca rupees, one crore and a half. The net deterioration therefore was, in April, 1818, something less than a crore, 98,03,529 sicca rupees.

Thus, upon the supposition, that the supplies annually furnished to England had been sufficient to meet the demands of England, the whole object of the Marquess of Hastings' plans would have been gained, at a sacrifice, up to this period, of less than one crore of rupees. But the supplies, though averaging annually one crore and thirty-five lack, were not equal to the home demand. On this point some explanation is necessary.

By the provisions of the last act for renewing the Company's charter, the revenues of India are chargeable, first, with the military establishments of the country; secondly, with the interest of the territorial debts, and pay of the civil establish-

* Total debt incurred	-	-	3,43,73,932
Deduct cancelled loan	-	-	95,68,750
			2,48,05,182

The crore thus cancelled was in Lukhnâo rupees, the conversion of which into Calcutta siccas occasions the apparent difference.

ments. All these are primary charges, to be defrayed before any surplus can arise, applicable to an increase of dividend on the Company's stock, or to the liquidation of the principal of any territorial debts. Coupled, however, with the above debts and civil establishments in India, are sundry debts and civil establishments contracted or maintained in England; the interest on which debts, and the pay of which establishments, is directed to be made good *pari passu* with similar items of territorial charge incurred in India; so that there can be no such surplus till these also are provided for. These several items are to be advanced from India, at the fixed exchange of *2s.* for the current, or *2s. 3d.* $(\frac{84}{100})$ for the sicca rupee, out of the territorial receipts; and the Company, in its commercial capacity, undertakes the risk of loss or profit upon the remittance, as the case may be.

It would seem, that the home territorial disbursements have every year amounted to near two millions pounds sterling, while the Indian supplies have, as above explained, averaged no more than one million and from six to seven hundred thousand pounds. To the above increase of Indian debt, there will thus remain to be added a further deterioration, to be reckoned as part of the charge of carrying the plans of the Indian executive into effect: viz. that resulting from the deficit of the home remittance, as compared with the home territorial charges; a deficit, that, under the operation of the act of Parliament, must be regarded as a territorial debt, payable by the country out of its territorial resources. We subjoin a statement, in which this deficit will be found to be incorporated, and by the result of which the recent change of our relations will be seen to have cost in the acquirement upwards of two crore and fifteen lack, besides about sixty-two lack more remitted in bullion from England over and above the payments on account of the British Government—a casual resource, unexpected by the Indian Exchequer; and, whether remitted in payment of old debts of the nation, on account of Java, the Mauritius, and other such expensive acquisitions made before the passing of the Act, or advanced on any or what other account, is not distinctly known to the Indian administration.

1814-15.		1815-16.	1816-17.	1817-18.	Total of 4 Years.
Indian revenues S^a R^s	14,69,84,106	14,66,86,016	15,44,08,916	15,68,71,060	
Ditto charges -	13,51,26,694	14,31,08,528	14,34,71,678	15,27,00,957	
Indian surplus -	1,18,57,412	35,77,488	1,09,37,238	41,70,103	3,05,42,241
Loan, resources, &c.	1,01,26,858	1,45,98,442	36,68,705	59,79,927	3,43,73,932
Total means -	2,19,84,270	1,81,75,930	1,46,05,943	1,01,50,030	6,49,16,173
Supplies to commerce for home territorial charges -	1,17,88,659	1,51,91,847	1,25,62,050	1,46,15,862	5,41,58,418
Demands of England	1,65,41,629	1,70,35,446	*1,62,50,000	*1,60,79,647	6,59,06,742
Remains due to England - -	47,52,970	18,43,619	36,87,950	18,13,785	1,17,48,324

		S^a R^s
Result debt gross -		†3,43,73,932
Deduct cancelled loan -	95,68,750	
Also amount increase of balances -	1,50,01,653	2,45,74,030
Net debt - - -		98,03,629
Add debt to England -		1,17,48,324
		2,15,51,853
Bullion from London in the four years in excess of payments on account of the British Government		62,06,552
		2,77,58,405

	S^a R^s
Debt bearing interest in 1814 - - - -	23,15,86,634
Debt ditto in 1818 -	25,28,04,984
Difference - - -	2,12,18,340
Add cancelled loan -	95,68,750
Total interest debt incurred	†3,07,87,090

* These two are upon estimates, the actual accounts not having been received from home.

† That this does not correspond with the amount exhibited per contra, (3,43,73,932 sicca rupees) is owing to the latter's including the floating no-interest debt and every thing else that appears in the accounts, on which the annual balance is struck.

By the above account, the net deterioration incurred, up to April, 1818, in the prosecution of the plans of the Indian Government, would appear to be, two crore and seventy-seven lack. We will suppose, that, when the accounts of the present year come to be made up, the general result will show an additional burthen of four crore, or, as the cash balances cannot again be reduced so low as they stood in 1814, four crore and a half: the campaigns will then appear to have ended with adding thus much to the debt of the Indian governments; so that, instead of twenty-three crore and fifteen lack, the amount in 1814, the debt in India will have been raised to between twenty-seven and twenty-eight crore, or near thirty-five million pounds sterling. The excess, at an interest of six per cent per annum, will entail an additional burthen of twenty-six lack on the territorial revenues of the country. In order, therefore, to show that financial advantage will have resulted from the late operations, it will be necessary to prove that the additional territorial resources acquired, added to the practicable reduction of Indian expenditure we shall, by the late operations, have been enabled to make, will be capable of supporting the whole of this burthen, in addition to that of the total home territorial demand.

It is one of the disadvantages resulting from the very recent date, at which the compilation of this account has been undertaken, that there are yet no satisfactory materials wherefrom to calculate either the value of the resources required, or the probable degree, in which it will be practicable to reduce the Indian expenditure. With respect to the former, we can only state the annual rate, at which the territories stood in the accounts of the displaced governments; neither can we undertake to say, with any approximation to certainty, either at what time they are likely to become equally productive in our hands, or what intermediate allowances we shall have to make for the unsettled state of the country, and for the expense of management. The following rough sketch must for the present suffice; and, if the curiosity of the public should wish to be farther satisfied in this particular, and this narrative should chance to run through a second edition, the accounts of succeeding years will have furnished the materials of a far more accurate statement of the real benefit, that shall be found to have resulted from the events above detailed; and the narrator will then be able to present a clearer view of the actual condition of this national concern at the close of the campaigns, drawn from the comparison of financial returns. In the mean time, he has only to regret, that he can now offer no more satisfactory information.

The territorial revenue of the Pêshwa, exclusive of assignments of land on military tenure, was estimated, in 1815, at a total of 96,71,753 rupees, the average rate of the accounts of that government. Mr. Elphinstone estimates the incumbrances arising from the provision for the Suttara Raja, the stipend of eight lack per annum to Bajee Rao, of three lack to his brother Chimnajee, with other necessary charges resulting from the operations, at no less than thirty-four lack per annum. The net gross acquisition will, therefore, be but sixty-two lack, inclusive of the cessions by the treaty of Poona, which were destined to the maintenance of an auxiliary force: and, though such a force may perhaps now be dispensed with, it will nevertheless be necessary to make some addition to the regular military establishment in lieu of it. From the resumed Jageers and Surunjamee tenures of the Poona state, a permanent further revenue of about 24,40,000 rupees is anticipated. Wherefore, after a very liberal allowance for any addition to the military establishments requisite for the acquired district, and for the expense of civil administration, which, in the western provinces of the Bengal presidency, averages a rate of sixteen per cent on the receipts of revenue, we may assume that the dominions, late of Bajee Rao, will yield a net revenue of fifty lack.

The ceded lands of the Bhoosla were entered in the accounts of that state at 22,47,000 rupees. Those of the treaty of Mundisor, which have been retained in our own hands, appeared, by Holkar's accounts of the year 1814, to have yielded no more than 4,42,500 rupees; but this must have been owing to the complete anarchy that prevailed at that period; for the same territories, in 1766, yielded to Tukojee Holkar no less than 17,03,000 rupees. A produce of ten lack may therefore be fairly assumed on this account. From Sâgur and other retained territories in its neighbourhood, we may reckon upon a product of at least five lack, including the cession of Mohaba by Govind Rao of Jaloun. Four lack more must be added for Ajimeer; and the Rajpoot tributes, including those formerly paid to Sindheea and Holkar, cannot be assumed at less than fifteen lack. The Jypoor tribute alone will ultimately amount to that sum; but, as it must be some years before this can be expected, it will be fairer to confine the present view to the prospects of a more limited period. The gross receipts on this side of India are thus taken at a little less than fifty-six lack and a half*. Allowing liberally for the additional civil charges incident to our present extended possessions, and for the new political as well as

* Recapitulation.

Bhoosla	- - -	Rs 22,47,200
Holkar	- - - -	10,00,000
Sâgur	- - - -	5,00,000
Ajimeer	- - - -	4,00,000
Tributes	- - - -	15,00,000
	Total	56,47,200
	Poona gross	87,11,753
		1,43,58,953

administrative establishments, that have become necessary in consequence, we will assume the advantages gained from other states, exclusive of the Pêshwa territory, to yield a net revenue of no more than forty lack. Thus, in ensuing years, when time shall have allowed the new acquisitions to reach the full measure of their productive power, we may look for a gross addition to the territorial resources of the Indian government of eighty-seven lack from Poona, and fifty-six and a half from cessions in other quarters: and the net advantage of both may be fairly taken at about ninety lack.

In the year 1817-18, part of these resources had become available: we will make the calculation, therefore, upon the result of the year preceding it, as exhibited in the above schedule. Supposing both the receipts and the charges of that year to be increased by the new acquisitions, in the ratio of the above rough estimate, then the Indian surplus, instead of one* crore and nine lack of rupees, would amount within a lack of two crore. If we can anticipate for the future a result of this nature from the increased resources only, without reference to any reduction of the expenditure, we may well be satisfied with the improvement in our financial prospects, consequent upon the late operations.

The principal obstacle to our at once reckoning upon this permanent result may arise from an apprehension, that an excess of fifty-three lack, on the expenditure of 1816-17, will not provide sufficiently for the additional charges of future years: for

* Receipts	1816-17	Charges
15,44,08,916		14,34,71,678
1,43,58,953	New	53,58,953
16,87,67,869	Total	14,88,30,631
14,88,30,631		
1,99,37,238	Supposed future surplus.	

ninety-three lack was the difference between those of 1817-18, and of the year preceding; and it is more than probable, that the disbursements in 1818-19 will be on the same high scale, if not indeed upon one yet higher. Considerably more than forty lack of the charges of 1817-18 were, however, expended in bringing the immense armies employed in that campaign into the field, an item which cannot recur; while many of the temporary establishments and levies of the period must, in the end, if not very shortly, be reduced. It will, therefore, only be in the year of actual exertion, and in that immediately subsequent, when its accounts come to be wound up, that such a rate of charge will be experienced; and we may still safely assume, that the permanent expenditure need not exceed the rate of 1816-17, by more than fifty lack; and this without reckoning upon any reduction of the war establishments; while, by practicable reductions, we may fairly expect, that the charges might be brought to an equality; for even the year 1816-17 was a season of very chargeable precaution.

The above estimate is necessarily an extremely rough one; but is by no means intentionally exaggerated. Its result must needs be satisfactory to the nation; as it shows, that, without making any allowance for possible reductions of charge, the consequence of the late operations will be, to raise the surplus revenue beyond the expense of Indian management of its concern, to two crore of rupees, unless some serious disappointment occurs, in respect to the productive powers of the acquired territory. If the surplus be raised to this amount, the national tribute of two million will be secure, and there will be a farther annual excess of forty lack, applicable to the payment of the interest of the additional debt incurred in the acquirement of these advantages, as well as to the gradual extinction of the principal also, if that should be thought expedient.

The British public is probably little aware of the prosperous and improving condition of its Indian concern. For the twenty years, from the close of 1792-93 to that of 1812-13, the average annual balance furnished by India to England, beyond its receipts from that country, did not exceed 24,40,734 sicca rupees, though it has since averaged more than a crore and sixteen lacks per annum. Yet, to effect the very moderate remittance of the former period, and maintain the then establishments in India, was that debt contracted, which will now, by the late excess of war charges, have been raised to about* twenty-seven crore. This is the average result of the seasons of war and of peace taken one with another. But, heretofore, whenever circumstances called upon the Indian authorities for any extraordinary exertion, not only was this moderate remittance wholly withheld from England, but besides, the annual expenditure in India very greatly exceeded the revenue. During the administration of Lord Cornwallis, the accounts were not kept in such a form, as to show readily the Indian deficit occasioned by the wars of that period. But of the Mahratta war of 1803 we have distinct financial accounts; by reference to which it appears, that the annual extra charges, on the average of the four years to 1807 inclusive, exceeded the annual income of India by †1,89,30,388 sicca rupees. Thus, the Indian resources at that time were to that extent incompetent to provide for exertions, which can now be made without occasioning any deficit, but on the contrary,

* The Indian debt bearing interest was, in April, 1793, no more than 5,33,68,683 sicca rupees.

	† 1803-4	1804-5	1805-6	1806-7
Indian receipts	11,88,95,032	13,06,49,241	13,58,38,952	12,97,16,627
Do. disbursements	12,87,90,378	15,76,18,750	16,44,88,747	13,99,23,531
Deficit	98,95,346	2,69,69,509	2,86,49,795	1,02,06,904

Total deficit for four years 7,57,21,544

Average for each year 1,89,30,388

still leaving a surplus. In the single year 1805-6, the extra charge, consequent upon the rupture with the Holkar, was larger than in the year 1817-18, when the whole strength of the three presidencies was last brought into the field. The consequence was, that the Indian deficit of that year alone exceeded the whole deterioration of the four years of the late operations, being no less than two crore and eighty-six lack; whereas, including the home demand at the average annual of rate of more than two million pounds sterling, an item which forms no part of the above deficit for 1805-6, the additional burthen of debt thrown upon India, up to April, 1818, has been shown, in the statement before given, not to have exceeded * two crore and seventy-seven lack.

The improved condition of the national interest in India may well be inferred from the above comparison. To wage a four years' war with the Mahrattas, cost, from 1803 to 1807 inclusive, no less a sum than seven crore and fifty-seven lack beyond the income derived from the country, and without allowing for the supplies to England, which of necessity were suspended during that period. But, on the late occasion, four years of active and most extensive exertion have been surmounted, not only without the occurrence of any deficit, but with an actual surplus of three crore and upwards, available for the purposes of the nation in England. Therefore, had the home demand been limited to this amount, the exertions India has been called upon to make would have produced no incumbrance whatever. It is because of the necessity of a still larger remittance, a necessity acknowledged whether in war or in peace, that the Indian administrations have found it necessary

* The deficiency in the supplies home, though considered throughout as part of the burthen incurred, is not of the same nature as a debt incurred in the country; for, if met by loans raised at home, it will not involve an annual charge of more than four per cent, or five under the most disadvantageous arrangement that could be made.

to provide funds for the execution of their object, by incurring new debt to the amount that has been mentioned. But no part of the sum has been raised on terms, that will leave a permanent incumbrance of more than six per cent: whereas heretofore, in seasons of financial difficulty, loans were never negotiable at a lower rate of interest than twelve per cent.

It should be observed too, that no fresh impost has been laid upon the territory, and that the receipt of the Indian revenue arises, not from the expedient of temporary taxation, in its nature liable to change or remission; but the whole of these results have been produced from land revenues, the property of the nation by right of conquest, fixed in their ratio, which no one is entitled to dispute, and for the administration of which the nation is accountable to no one upon earth.

A word or two may be necessary on the subject of the home* territorial charges, the extent of which might else excite astonishment. A considerable portion goes towards paying the interest, and some part into a sinking fund, on loans raised from the British public, in anticipation and aid of the Indian finances, or to defray charges of home management, for which India had not provided funds. Another considerable portion is expended

* The following were the items of these charges for the two years 1814-15, and 1815-16.

	1814-15	1815-16
Passage of military - - - - - -	£ 79,109	£58,976
Freight—demurrage - - - - - -	72,610	182,222
Military officers on furlough and the retired list	283,993	205,142
Carnatic debt - - - - - - -	182,831	137,408
Loan of 1812, with sinking fund - - - -	244,044	243,982
St. Helena—Bencoolen - - - - -	53,083	47,724
Political charges general - - - - -	266,842	301,338
Stores sent to India - - - - - -	483,343	439,080
Payments in England for King's regiments -	252,974	360,236
Total per annum	£1,918,829	1,976,114

in pensions to military officers on the retired list, or in the pay of officers on furlough, which are legitimate Indian charges; so likewise are the recruiting and depôt expenses, and the charge of sending out men for the King's regiments in India. A third large item of home expenditure is on account of military and naval stores furnished to the country, and, therefore, is a payment for value received. It is only the remainder, after all these deductions, that can be fairly considered as the expense of establishments, maintained in England for the due administration of the affairs of India. This residuary item is more particularly under the control of the British parliament.

It may possibly be objected, that, unless India have provided an annual revenue, equal to the whole amount of these charges, plus the total expense of its local administration, and without incurring debt for the purpose, it must be regarded as a losing national concern; the answer is, that, even supposing the sums raised to meet these charges to be money absolutely thrown away, without the least hope of any future return, the question would still remain behind, whether there be no other advantages arising from the dominion of India, to compensate for such an annual loss. The most obvious and striking benefits, that present themselves to our view, are the maintenance, and means of accumulation too, which the management of so large a concern affords in its various departments to many thousands of British subjects, and the annual accession to the national capital of numerous private fortunes remitted to England, to say nothing of other funds supplied to British consumption from income drawn in India. But, if the inability to meet the full amount of present charge, without incurring debt, be taken to arise from the necessity of making a still further outlay to secure and improve what we before possessed; and, if there be a prospect of national advantage to be derived from the sums so expended in improvement, then is the case completely altered. Undoubtedly, the value of the concern must heretofore have been affected by the extent of outlay still requisite to secure the full benefit, of which it could be made productive; but, so long as there remained a rational probability of ultimately securing that benefit, there could be no wisdom in withholding the outlay, through fear of receiving no present adequate return. Would an individual, that has three parts of an estate, and a title to the remainder, which could be established at the expense of a very few years. rent of the remaining portion, act wisely, in allowing himself to be deterred by the amount of present advance, from any exertion to make himself master of the whole?

Apply the same principle to the recent acquisitions of the empire in India, and to the outlay of debt, of which they are the returns. We have now got possession of the whole estate, and hold it without a parcenor or competitor. We may therefore expect, for it is in our power, henceforward to derive the full benefit that it can be made to yield, though we yet know not its real extent. The accumulation of new debt is the price, by which this entirety of possession has been effected. The sums last borrowed were taken up merely to complete the object of former outlays: the one expense was a necessary consequence of the other. But this at least may be asserted with confidence; that, of all the national acquisitions successively made by the application of such means, no part of the estate will be found to have been purchased so cheaply, as this last portion of territorial sovereignty over the vast expanse of Asia, that lies within the natural barriers of India.

With this summary of the present condition and prospects of Indian finance, we take leave of the reader, whom curiosity or past recollections shall have conducted thus far, through a simple narration of facts, perhaps uninteresting to the generality of Europeans. But it is fit, that the British public should know the motives and the conduct of their countrymen in the East, and keep a vigilant eye upon the measures of delegates, who exercise an incalculable influence over the wealth and happiness of that large proportion of the human race, which Providence has subjected to British dominion. The depositaries of this important trust court publicity, and invite inquiry. They are anxious to be judged by British feelings and principles, tempered only by a due regard to the peculiar circumstances, under which the Indian dependencies of the empire were first acquired, and to the moral duties, that have been entailed by this possession. To the approbation of their country they look for the chief reward of no common exertions, and of what, with all its splendour, can never be other than exile: and they are not afraid to place their labours, in every department of national administration, even that which they may be supposed to be least attentive to, the observance of public economy, in competition with those of their fellow countrymen, whether at home or in any other part of the world.

THE END.

LONDON:
PRINTED BY T. DAVISON, WHITEFRIARS.